A Legend of Retailing
HOUSE OF FRASER

£1 ¹⁵

A Legend of Retailing
HOUSE OF FRASER

Michael Moss and Alison Turton

Weidenfeld and Nicolson
London

Published in Great Britain by
George Weidenfeld & Nicolson Limited
91 Clapham High Street
London SW4 7TA

Designed by Trevor & Jacqui Vincent

ISBN 0 297 796801

Printed in Great Britain by
Butler & Tanner Ltd, Frome and London

ENDPAPERS
Buchanan Street, Glasgow, 1914.

FRONTISPIECE
Harrods' Food Hall.

Contents

Acknowledgements 7

1 1780–1849: Shopping Transformed 11

2 1849–1873: Hugh Fraser Starts Out 32

3 1873–1909: Palaces of Commerce 47

4 1909–1924: Going up with Leaps and Bounds 93

5 1924–1948: To be Developed by Local Men 123

6 1948–1966: Scottish Retail Drapery King 168

7 1966–1976: No Easy Path 206

8 1976–1985: Retailing out of the Recession 227

9 1985–1990: The Store is King 257

Selected Store Histories 271

Sources 375

Index 377

Acknowledgements

This history of Britain's largest department store group has its origins over ten years ago when James Cathcart Stewart, a long time associate and friend of Lord Fraser, began to piece together an account of the remarkable growth of the enterprise. In pursuing this task he became increasingly concerned about the fate of the archives of the Group. As a result Sir Hugh Fraser and the board of House of Fraser invited Glasgow University Archives to conduct a survey of the records of all the companies in the Group and Alison Turton was appointed to carry out this task. Out of her work emerged the House of Fraser Archives, now part of the well-known Business Records Collection at Glasgow University. We are grateful to the late Sir Hugh Fraser and the late James Cathcart Stewart for their vision in promoting and supporting this project, out of which naturally grew the conception of this book, not just as a study of House of Fraser, but of the development of the idea of a shop with many departments supplying a variety of goods and services. We thank Ali Fayed, the chairman of House of Fraser, and his colleagues George Willoughby, Philip Wright and Richard Scott, for encouraging us to complete this fascinating task and for publishing the book, a monument to all those shopkeepers and warehousemen who, for more than two centuries, have contributed to the development of the many businesses that now comprise the Group.

We are grateful to librarians and archivists up and down the country who have helped us in our quest, particularly the staff of the Glasgow Room of the Mitchell Library; the British Newspaper Library at Colindale, London; Bath City Library; Plymouth Central Library; Southwark Local Studies Library; Kensington and Chelsea Borough Libraries; Tower Hamlets Local Library and Archives; Essex Record Office; and West Yorkshire Archives. The staff at the Group's stores have answered many of our queries and we thank, especially, Linsey Watson, Susan German and Nadene Hansen of Harrods, Colin Hehir of Rackhams of Bradford, Nigel Jones of Jollys of Bath, and Colin Pickersgill of Schofields of Leeds. We are also indebted to former directors and employees for their reminiscences, notably Kenneth Marley and Winston Brimacombe. We thank Ralph Davies, the company secretary, and his assistant Granville Prosser in London, and Nigel Dewar Gibb in Glasgow, for continuing to unearth more and more records just as we thought our task was complete. We thank Alan Cameron of the Bank of Scotland Archives for supplying information about the early banking business of the Frasers; Robin Harrod for allowing us to draw on his extensive knowledge of his family's history and George Dixon for unearthing many references to the early history of Arthur & Fraser during the course of his research into the history of Sir Robert McAlpine & Sons. At Glasgow Univerity we regularly disrupted the work of Lesley Richmond, deputy archivist, and Alma Topen, the manager of the Business Records Collection who cares for the House of Fraser Archives, and we thank them for tholing us.

We could not have written this book without the able assistance of Iain Russell, our research officer, who cheerfully responded to all our unreasonable demands and constantly corrected our misinterpretations. He travelled far and wide in search of information, doggedly pursuing even the most obscure leads. While attending to our needs Iain Russell was assisted by three part-time researchers, Eilean Malden, Iain Patteson and Vanora Skelley, who have worked for us through volumes and volumes of trade periodicals and Group archives to help us with our inquiries. We thank them. We are especially grateful to Rita Hemphill, who translated our scribblings and crossings out into a clean, unblemished typescript with great skill and patience. We are also indebted to Lynne Moss and June Turton who have worked hard to ensure that we were consistent in our references and felicitous in our grammar.

Michael Moss and Alison Turton
Glasgow and London

ILLUSTRATION ACKNOWLEDGMENTS
In the preparation of the illustrations we have been ably assisted by Glasgow University Photographic Department and Trevor Graham. Most of the illustrations have been drawn from the Group Archive at Glasgow, we thank the following for permission to use illustrations: Aberdeen University Library, G. W. Wilson Collection: 86; Baring Brothers & Co. Limited, London: 4, 41; Edinburgh City Libraries: 351; Mary Evans Picture Library, London: 17, 43; John Freeman: 2, 234, 235; *Glasgow Herald*: 152, 154, 186, 224, 350; Glasgow University Archives: endpapers, 90, 146, 147; Trevor Graham: 24; The Guildhall Library-/Bridgeman Art Library, London: 14, 21, 34; Robert Harding Picture Library, London: 237, 245, 268, 270; Kensington and Chelsea Borough Libraries, London: 59; Lewisham Local History Library, London: 302; Mitchell Library, Glasgow: 25, 26, 28–9, 30, 36, 38, 72, 82, 369; People's Palace Museum, Glasgow: 12–13, 19, 20, 40; Rex Features: 247; Scottish Tourist Board: 241; Strathclyde Regional Archive, Glasgow: 279; West Yorkshire Archives, Leeds: 181, 356, 357, 358.

OPPOSITE *Hugh Fraser, later Lord Fraser of Allender, and his son in discussion at the Group's Glasgow head office, c. 1958.*

I 1780–1849
Shopping Transformed

Today House of Fraser is a vast department store group, stretching from Aberdeen in the north to Plymouth in the south, with a turnover in excess of £1.2 billion. Yet 140 years ago department stores were unknown, and famous emporia like Harrods of Knightsbridge, Dickins & Jones of Regent Street and Jollys of Bath, were no more than tiny, family-owned concerns specialising in drapery or groceries and serving an exclusively local market. Towards the end of the nineteenth century a small number of these speciality shops responded to the changed trading conditions of late-Victorian Britain by embarking upon the sale of additional lines and expansion into adjoining premises, thereby creating a new kind of retail enterprise. The seeds of the department store were, however, sown much earlier and their arrival anticipated in the emergence of the first permanent shops and changing patterns of consumption during the late eighteenth century.

In medieval and Tudor times the word 'shoppe' was used to describe anywhere that selling took place, ranging from a market stall to a hawker's tray. By the late seventeenth century, 'shop' had largely come to mean the ground floor of a house where retail business was conducted. Initially, wares were sold through the open window of the shopkeeper's parlour and displayed on the roadway outside. Gradually open windows were glazed, counters installed and transactions began to take place inside. The emergence of the permanent shop was, in part, a response to the growing inadequacy of the traditional system of retail distribution which had been based upon a variety of fairs, markets and itinerant dealers. Fairs, which had evolved during the Middle Ages to evade municipal controls on long-distance trade, were less frequent and less controlled than markets and dealt primarily in agricultural products. By the end of the eighteenth century increased industrial production, the growth of towns and improved transport links had undermined the vital wholesaling role of the fair, and, where they persisted, fairs had become little more than recreational events for the purchase of novelties. Markets, by contrast, remained vigorous well into the nineteenth century, supplying food and household goods at competitive prices. Their familiarity made markets attractive to the labouring classes and in urban areas their original function, of providing a forum for the exchange of local production, was supplanted by that of distributing goods from distant sources of supply. Gradually markets in the major industrial towns, such as London, Birmingham, Leeds and Manchester, were improved by the provision of covered and supervised sites. Similarly, itinerant traders persisted purveying a wide variety of easily transportable goods ranging from haberdashery to provisions. Some sold for cash, others, known as tallymen or Scotch drapers, serviced regular customers and sold on credit. By 1800 most of the villages in Britain had at least one permanent shop, and as early as 1784 Prime Minister William Pitt discovered that a shop tax could be a remunerative device.

During the 1780s the city of Glasgow, where House of Fraser originated, was a flourishing and attractive town sprawling along the north bank of the River Clyde. Daniel Defoe, touring Scotland as early as 1710, had declared that

Trongate, the heart of the city of Glasgow, in 1826. The statue outside the Tontine Hotel was a popular meeting place for local merchants.

VIEWS of LONDON. N:4

'Glasgow is, indeed, a very fine city; the four principal streets are the fairest for breadth, and the finest built that I have ever seen in one city together. The houses are all of stone ... the lowest storey generally stands on vast square Doric columns ... and the arches between give passage into shops ... 'tis the cleanest and beautifulest, and best built city in Britain, London excepted.' Since the Act of Union (1707), Glasgow had enjoyed an unprecedented prosperity based on a profitable tobacco trade with England's American colonies. The voyage from Glasgow to Virginia was far shorter than from London and the value of Scotland's tobacco imports, largely landed at Glasgow and re-exported to Europe, increased from £2.5 million in 1715 to £39 million in 1770. The wealthy tobacco merchants built huge mansions on the western outskirts of the city and created an important customer base for the increasing number of coffee rooms and luxury shops. The outbreak of the American War of Independence in 1775 disrupted the tobacco trade but the postwar period witnessed its replacement by an equally successful cotton import business. The number of cotton mills in and around Glasgow multiplied rapidly and the Clyde was deepened to allow ships to sail up the river to the Broomielaw Quay in the heart of the city.

During the last sixty years of the eighteenth century the population of Glasgow more than quadrupled, growing from 17,034 in 1740 to 83,769 in 1801, and the city continued to develop westward as villas were erected on the fringes of the built-up area. Although this expansion was entirely unplanned, an overall grid pattern began to emerge. During the early eighteenth century a successful maltster, George Buchanan, put up a substantial mansion in open countryside on the north side of Argyle Street. In 1760, his eldest son, Andrew, a wealthy tobacco merchant, built a two-storey villa on a nearby site. When the tobacco trade collapsed during the late 1770s Buchanan began to sell off plots of land, along a broad avenue to the north of his own house, for the development of exclusive homes. The new thoroughfare became known as Buchanan Street. Likewise Jamaica Street was laid out for feuing in 1763, Miller Street in 1773, Queen Street in 1777, St Enoch Square in 1777, Ingram Street in 1781, and George Square in 1787. The first Glasgow Bridge was opened in 1772. To the west of these developments lay marshy fields but the heart of the city had already shifted south, away from the cathedral at the top of High Street, to the fine shopping streets of Trongate and Saltmarket which had been so admired by Defoe. In 1803 William Wordsworth's sister, Dorothy, was delighted and surprised to find that 'the shops at Glasgow are large and like the London shops.'

London, however, was unsurpassed in the number, variety and sophistication of its shops. By 1803 the shopping area was itself extensive, stretching from Whitechapel and Shoreditch in the east to Charing Cross and Oxford Street in the west, along two parallel and well defined lines of streets. The City was the centre of the drapery trade but from the 1770s promenades like Oxford Street became increasingly celebrated for the sale of fashionable fripperies. In 1786, when Sophie von la Roche, a German visitor to London, took an evening stroll along Oxford Street, she described the spectacle to her family in minute detail: 'Just imagine, dear children, a street taking half an hour to cover from end to end ... and the pavement, inlaid with flag-stones, can stand six people deep and allows one to gaze at the splendidly lit shop fronts in comfort. First one passes a watchmaker's, then a silk or fan store, now a silversmith's, a china or glass shop ... Just as alluring are the confectioners and fruiterers, where, behind the handsome glass windows, pyramids of pineapples, figs, grapes, oranges and all manner of fruits are on show.' Such an environment bred innovation as shopkeepers strove to attract custom and to offer a unique service.

OPPOSITE BELOW
The entrance to Oxford Street, at Tyburn Turnpike, in 1798. This end of the street was less developed for shopping and marked the western extent of the principal built-up area.

OPPOSITE ABOVE
Small shops near the Pantheon, at the eastern end of Oxford Street, during the 1790s.

During the early eighteenth century it was generally believed that demand was finite and that one shop might only increase its sales at the expense of another. In such a climate a growth in the number of shops was considered to be undesirable and competitive retailing was frowned upon. By 1800, however, contemporaries had begun to recognise that an absolute increase in demand was possible and, indeed, beneficial to society, and Georgian Britain was soon overwhelmed by a new passion for being in vogue. Fashions in clothes changed incessantly; bustles and hoops were abandoned in favour of light, high-waisted muslin shifts, new accessories such as the handbag were introduced, and even such minor adornments as buttons and buckles altered drastically in shape and size from one season to the next. Consumer goods such as furniture, chinaware and cooking utensils, which had once been handed down from one generation to another, became disposable and were more frequently replaced. Architects like the Adam brothers were commissioned to design elegant, modish houses, boasting unusual decorative colour combinations and beautifully landscaped gardens. Painters like Gainsborough and Stubbs executed fashionable family portraits.

Fashion held sway but its potency was rooted in deep-seated changes which were taking place in British economy and society. During the latter half of the eighteenth century, industrialisation swelled the ranks of the middle classes who began to enjoy a significant margin of income over essential expenditure. The employment of women and children in factories also boosted the disposable income of families of the labouring classes. The divisions between the classes remained clear but it was possible to climb the social ladder. Under such circumstances conspicuous consumption became a means to achieve social mobility. The response of both the middle classes and the gentry to such emulative spending on the part of the lower ranks was a tendency to spend more frantically themselves in order to outdistance their challengers. Such spending had a spectacular effect on the clothing trade where changes in fashions, which would previously have taken decades, now happened yearly or even monthly.

London and Paris became the arbiters of British fashion and, from the 1770s, news of changing colours or styles was spread by the paper fashion doll (a flat cardboard model accompanied by sets of cut-out clothing) and by a growing number of ladies' journals and national newspapers. Reports of the latest retailing and fashion initiatives were circulated by the well-to-do who spent the season, from October to Easter, in the capital before returning to the provinces. London retailers also played a significant role in disseminating information by acting as wholesalers for trade customers from all over the country. Shopkeepers themselves, in their advertising and buying policies, encouraged a devotion to fashion by changing their entire stock with every season and selling off merchandise which was out of date. The premature obsolesence of consumer goods, which would previously have been made to last, greatly heightened demand. Looking back on Glasgow in the 1820s a contemporary observer remarked that 'the wants of the people have increased even faster than the population, and it will also be seen that these wants are nearly all of an artificial nature.'

Changes in spending habits were encouraged by the huge migration of agricultural labourers into such nascent industrial towns as Manchester and Glasgow. Displaced from their traditional rural life the new factory workers were no longer self-sufficient. What they might previously have grown or bartered they were now forced to buy from middlemen. Provided with enhanced cash wages from factory employment on the one hand, yet deprived of the time and means to supply their needs on the other, they turned eagerly to the new shops. The growth of towns also encouraged the centralisation of retail functions, and

OPPOSITE *Simple, high-waisted gowns became fashionable during the late 1790s. Bustles and corsets were abandoned in favour of flimsy garments and a new range of accessories.*

N.º 15.

LONDON DRESS, MAY, 1799.

shopping centres began to emerge. The implementation of town improvement schemes, including the provision of lighting, paving and sewerage and the removal of nuisances, encouraged this trend by making shopping streets more attractive social centres.

By the early nineteenth century small rural shops were well established, selling on credit to a regular and local clientele, processing bulk stocks of foodstuffs into small parcels and purveying fabrics and trimmings. During the 1820s a contemporary described her own local shop as 'like other village shops, multifarious as a bazaar; a repository for bread, shoes, tea, cheese, tape, ribands, and bacon.' In the growing town centres a very different kind of shop was emerging, prompted to adopt new sales techniques in order to attract custom in an increasingly competitive marketplace. This new breed of retailer appeared in London during the closing years of the eighteenth century, but was rarely in evidence in provincial towns until several decades later. 'The first class retail shops in Glasgow', recalled a contemporary describing their unhappy condition as late as 1810, 'were lighted by projecting bow windows. The manner in which some of these places were fitted up internally, was generally characterised by plainness and simplicity ... Many of the shopkeepers of those days, kept a little of everything, and if age was any advantage to their wares, their customers were sure to be well suited.' The early shops were sombre and ill lit. Stock was not displayed but stored in drawers and cabinets behind the counter. Customers were not encouraged to browse and mere entry into a shop was, at least in part, a commitment to buy. Most shopkeepers tended to rely on a known circle of regular customers, termed at that time 'a connection', rather than seeking to attract new ones. Prices, which were hardly ever marked, tended to be pitched as high as individual customers might afford, a deal being struck after time spent haggling. Many shopkeepers were entirely without scruples. Deception was more typical than service, and returns and exchanges of merchandise were unknown. Whilst these traditional methods of selling certainly persisted, a growing number of urban retailers began to experiment with more adventurous sales techniques.

The manipulation of prices was an obvious means to influence spending. The same compulsions which prompted conspicuous consumption as a measure of wealth made high-priced goods an attractive symbol of social status. Josiah Wedgwood, the Staffordshire potter, used high prices as a means of product differentiation to attract aristocratic custom. 'A great price', wrote Wedgwood to his partner in 1772, 'is at first necessary to make the vases esteemed ornaments for palaces.' He aimed to sell his products to the aristocracy as a means of making them coveted by the lower classes. Most shopkeepers, however, aimed to increase sales by lowering prices. In 1837 Nathaniel Whittock, author of *The Complete Book of Trades*, maintained that the 'substitution of quick for slow sales is precisely like an improvement in the machinery which cheapens the cost of production.' Many of his contemporaries found it difficult to accept these new ideas, an aversion which stemmed from traditional economic theory based on the inelasticity of demand and of profit potential. The idea of the 'just price' persisted and many believed that 'pushing' shops, as the low-price retailers were known, sold merely at the expense of others and could not create new demand. In 1819 *The London Tradesman* warned the public that 'cheap shops are a great evil, and a much greater eyesore to the regular trader ... because cheap selling is usually a mere pretence ... manufactured goods of nearly every description having standard prices, at which they are retailed in the market.' Low price tactics were made feasible by the lower cost of mass production and improvements in transport which reduced costs and breakages, whilst the more rapid turnover sustained

BATH EMPORIUM,

No. 12, MILSOM STREET.

JOLLY and SON have the honour to return their sincere thanks for the Patronage they have experienced at their Establishment in Old Bond Street, which has induced them to open

EXTENSIVE PREMISES at

No. 12, MILSOM STREET.

From the novel nature of their new Establishment, which will combine a SHOP and BAZAAR, they deem it requisite to point out *the peculiar advantages it will offer to Purchasers.* The distinguishing feature of the EMPORIUM will be

ECONOMY, FASHION, and VARIETY.

The FIRST can only be obtained by an exclusive Ready Money System, *no Article being delivered unless upon prompt payment.* The advantages of this System are great. By it the Tradesman is enabled to purchase on the very best terms, and from the quickness of his return, and his not incurring any risk of loss from bad debts a very small profit will remunerate him; *the benefit thus arising to the Consumer can only be judged of by comparison.*

For FASHION and VARIETY, JOLLY and SON trust the EMPORIUM will be unrivalled, they having just completed most extensive Purchases in *London* and *Paris*, combining, with their former FOREIGN STOCK, a general Assortment of

LINEN DRAPERY, SILK MERCERY,

Hosiery, Haberdashery, Shawls, Merinos, Lace Nets, &c.

The BAZAAR Department will contain a Splendid Selection of

FOREIGN CHINA and BIJOUTERIE; OR MOLU and ALABASTER CLOCKS, Italian ALABASTER URNS, VASES, and FIGURES;

British and Foreign Cabinet Goods; Jewellery; Perfumery;

STATIONARY; COMBS; BRUSHES; CUTLERY; a great variety of TOYS;

And almost all the multifarious Articles usually kept in Bazaars.

There will be no abatement made from the price asked, the profit on each article being too small to admit of any reduction.

The EMPORIUM will OPEN on THURSDAY, November the 3d, 1831.

ABOVE *Advertisement from the* Bath Chronicle *which heralded the opening of Jolly & Son's Milsom Street shop in October 1831.*

RIGHT *A small grocery shop in eighteenth-century Glasgow. The cone shaped packages are loaves of sugar.*

Wylie & Lochhead's pioneering iron-framed warehouse in Argyle Street, Glasgow, in 1845. This new style of construction allowed an unprecedentedly large expanse of window.

OPPOSITE ABOVE
A typical Georgian bow-fronted shop.

OPPOSITE BELOW *Inside London's new Burlington Arcade during the 1820s.*

profit levels. The textile industry, on account of early mechanisation, was one of the first to reduce the cost of its manufactures and it was often drapers who pioneered the new forms of salesmanship.

Other pricing innovations were introduced during these years, including the notion of fixed and ticketed prices. A draper, recalling his apprenticeship in the City of London during the 1800s, noted that 'the healthy system of sticking to one price was just coming into vogue.' By the late 1820s the practice was not uncommon in the provinces. In 1831 when Jolly & Son of Bath (see page 337) moved their showrooms to larger premises at 12 Milsom Street they announced that 'there will be no abatement made from the price asked, the profit on each article being too small to admit of any reduction.' Haggling became unworkable as shops grew in size and the emphasis shifted from high prices to swift stockturn. Bargaining was not only extremely time consuming but it also complicated accounting and required high standards of ability and honesty from shopmen. The increasing use of fixed prices was associated with the ticketing of goods on display. This practice was shunned by shops catering for the gentry but greatly quickened trade for those bold enough to mark merchandise plainly. Enterprising retailers seized every opportunity to attract attention by special price promotions – clearances of soiled merchandise, of oddments or of the previous season's stock and special purchases of cheap goods or the stock of a bankrupt or retiring warehouseman were all popular. Generally only selected goods were offered at reduced prices and bargains were heavily advertised. Kendal Milne & Faulkner of Manchester (see page 343), Brown & Muff of Bradford (see page 293) and Jollys of Bath all indulged in such tactics through the 1840s.

Another effect of the growth of towns was the severing of the old kinship and friendship nexus within which retailers had previously operated. Contract replaced custom, and the offering of credit became a risky business. The insolvency rates amongst shopkeepers were extraordinarily high and all too often bankruptcy stemmed from a mass of debts owed by dilatory customers. During the late eighteenth and early nineteenth centuries most business enterprise depended heavily on credit – not only between retailers and their customers but also between manufacturers, wholesalers and the shops which they supplied. During these years banks began to emerge on a significant scale to administer and extend the availability of credit, and the transferrable bill of exchange became a popular means of payment. The ubiquity of credit, however, pushed up the prices of goods and made some shopkeepers extremely vulnerable to bad debts. Consequently, enterprising retailers began to insist on cash payment. In 1784 Robert Owen, later to become a famous cotton manufacturer at New Lanark in Scotland, secured a situation at Flint & Palmer's shop on London Bridge which he described as 'a house established, and I believe the first, to sell at small profit for ready money only. The house was already wealthy, making all their purchases with money and continuing very successful.'

In 1831 James Jolly not only insisted on fixed prices but also on 'an exclusive ready money system, no article being delivered unless upon prompt payment. The advantages of this system are great. By it the tradesman is enabled to purchase on the very best terms, and from the quickness of his return, and his not incurring any risk of loss from bad debts, a very small profit will remunerate him; the benefit thus arising to the consumer can only be judged of by comparison.' Jolly's unusual style of retailing proved to be extremely successful. A friend with lodgings across the street watched the shop on the opening day: 'The number of sedan chairs and carriages were very great ... your shop was, at times, so crowded that ladies had to wait outside until others came out to give them

room. Indeed, I thought that, of all the ladies who passed on that side of the street, eight out of ten went in.' Many of the shops which were to develop into major department stores instituted ready-money and fixed price policies at an early stage. Nonetheless the widespread adoption of such devices was slow in rural areas and amongst shops catering for the gentry, where custom continued to derive from connection and the offering of credit remained a vital means to retain goodwill.

Manipulation of the level and mode of pricing was not the only tactic used by the more adventurous shopkeepers to attract custom. Window display and advertising began to be used, albeit crudely and haphazardly, to push sales. The art of window display developed alongside changes in the architectural design of shopfronts. By the 1780s the ugly and unfunctional construction of the early years of the century had given way to glazed bow windows, elegant fanlights, ornamental pilasters and imitation marble in classical designs. After 1762, when projecting shop signs were banned, elegant flat fascia boards proliferated. Advances in glass-making technology, with the introduction of clear glass and later plate glass, had a dramatic effect on shop design, allowing the introduction of bold glass facades admitting light into the interior and encouraging exciting display. Shopping arcades, such as the Burlington Arcade in London's Piccadilly, were opened. In 1819, when a parliamentary select committee was established to investigate the potential loss of government revenue should shops be assessed for window duty only on their value as dwellings, the probable shortfall was estimated

INTERIOR OF BURLINGTON ARCADE, LONDON.

Harding, Howell & Co of Pall Mall, London, in around 1800. The manner of fabric storage and display shown here was typical of the period.

at around £160,000. The cheapening of plate glass, consequent upon the repeal of glass duties in 1845, further encouraged the adoption of glass shopfronts. The aim of window displays was to tempt the passerby to enter and to spend. In 1786 Sophie von la Roche described Oxford Street in her letters, noting that 'behind the great glass windows absolutely everything one can think of is neatly, attractively displayed, in such abundance of choice as almost to make one greedy ... There is a cunning device for showing women's materials. Whether they are silks, chintzes, or muslins, they hang down in folds behind the fine, high windows so

Jolly & Son of Bath, showing the handsome frontage erected during the 1830s. Pilasters and ornate fascia boards were commonly used to create an imposing shop front.

*Debenham, Pooley &
Smith, later Cavendish
House, of Cheltenham, as
depicted in George Rowe's*
Illustrated Cheltenham
Guide *in 1845.*

that the effect of this or that material, as it would be in the ordinary folds of a woman's dress, can be studied.' Such methods were typical of the 1780s when the display of fabrics largely involved draping lengths of cloth in windows, around the shop door and from pillars and walls in the interior. A handful of more adventurous shopkeepers did, however, begin to use techniques which were to become far more popular in the mid-Victorian period, displaying a mass of goods of one type only. During the 1820s a Bristol draper, recently removed from London, described how he 'opened shawls in rows, one behind the other, commencing with a low height and gradually filling the window into the back.' He added, 'people did not know quite what to make of it.' Sophisticated and accessible displays inside shops did not arrive until much later although as early as 1765 Josiah Wedgwood, having opened his first showrooms in London, set out services as if for a meal which were to 'be so altered, reversed and transformed as to render the whole a new scene' every few days. He believed extensive and changing displays would encourage frequent visits from customers as 'business and amusement can be made to go hand in hand.'

From the 1790s, advertising, or 'puffery', was similarly used by retailers to provoke interest. Newspapers, however, had a limited circulation and advertisements tended to be extremely deferential and repetitive. 'Blowing one's own trumpet' was regarded as contemptible in many quarters and advertisements were often disguised as unattributed commendations of particular products or services. Nonetheless, by the 1840s the front pages of most local newspapers were filled with advertisements, causing an infuriated Glasgow observer to complain that 'our wives and daughters are puffed into fashionable dresses by puffing drapers at half their real value.'

Thus during the sixty years after 1780 shopping in Britain was transformed and the preconditions set for the emergence of a new genre of retailing. These momentous changes did not escape the notice of one of the period's best-known authors, Charles Dickens. 'Six or eight years ago', he wrote in *Sketches by Boz*, 'the epidemic began to display itself among the linen-drapers and haberdashers. The primary symptoms were an inordinate love of plate-glass, and a passion for gas-lights and gilding. The disease gradually progressed, and at last attained a fearful height. Quiet dusty old shops in different parts of town, were pulled down; spacious premises with stuccoed fronts and gold letters, were erected instead; floors, were covered with Turkey carpets; roofs, supported by massive pillars; doors, knocked into windows; a dozen squares knocked into one; one shopman into a dozen.'

Glasgow's shops, despite the prosperity of the city, were slow to adopt the new

The Argyll Arcade, built in 1829, which remains an attractive feature of Glasgow's central shopping district.

retailing techniques which had become popular in London and such fashionable resorts as Bath and Cheltenham. By the 1820s a few drapers were selling at fixed prices, glass frontages had arrived in the principal thoroughfares and the newspapers were filled with advertisements. For the most part, however, the trade was dominated by old-fashioned shops selling at high prices and with little flair. Few retailers kept large stocks and trade was largely conducted to order. The main warehouses were clustered around Trongate, although nearby Argyle Street had also become a busy shopping promenade. By contrast Buchanan Street, which led off the north side of Argyle Street, remained entirely residential. During the mid-1820s, however, a handful of tradesmen moved into Buchanan Street attracted by the relatively low rents and fine location close to Glasgow Bridge. A contemporary later recalled these early days 'when shops were first attempted in Buchanan Street ... It was thought by many people to be perfectly absurd, and that they would never pay. Who would think of overlooking the thriving shops in the then fashionable lounges of the Trongate, Glassford and Hutcheson Streets, the Candleriggs, or even Stockwell, for such an out of the way place as Buchanan Street where shop tenants must infallibly starve for want of custom?'

OPPOSITE *Buchanan Street which, by the 1890s, had become one of Glasgow's most fashionable shopping promenades.*

Robertson Stewart and John McDonald had no such misgivings when, in 1826, they opened their new wholesale drapery warehouse at 5 Buchanan Street. The business flourished and the partners' boldness was rewarded three years later when a fashionable arcade of shops, built in an L-shape between Argyle Street and Buchanan Street, enticed promenaders and shoppers further west. During

Tallis's view of Buchanan Street, illustrating Stewart & McDonalds' large warehouse, in around 1842.

the early nineteenth century larger shopkeepers often engaged in both retail and wholesale activities, although specialised wholesalers, like Stewart & McDonald, had also begun to emerge on a significant scale in the drapery trades. At the same time the term 'warehouse' came to be used indiscriminately to describe any retail or wholesale establishment which the owner considered to be so substantial as to merit a more impressive description than that of shop. By the late 1830s Stewart & McDonald had grown large, acquiring adjoining rooms and additional premises around the corner in Argyle Street and supplying retailers from Glasgow and surrounding districts with drapery of every description.

Meanwhile James Arthur and Hugh Fraser, who were to found House of Fraser by commencing in business together as drapers, were growing up in very different circumstances not far from Glasgow. James Arthur was born on 21 March 1819 in Paisley, a flourishing industrial town some eight miles west of Glasgow, which had grown rich upon the success of the local textile manufactories. His father, a Renfrew bleachfield manager, appears to have provided him with financial backing and in 1836 he acquired, for the sum of £800, the stock and business of a bankrupt draper and hosier. The shop at 18 High Street, Paisley, was renamed and Arthur swiftly augmented the trade by the addition of a new line in 'men's cloths' and the acquisition of adjoining premises. By the mid-1840s he was advertising heavily and operating a low-price policy with 'all goods marked in plain figures.'

Hugh Fraser's family, by contrast, had no links with the drapery business. Fraser's mother, Elizabeth Lennox, had married Robert Barr, an innkeeper's son, in around 1800. The couple lived at Burnfoot in the small agricultural village of Cardross, some eighteen miles from Glasgow in Dunbartonshire on the northern bank of the Clyde. Barr kept a local ferry house and also sold liquor. The Barrs had four children before Robert died suddenly of cholera in 1810 at only thirty-one years of age. Elizabeth determined to implement his plan to build a combined inn and ferry house, and acquired Bainfield Inn on the south side of the main highway. Within two years of Robert's death, Elizabeth, having conceived a child, was remarried to John Fraser, a young man in her employ from Boleskine in Inverness-shire. Elizabeth and John had six children, two boys and four girls. The eldest boy, Hugh, was born in Cardross on 19 May 1815. The family was not particularly wealthy and, although his eldest stepson, John Barr, succeeded him as ferryman during the 1840s, John Fraser continued to run Bainfield Inn until he was in his seventies. Hugh lived at the inn, which became known as Fraser's Inn, for many years and is described as a cloth salesman in the Cardross enumerator's handbook for the 1841 census. It is possible that he was acting as an itinerant dealer in drapery goods providing a retail service in an area where shops would have been few and far between. During the mid-1840s Hugh Fraser appears to have obtained a position as lace buyer at Stewart & McDonald in Buchanan Street and was later promoted to warehouse manager. Dealing with customers from all over the west of Scotland, Fraser quickly built up a large connection, becoming particularly friendly with James Arthur who bought extensively at the warehouse to stock his Paisley shop.

By the late 1840s the population of Glasgow had reached 300,000. Geographically the city had grown enormously, absorbing the barony of Gorbals and burghs of Calton and Anderston in 1846. More importantly for the large warehouseman, significant clusters of middle-class housing were developing in elegant terraces and crescents around Woodlands Hill and along Sauchiehall Street and Great Western Road. The middle classes, essentially those employed in non-manual professional and business jobs, assumed increasing importance as

Hugh Fraser (1815–73), founding partner in Arthur & Fraser.

the manufacturing and service industries developed. They were not, however, a homogeneous group, and ranged from teachers and clerks, earning as little as £60 per year, to affluent bankers and lawyers bringing in salaries of £300 to £400. Their class-consciousness was acute and was manifested in an increasing expenditure on consumer goods. Although determined to follow the latest fashions, they formed a discerning and cost-conscious market to whom the new ready-money warehouses held great appeal. The cult of the home became particularly pronounced during these years when books on domestic economy abounded. Whether home was a cramped terraced house or a modest villa with live-in servants, its adornment with furnishings of an appropriate quality and style became paramount. Carpets, curtains, paperhangings, mahogany furniture and porcelain were all essential ingredients. Similarly, dress was perceived by the middle class as a way of 'keeping up appearances'. Middle-class ladies flocked to

*Map showing the large
extent of Glasgow's built-up
area in 1847.*

Cartoon portrait of John Anderson, an innovative retailer and founder of the Royal Polytechnic warehouse.

the ready-money warehouses to buy dress materials and trimmings (tartans and rosebuds were popular during the 1840s) which could be made up into garments at home.

Meanwhile, central Glasgow had come within easy reach of a far larger population than ever before, vastly increasing the potential market of the principal shops. Horse-drawn omnibuses began to ply routes to the suburbs during the mid-1840s. Initially these were operated by private firms like Wylie & Lochhead, a popular retailer of furnishings which diversified into transportation (see page 366), and Andrew Menzies, and extreme competition kept prices low. At the same time the arrival of the railways made shopping trips to the city from further afield more practical. In 1840 the Glasgow to Greenock line was opened for passenger traffic, swiftly followed by routes to Edinburgh and Helensburgh. Queen Street railway station was built in 1842 and Buchanan Street station in 1849. Steamships also began to bring passengers to the busy quays at the Broomielaw in the centre of the fashionable shopping district.

During the late 1840s the growth of the market and sophistication of consumer demand started to transform Glasgow's shops. A handful of retailers, grasping the vast market opportunities available, began to devise bold and innovatory marketing techniques to attract custom. Most enterprising of the early Glasgow shopkeepers was John Anderson. In 1837 Anderson opened a small drapery shop in Clyde Terrace on the south side of the river. There he introduced the novel idea of 'universal trading' which was to become the most basic characteristic of the department store. 'The old fashioned system of keeping the drapery trade strictly confined to dress materials was then in full swing', recalled a contemporary, 'but Mr Anderson determined to take up a branch of business which would be sure to bring customers to his warehouse, whether they required drapery goods or not.' In 1845 he added toys to the usual drapery lines and later also perfumery, books and patent medicines. Alongside diversification of stock Anderson began to use low prices as a device to attract customers. 'He was not afraid of purchasing large stocks to show them, and he thought nothing of clearing out a "remainder" stock from a manufacturer which would have appalled the proprietors of many larger establishments. His method was to purchase one particular article, to advertise it strongly, and for some days to show nothing else for sale. As these "remainders" were bought by him at discounts varying from fifty to seventy-five per cent, he could sell them cheaper than other traders could purchase them and yet have a large profit.' Anderson never missed an opportunity, making four trips to Paris during 1848, when the revolution depressed trade, to buy fashionable French goods on advantageous terms.

Anderson's tactics, typical of those of the early department store proprietors, were hugely successful and on his sale days the crowds of shoppers often blocked Clyde Terrace entirely. As turnover increased, new storeys were added to the showrooms and his promotions and advertising became more flamboyant than ever. His success was not popular amongst more traditional colleagues. At a banquet to celebrate the firm's jubilee in 1887 Anderson recalled that 'the offence of combining different branches of trade under one roof made many enemies. I was assailed – boycotted, etc. – for the simple reason of reducing the prices of useful articles within the reach of all classes.' Anderson persisted in the face of this opposition and his success demonstrated that diversification, display, advertisement, price manipulation and sheer spectacle could, in the context of mid-nineteenth-century Glasgow, create a new kind of consumption.

2 1849–1873

Hugh Fraser Starts Out

By the early 1840s the commercial centre of Glasgow was shifting away from the area around the Cross at the eastern end of Trongate. Argyle Street had become a fashionable promenade and in Buchanan Street Stewart & McDonald's wholesale drapery warehouse had been joined by shawl and millinery showrooms, print, book and music sellers, grocers, apothecaries, stationers and silk mercers. The Argyll Arcade alone was lined with some sixty-three shops purveying luxuries of all kinds. Despite this huge influx of tradesmen the buildings largely retained the character of individual town houses, their doors approached up steps flanked by iron railings. Few of the shops had glass frontages and the bow windows of Hunter & Co's hatters shop and W. Mitchison's music warehouse, projecting where Argyll Arcade emerged on to Buchanan Street, were at odds with the general character of the thoroughfare. Rents were still low in Buchanan Street and premises more easily available than was the case further along Argyle Street. Consequently, during the summer of 1849, when James Arthur and Hugh Fraser conceived the idea of starting in business together, the partners rented premises in Andrew Buchanan's former mansion on the corner of Argyle and Buchanan Streets. Arthur was clearly the senior partner although it is not known precisely how the capital investment was divided. In 1856 Arthur's stake was £36,000, six times as large as that of Fraser, and it is likely that their respective shares were of similar proportions in 1849. In order to devote his entire attention to the new business, Arthur withdrew from direct involvement in the Paisley shop, appointing John Cattanach as managing partner. Fraser, who had recently married

NEW SILK MERCERY. LINEN AND WOOLLEN DRAPERY ESTABLISHMENT, 8 BUCHANAN STREET.

ARTHUR & FRASER

BEG to announce that they intend, on MONDAY, 15th inst., OPENING these Premises,

EAST CORNER OF BUCHANAN STREET AND ARGYLL STREET,

with a LARGE STOCK of NEW GOODS, comprising every article in connexion with the above Business.

In soliciting a share of public patronage, ARTHUR & FRASER respectfully intimate that they intend conducting their Business exclusively on cash principles.

In thus avoiding the expense and risk connected with a credit giving Establishment, it will be in their power to adopt a scale Profits not attempted hitherto in Buchanan Street.

Observe the New Entrance from Buchanan Street

Glasgow, 6th Oct., 1849.

Arthur & Fraser's opening advertisement which appeared in the Glasgow Herald *on 8 October 1849.*

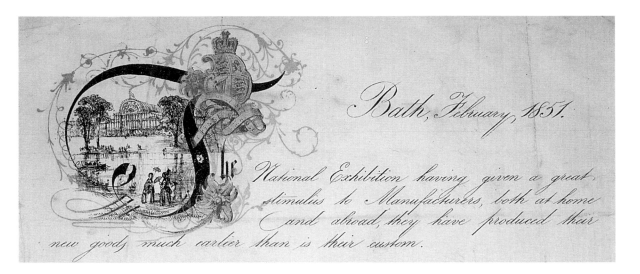

Bath, February, 1851.

National Exhibition having given a great stimulus to Manufacturers, both at home and abroad, they have produced their new goods much earlier than is their custom.

The Crystal Palace, as featured on a circular issued by Jolly & Son of Bath to describe the store's new spring stock in 1851.

Jane Bunting, resigned from his position at Stewart & McDonald. Both men had considerable experience in the trade and determined to embrace the most modern commercial practices. Consequently, they decided to adopt the same ready-money policy which Arthur had already employed to advantage in Paisley. The shop, specialising in the staple drapery lines of silks, linens, and woollens, was to trade as Arthur & Fraser.

The first-floor premises which the partners rented in the autumn of 1849 had to be extensively altered and a new entrance built for access from Buchanan Street. The refurbishment took longer than expected and the opening of the showrooms had to be deferred for two days whilst work was completed. Finally, on Wednesday 17 October 1849, the new shop opened at 8 Buchanan Street. An advertisement, placed in the *Glasgow Herald*, announced the opening of a 'new silk mercery, linen and woollen drapery establishment' with 'a large stock of new goods'. The advertisement also explained the partners' trading policy: 'In soliciting a share of public patronage, Arthur & Fraser respectfully intimate that they intend conducting their business exclusively on cash principles. In thus avoiding the expense and risk connected with a credit-giving establishment, it will be in their power to adopt a scale of profits not attempted hitherto in Buchanan Street.' Fraser had been popular at Stewart & McDonald and attracted many of his former customers to the new concern. Stocks of delaines, cashmeres and prints were purchased and staff recruited to make up cloaks and dresses. As trade increased Arthur & Fraser took the flat above the original showrooms and installed a small inner staircase to provide access. The first-floor location, however, afforded little opportunity for window display and for many years the firm had no more than 'a little narrow window at the foot of the stair, which faced up Buchanan Street and readily caught the eye of the promenaders.'

Two years after the establishment of Arthur & Fraser's new drapery business the attention of the whole country was focused on the 'exhibition of the works of industry of all nations' which opened in London in May 1851. The Great Exhibition, conceived as a means of advancing industry and art across international divides, attracted over six million visitors. Housed in an immense hall of iron and glass the profusion and variety of 'all that is beautiful in nature or in art' was overwhelming. The exhibits, arranged in discernible sections along ten miles of frontage in the vast galleries of the Crystal Palace, set new standards in the display and arrangement of manufactured goods. Visitors were free to wander

The British Department at the Great Exhibition. The well-stocked displays were similar to those beginning to appear in the larger shops.

through the various departments enjoying not only the spectacle but also the musical diversions and refreshment facilities. The similarities between the Exhibition and the stores of such innovators as Glasgow's John Anderson were apparent even to contemporaries. 'It was neither crystal nor a palace', wrote Leigh Hunt, 'it was a bazaar, admirably constructed for its purpose and justly surprising all those who beheld its interior.' The popularity of the Great Exhibition undoubtedly led the public towards the acceptance of a new style of retailing and lent respectability to the large warehouses with their emphasis on magnificent showrooms, freedom to browse without obligation and vast ranges of unassociated merchandise. In anticipation of the Exhibition, manufacturers at home and abroad produced their new season's goods much earlier than usual and shops all over Britain bought stocks of wares which were to be exhibited. In May 1851, Wylie & Lochhead announced the arrival of their new carpet stocks which included 'several exhibition patterns ... which are most perfect and exquisite description, the designs and colourings being beautifully and harmoniously blended.' Typically, John Anderson went one better by visiting

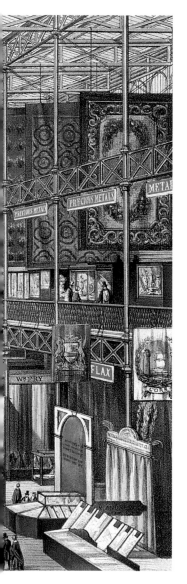

London towards the end of the Exhibition and buying up cheap stock from those exhibitors loathe to carry their display goods home.

Meanwhile Arthur and Fraser were working hard to build up their new business. Further premises had been acquired around the corner at 118 Argyle Street and there Arthur established a modest wholesale branch. Fraser concentrated his attention on the retail trade, continuing to sell only for cash, marking all prices 'in plain figures' and coupling a low-price policy with an insistence that 'they keep no class of goods but such as they can with confidence recommend.' The firm was then selling a broad range of drapery goods, including silks, shawls, merinos, cloaks, cashmeres, laces, collars, straw hats, ribbons and flowers, blankets, flannels, sheetings, table cloths, damasks, linens, hosiery, gloves, black mourning goods and tartans. Tartans became a particular speciality, 'in all the different clan and new fancy patterns', and were pushed during the summer months when the city was filled with visitors.

By 1853, to allow more room for growth, Arthur & Fraser had also moved into premises at 116 and 120 Argyle Street and 10 Buchanan Street, all of which were shared with other tenants. The wholesale trade, which had initially been unremunerative, continued to be serviced from 118 Argyle Street where credit began to be offered to wholesale customers for the first time. Meanwhile retail stocks became more adventurous with the purchase of French shawls, Irish and Norwich poplins and German goods. In September 1855 Arthur & Fraser announced the opening of a new fur department based on extensive 'purchases from the best London furriers.' The partners, who were very different in character, appear to have complemented each other well. A contemporary was later to describe them in the following terms: 'The mild, suave disposition of Mr Fraser was of very great advantage. He was always a favourite with customers, many of whom were rather repelled by the brusque and funny manner of Mr Arthur. Whilst the latter was a stern disciplinarian who would adhere strictly to his bargain regardless of circumstances, Mr Fraser took a less rigid view of life and was willing to come and go as prudence might dictate. He had, therefore, the art of keeping good customers when he had got them, and of smoothing down the asperities of business life.'

By the mid-1850s Glasgow had become an extremely competitive and sophisticated retail environment. A large number of warehouses were, like Arthur & Fraser, pursuing low-price, ready-money policies. Arnott, Cannock & Co and Robert Simpson & Sons in Jamaica Street, Daly, Spence, Buchanan & Co in Trongate and Thomas Muirhead & Co in Argyle Street all adopted the ready-money system. Retail and wholesale drapery businesses of enormous proportions had also begun to emerge, labelled by contemporaries as 'monster houses'. J. & W. Campbell, for example, divided into eighteen distinct departments, operated huge warehouses in Candleriggs and Ingram Street handling sales in excess of £1 million each year. John Anderson, on the south side of the river, had pioneered the idea of universal trading and, as a contemporary noted, 'having now thoroughly shaken off the trammels which bound the old-fashioned draper, Mr Anderson no longer limited his purchase to articles connected with the drapery trade. His stock was now a heterogeneous one including bric-a-brac of all kinds of the best quality, which he was able to sell at a profit at very reasonable prices.'

Warehousemen like Anderson had begun to appreciate that turning stock quickly was more important than high mark-ups because it kept capital effectively employed. A new eagerness to undersell competitors developed alongside widespread indulgence in such tactics as fixed, ticketed prices and remorseless

Daly, Spence, Buchanan & Co's trade card, depicting the firm's warehouse in Trongate, Glasgow, in 1850.

advertising. Low prices alone would have been ruinous, but, coupled with insistence on ready money and bulk discounted purchases from suppliers, rapid turnover ensured the constant availability of capital for further expansion. Indeed, modest mark-ups meant that an increase in turnover constituted the principal means to boost profits, and such growth was usually achieved by diversification into new lines of merchandise. As property values and rentals in town centres began to rise, an extension of the sales area also became the obvious route to reducing operating expenses as a proportion of turnover. Back buildings, upper floors and offices began to be converted for selling. As John Anderson's trade soared during the late 1840s he built storey upon storey over his original showrooms in Clyde Terrace. In London Charles Henry Harrod (see page 321), who had acquired a tiny grocery shop in London's Knightsbridge around 1853, laid the foundations of Britain's largest and most famous department store by taking similar steps to expand his sales area. During the 1860s, Harrod removed his family to the suburbs and built a new shop front and two-storey extension in the garden for the sale of flowers, fruit and vegetables. Thus economic logic hastened the growth of the nascent department stores.

In addition to considerations of price and scale, a few adventurous ware-housemen also began to pay more attention to the appearance and design of their showrooms. In 1855 when Wylie & Lochhead were forced to move out of their Argyle Street premises for want of space, the partners seized the opportunity to create a purpose-built shop of unparalleled magnificence in Buchanan Street. Designed by William Lochhead himself, the new building, of iron-framed con-

Inside Wylie & Lochhead's
magnificent Buchanan
Street store in around 1870.

*James Arthur (1819–55),
founding partner in Arthur
& Fraser.*

struction, was 200 feet in length by 70 feet high. 'The main salon', reported the *Glasgow Herald*, 'consists of a spacious street floor, and three lofty open galleries, rising one above another, and extending round the whole building in a semi-circular form. A magnificent cupola of ground glass, extending the whole length of the galleries, throws down a perfect flood of light but at the same time so well subdued and tempered as to fall softly all around, and exhibit with the best effect the elaborate decoration of the structure, and the goods of every kind and hue with which it is so abundantly stored.' The interior was beautifully appointed with more than 200 gaslights, 'their globes appropriately and harmoniously dispersed throughout the place.' The design, with its glass barrel roof, was strikingly reminiscent of the Crystal Palace. The building attracted so much interest that for several weeks no business could be conducted on Saturday afternoons. Instead free admission tickets were issued and crowds of curious visitors flocked to view the gracious salons at first hand. On the opposite side of Buchanan Street Arthur and Fraser must also have been filled with wonderment. Wylie & Lochhead had never espoused the ready-money system, but the magnificence of their new warehouse posed a different kind of challenge to competitors.

By 1855 Arthur & Fraser's wholesale department was flourishing, its turnover far exceeding that of the original retail business. Arthur had invested heavily in a wide range of stocks, and the cramped premises at 118 Argyle Street were abandoned when a larger wholesale warehouse became available in Miller Street. The new premises were opened on 7 January 1856, and boasted twenty-one departments, including clothes, merinos, tartans, printed cottons and cambrics, ribbons, silks, muslins, laces, haberdashery and trimmings, hosiery, shirts and shirtings, gloves, shawls, handkerchiefs, flannels, linens, sheetings, carpets and floorcloths. Arthur and Fraser created a separate partnership, Arthur & Co, to operate the relocated wholesale business, which had assets worth in excess of £230,000. Arthur, as senior partner with an investment of £58,519 in the new concern, took thirteen-sixteenths of the profits and Fraser, with a smaller stake of £10,302, took three-sixteenths. Fraser, as managing partner, also drew an annual salary of £200.

The wholesale business quickly began to demand the attention of both partners and, as Fraser's absences became more frequent, Thomas Kirkpatrick, was appointed to manage the retail branch. Kirkpatrick, fifty years of age and formerly of Campbell & Co of Buchanan Street, was a talented and experienced retailer. Sales increased and a number of departments were moved into the Argyle Street premises vacated by the wholesale business. For the first time the retail branch had a main entrance and display windows, and soon afterwards new buildings were erected at 12 Buchanan Street, on the other side of a lane to the north of the existing block. Both Arthur & Co and Arthur & Fraser flourished during the first half of 1857, the wholesale business returning a profit of £6,000 after six months' trading. This success was, however, cut short during the following months by the onset of an unexpected and severe commercial crisis. Interest rates rose and there was a rash of bankruptcies across the country. The wholesale trade was brought to a standstill, and in Glasgow the crisis was heightened by the collapse of the Western Bank in November 1857. 'Who would have imagined six months ago', lamented a commentator in the *Glasgow Herald*, 'that amongst our merchant princes ... there would have been so many men of straw.' A few enterprising retailers took advantage of the situation. In Clyde Terrace Anderson bought bulk stocks of drapery at rock-bottom prices, advertising 'waggon loads of new bargains' in the local press. By contrast, Arthur & Co, in common with many of the city's wholesale warehouses, quickly began to experience severe cash-flow problems.

Arthur knew that the firm was basically sound and he was determined to avoid the crash which would certainly ensue if all the firm's creditors demanded immediate repayment. In January 1858 he wrote to every creditor explaining that the firm's books had been placed in the hands of an accountant and that a balance sheet would shortly be circulated. 'When making this announcement', he added, 'it is proper to explain that our ordinary half yearly balance taken towards the end of last month showed us a very large surplus, that we have the most perfect confidence of being able to pay off all our liabilities with interest within a short time, and of continuing to carry on the business with increased

OPPOSITE *Arthur & Fraser's warehouse, showing the double frontage on Buchanan and Argyle Streets. This illustration appeared on the firm's billheads during the 1860s and 1870s.*

The foot of Buchanan Street looking south toward St. Enoch Square, in around 1880. Arthur & Fraser's warehouse is shown on the left-hand side.

confidence on the part of our friends.' It was a bold initiative. Two weeks later Arthur & Co's creditors gathered in the Carrick Hotel to discuss the firm's affairs. A representative committee had already examined the stock *in situ* and the financial statement clearly demonstrated that the firm's assets greatly exceeded its liabilities. The meeting agreed that the larger debts might be paid off in equal instalments over nine months, thereby allowing Arthur & Co time to weather the crisis. 'In the annals of commerce', declared the chairman of the proceedings, 'a statement more creditable to the partners had never been submitted to a meeting of creditors. Indeed, in every respect it redounded so much to their honour that he could scarcely esteem their suspension a calamity; and he felt assured that in its results to them it would prove the very reverse. It placed them above all calumny; and for the future, they would enjoy an untainted and almost unlimited credit.' Subsequently Arthur & Co's bankers, the Union Bank of Scotland, advanced £40,000 to cover the partners' liabilities whilst their debts were discharged. The firm's profits, which had fallen away at the end of 1857, swiftly recovered as the commercial crisis passed. During 1858 Arthur & Co's trading profit exceeded £9,500.

In the midst of these problems Thomas Kirkpatrick announced that he wished to quit Arthur & Fraser in order to start up a drapery business on his own account at 160 Argyle Street. The retail branch, buying and selling largely for cash, had been little affected by the commercial crisis but Kirkpatrick's departure was untimely. In January 1858 Arthur & Fraser announced a clearing sale 'preparatory

to alterations in the management of their business.' Alexander McLaren, merino buyer at Arthur & Co, was transferred to superintend the retail business. Initially the appointment was not a success as McLaren had little experience outside the wholesale trade, and the profits of the retail branch began to fall away. In October 1860 an overhead passage was constructed between numbers 10 and 12 Buchanan Street, uniting the new building with the main Argyle Street showroom. The store then comprised thirty-two departments on the ground and second floors. Meanwhile Arthur & Co expanded rapidly establishing representation in London and Londonderry and conducting a large trade in England as well as the West of Scotland. During 1860 William, Arthur's elder brother, was assumed as a partner in both Arthur & Co and Arthur & Fraser. William was an extremely wealthy warehouseman in his own right and appears to have returned from England to join his brother's business. Later in 1860 William Ogilvie, formerly of Mitchell, Miller & Ogilvie, wholesale warehousemen, also joined the partnership, presumably to furnish further funds for expansion. Four years later Arthur & Co acquired the wholesale firm of Wingate & Co which provided an extensive warehouse as well as a large connection. William Wingate was also made a partner.

As Arthur & Co grew in size the retail trade became less relevant to the firm's mainstream activities. Relations between Arthur and Fraser, which had once been close, became strained and Fraser was eager to gain more control over the retail operation. On 5 December 1865, by mutual consent, the firm of Arthur & Fraser was dissolved. Fraser retired from the co-partnership of Arthur & Co which was continued by the remaining proprietors as a separate concern. Fraser's investment of some £43,000 was withdrawn in its entirety and presumably used to buy out his co-partners' interests in Arthur & Fraser. The retail branch, worth some £42,000 in 1866, was modest in comparison with the wholesale business which had an asset value of almost £1 million at the end of 1865. On 6 December, close upon the dissolution of the partnership, a massive sale was held in an effort to dispose of the entire stock, worth over £50,000, so that the proceeds could be divided. Arthur & Co later became one of the largest wholesale drapery businesses in Scotland.

By the end of March 1866, Fraser had entered into a partnership with Alexander McLaren, who had been managing the retail branch for some years. Fraser now became the senior partner, investing £40,622 in the firm compared with McLaren's much smaller stake of £1,525. Accordingly, Fraser took three-quarters of the net profits and the new business traded as Fraser & McLaren. By this time the firm had diversified away from drapery and was also selling dining-room, drawing-room, parlour and bedroom furniture alongside carpets at 8 Buchanan Street. Later a new department was set up for furnishing ships built in the Clydeside yards as well as hotels and private houses. Such orders could be lucrative; the napery contracts for sizeable ships comprising large numbers of towels, tablecloths, napkins, dishtowels, blankets and pillow slips. In April 1867 Fraser purchased the Argyle Street and Buchanan Street showrooms for £26,000 having borrowed £20,000 on the security of the property. Shortly afterwards the back building was demolished and a new warehouse erected at a cost of £3,500. By this time the store occupied a number of buildings in a square area bounded by Argyle Street on the south, Buchanan Street on the west and Morrison's Court on the north and east. The Argyle Street frontage comprised four storeys, occupied by the woollen and linen drapery departments, and a sunk flat and attics used for storage and staff accommodation. The upper floors of the adjoining building, a tenement on the corner of Argyle Street and Buchanan Street, were also occupied by Fraser & McLaren and housed the furniture, carpets, upholstery and general house and ship furnishing departments. These premises were shared with a jeweller, hosier and brush dealer. Behind the Argyle Street frontage the new four-storey tenement was connected to a three-storey building on Buchanan Street, both wholly occupied by the firm and used for dress materials and fancy goods.

The middle classes remained the principal market for stores like Fraser & McLaren and, by the 1860s, clusters of elegant villas and town houses had developed further west in Park Circus, Dowanhill and Partick, as well as on the south side of the river at Pollokshields. Hugh Fraser's own home moved gradually westward from a tenement in the city centre, where he resided when Arthur & Fraser was established, to fashionable town houses in Bath Street and Elmbank Street during the 1850s. By the late 1860s his business success allowed him the luxury of a substantial detached villa in Partick. The Fraser family was typical of the rising middle class whose demand for draperies and fancy goods of all kinds became more pronounced than ever during the mid-nineteenth century. Fashionable costumes and furnishings were extremely elaborate during these years when ornamentation won out over comfort. This was the age of the crinoline – an enormous circular skirt supported by a cage of flexible steel hoops. The crinoline, which achieved its most exaggerated form in 1860, was of great benefit to the drapery trades as a single dress generally required in excess of thirty-five yards of material. Similarly, mid- and late-Victorian houses were cluttered with furnishings. Windows were hung with velvet and lace curtains; sideboards, pianos, fireplaces and chairs draped with runners, cloths and anti-macassars; mantelpieces laden with clocks, glassware, china figures and wax fruit, and walls adorned with gilded papers and hung with a plethora of plates, paintings, photographs and samplers. Whilst the middle classes enjoyed these trappings of an upper-class lifestyle, they still sought to make their purchases as economically as possible. The growing department stores, therefore, satisfied a new and important market and reflected middle-class aspirations and expectations in their merchandise ranges and trading policies.

The Lovers cannot go out for a walk, Turn—stiles and Gate-posts are perfect barricades between them, and the pleasant fields.

Cartoons ridiculing the enormous size of the fashionable crinolines, from Cupid and the Crinoline *(1853).*

Adolphus can never approach his beloved near enough to get 'such a thing as a KISS.'

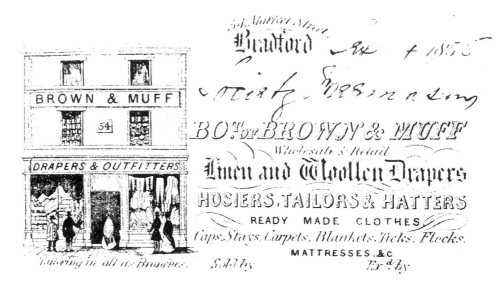

One new kind of merchandise which was to play an important role in the development of the department store was ready-to-wear clothing. Until the mid-nineteenth century few clothes were available off-the-peg. Drapers primarily sold lengths of cloth to be made up by the customer's own tailor or dressmaker. Part-sewn garments, supplied with the necessary trimmings, and simple clothes like mantles and cloaks were available by the 1830s, but the acceptance of ready-to-wear, as a stylish alternative to bespoke tailoring, was slow. By the mid-1850s Arnott & Co of Glasgow (see page 278), Brown & Muff of Bradford and Jollys of Bath were all purveying ready-made clothes. The advent of the sewing machine, however, accelerated the pace of change. Invented in America and patented by Isaac Singer, the sewing machine had become commonplace in Britain by the 1860s, allowing the mass production of fashion garments. In 1856 Singer & Co's first British premises were opened in Glasgow's Buchanan Street. Ready-to-wear garments required less time and skill to produce and could be sold quickly and cheaply for cash. Such merchandise was well suited to the new department stores' philosophy of ready money and quick stockturn. Fraser & McLaren do not appear to have been early purveyors of ready-to-wear clothing, although such garments were clearly available in many Glasgow stores by the 1870s.

During the first half of March 1872, Fraser & McLaren began, as usual, to receive their spring stock. On 18 March the partners invited inspection of a 'large and choice selection of goods in every department.' The following week the costume buyer returned from London with 'the newest styles in jackets and mantles.' The furniture showrooms likewise were 'replete with a large and carefully assorted stock of first class goods.' A few days later, in the early hours of the morning of 27 March, fire broke out in Fraser & McLaren's Argyle Street showrooms, and the back buildings in Morrison's Court were soon enveloped in flames. From there the fire spread to the connecting Buchanan Street showrooms. In Argyle Street the iron shutters, which had been tightly closed, hindered the fire fighting and on the following day the *Glasgow Herald* reported that 'all hope of saving the front building was soon abandoned; the fire raged from floor to floor with resistless fury, and all that could be done was to keep pouring water in by way of moderating the flames, without hoping to extinguish them, until everything which would burn was consumed. The floors gave way one after the other as the morning wore on, and at last only the roofless wall remained.' The front portion of 12 Buchanan Street was, however, saved and thick walls also preserved the corner building at 8 Buchanan Street. Within a week temporary premises were found for the carpet and furniture showrooms at 195 Argyle Street and a new stock of silk mercery, drapery, millinery, mantles and underclothing was secured for sale at the surviving showrooms on the first floor at 8 Buchanan Street. Fraser's insurances amounted to £46,900 for stock and fittings and £13,470 for the buildings. In the event a little over £11,500 was claimed for reinstating the warehouse and, once the insurance money had been gathered in, William Spence, a local architect, was commissioned to design new showrooms for the entire site. Demolition work began at the end of May 1872 and by July the builder, John Morrison, had laid the foundations of the warehouse.

The new building was, however, only partially complete when, on 12 February 1873, at the age of fifty-seven and after a long illness, Hugh Fraser died at his villa in Partick. He left an estate worth nearly £56,000. Under the terms of his will the trustees were to carry on the business with Alexander McLaren, Fraser's widow, Jane Bunting, and his eldest son, James Arthur Fraser, then eighteen years of age, until the expiry of the co-partnery contract with McLaren. If McLaren's co-partnership agreement was renewed the trustees were instructed not to allow him more than one-eighth of the profits nor any power to make purchases. Additionally, if an opportunity arose, the trustees were urged to purchase the corner building at 8 Buchanan Street which had split the store's two fronts for so long. Fraser's property was to be shared equally amongst all his children, and, although the business was to remain intact, each of his other four sons, John, Hugh, David and Matthew, who desired to enter the firm was to be able to purchase a share in its heritable property for the sum of £8,000. All bequests were directed to be paid with due regard to the interests of the business, and those due to his wife and children were to be held as interest-bearing investments in the firm. James Arthur Fraser was immediately assumed as a partner to manage the business alongside Alexander McLaren and his father's trustees – Jane Bunting, Matthew Pettigrew, Murray Cowbrough and John Snodgrass, the son of Fraser's step-sister who had married a farmer in Cardross. Apart from Fraser's wife, the trustees were all able businessmen involved in manufacturing, warehousing and commission agency businesses in Glasgow. In the absence of an obvious and immediate successor the death of Hugh Fraser was a severe blow to the business. However, the new team quickly began to lay plans for the future and determined to complete the half-built warehouse according to the designs which Hugh Fraser had already approved.

*Buchanan Street in 1880,
looking north. Wylie &
Lochhead's warehouse is
shown on the left-hand side.*

3 1873–1909
Palaces of Commerce

Construction work on Fraser & McLaren's new warehouse, superintended by the architect, William Spence, continued throughout 1873 and the new show-rooms were opened in their entirety in the spring of 1874. Forming a right angle between Buchanan Street and Argyle Street, with entrances to the retail departments from both sides, the new warehouse was built in the Venetian style favoured by contemporary architects. 'The Argyle Street front', commented *Building News*, 'has one central doorway, with two pilasters on each side, which project on the pavement. The projection caused by the entrance is carried up the entire height of the building. The Buchanan Street front presents a similar appearance, while the court is designed like an arcade.' Inside, light and airy showrooms stocked with a wide range of drapery goods and house furnishings were supplemented by costume, shawl and millinery workrooms, an upholstery workshop, carpet sewing room and counting house. The windows of the upper floors were decorated with eighteenth-century ornamental keystones, the 'Tontine faces', which had been acquired by Hugh Fraser before his death. These grotesque carvings had, until 1869, adorned the old town hall in Trongate. John Tweed, compiler of a city guide, noted that 'the beauty of the Tontine has disappeared; even the sculptured masks which stretched along the whole front have vanished, and nobody seems to know what has become of them.' Several letters had appeared in the press debating their whereabouts, and so the incorporation of a number of the faces in the facade of Fraser & McLaren's new warehouse stirred considerable local interest. On 2 March 1874 Fraser & McLaren took an entire column on the front page of the *Glasgow Herald* to advertise the opening of their new premises, listing departments for silk, millinery, underclothing, clothes, stuff, costumes, ribbon and lace, muslin, prints, napery, haberdashery, mantles, hosiery, gentlemen's accoutrements, shawls, mourning, dressmaking and carpets.

The business traded profitably for the next three years, advertising vigorously and carrying a broad range of stock. Average sales amounted to over £75,000 per annum and trading profits were in excess of £15,000. On 31 July 1875 Alexander McLaren retired from the partnership. His investment in the firm, which had diminished since Fraser's death, then stood at £414. James Arthur Fraser was yet but a youth of twenty years and his younger brothers, John and Hugh, were still in their early teens. The trustees, therefore, continued to administer the business, which was renamed Fraser Sons & Co, appointing an experienced draper, John Towers, as managing partner. Towers' agreement was to run for seven years and he invested a sum of £1,200 in the firm. During the following months trade became sluggish and an effort was made to collect outstanding debts. However, with sales down by twenty per cent, trading profits contracted. James devoted himself to the business, drawing a salary of £100 per annum, and appears to have been joined by both John and Hugh as soon as they left school.

During the late 1870s the returns of the business remained unspectacular. In 1878 the situation was worsened by the collapse of the City of Glasgow Bank which precipitated a general commercial crisis. Demand diminished and many retailers throughout Scotland were forced into bankruptcy. For four years between 1879 and 1882 Fraser Sons & Co suffered severe trading losses which were borne by John Towers and James Arthur Fraser alongside the trustees. However, buying and selling largely for cash, the firm never owed more than a few thousand pounds, and during the first half of 1883 a small profit of £700 accrued. Meanwhile John Towers' partnership agreement had been renewed. The following year John Fraser, having reached the age of twenty-five, was assumed as a partner. By then sales had begun to recover and land values in Buchanan Street were rising rapidly. In 1884 the firm's property was valued at £57,000. Despite a recurrence of trading losses during the years between 1885 and 1888, in 1887 Hugh Fraser also joined the partnership. The two youngest Fraser brothers showed no interest in the business. David, apprenticed as a lawyer, later became a merchant in New York and Matthew farmed in the Borders.

Hugh Fraser (1860–1927).

By early 1888 Glasgow was in a fever of excitement in anticipation of the opening of the Glasgow International Exhibition. Such events were extremely popular during the 1880s and there had been exhibitions in both Edinburgh and Manchester during the previous two years. The Glasgow International Exhibition, housed in specially built pavilions in Kelvingrove Park, was, however, to be the largest of its kind since that held in London in 1862. The entire city was transformed by the remaking of roads and beautification of the fashionable shopping promenades in preparation for the vast influx of visitors. Opened on 8 May 1888, the Exhibition attracted over four-and-a-half million visitors in just six months and included displays of manufactured goods from all over the world. Local businesses were quick to recognise the immense promotional opportunities offered by the Exhibition and several of the large Glasgow warehouses took stands or created 'exhibition displays' in their showrooms. Unlike the Great Exhibition of 1851 all wares on display could be priced, although the sale of articles for their immediate removal was not permitted.

Manufacturers and purveyors of fine furniture were assembled in Court 29 where Frasers displayed an oak sideboard, couch, bedroom suite, dressing table, wash-stand and 'Fraser's Patent Telescope Table'. Amongst the textile stands Walter Wilson & Co showed a mass of millinery, tartans and napery. Wylie & Lochhead were also much in evidence, having been invited to furnish the royal reception rooms. Throughout the Exhibition the city centre bustled with activity, and Frasers, like other stores, pushed sales with discounts and advertising. In August the store launched a huge summer sale, reducing the charge for making up dresses to only ten shillings. By the end of September Frasers had already received their new season's stock and the Buchanan Street windows were attractively dressed with a suite of bedroom furniture and a wide range of winter fashions.

Two weeks later the entire western wing of Frasers' fine Buchanan Street warehouse was utterly destroyed in the aftermath of a huge conflagration. On Sunday, 14 October 1888, a fire began inside a drapery warehouse in Buchanan Street and spread rapidly until the two blocks between Argyll Arcade and Frasers' premises were a raging inferno. The heat of the blaze shattered the windows of Stewart & McDonald's warehouse on the opposite side of the street and the walls of Wylie & Lochhead's new building were blackened and blistered. Despite this destruction the thick gable walls and hoses playing over the roof served to protect Frasers' warehouse and by evening the flames had been extinguished. The store appeared to have been saved but, early on the Monday morning, most of the Buchanan Street portion of the warehouse collapsed without warning, undermined by water which had flooded into the cellars. The manager, Mr Smith, who had stayed in the store overnight to keep watch, was forced to make a hasty escape. The reverberations of the collapse sent debris hurtling in all directions, breaking most of the nearby plate-glass windows which had not been lost on the previous day. The *Drapers' Record* reported the fire at length: 'The appearance presented by the street the following day was something not easily to be forgotten, the most striking feature being Frasers' warehouse cut through the centre as if with a knife, the several flats being exposed to view, with the goods in the respective departments.' Buchanan Street was quickly cordoned off and Frasers were forced to suspend business in the surviving Argyle Street building. The trustees immediately set about finding alternative premises and announced the selling off of damaged stock as soon as the loss adjustors were satisfied. The insurance claim was uncontested and the payment of £6,207 covered a large portion of the reinstatement costs. On Tuesday 23 October Frasers launched an

THE GLASGOW HERALD, TUESDAY, OCTOBER 16, 1888.

THE BUCHANAN STREET FIRE.

This sketch shews the whole of the space on the east side of Buchanan Street which has been affected by the fire that broke out on Sunday afternoon. On the extreme left, the low building is the Argyll Arcade. Next, comes the structure in which the conflagration originated. The thin upright columns and cornice are all that now remains standing, for in the course of yesterday the gaunt gable and back walls were pulled down to prevent their falling unexpectedly and injuring the firemen who were pouring water on the ruins. The low building with the arched beam and chimney stack further to the right represents the premises of Messrs Brown, Smith & Co., and Austin & M'Aslan, wherein the fireman was imprisoned; while on the extreme right are the ruins of Messrs Fraser, Sons & Co.'s warehouse, which fell so unexpectedly yesterday morning.

Fraser Sons & Co's fire-destroyed warehouse, as sketched by a Glasgow Herald *reporter in October 1888. The L-shaped building was cut in half exposing all four floors to the elements.*

immense sale of damaged stock. The *Drapers' Record* reported that 'every day this week the pavement has been impassable for the crowds of people crushing to obtain admission ... Frasers are getting rid of enormous quantities of goods, and, so far as one could judge from the windows, the articles are fetching good prices.'

Work on the rebuilding began in mid-January 1889. By June the roof had been completed and the fitting out of the interior began. The showrooms were expected to be ready in August and new stocks were ordered which had later to be sold off at a discount when completion was delayed. The new warehouse was finally opened at the end of October, occupying the same site between Argyle Street and Buchanan Street. Built on six floors with a fine stone facade it boasted the most modern fittings, including electric lighting and heating equipment. 'The stocks in all the departments', announced an advertisement on 21 October, 'will be found fresh and fashionable, bought from the first and best sources of production for cash, and which we continue to mark on our well-known minimum profit system.' The following year the Argyle Street entrance was substantially altered to fit in with the new frontage on the Buchanan Street side.

Frasers' lavish new building was in keeping with the spirit of the times. By the late 1880s Glasgow had become one of Britain's most sophisticated shopping centres. 'Its shops', commented the *Drapers' Record*, 'are almost all lofty, well lighted and ventilated, and certainly in all the leading thoroughfares are dressed with as much taste as though they were situated in the heart of London. The goods shown are of the latest fashions and styles; the prices are low and they are

OVERLEAF *Various departments at Jolly & Son of Bath during the 1890s: the parasol and fan department; the Manchester goods department; the lace and embroidery department.*

displayed to the best advantage.' Competition was fierce and the large warehouses could no longer rely on their early innovations to sustain market leadership. Their advantage over the speciality shops had begun to be eroded. Low margins, fixed marked prices, window display and sales had all been adopted by other retailers. An emphasis on rapid stockturn and the economies of scale persisted but, alongside these, the nascent department stores began to pioneer new ways of attracting customers and of inducing them to spend. Whilst their initial success had been based on the manipulation of price, the late-Victorian and Edwardian department stores thrived on the seduction of the customer. Enterprising owners determined to make their stores centres of spectacle and showmanship, encouraging shoppers to linger by making a visit to the store an event in itself. Once inside the profusion and variety of goods and adventurous and accessible displays created an irresistible urge to buy. In 1895 Lady Jeune noted, with some disapproval: 'What is shopping in these days, but an unsuccessful struggle against overwhelming temptations? We go to purchase something we want; but when we get to our shop, there are so many more things that we never thought of till they presented obtrusive fascinations on every side. We look for a ribbon, a flower, a chiffon of some sort or other, and we find ourselves in a paradise of ribbons, flowers, and chiffons, without which our life becomes impossible, and our gown unwearable.' By the 1890s the discount warehouses of the mid-nineteenth century had been transformed into 'palaces of commerce' – the golden age of the department store had arrived.

Punch *comments on the enormous size of the growing department stores.*

OUR MAMMOTH STORES.

Shopman. "EXCUSE ME, MADAM, BUT AM I NOT RIGHT IN PRESUMING YOU COME FROM THE TOY DEPARTMENT?"   *Lady.* "CERTAINLY. WHY?"
Shopman. "WOULD YOU VERY KINDLY DIRECT ME TO IT? I'M ONE OF THE ASSISTANTS THERE AND I'VE LOST MY WAY."

The store buildings were an important part of the new strategy. Initially the department stores had grown by the haphazard acquisition of adjoining premises, creating rambling and often cramped showrooms which clearly betrayed their origins as separate lock-up shops. Where space could not be gained by acquisition new storeys were added to existing buildings, workrooms and offices converted and salons erected in gardens to the rear. In London, early building regulations required large retail showrooms to be subdivided by walls and doors to prevent the spread of fire. Consequently the adoption of the open plan interiors common in contemporary Parisian and American department stores was slow in Britain. Instead, London stores tended to be planned, as was Harrods, with the shop on the lower floors, divided into discrete showrooms, surmounted by flats or work-shops which were accessed by a separate entrance. Nonetheless, by the 1890s a new generation of purpose-built department stores had been created. Outside they were impressive and monumental, often classical in design, incorporating stately columns and vast arcades of plate glass. Inside they were opulently fitted out with large areas of sales space, well adapted to enticing display. In 1885 when Wylie & Lochhead erected their new warehouse in Buchanan Street it was a model of its kind and, although broadly similar in design, totally eclipsed its predecessor of thirty years before. The unusual terracotta facade was 'one huge window' attractively complimented by an ornamental doorway. The internal arrangement was also stunning with 'several successive tiers of immense galleries running round the entire edifice, one above another, and leaving in the centre a space entirely unoccupied, from the ground floor to the immense ellipsis of glass and ironwork that roofs the whole.' The circulation of customers was encouraged by the provision of modern passenger lifts and sweeping iron and walnut stair-cases, and the entire establishment was gently lit by the ample admission of daylight. National and local journals reported enthusiastically on the new store: 'To stand in any part of this warehouse and survey all that is visible from any one point of view of the magnificent display of superior goods it contains is simply a privilege, an artistic treat, which should certainly enhance the pleasure of making a purchase in an establishment where the convenience and satisfaction of customers constitute at all times considerations of paramount importance.' Thus the building itself lent a respectability to the raw commercial machine within, emphasising the unity of the store despite the disparity of the various departments and providing a suitable stage for the showmanship of display and promotion.

Technological advance had made such warehouses possible. Until the advent of iron-framed construction, showrooms with broad column spaces, light wells and integrated plate glass frontages would not have been possible. Glasgow, with its buoyant local iron trade and daring school of architects, was one of the first cities to adopt iron-framed construction on a significant scale. Wylie & Lochhead's earlier Argyle Street warehouse, built in 1845, had pioneered the use of iron-framed construction for retail shops. The introduction of cast-iron piers, common by the 1850s, provided structural support and allowed shopfronts to be built in the same plane as the upper facade. Similarly, the reduced need for internal supporting walls allowed, where local building regulations permitted, the creation of magnificent open salons. The grace and versatility of the new building material, well suited to flamboyant and decorative structural features, soon made it popular for the construction of retail warehouses. Its principal drawback was that iron lost its strength in intense heat, a susceptibility to fire compounded by the Glasgow custom of laying timber floors on iron girders. Later warehouses over-came this problem by bedding the iron frame within fire-proof bricks. The

OPPOSITE *The impressive Buchanan Street facade of Wylie & Lochhead's new warehouse.*

magnificent architecture of the new generation of store buildings was easily matched by the opulence of the internal decorations and fittings. Mahogany panelling, thick pile carpets, a profusion of mirrors and elegant light fittings were all common by the 1890s. Every detail of the elaborate ornamentation was carefully calculated to create an atmosphere conducive to spending.

The vastness of the new department stores tended to discourage the circulation of customers to upper floors and to corners at a distance from the main doors. The large warehouses were, therefore, amongst the first public buildings to introduce passenger lifts. As early as 1855 Wylie & Lochhead's new Buchanan Street warehouse had included a crude lift described in the *Glasgow Herald* as 'a very ingenious hoisting apparatus, worked by a neat steam engine, which is intended not only to lift up bales from the waggon entrance to the upper parts of the building, but to elevate those ladies and gentlemen to the galleries to whom the climbing of successive flights of stairs might be attended with fatigue and annoyance. Parties who are old, fat, feeble, short-winded, or simply lazy, or who desire a bit of fun, have only to place themselves on an enclosed platform or flooring when they are elevated by a gentle and pleasing process, to a height exceeding that of a country steeple, and from the railing of the upper gallery they may look down on a scene of industrial activity and artistic magnificence which as yet has not a parallel amongst us.' The Wylie & Lochhead lift was an extremely early device. The first safe lift, with brakes, was developed by Eliza Otis in America in 1852 and powered by hydraulic motor. 'Passenger hoists', as early lifts were known, remained relatively uncommon until the 1880s when the application of electric power considerably increased their efficiency.

The first 'moving staircase' installed at Harrods in 1898. Escalators subsequently became a popular feature of large stores throughout the country.

By the late 1890s many large stores throughout the country boasted passenger lifts on every floor. Harrods alone, amongst the major department stores, had resisted their large-scale installation, reputedly because managing director, Richard Burbidge, did not favour the new machines. By the spring of 1898, however, the Harrods board was locked in discussions with a French company, Piat et ses Fils, for the purchase of the exclusive patent rights to a new invention, the 'revolving staircase' or escalator. In May agreement was reached and construction work began immediately. Piat vouchsafed that no similar staircase would be erected elsewhere for six months and that Harrods, as sole patentee, would have its name branded on the leather belt. During the autumn of 1898 the Harrods escalator was completed. Comprising a flat conveyor belt rising up a gentle gradient of one in three between two handrails, it ran some forty feet between the ground and first floors. In his diary Burbidge reported enthusiastically on the final tests, noting '700 staff coming up in fifteen minutes' and 'perhaps 4,000 people per hour can travel by it.' The experiment attracted much publicity and on the opening day in November shopmen were stationed at the top to revive customers who had been unnerved by the experience with free smelling salts or cognac. 'The traveller', reported the *Daily Chronicle*, 'puts his feet on the moving staircase, his hand on the rail and is wafted by imperceptible motion to the place where he should be.' In February 1899 the board granted an escalator licence to Owen Owen's store in Liverpool and within a few months had also negotiated the formation of a joint company with the Reno Inclined Escalator Co of New York to exploit the Halle and Reno escalator patents. During 1900 an additional Reno escalator was installed in the store at a preferential price of only £500.

Until the late nineteenth century, the provision of adequate lighting in large stores had presented a problem. The early department stores were designed to maximise the admittance of daylight by the use of plate glass facades and the arrangement of departments around a central, roof-lit well. By the 1850s gas lighting was general in the larger shops but it was not until the advent of electric lighting that stores could be configured in a different way to make more intensive use of floor space and to allow the colour and opulence of merchandise displays to be exploited to the full. In Glasgow, although the railway stations and post office had electric lighting as early as 1879, electricity was not provided by the Corporation until 1893. Enterprising shopkeepers were quick to see the attraction of the new form of illumination. In 1882 Walter Wilson of the Colosseum introduced three forms of electric lighting (Crompton, Weston and Swan) and installed sixty lamps in the toy salon to create a 'dazzling hall of light' as a promotional feature. In 1889 Frasers' new showrooms also boasted electric lighting. By the 1890s electricity was, in addition, being used to power fans for the provision of heat in winter and ventilation in summer.

Administrative problems caused by the size of the new warehouses were also overcome by new inventions. Change owing on cash transactions was generally dispensed from a central point. During the mid-nineteenth century young boys were employed as 'cashs' to run between the showrooms and the counting house. During the early 1880s the need for such lads was ended with the invention of Lamson's cash balls, which allowed money and bill to be placed inside a hollow ball and propelled along overhead tracks to the change desk. Later the balls were replaced by railways and pneumatic tubing. The first Scottish cash-carrying system was installed in Glasgow at Arnott & Co's Jamaica Street warehouse in 1885. Walter Wilson swiftly copied the idea installing a cash railway in his Colosseum warehouse in the same year.

N. 98   Polished brass........................ 11/10

No. 92. Wrought iron and copper with amber or opalescent shade ....price 12/4
Extra shade......each 2/0

ALL GLOBES AND BURNERS EXTRA.

John Barker & Co of Kensington High Street during the late 1880s. The store already sold a wide range of goods and boasted most impressive premises.

Customers were, however, attracted not only by the magnificence of the buildings and novelty and opulence of the fittings and services, but also by the variety and profusion of goods available. By the late 1880s, London department stores were offering a vast range of wares quite unconnected with their original specialities. William Whiteley pioneered merchandise diversification on a large scale in his Bayswater store, and became known as the 'Universal Provider'. Whiteley took a pride in being able to supply any merchandise requested and offered departments ranging from jewellery and furniture to railway tickets and forage. The store was described in *Modern London* as 'an immense symposium of the arts and industries of the nation and of the world; a grand review of everything that goes to make life worth living passing in seemingly endless array before critical but bewildered humanity; an international exhibition of the resources and products of the earth and air, flood and field.' John Barker, who had served as a department manager at Whiteleys for some years, carried a similarly diverse stock at his showrooms in Kensington High Street. Barker (see page 281), having opened a small drapery shop in 1870, rapidly acquired adjoining premises and added new lines until, in 1889, he was trading in an imposing six-storey warehouse with a magnificent plate-glass frontage and offering departments as varied as books, groceries and furniture.

Even in Glasgow diversification had become commonplace. In 1889 an observer reported, 'The term "general draper" has long since lost its original significance and now within the limits of an establishment whose title would denote its devotion to trade in cloths and such things, the public embrace the opportunity of purchasing nearly every article their requirements dictate.' Lady Jeune, although concerned about the ethical propriety of the new department stores, acknowledged that 'the convenience of being able to buy everything one wants under one roof is very great, and as the easy means of communication brings so many more people than formerly ... to the large centres, to do their shopping, they prefer to make their purchases where they can concentrate their forces and diminish the fatigue ... What an amount of trouble and expense is avoided where one can order one's New Zealand mutton downstairs, buy one's carpets on the ground floor, and deck oneself out in all the glory of Worth or La Ferrier, on the top floor, to all of which one is borne on the wings of a lift, swift and silent.' Initially new lines were added in the same way that they had previously been sold by the speciality shops – silks, mantles, fancy goods, bazaar goods, china and so on. Occasionally, new merchandise was tried in an existing department until sales expanded to the point where a separate department was justified. Frequently the creation of totally new departments in a mature form was prompted by the acquisition of adjoining premises or the stock of a retiring tradesman. In the larger stores a third party might be introduced to initiate a new department, or agency agreements were signed with particular manufacturers. Harrods introduced several departments in this way, engaging Lombardi & Co, for example, to begin a photographic studio in spring 1894 which was taken over by the store itself a year later. As store operations grew in size, departments became distinct operating units with their own managers and buyers, their sales and profit figures clearly distinguished in the accounts. Gradually the merchandise was regrouped so that previously unrelated stock was associated by location and displays. Ladies' clothing and accessories, for example, previously split into a number of separate departments began to be sold together in novel combinations.

Alongside the diversification of merchandise the large stores began to offer an increasing range of services. From the early nineteenth century many drapers had provided funeral undertaking facilities but the new department stores also began to offer building and decorating, catering, cleaning and dyeing, and hairdressing services alongside the sale of theatre and travel tickets and the provision of house agency and auctioneer departments. Customers were also encouraged to linger in the stores by the provision of tearooms, restaurants, reading rooms and cloakrooms. Such facilities were a potent attraction at a time when there were few places that a lady could have a meal alone and nowhere for women to meet friends outside their own homes. The stores became social rendezvous, particularly attractive to the out-of-town shopper on a day visit. Several London department stores boasted tearooms by the mid-1880s and a refreshment room was launched at the Army & Navy Stores in Westminster as early as 1877. Manchester was reported as having several shops with tearooms and ladies' lavatories in 1889 and the refreshment room at Kendal Milne, decorated extravagantly in Moorish style, was opened in 1890. In Glasgow Walter Wilson & Co opened a suite of rooms for the supply of temperance refreshments in July 1888. These were the first tearooms in a Scottish warehouse and were described in some detail in the *Drapers' Record*: 'The rooms are fitted up most sumptuously, the draping being of Japanese silk and cloth. There are two large saloons, where either ladies or gentlemen may have refreshment, and one very neat saloon specially reserved for ladies. A good deal of the continental element has been introduced, prominence being given to *café au lait* and French pastries. There are also reading and writing rooms attached.' In 1898 Pettigrew & Stephens of Sauchiehall Street advertised: 'The tearoom, a cosy resting place, is at the disposal of country visitors, light refreshments can be had. Resting rooms adjoining.' The tearoom had been opened in 1895 on a complimentary basis but, after considering comments from customers, a moderate charge was introduced 'to remove all idea of indebtedness from the minds of their patrons.' In Edinburgh,

THE TEA ROOM AT
MAULE'S, EDINBURGH.

when Robert Maule opened his new warehouse at the western end of Princes Street in 1894, the restaurant, known as The Rendezvous, became the social focus of the store which adopted the advertising slogan 'Meet me at Maule's.'

In the larger stores the range of services could be phenomenal. By 1909 Harrods boasted 'elegant and restful waiting and retiring rooms for both sexes, writing rooms with dainty stationery, club room, fitting rooms, smoking rooms, etc … free of charge or question. Public telephones … provided in all departments, a post office, theatre ticket office, railway and steamer ticket and tourist office, appointment boards where one can leave notes for friends, a circulating library and music room.' Within the store it was possible 'to insure life, property and servants, buy, sell or let houses and estates, buy or sell stocks and shares, rent a safe in which to keep valuables, open a banking account, book theatre seats, secure tickets for railway journeys, book sea passages, despatch household and other property to any part of the world … get your hair dressed, hire a carriage or motor car, lunch or dine on the premises, enjoy the club and reading room, join an up-to-date library, and store furs, tapestries, etc., in a specially constructed cold air chamber.' In the Grand Restaurant, afternoon tea was served 'to the strains of Harrods' Royal Red orchestra.'

By 1911 Harrods of Knightsbridge offered a huge range of departments: the grocery department (below); the meat hall (opposite above); and the millinery department (opposite below).

Harrods' delivery vans lined up in Brompton Road, in front of the store, in 1912.

OPPOSITE
A Brown & Muff's delivery cart in Bradford during the 1890s. Horse-drawn vehicles were commonly used by department stores until after the First World War.

In addition to a broad range of merchandise and services, the department stores began to offer an extensive delivery service so that customers no longer needed to be burdened with their purchases whilst shopping. Initially, horse-drawn carts were employed and the large stores maintained huge stable establishments – in 1906 Harrods owned 410 horses, 10 motor vans, 157 despatch vans and 52 removal vans. Later, motor vehicles were used, particularly the model T-Ford. In Glasgow Walter Wilson's Colosseum was the first to adopt the motor car, and the store's Daimler, leaving Jamaica Street at ten, twelve, two and four o'clock every day, attracted much attention. The expense of running a delivery service was enormous and, although a small charge was levied, keen competition generally meant that costs were not recouped in their entirety. Later, in 1905, Harrods threw the trade into disarray by announcing free delivery for any item throughout England and Wales regardless of value.

A number of shops also began to integrate backwards into production. All large warehouses engaged in manufacturing of some kind, commonly related to making up lengths of cloth into dresses or mantles. Frasers themselves had a range of costume and upholstery workshops by the 1880s. Other stores manufactured on a much larger scale in order to gain more control over the quality and quantity of supply and also to reduce costs. Walshs of Sheffield, Kendal Milne of Manchester, and Wylie & Lochhead of Glasgow, all operated important cabinet-making factories. Stores such as John Barker's in Kensington had sizeable building and decorating workshops and Harrods owned a range of factories as well as a model bakery, nursery gardens and farms. The Army & Navy Co-operative Society was particularly active in manufacture. Within two years of its establishment, several selling departments, including printing, perfumery, shirts and portmanteaus, were producing merchandise and by 1878 separate workshop premises were acquired and a manufacturing manager appointed. During the next ten years the number of Army & Navy employees involved exclusively in manufacturing increased four-fold to over 1,200.

When, in 1896, John Walsh commissioned local architects to design a warehouse for a vacant site in Sheffield's High Street it was typical of the new genre of magnificent department stores. The premises, with a frontage in excess of 370 feet, comprised three-and-a-half acres of sales space. *The Sheffield and Rotherham Independent* reported that 'the ground floor of the building will be 150 feet wide by 200 feet long, and a feature will be the absence of all internal walls. This floor will be divided, however, into six sales shops, each 25 feet wide by 200 feet long, by columns, which will be so placed as to cause no obstruction to either passengers or counters. Another feature which is sure to be appreciated by the numerous ladies and others who will visit the establishment will be the arrangement of the counters, which will be so placed that in every part the full light of day will be available.' The basement showrooms extended in an L-shape along both frontages and elevators provided easy access to every floor. Behind the sales area there

OVERLEAF LEFT Printing and binding the Army & Navy Stores' substantial price lists during the 1890s.

OVERLEAF RIGHT Staff arriving at the Army & Navy Stores during the 1890s. Such warehouses employed an immense workforce, and department store owners often led the way toward improving shop assistants' conditions of work.

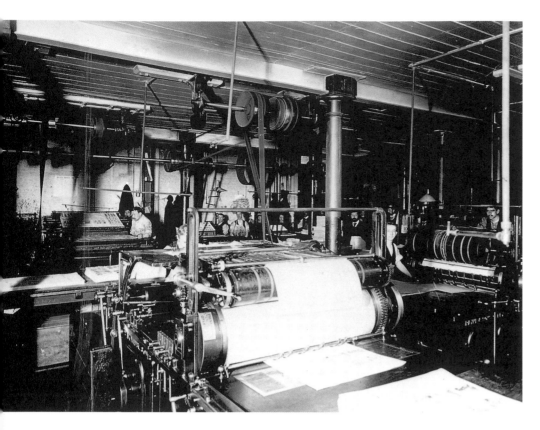

John Walsh's magnificent new store in Sheffield, shortly after its completion in 1899.

were rooms for receiving, marking and despatching goods, a covered yard and a counting house. Above the sales rooms were four floors of bedrooms and other facilities to accommodate more than 100 staff, and behind these were two floors of workshops. Inside, the store was fitted with thick carpets, mahogany counters and brass fixtures. Completed in 1899, the building cost more than £60,000.

Shoppers, attracted to the stores by their palatial buildings and novel facilities, were then tempted to spend by seductive display. During the mid-nineteenth century shopkeepers had concentrated their attention upon new kinds of window displays. By the 1890s, however, the creation of attractive and accessible displays inside the warehouses had assumed more importance. From the early 1880s shopfitters began to provide lady-like figures for showing dress goods. A few had wax heads and hands but most were simply padded bodies on a stand with wooden knobs to serve as heads. By the turn of the century more sophisticated equipment became available. In 1900 Arnott & Co of Glasgow attracted considerable attention by showing a mannequin advertising the 'I.L. Persephone' corset, 'the movement of the head and eyes and the heaving of the chest being wonderfully life like.' Other equipment was also available, such as muff, fan, open parasol and boot stands; glove hands; mantle shoulders; and enamelled legs and feet for displaying shoes and hosiery. Furniture began to be displayed in room settings, and china and cutlery laid out on tables. Even rolls of cloth were

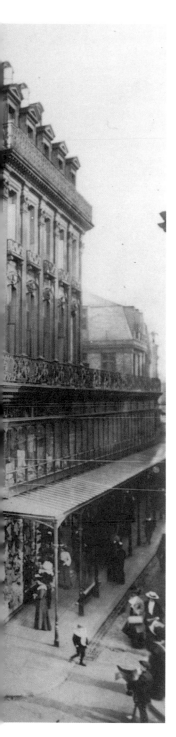

Display stands or 'figures' for dresses.

brought out from behind the counters on to purpose-made cloth stands. The aim was to make goods touchable and attainable in order to encourage purchases. During sale periods bargain goods would be piled together inviting self-service. Emile Zola's *Au Bonheur Des Dames*, a fictional portrait of a Parisian department store in the 1880s, described the exciting preparations made for the white sale: 'The counters disappeared beneath the white of silks and ribbons, of gloves and fichus. Around the iron pillars froths of white muslin were twining up, knotted from place to place with white scarves. The staircases were decked with white draperies, draperies of pique alternating with dimity, which ran all along the banisters, encircling the halls right up the second floor; and the ascending whiteness was taking wing, thronging and disappearing like a flight of swans.' Such open displays brought with them a new problem, shoplifting, which particularly affected the department stores. 'Kleptomania', as shoplifting was known, worried contemporaries who saw it as a symptom of declining moral standards. In 1888 the *Drapers' Record* reported 'that it may seem incredible, but during the periodical sales the great shopkeepers find it absolutely necessary to employ a goodly staff of detectives, whose duty it is to put a stop to petty pilfering.' It was hard to secure a conviction and storeowners generally played down the crimes provoked by sales techniques which were otherwise enormously successful. At the same time the trade press began to complain of 'tabbies', the name given to ladies who visited the larger stores on a regular basis to enjoy the displays and facilities without any intention of buying.

In contrast to the sophistication of merchandise arrangement inside the stores, the art of window display was less progressive during these years. The practice of filling windows with a mass of goods and tickets persisted, encouraged by a belief that customers rarely entered shops unless they could see what they required in the window. The importance of window display was, however, well understood. 'Business', noted the *Drapers' Record*, 'is done less and less between the public and the tradesmen and more and more as between the public and the shop windows.' Window displays changed with the seasons, reflecting the stores' calendars of sales and the new season's arrivals. Window dressing became an art in its own right and special staff were appointed exclusively to devise and execute displays. None of the large stores could afford to ignore this side of the business. In 1888 a Glasgow observer noted: 'There is a marked change in the attitude assumed now by certain old-established firms, such as Fraser Sons & Co, Stewart & McDonald, and Arnott & Co, who long held by the conservative plan of simply displaying their goods in the windows, and trusting to their well-known name bringing custom. Judging from the style adopted now they evidently find they would soon get relegated to one side in the race for business, if the old-fashioned tactics were pursued; each of these firms now gives large orders to the ticket writers and go in for labelling their goods with the modern legends of "great bargain at so-and-so," "big purchase," "so many grosses to be cleared out at so-and-so," and even in some cases do not disdain to use the catching elevenpence-halfpenny; it certainly shows wisdom to keep up with the times, as, if that is not done, one might as well retire from trade altogether.'

By the 1900s continuing improvements in the manufacture of glass allowed the production of massive plate-glass windows. Panes were no longer confined to the narrow widths which had given earlier shopfronts a pronounced vertical emphasis. Instead the new department stores boasted majestic and unending arcades of glass. In addition, the development of electric lighting encouraged stores to light up their windows until late into the night. However, by modern standards, window dressing remained rather mundane and the use of mannequins

OPPOSITE *Window displays at Mawer & Collingham of Lincoln in 1888. The plate-glass windows were divided into a number of small panes, cheapening the cost of construction and replacement.*

and arrangement of a few choice items did not become common until some years later. Nevertheless, the larger stores did occasionally exhibit novelties 'as a sort of magnet to rivet the attention of the passerby at first, after which, of course, from the contemplation of the curiosity to the examination of the ordinary goods the transition is easy.' In 1900 Arnott & Co showed the mechanical mannequin modelling the Persephone corset. In 1904 Swan & Edgar were fined 40 shillings for causing an obstruction with a live model, 'Phroso', who stood in the store window in Piccadilly daring shoppers to make him smile for a £10 prize.

The earliest exceptional window displays were often linked to a special promotion. Apart from sales the most popular promotions during the 1890s were undoubtedly the Christmas bazaars. By November these were generally well in hand, focused on a particular theme, such as Father Christmas, zoos or nursery rhymes. Introduced during the mid-1880s, in Glasgow the Christmas bazaar was pioneered by Walter Wilson's Colosseum, and quickly imitated by such stores as Copland & Lye and Pettigrew & Stephens. Each year Wilson's Christmas events became more and more spectacular. In 1893 he provoked much interest with a mirror maze, which, 'once in, the visitor is so surrounded with apparently long vistas and duplications, that he is utterly at a loss as to how to get out. Some of the combinations are of a comical character.' In 1895 workmen spent months preparing a reproduction of Beethoven's house in Bonn and a model of the market place and town hall of Leipzig. These bazaars not only sold toys but, as Christmas cards to friends began to be replaced by small presents, also featured books and fancy goods. Other kinds of promotion were intended as pure spectacle to boost the number of shoppers visiting the stores. Walter Wilson was by far the most inventive in this area, holding competitions, distributing free gifts and posting thousands of circulars from the top of the new Eiffel Tower in Paris. In 1890 he paid £6,000 to show John Lavery's painting of Queen Victoria opening the 1888 Glasgow International Exhibition, and, on a single day, attracted over 10,000 visitors.

During the early 1870s, shops advertised almost exclusively in the classified columns of newspapers and magazines, reaching a limited audience. By the 1890s, however, press advertising had become a more influential weapon. Technical advances in printing allowed mass production of penny and half-penny dailies which enjoyed a large circulation. In 1880 the *Daily Telegraph* claimed 300,000 readers and by 1900 the *Daily Mail* had over one million. The number of ladies' magazines and daily newspapers circulating outside London also increased dramatically. A few enterprising store owners began to publish flamboyant advertisements, adopting a novel format or unorthodox copywriting style. Manufacturers of branded goods often led the field, repeating a brand name or slogan for several column inches as an eye-catching device. From the 1880s, illustrations became more common. 'One little block', remarked the advertising manager of D.H. Evans, 'is worth a page of letterpress.' Typically, in Glasgow, the new genre of advertising was pioneered by Walter Wilson of the Colosseum who was continually trying such new ideas as shocking headlines and advertisements written in code. He also began to use new media, actively linking advertising with sales promotion. In 1884, under the headline, 'A Colossal Advertiser', the *Evening Times* reported: 'Walter Wilson of the Colosseum, in the enterprise of his advertising proposals, seems in a fair way of outstripping any of his competitors ... His proposal to engage Mrs Langtry, his huge lorry processions, and £100 prize, are all familiar; but his supreme effort is his latest, in which he has made an offer to the Glasgow authorities to provide clothing, free of charge, for the whole police force for the next five years, provided he is allowed to put the words "The Colosseum Tea" on the bands of the policemen's helmets.'

By the early 1890s, Glasgow newspapers were filled with advertisements for local shops. 'In no other important town in the United Kingdom', reported the *Drapers' Record* in 1892, 'do drapers advertise so fully as in the second city of the Empire.' Two years later a Glasgow shopkeeper disclosed that 'warehousemen

THE QUEEN, THE LADY'S NEWSPAPER.

EXCLUSIVE MODEL SATIN BRIDAL GOWN, exquisitely embroidered in Silk and Pearls, or Paste Diamond and trimmed with Chiffon and Lace. Price according to quality of Satin selected.
BRIDAL GOWNS complete from **18** Guineas.
BRIDAL VEILS.—In Real Brussels Appliqué, from **7½** to **20** Guineas. **TAMBOUR** from **69/6.**
JUST PUBLISHED.—Ful'y Illustrated and Detailed CATALOGUE of WEDDING TROUSSEAUX and GENERAL OUTFITTING Post Free on Application.

DICKINS & JONES, 232 TO 242, REGENT ST., LONDON, W

A Dickins & Jones advertisement for bridal gowns in The Queen *(1897).*

like myself must keep himself before the public and the only way to do this is by advertising in the newspapers.' In London the large stores spent thousands of pounds on advertising. In February 1904 Harrods spent £2,500 on one day alone and, a few years earlier, had been the first store to take a whole page in the *Daily Telegraph.* Richard Burbidge, managing director of Harrods, had visited the large stores in the United States and was persuaded of the value of advertising along American lines. 'To be successful,' he is reported as saying, 'advertising should be carried out systematically and must have a well thought out scheme or design. It wants a man to give his whole attention to it.' By the early 1890s Harrods had set up an advertising department with its own manager.

Illustrations from an autumn fashions circular issued by Jolly & Son of Bath in 1890.

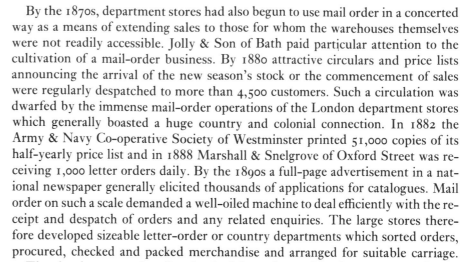

OPPOSITE ABOVE *Harrods'*
telephone order room in
1909. The store was the first
to introduce a twenty-four
hour telephone enquiry
service.

OPPOSITE BELOW *A*
Dallas & Co of Glasgow
circular issued during the
1890s, concerning ladies'
clothing.
The instructions for self-
measurement are exacting as
standard sizes were not
introduced until much later.

By the 1870s, department stores had also begun to use mail order in a concerted way as a means of extending sales to those for whom the warehouses themselves were not readily accessible. Jolly & Son of Bath paid particular attention to the cultivation of a mail-order business. By 1880 attractive circulars and price lists announcing the arrival of the new season's stock or the commencement of sales were regularly despatched to more than 4,500 customers. Such a circulation was dwarfed by the immense mail-order operations of the London department stores which generally boasted a huge country and colonial connection. In 1882 the Army & Navy Co-operative Society of Westminster printed 51,000 copies of its half-yearly price list and in 1888 Marshall & Snelgrove of Oxford Street was receiving 1,000 letter orders daily. By the 1890s a full-page advertisement in a national newspaper generally elicited thousands of applications for catalogues. Mail order on such a scale demanded a well-oiled machine to deal efficiently with the receipt and despatch of orders and any related enquiries. The large stores therefore developed sizeable letter-order or country departments which sorted orders, procured, checked and packed merchandise and arranged for suitable carriage.

The development of mail order had been fostered by improvements in the national postal service and the growth of a comprehensive rail network. In 1856 the preferential postage rate for books was extended to include printed papers sent in open covers, thereby reducing the cost of the mass circulation of price lists. In 1863 an additional pattern post was introduced for fabric samples. The despatch of ordered goods was facilitated by the Post Office's inauguration, in 1883, of a flat-rate parcel post operated in conjunction with the Railway Clearing House. The railway companies also continued to operate their own services for the carriage of parcels and the resultant competition kept prices low. Consequently, in 1892 and later in 1902, when the Caledonian and North British Railway Companies negotiated agreements which would have stifled freight price competition, the Glasgow department stores launched bitter protests. Customers were generally charged according to distance from the store and the mode of carriage, although orders above a certain value or within a specified radius were delivered free. Empty packaging was returned to the stores for re-use. From the late 1880s the letter-order departments were often complemented by a telephone enquiry service. The first telephones arrived in Britain in 1878 but their commercial use evolved hesitantly and they did not become common in department stores until the mid-1890s. Frasers had installed a telephone by 1892 and in 1905 Harrods pioneered the provision of a twenty-four hour telephone-order department.

By the 1890s, mail order could constitute as much as a third of a large store's turnover and was most popular during sales periods. In January 1907 the *Drapers' Record* commented on the increasing popularity of 'shopping by post' during the sales: 'All the firms have adopted this handy method of extending trade, and at the same time meeting the wants of distant customers who cannot find it convenient to travel to the city. These letter orders of a morning can be counted by the hundred, and special staff have had to be deputed to see to their execution.' The Army & Navy Co-operative Society was unusual in that it originated primarily as a mail-order business, circulating a huge annual price list to its membership of army and navy officers and their families. So enormous was its postal business that the Society's low, 'co-operative' prices began to have a depressive effect on provincial retailers. As early as 1879 when a parliamentary select committee was appointed to inquire into the middle-class co-operatives, it heard complaints from as far afield as Bournemouth, Cardiff and Cambridge that the Army & Navy catalogue business was bankrupting local firms. *Punch*, quick

to comment on issues in the public eye, swiftly printed a cartoon depicting a country grocer who had laid off staff 'owing to the rector and other gentlemen getting their supplies from the Stores in London.'

Mail-order circulars were generally sent to regular customers and others upon application. Price lists ranged from simple broadsheets to substantial sewn and bound books. Often small samples of cloth were included, and in the larger stores entire departments might be devoted to cutting and pasting these patterns. Occasionally, fashion catalogues offered instructions for self-measurement or ladies were advised to send in an old bodice as a model for the store's dressmaker. By the late 1890s Harrods and Army & Navy were despatching illustrated price lists running to over 1,000 pages. The production of these catalogues was, in itself, a major operation and by the 1880s Army & Navy had begun to print and bind the catalogues in their own workshops, reporting a saving of some twenty per cent on production costs. The seasonal catalogues were eagerly awaited by ladies as the authoritative pronouncement on the latest styles, and were passed from hand to hand like a popular journal. Harrods described their price list as a 'veritable shopping encyclopaedia . . . handsomely bound in cloth, lettered in gold and . . . worthy of a place in the domestic library.'

The massive growth which most department stores underwent during the last quarter of the nineteenth century was not accompanied by a reduction in costs. Instead the maintenance of opulent buildings, the provision of facilities like cloakrooms and a delivery service, the growing importance of fashion goods such as ready-to-wear clothing which became worthless once outdated, the adoption of lines like furniture which enjoyed lower stockturn, large-scale advertising and an emphasis on display which increased wastage by soiling, all contributed to higher operating expenses. In part these increased costs were counter-balanced by the overall growth of turnover and purchase discounts procured by the stores on the strength of their huge buying power. However, they also found expression in increasing mark-ups which averaged around twenty per cent during the 1880s. Department store prices, however, remained relatively low. In part this was due

A Harrods own-brand coffee label dating from the 1900s. The red, white and blue livery was subsequently replaced by a less garish olive green.

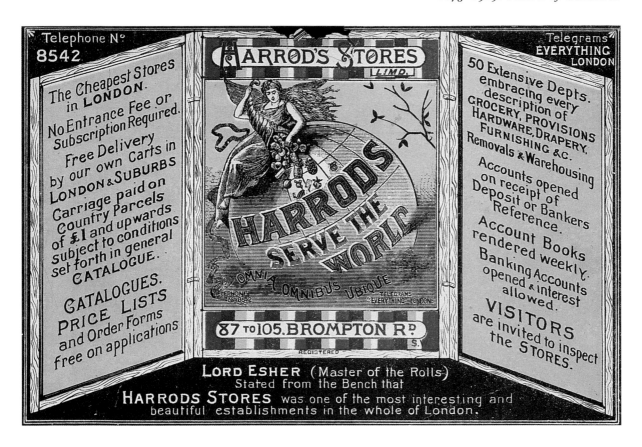

'Harrods Serves the World'. The globe and cornucopia had been adopted as the store's trademark by the 1890s.

to the influence of middle-class co-operatives like the Army & Navy Co-operative Society which, pledged to avoid the accumulation of profits, sold at extremely low prices. For the first time, consumers were made aware of the real value of goods, and Harrods' initial success in the 1870s was based upon a policy of adopting 'co-operative prices' and advertising them widely.

Price competition was intensified by the introduction of proprietory goods, pre-packaged and manufacturer advertised, which could be sold cheaply in large shops by unskilled staff. Such branding was initially confined to groceries and medicines but spread to other merchandise such as off-the-peg fashions. Branded goods were readily adopted by the large stores, and small shopkeepers who could not compete on price began to demand resale price maintenance. Manufacturers, however, were rarely willing to lend their support to such price fixing as they depended heavily upon the custom of the large stores which otherwise replaced protected items with own-brand goods. Many department stores quickly developed trade marks. In 1890 alone D.H. Evans of Oxford Street registered two clothing labels, 'The Mifit' for corsets and stays and 'A La Scintillante' for general purposes. Indeed, as their local and national reputations grew, protecting a large store's name and labels became an economic necessity. In late 1887 Lewis & Co of Manchester became the first business to bring an action under the new Merchandise Marks Act. A few stores had, like Harrods, already begun to develop large ranges of branded goods. In the grocery and provisions departments, Harrods used branded goods to spearhead its low price policy, adopting a distinctive red, white and blue striped livery to make 'own wares' recognisable.

During the 1850s and 1860s, price promotions largely comprised occasional sales of salvage from fires or the stocks of bankrupts. During the last quarter of

A delightful postcard, sent to the regular customers of Robert Maule & Co of Edinburgh in 1909, announcing the imminent winter sale.

the nineteenth century, however, the department store year became punctuated by a regular series of sales from stocktaking or white sales in January, through clearance sales at the close of the spring, summer and autumn seasons. In between there were promotions based on special purchases of particular goods. Occasionally stores used loss leaders, that is the selling of a particular article or the stock of an entire department at a loss in order to attract interest. Octave Mouret, the Parisian store owner in Zola's novel, understood the value of loss leaders: 'We shall lose a few sous on the stuff, very likely. What matters, if in return we attract all the women here, and keep them at our mercy, excited by the sight of our goods, emptying their purses without thinking?' In Glasgow special price events were also held in July for the benefit of holiday visitors and later for ladies who, returning from the coast, were anxious to replace their well-worn wardrobes. In August 1887 the *Drapers' Record* bewailed that 'frontages which have hitherto preserved a perfectly wholesome appearance, have, as it were, broken out in an eruption of red blotches. Gaudy window bills inform the world that "to make room for autumn purchases the remaining stock will be sacrificed at less than cost price."'

As department stores grew in size owners sought both protection and funding by conversion to limited liability. The late 1880s and 1890s witnessed a general upswing in company registrations across all sectors of the economy. Many of these were private company formations prompted solely by a desire to limit the liability of the proprietors for the firm's debts. Retail partnerships which converted to private companies included Wylie & Lochhead Ltd in 1883, Cavendish House Ltd in 1883, Arnott & Co Ltd in 1891, John Walsh Ltd in 1902 and Jolly & Sons (Bath) Ltd in 1903. In most cases the founding families retained total control of the business. Other store owners, however, sought public flotation as a means to fund expansion on a scale which could not be supported by profit ploughback alone. Shares were generally offered primarily to customers and staff and were frequently subscribed several times over. Cavendish House Co Ltd of Cheltenham went public in 1888, Harrod's Stores Ltd in 1889, D.H. Evans & Co Ltd in 1894, J.J. Allen Ltd of Bournemouth and H. Binns Sons & Co Ltd

OPPOSITE *A colourful broadsheet advertising the flags, banners and buntings available at Cavendish House of Cheltenham during the Queen's Diamond Jubilee in 1897.*

CAVENDISH HOUSE, CHELTENHAM.
THE QUEEN'S DIAMOND JUBILEE.
ILLUMINATIONS AND DECORATIONS — GREAT REJOICINGS.

In anticipation of a large demand for Flags, Banners, Bunting, and other decorative materials, we have made very extensive preparations, having placed large orders at an early date on very advantageous terms.   Particulars and prices are as follows:—

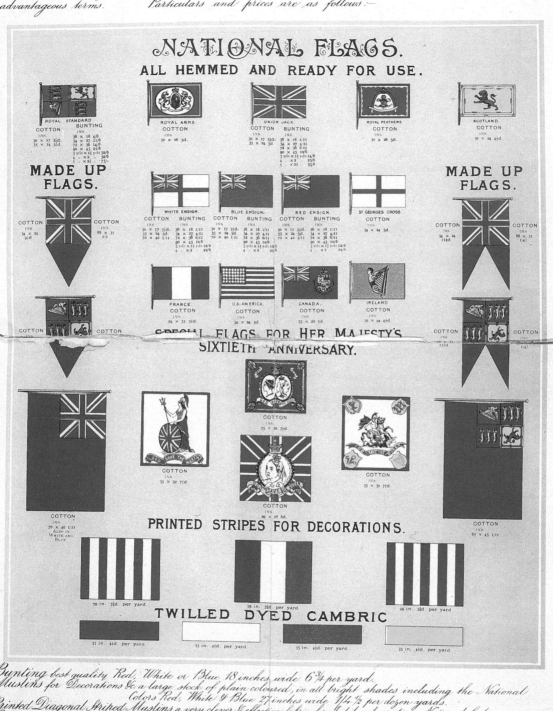

NATIONAL FLAGS.
ALL HEMMED AND READY FOR USE.

MADE UP FLAGS.

MADE UP FLAGS.

SPECIAL FLAGS FOR HER MAJESTY'S SIXTIETH ANNIVERSARY.

PRINTED STRIPES FOR DECORATIONS.

TWILLED DYED CAMBRIC

Bunting best quality Red, White or Blue 18 inches wide 6¾ per yard.
Muslins for Decorations &c a large stock of plain coloured, in all bright shades including the National Colors Red, White & Blue 27 inches wide 1/4½ per dozen yards.
Printed Diagonal Striped Muslins, a very clever & effective fabric for Jubilee decorations National Colours 40 inches wide 3¾ per yd.
Patterns of Muslins &c for Jubilee Decorations free on application.
Japanese Lanterns for Decoration various shapes 4½ to 10½ per dozen.
Japanese Lanterns larger sizes, 2ᵈ, 5ᵈ, 1/- & 1/4ᵈ each.
Japanese hand Screens from 6ᵈ per doz., Japanese Fans 4ᵈ & 6ᵈ each.

Cavendish House Company, Limd.

of Sunderland in 1897, Dickins & Jones Ltd in 1900 and John Barker & Co Ltd in 1904. Initially, the limited liability was disliked and misunderstood by the public who considered shareholders to be foisting their responsibilities on to customers and suppliers and feared that salaried directors would be devoid of incentive to efficiency. As late as 1898 a columnist in a ladies' magazine could write that 'there seems to be a small scare amongst certain numbers of my correspondents who imagine that their dearly beloved Marshall & Snelgrove's is going to be altered out of all recognition simply because it has turned into a limited liability company.' In fact, since control rarely passed out of the hands of the founding families, the stores themselves were outwardly unchanged. Besides, the generalisation of smaller uncalled liabilities and share denominations and the emergence of bankers and solicitors as respectable financial intermediaries soon quelled public fears.

In 1894 when Dan Harries Evans was interviewed on the recent flotation of his business, the journalist reported: 'As evidence of the reception the prospectus had received, Mr Evans picked up at random half-a-dozen letters from customers, and read extracts from their expressions of goodwill towards the new venture,

Glasgow's Sauchiehall Street in around 1902.

82

and an anxiety to be allotted a holding. He explained that the prospectus had been sent out to every customer as a desire was to give the preference to everybody who was already connected in any way with the firm, and the response he said, had exceeded even his utmost expectations. Until the country applications had all been received, it was impossible to say precisely how the thing had gone, but it was obvious it was to be applied for several times over. The eagerness with which the staff also had applied for shares was marvellous, everyone on the premises who had any money to invest having apparently determined to throw it into the business.'

Subsequently department stores ventured further afield than their own customers to dispose of shares and in 1899, when H. Binns Sons & Co Ltd of Sunderland made a new share issue, subscriptions were invited from City houses. The editor of the *Drapers' Record* disapproved of the rash of flotations but admitted that 'money is cheap and the spirit of investment is in the air.' Yet, whilst other companies, such as brewing, textile finishing, tobacco and wallpaper concerns, grew by merger, department stores largely developed by accretions to their existing trade. There were undoubtedly some mergers. During the 1900s Dickins & Jones Ltd of Regent Street acquired several other famous firms, including Lewis & Allenby of Conduit Street and George Hitchcock of St Paul's Churchyard, both silk mercers. For the most part, however, department stores tended to combine only through casual trade associations for the discussion of such issues as pricing policies and opening hours.

Fraser Sons & Co remained a fairly traditional dry-goods warehouse and never indulged in flamboyant advertising or promotions nor diversified to the same extent as the adventurous London department stores. During the early 1890s the business was effectively managed by James and John Fraser, Hugh being obliged by ill-health to spend some time overseas in the warmer climes of Australia. In 1892 the youngest of the late Hugh Fraser's sons reached the age of twenty-five and the trustees determined to transfer Fraser Sons & Co to James, John and Hugh, who had been assumed as partners. The other two sons, David and Matthew, promptly contested the transfer demanding an opportunity, as stipulated in their father's will, to purchase a share in the heritable property for £8,000. Additionally, the surviving daughters protested against the conveyancing of any of the property. The trustees took the case to the Court of Session in Edinburgh, and in January 1894, the Lords judged that David and Matthew Fraser were not entitled to demand assumption as partners and that the business and property might be transferred to James, John and Hugh Fraser in its entirety. Consequently, during the summer of 1894 the existing co-partnership was dissolved and the three brothers commenced in business as sole partners.

These were unauspicious years for the retail trade with the country in the grip of a general recession and prices falling. Frasers must also have been concerned by the westward drift of the fashionable shopping district from Buchanan Street to Sauchiehall Street. Straightened, drained and planted with trees in 1809 to provide a promenade for the elegant residential area to the south, by the 1870s Sauchiehall Street was lined with tenements which were crammed with shops on all floors. By the 1890s a significant number of large stores were established in Sauchiehall Street, including Copland & Lye (1878), Pettigrew & Stephens (1888), Tréron & Cie, a branch of Walter Wilson's Colosseum (1890), and James Daly & Co (1894). The trade press observed that 'Sauchiehall Street is improving almost every month as a shopping thoroughfare' and 'fast becoming the Regent Street of Glasgow.' During the last five years of the nineteenth century property values in Sauchiehall Street leapt by a phenomenal forty per cent.

Frasers endeavoured to sustain sales by continued advertising and the inauguration of a bonus system for staff. Profit sharing was then a novel concept. In
1891 the *Drapers' Record* reported that 'there is no concern in our trade which
has adopted the profit-sharing system of trading in any of its existing forms.
There may be instances where heads of departments participate in the profits of
the section over which they preside, but we are not aware of a single business
where the rank and file of the house have an individual interest in the welfare of
the establishment.' A few stores had begun tentative schemes when, at the end
of 1897, the Fraser brothers 'agreeably surprised their employees by giving each
of them a handsome present as their share of the year's profits. They were
promised that if the turnover exceeded a certain amount the gift would be
repeated.' The incentive scheme, which coincided with a general return of
prosperity, was tremendously successful and sales increased substantially during
1898 and the first half of 1899. Initially, the outbreak of the Boer War in October
1899 depressed trade. In a climate of austerity, as news of the early Boer victories
arrived, social functions diminished and the demand for fashionable trinkets
collapsed. Later a craze for khaki took hold and large quantities of ties, handbags
and even handkerchiefs were sold in military green. The relief of Ladysmith was
followed by a huge demand for 'patriotic drapery' and souvenirs, such as flags
and buttons emblazoned with portraits of the commanding generals. Meanwhile,
work had begun on the redevelopment of Stewart & McDonald's warehouse in
Buchanan Street opposite Frasers' store. The new building was to be set back in
line with the rest of Buchanan Street, thereby relieving the congestion hitherto
caused by the narrowing of the southern end of the thoroughfare.

In January 1901 Frasers, in common with every department store and large
drapery shop in the country, were preparing for the seasonal sales when the news
of Queen Victoria's death was received. An assistant at Dickins & Jones of
London recalled the event vividly: 'The day Queen Victoria died we were on the
eve of the white sales. By the next morning everything was turned to black – it
was one of the biggest transformations in the history of the trade. Everything
that could be dyed was used to meet the colossal demand.' Throughout the
country sales of mourning goods increased dramatically, not only for personal
wear but also for the sombre decoration of public buildings. The *Drapers' Record*
reported that in Glasgow 'practically the whole population of the city are wearing
either black clothes or black ties.' The end of the period of general mourning in
mid-April was eagerly awaited by retailers who anticipated a 'rush for coloured
stuff'. By the first week in May trade was once again brisk. Good weather, a
release from mourning and the opening of the 1901 Glasgow Exhibition encouraged sales. Glasgow's streets were thronged with visitors and the *Drapers' Record*
noted that 'many of them have found their way into the dry goods emporiums.'

That week Pettigrew & Stephens opened their new department store at 181–
193 Sauchiehall Street after two years of rebuilding and refurbishment. 'Next
to the exhibition', announced the firm's advertisements, 'Pettigrew & Stephens'
great warehouse and department store is the sight of Glasgow.' Featuring a gilt
dome, originally designed by Charles Rennie Mackintosh for a chapterhouse, the
store boasted seven floors, departments ranging from silks to confectionery and
carpets to china, tearooms and reading rooms, lifts serving every floor and a
pneumatic cash-carrying system. It was one of the most diversified and stylish
stores in Scotland and, in order to see the warehouse properly, ladies were
enjoined to 'take the passenger lift to the very top, inspect the model kitchens
and make their way down through the ironmongery and furniture departments
to the charming restaurant, from which, after resting and refreshing, they can

A 1901 trade card illustrating Stewart & McDonald's new building, on the corner of Buchanan and Argyle Streets, which was completed in 1903.

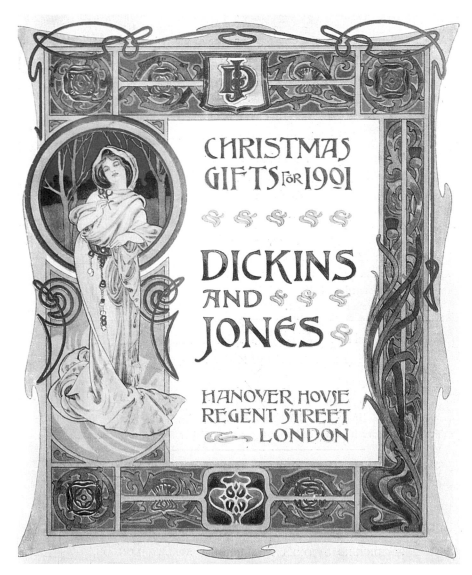

The cover of Dickins & Jones' 1901 fashion catalogue reflected the contemporary popularity of Art Nouveau.

Union Street, Aberdeen's main shopping street, showing John Falconer & Co's flourishing store on the right, next to a branch of Lipton's grocery chain.

set out again on a visit of delight through the charming costumes and millinery salons, boot salons, underclothing section, down the grand staircase to the street floor, and finish up with the china and glass and the gents' hat and cap department in the basement. They will have traversed seven complete floors, and will acknowledge, when finished, that no such shopping centre, where the whole wants of the family can be supplied, exists in Scotland.' Members of the press, invited to a preview inspection, were equally eulogistic: 'The interior is divided into three bays of galleries, and, standing on the ground floor, one has an uninterrupted view right up to the top storey, the roof of which is fitted with an

expanse of clear glass, which sheds light into the whole interior. The walls of the main staircase are adorned with Grecian marble of beautiful colours, and the windows are fitted with stained glass depicting the industry and costumes of a long line of centuries.' Every day for a week a souvenir gift, commemorating the opening, was given to each customer entering the store.

The following month, upon the occupation of Pretoria and trouncing of the Boers, Glasgow's shopping streets were decked out for victory whilst at the Exhibition in Kelvingrove many of the city's large stores competed to achieve the most eye-catching displays. Pettigrew & Stephens built a large Moorish pavilion showing lace wares on a daring Mackintosh-designed stand, whilst Wylie & Lochhead once again furnished the royal reception rooms and created a magnificent Art-Nouveau pavilion in the new 'Glasgow style'. When the Exhibition closed in November the city's retailers were already looking forward to the Coronation year. Queen Victoria and her long widowhood had cast gloom over the country, and the department stores confidently expected that Edward VII and his queen, who were enthusiastic theatre-goers and socialites, would give fresh impetus to the fashion trades.

During the last quarter of the nineteenth century, the retail trade had been afflicted by a multitude of short-term setbacks. Sensitive to the slightest change in the disposable incomes of the middle classes, the department stores were disproportionately affected by local recession and even by the less predictable vagaries of the weather. Again and again a prolonged summer proved ruinous in the autumn and an untimely spell of fog killed the Christmas trade. Yet, during the late-Victorian period, the department stores flourished and achieved an unprecedented degree of size and sophistication. The cyclical economic booms of the 1880s and 1890s undoubtedly underlay their success. The stores were, however, also a tangible expression of the new culture of self gratification, reflecting the confidence of a nation at the peak of its economic, political and military might and boasting an Empire which stretched around the world.

The general prosperity which Britain enjoyed during the closing years of the nineteenth century gave way to a period of recession at the beginning of the twentieth, and the average weekly wage fell sharply. Many retailers began to experience severe problems, particularly in the face of the growing price competition offered by the increasingly successful multiple and co-operative stores. Multiple shops, such as Liptons and Home & Colonial Stores, had originally been confined to the grocery and provision trades. They sold cheaply, practising the same bulk buying exercised by the department stores but retailing through a number of remote branches. By the 1900s, multiple selling had penetrated other trades. Freeman Hardy & Willis and Thomas Lilley were selling boots and shoes; Hepworth and Dunns men's clothing; Fleming, Reid, ladies' hosiery; and Boots, patent medicines. Department stores had, however, generally traded up during the 1890s and, despite fierce competition, continued to prosper during the slump. By concentrating on providing better standards of service, new facilities and more luxurious surroundings for their customers, rather than cutting margins, store owners had reinforced the popular perception of the department stores as emporia for the middle classes. During the opening decade of the new century they traded on this growing reputation for comfort and gentility with great success.

Britain's middle classes had swollen in numbers and confidence during the reign of Queen Victoria. From the 1870s there had been a great increase in opportunities to enter such professions as the law, accountancy and engineering, whilst the powers and responsibilities of the civil service and municipal government were broadened creating a new bureaucracy. Salaried professionals and

MADE-UP LACE DEPARTMENT.

Smart Russian Blouse in Black Chiffon and Chantilly Lace over Bright Blue Chiffon, or color to tone with Skirt.
Price 5 Gns.

New Smock in Shot Ninon de Soie, trimmed Old Gold or Aluminium Gaion.
Price 42/-
In Black. **Price 35/9**

Charming Fichu in Black Chantilly Lace and Chiffon, with pretty Tassel Ends.
Price 49 6

ALL PURCHASES of Drapery Goods sent Carriage or Post Free in the United Kingdom or Channel Islands.

OPPOSITE AND RIGHT
A selection of the made-up lace and millinery goods available at Dickins & Jones in around 1902.

No. 670. Broderie Anglaise Soft Muslin Embroidered Collar.
4/11

No. 8953. Heavy Guipure Lace Collar with deep pointed back, in the new Ochre shade. **15/6**
In **Black** two shillings extra.

No. 8952. **Fine Hand-Embroidered French Muslin Collar** with deep back and small revers in front. The latest shape.
7/11
Also with **Square Back** at same price.

No. 8701. **Real Point de Venise Lace Collar,** the new deep back shape, finishing on the shoulders without fronts. particularly suitable wear with outdoor coats. White only.
17/6

officials generally had greater job security as well as higher incomes than industrial workers. By the 1900s the purchasing power of the middle classes had also increased alongside their growing importance. A considerable number of single middle-class women were beginning to earn a living as governesses, teachers, typists and shop assistants, and had regular independent incomes. In addition, as the birth rate fell, two or three children replaced the enormous families of the previous century, and expenditure on necessities diminished with increasing imports of cheap food from the Empire. Towns grew markedly with the construction of large numbers of elegant semi-detached villas. Between 1901 and 1911 almost a million new houses were built. Furnishings remained rich and elaborate, although well-designed machine-made furniture, touched by the exciting Art Nouveau styles, was also much in evidence.

The new King, Edward VII, was a famous *bon viveur* with a taste for champagne and large cigars. Edwardian high society modelled itself on the King. Dinners, balls and country house parties assumed a sudden popularity and more money was spent on food and clothes than ever before. The middle classes were willing and able to emulate this new cult of consumption. Women were particularly pleased to discard the sober fashions and stifling social conventions of the late-Victorian era. Until 1910 basic clothing styles remained unchanged and the fashionable 'S' shape of the 1890s persisted, with its exaggerated bustline and highly corseted waist. The trade in accessories and trimmings was, however, revived. Heavy jewellery, furs, feather boas and elaborate millinery became the rage. In 1905 George Bernard Shaw complained bitterly about a woman at the opera wearing a complete bird as a hair ornament. Pastel shades of pink, blue and mauve replaced the sombre hues of the 1890s and dresses were heavily adorned with lace, ribbons and sequins. Meanwhile middle-class wives, with smaller families to manage, had more time for leisure as well as more money to spend. The department stores were quick to provide the restrooms, restaurants, tearooms and other facilities which would attract them to the stores. In 1902,

The elaborately furnished living-room of a typical well-to-do Scottish household during the 1890s.

Harrods' directors were told that recent developments proved 'that business promptly responds to increased trading facilities.' Confident of a bright future, many department stores embarked upon major refurbishment schemes. In London the entire Brompton Road frontage of Harrods was rebuilt in extravagant style and construction work on the famous meat hall was completed. Barkers in Kensington and D.H. Evans in Oxford Street also commenced the erection of new buildings and, in the provinces, Jollys of Bath, Howells of Cardiff and Arnotts of Glasgow were all extensively remodelled.

Frasers, determined to attract new custom, altered the Argyle Street frontage of the store in August 1903. 'The design is artistic', noted the *Drapers' Record*, 'and should give scope for attractive window display.' A few months later disaster was narrowly avoided when the seven-storey warehouse of Brown Smith & Co, adjoining Frasers' Buchanan Street showrooms, was utterly destroyed in a massive fire. In November 1905 John Fraser, in his late forties, withdrew from the business and James and Hugh immediately appointed an experienced assistant manager, William Pollok, formerly of Mann, Byars & Co and Pettigrew & Stephens. Scarcely three months later, in February 1906, James Fraser was also compelled to retire on grounds of ill-health, leaving Hugh Fraser in sole command. Hugh immediately embarked upon an extensive refurbishment programme, erecting fitting rooms, creating a new dress and costume salon and totally redecorating the warehouse.

At a time when wealthy Glaswegians were drifting away from Buchanan Street to shop at the increasingly popular department stores in Sauchiehall Street, and on the eve of the severe local recession of 1907–9, Fraser's energetic efforts to improve his store were well timed. Whilst the turnover of even the most exclusive of Glasgow's stores diminished during the short recession, Frasers were able to maintain sales at a level of just over £50,000 per annum and contain losses and bad debts. By the beginning of 1909 there were strong signs of recovery in Glasgow's economy. Elsewhere in Britain the depression had never been so severe as in the west of Scotland. In 1908 the *Drapers' Record* reported that 'the present course of business shows clearly that "the great middle class" is holding its head up to an unexpected degree, and there is now no reason for anticipating that those who cater for its wants will find any very extraordinary falling off in business.'

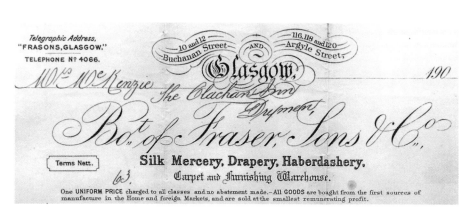

The Manœuvres of the Aeroplane.

This group shows some of the newest models. Of the two standing figures, one wears a frock of blue drap cotéle laced with silk cords, and a black hat trimmed lilies, the other a biscuit-coloured gown with soutaché embroideries and large picture hat. The sitting figure wears a dress in marquisette and a blue straw hat with pansies.

(PATTERNS AND ESTIMATES ON APPLICATION)

4 1909–1924
Going up with Leaps and Bounds

In late May 1909 the summer sales in Glasgow's warehouses were at their height. Every day during the month the city's daily newspapers carried front-page page advertisements declaring the bargains to be had at the leading stores. Pettigrew & Stephens, Anderson's Royal Polytechnic, Arnott & Co, Copland & Lye, Trérons, and Fraser Sons & Co, vied with each other for imaginative copy and the best bargains. All were keen to tell customers that they stocked the latest London and Paris fashions. By the beginning of the month, Frasers were 'radiant with everything new in the realm of dress.' At the time, couture was being transformed by the introduction of simpler, looser garments and the rejection of the tight corsets designed to produce the 'S' shape so popular with Edwardian women. With the economy expanding quickly, people had money to indulge in the new styles. Frasers were fortunate to secure the services of Miss Grace Hutcheson, 'the authority on proper corset fitting and deep breathing', to demonstrate and fit her new 'hygenic corset' during the first week of May – 'demand was beyond all expectations'. With this success behind them, Frasers promoted in the second week of May their sale of 'gowns, coats, blouses and Paris and London millinery,' and in the third week 'needs for the home' – 'Belfast bedroom and table linens,' 'carpets, exquisite curtains, furniture, hardware, Georgian bedroom suites and Sheraton cabinets.' Bold as Frasers' advertisements were, they were overshadowed by the more ambitious declarations of Trérons, 'Scotland's greatest fashion warehouse', and Anderson's Royal Polytechnic, 'supreme in the drapery trade for three generations,' which, in a topical reference to the latest battleship, boasted a 'Dreadnought competition.'

Despite the optimism that permeated the summer sales in 1909 with their exciting new styles, warehousemen and their middle-class customers were troubled by the contents of the Liberal Government's budget introduced in the last week of April. Newspapers were crammed with comments on the budget which the *Glasgow Herald* condemned as 'penalizing' and 'a ransom to the well-off.' Throughout Britain many business families took emergency action to defend their enterprise from what they conceived to be the damaging effects of the Chancellor's proposals. Commonly, shareholdings were dispersed to reduce exposure to taxation, and firms that had not already sought the protection of limited liability hastily did so. Fraser Sons & Co was registered as a private limited company on 26 May, with the three former partners, Hugh, James Arthur, and John as directors. The new company took over the business but not the Buchanan Street warehouse premises, which remained the three brothers' personal property. The business was valued as a going concern at £30,316, which was met by the issue of 10,000 five-per-cent-cumulative preference shares of £1 and 17,200 ordinary shares of £1, and the payment of the balance in cash. As the eldest brother and senior partner, Hugh Fraser held the bulk of the ordinary shares, receiving 15,206, James was given 2,001, and John 1,000. The clan badge of the Frasers, a stag's head, was chosen for the company seal. Fears that the budget would jeopardize burgeoning retail sales were borne out by the new

1909

Supper at the Savoy.

The above scene depicts two new models for evening wear. The gown on the left is amethyst satin, exquisitely embroidered in shaded silks and silver. On the right is a soft satin gown, of palest green with gold thread and crystal bugle embroideries. The sleeves of this gown are of gold bugle net, veiled with lilac chiffon.
(PATTERNS AND ESTIMATES ON APPLICATION.)

company's experience in the summer months with turnover only inching forward at a time of rising prices. The only good news was a return to profitability, albeit at just two per cent of total sales, after the loss in the winter season. This low level of return reflected the continuing price struggle with the co-operative societies and emerging multiple chains that had bedevilled the whole of the retail trade since the beginning of the century.

Competition in London, where the biggest stores had ten times Frasers' turnover, became intense in the spring of 1909 with the opening, by Gordon Selfridge, of a giant new store at the unfashionable end of Oxford Street. An American, who had made a fortune working for Chicago's biggest store Marshall Field's, Selfridge brought new concepts in management, and particularly in promotion, to the formality of Edwardian England. His preliminary advertising campaign alone cost £30,000 and set new standards in its use of illustrations rather than drab bold type. With no pretence of secrecy he revolutionized the conduct of personnel relations through higher wages and improved working conditions. He changed attitudes to stock control, maintaining higher levels of stock which was to be turned over more rapidly than most of his competitors. London was agog with excitement in the days leading up to the opening on 15 March, and crowds thronged to see the new store which Selfridge himself described as 'a social centre, not a shop.' Under the heading 'A Battle of Giants', the *Drapers' Record* commented at the end of February: 'The West End ... is to be a great battlefield of opposing business firms. Not only between West End firms, but as suburban and provincial stores try to counter the pull of the West End.'

London's established stores prepared vigorously for the fight. Harrods arranged to celebrate its diamond jubilee in the same week, with daily concerts in the store performed by the London Symphony Orchestra. Woodman Burbidge, the store's general manager, maintained that this was a mere coincidence, asserting that 'the day selected was the actual birthday of the famous Brompton Road establishment and that there was no deliberate intention of providing the public with a counter attraction.' His attempt to persuade the Secretary of State for War, Richard Haldane, to speak to the audience about the newly created Territorial Army was thwarted by the Prime Minister who was determined that the Government should not take sides. Retaliating against Selfridge, Harrods claimed to have pioneered shopping by telephone, particularly the provision of a round-the-clock service. Dickins & Jones, even though their store had been established in 1803, decided, belatedly, to celebrate their centenary, publishing a beautifully illustrated colour catalogue titled 'Upwards of a Century'. The introduction vaunted the company's accumulated experience: 'The aim of the founders of this business was to supply the finest and most reliable articles at the lowest possible prices which would allow a fair commercial profit. These successful methods eventually added a valuable asset, tradition, and the greatest testimonial a firm can receive – to be patronised year after year by successive generations of the same family.'

Throughout Britain warehousemen believed that tradition was their strongest weapon against Gordon Selfridge, who was condemned as a rich upstart who had used his money to poach their staff and customers. They banded together to deny him the commercial information they exchanged through their trade associations, and every store of any age began to advertise its heritage and the consistent quality of service. Dallas's, the Glasgow store with an extensive mail-order business in West Africa, incorporated 'Established in 1865' on all its literature, and announced the doubling in size of its warehouse with the slogan 'The business that stands still goes to the wall! Dallas's progresses by leaps and bounds!!!'

OPPOSITE *Ladies dressed for dinner at London's Savoy Hotel, from Dickins & Jones' catalogue, 'Upwards of a Century'.*

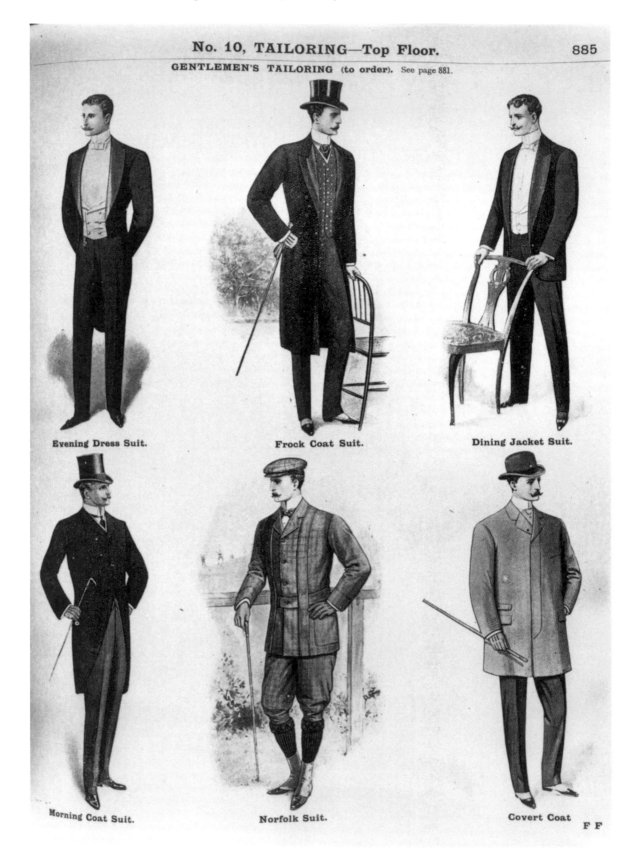

GENTLEMEN'S TAILORING (to order). See page 881.

Evening Dress Suit.

Frock Coat Suit.

Dining Jacket Suit.

Morning Coat Suit.

Norfolk Suit.

Covert Coat

F F

Illustration for the programme of Harrods' diamond jubilee celebrations, staged to coincide with the opening of Selfridges in 1909.

The cost of promotion to meet Gordon Selfridge's challenge was considerable, particularly for the London stores. Harrods and Dickins & Jones blamed the heavy expense of advertising and discounting for holding back profits in 1909. The following year Dickins & Jones were worried that the cost of promotion was driving up their prices. Some firms like Dallas's which had simply never been able to afford such outlays, continued to make a virtue of necessity by telling their customers, 'we can afford to give extra value as we do not spend reckless sums in bombastic newspaper advertising.'

However hostile their reaction to Gordon Selfridge's arrival in London, few stores up and down the country remained unaffected by the shock waves he sent rippling through the retail trades. Whiteleys planned a huge store in Bayswater to compete with their new Oxford Street rival. As early as 1909 Lieutenant-Colonel Stratchey, secretary of the Army & Navy Stores, began to review the company's organization 'with a view to bringing the Society's methods up to date by the utilisation of modern systems and inventions.' By July he had calculated

RIGHT *The ladies' tearoom of Mawer & Collingham of Lincoln, opened in 1910, and fitted out in the latest Art-Nouveau style, with fumed oak furnishings.*

ABOVE *An outing by the staff of Kendal Milne of Manchester in 1911 to celebrate the passing of the Shop Act which guaranteed weekly early closing. The photograph illustrates the large number of men and women who were employed in department stores prior to the First World War.*

that a pneumatic tube system would save enough boy labour to cover the interest on the cost of installation. At the end of the year arrangements were made for the London General Omnibus Co to carry the store's advertisements. Early in 1910 one of the directors, Captain Lewis, made a spying expedition to Harrods to compare prices and delivery times. In Cheltenham, between 1909 and 1910, Cavendish House commenced a programme of refurbishment and extension, adding a suite of fitting rooms to the costume department, opening a department for the sale of boys' outfits and building a new showroom for the millinery department and an all-important ladies' cloakroom and lavatory. Mawer & Collingham of Lincoln built a new tearoom to accommodate a larger clientele of ladies. In Glasgow on New Year's Day 1910, both Frasers and Muirhead & Co announced 'important extensions' that would be completed by the time of the sales. Other stores in the city followed suit. In midsummer Arnotts added an arcade to increase their window frontage by almost 500 feet. Many stores published new manuals for their staff, echoing those concepts. Copland & Lye's brochure emphasised that 'Good merchandise is useless without good service ... Small transactions well executed lead to big ones.' These investments and improvements were made against a background of continuing political uncertainty.

Although the Liberals won a landslide victory in January 1910, following the rejection of the budget by the House of Lords, the constitutional crisis remained unresolved. In the midst of the emergency, King Edward VII died suddenly on 6 May. For warehousemen, the King's death could not have come at a worse time. The summer sales had just begun and shops were crammed with stock. Windows were hurriedly cleared as the nation went into mourning and it was confidently predicted that the summer sales could be written off with large losses. The new King George V came to the rescue by declaring an abbreviated period of official mourning, finally dispensing with Victorian practice, and applied himself to searching for a solution to the political problems that beset the country. When talks collapsed there was a further election in December with another decisive Liberal victory. The crisis was finally resolved in August with the passing of the Parliament Act, which circumscribed the power of the House of Lords. Apart from the disruption in sales of the large London stores, caused by the departure of Members of Parliament and their supporters to constituencies during the election, the crisis was aggravated by labour disputes. Unrest on the railways and in the shipbuilding industry prevented a recovery in the retail trade during 1910. The following year more widespread disturbances of shipping, the railways, and road transport, not only disrupted the delivery of goods to stores and their despatch to customers, but also drove up prices, particularly of groceries, in the wake of wage settlements.

While the constitutional crisis was being played out, the hours and working conditions of shop assistants once again attracted the attention of Parliament. The subject of legislation for shops had first been considered in 1873, although it was not until 1886 that the Shop Hours Regulation Act was finally passed. In August 1909 the Liberal Government introduced a bill which, as well as demanding basic amenities for shop workers, prohibited them from working more than sixty hours a week and enforced early closing on one day a week. The Early Closing Association, which numbered among its members many of the larger stores and warehouses and was chaired by the Glasgow Member of Parliament, Cameron Corbett, was broadly supportive since most of the members already complied with the proposals. Smaller shopkeepers were much less enthusiastic, if not hostile. The passage of the bill was disrupted by the two general elections during 1910, but discussions between the trade and the Government continued

*The frontage of Mawer &
Collingham's Lincoln store
with its large ground floor
windows and arcade to
tempt the passer-by.*

throughout the year. So as to buy the support of this politically influential element
of the electorate, the Liberals agreed to amend the clauses that gave most
offence to small retailers. When finally passed in 1911, the Shops Bill was much
emasculated, but it did fulfil the objectives of the Early Closing Association for
weekly half-day closing, bringing other shopkeepers into line with the practice
of most warehouses and department stores. More significantly, the Suffragettes
who were actively campaigning for votes for women, apart from deriding those
females who were wasting their time amusing themselves at department stores,
intensified the attack on the living-in system.

In planning for the Coronation, Queen Mary made it known that only British-
made materials were to be used in her gowns. Wholesalers and retailers were
quick to espouse the patriotic cause and the trade press condemned the buying
public's preference for French fashions. An 'All British' shopping week was
arranged for the end of March with the support of the Union Jack Industries
League and organised by a committee of leading London stores, including
Harrods, Harvey Nichols and even Selfridges. Other cities followed – Bradford,
Leicester and Portsmouth, but none in Scotland. Glasgow warehousemen were
positively hostile, declaring that if they were 'to maintain good home trade, they

must be left a free hand to buy in all markets.' Although he was chairman of the Scottish National Exhibition which opened in Glasgow in May, Sir Andrew Pettigrew of Pettigrew & Stephens and Stewart & McDonald sympathised with such views expressed by his fellow warehousemen in the city.

By the time of the Coronation in June 1911, there was a prospect of better times ahead for the whole retail trade. Throughout Britain stores took advantage of the celebrations to sell souvenirs and flags and buntings. In Glasgow Anderson's Royal Polytechnic announced on 20 June: 'Now the decorators are getting busy – Phenomenal rush on the decorations department.' All the stores held Coronation sales to mark the occasion. Pettigrew & Stephens, flagrantly flouting the royal patronage for the 'Buy British' campaign, offered substantial discounts on dresses from French fashion houses, while Frasers preferred more prosaic, but patriotic, lines – Peter Pan collars, ladies' all-linen handkerchiefs, parasols and feather boas. As the Coronation approached, Frasers' advertisements were pushed off the front page of Glasgow newspapers by the city's leading stores. By the beginning of the following week Frasers had returned to their annual end-of-sales pitch – 'The period of quick selling at substantially reduced prices.' In the other Glasgow stores and elsewhere, particularly in London, the festivities continued into July. Despite the lack of enthusiasm for the 'Buy British' campaign in Glasgow, the impetus it gave to the domestic fashion industry soon became evident in the shops. Within two years it was reported that 'the great strides made by Bradford makers have resulted in the Yorkshire houses carrying off the great bulk of the orders ... there is scarcely a French agent to be seen within the doors of Glasgow houses.'

The upturn in trade during 1911 brought an increase in profitability and growing confidence, particularly in industrial centres like Glasgow and the north-east of England. Throughout Britain warehousemen planned further new buildings to bring their stores up to date. In many shops over the next three years the long rows of mahogany counters were ripped out and 'the main floors converted into salons with nicely decked glass cases.' Both the Army & Navy Stores in London and Mawer & Collingham in Lincoln refitted their floors in this way. In Glasgow Copland & Lye constructed a new warehouse alongside their existing shop in Bath Street, and their neighbours Pettigrew & Stephens, following a fire, extended their premises into the Fine Art Institute. Less ambitiously, Frasers installed new windows in their lace department and altered the layout of other departments at a total cost of £560. Within a year of their completion, James A. Fraser died after a long illness.

The decision by many stores to embark on yet more investment was premature. Industrial disputes continued into 1912, throwing into question the future course of the retail trade. A national miners' strike in March brought massive dislocation to the railways, leading to a sharp fall in sales at inner-city stores. The London West End department stores reported business down as much as a quarter during the six weeks of the strike. To make matters worse, Suffragettes began a campaign of breaking department store windows in March – Barkers lost twenty windows and Harrods two. No sooner was the miners' strike over than London tailors and tailoresses downed scissors in May. After an acrimonious dispute, the strike was settled early in the following month, by which time there were further disturbances on the railways and in the docks. Conditions were more or less back to normal in early August and shopkeepers again looked forward to an excellent autumn and winter season, but at first even this seemed to be denied them. The weather was atrocious, keeping customers at home and causing a wag to pen this parody of the popular rhyme for remembering the days in the months:

Dirty days hath September,
April June and November
February days are quite alright
It only rains from morn til night
All the rest have 31
Without a blessed gleam of sun,
And if a month had two and 30
They'd be just as wet and dirty.

In presenting the accounts of Dickins & Jones for the year, showing profits down from £67,000 to £60,000, the chairman, Sir John Prichard Jones, listed the various economic factors that might have contributed to this setback, but concluded: 'The factor which however more than any other is calculated to disturb such a business as ours is the weather and we take no blame to ourselves for not having been able to forecast the extraordinary bad weather conditions which prevailed throughout last summer.'

A fine September and smog-free November, combined with more settled industrial relations, at last presaged the boom in the retail trade which shopkeepers had been anticipating for over three years. As part of their preparations for this upturn, all sections of the retail and wholesale trade had made determined efforts through various local and national trade associations to bring an end to price cutting by agreeing to observe minimum prices and credit terms. This strategy was tested early in 1912 when J. & P. Coats of Paisley, the largest manufacturer of sewing cotton in the world, asked their customers if they would prefer thread prices to be fixed. There followed an intense debate in the trade press, but the retailers themselves were unequivocal in their support for 'price maintenance'. This decision paved the way for its introduction by other manufacturers and their trade associations – for example, in November the Bedstead Manufacturers' Association started a bedstead rebate scheme, whereby retailers received discounts against fixed prices for repeat orders. With sales advancing there was less difficulty in ensuring compliance with such schemes and preventing unauthorised discounting.

Y42. **Skating Boot**, of Box Calf, with Enamelled Box Calf Golosh, fitting closely to the leg, and has padded tongue, heels specially screwed to take the strain of the skate. **32/9**
Also in all Box Calf, 30/-
Suitable either for Rinks or Switzerland.
We always stock a large selection of Blades by the best makers, from **16/6**
Fixed under the supervision of our expert free of charge.

Y41. **Ladies' Ski-Boot.** This renowned Boot, designed by our expert Ski-Runner, has, after the most exhaustive tests, been still further improved. It is now lighter in weight and neater in appearance, built of specially prepared snowproof leather, stiffened toes, and waterproof stitching to exclude all damp. The very best workmanship is used, which enables us to guarantee every pair to give satisfaction in the severe test the sport entails. **35/-**

GOLFING

Golfing Suit, designed to give freedom of action, in a variety of useful Tweeds. **4½ Guineas.**

To measure 10/6 extra.

Useful Golfing Skirts in Shrunk Tweeds and Serges. **27/6**

Hat of soft Velour, trimmed Corded Ribbon and flat Bow. **39/6**

Golf Shoes, *as illustration,* Tan Willow Brogue, also Black. Finest quality. **25/9**

DICKINS & JONES Ltd., Regent Street, London, W.
8

Y 10. **Ski-ing Suit,** embodying all the latest ideas of an ideal Ski Suit, in "Oberland" Waterproof Cloth, in a variety of pretty colors and Black. Made in our own workrooms. To measure 10/6 extra. **6 Gns.**

OPPOSITE AND ABOVE
During the opening years of the century, women began to escape from the claustrophobic attitudes of the Victorian era, enjoying new sports and pastimes. The latest ski-ing outfit from Dickins & Jones included a velour hat and specially designed boots tested by 'our expert ski-runner.' For the less adventurous, golfing suits were more modest in their cut.

Optimism, resulting from rising prosperity, made customers less price sensitive and more fashion conscious. Younger women finally abandoned the long ornate skirts of their mothers and grandmothers, and even men began to dress informally out of the office. The growing popularity of the motor car amongst the better off and the participation of women in sport stimulated demand for simple, robust clothing. The new fashions quickly reached every part of Britain. At the opening of their new costume department in 1913 Guy & Smith of Grimsby offered the latest styles, including new sponge-cloth blouses, and three-quarter-length sports coats. At the same time William Henderson & Sons of Liverpool were offering easy-fitting suits, with hems off the ankle, and simple hats. These changes in fashion brought in their wake a growing preference for ready-made clothes instead of piece goods that were made up by dressmaking and tailoring departments. By 1913 piece goods departments, once the mainstay of large stores, were being reduced in size and the space taken by bigger departments – fancy goods, perfumes and toys. Many were outraged by the change in fashion, fearful that women would endanger their health: 'There is no doubt about it. Women, for some occult reasons, want to wear less and to show themselves in the most literal sense to expose their necks and their chests, their ankles and even their calves, more than they have ever done before … Women cannot go on in this direction until they perambulate semi-naked. Our climate will stop them.' Warehouses that catered principally for clients in the Empire and the colonies sympathized

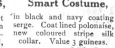
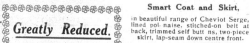

RIGHT *Although the design of women's clothes changed rapidly in the years before the First World War, many stores remained conservative in the lines they offered. This page of ladies' blouses from the 1913 catalogue of Dallas's of Glasgow shows styles that had been advertised for more than ten years. Dallas's enjoyed a large trade with the British colonies in West Africa.*

'54   **DALLAS'S, Limited, Milton House, Glasgow.**

LADIES' BLOUSES.

7/6

THE MILTON HOUSE, THE RIGHT SPOT FOR VALUE.

NOWHERE IS BETTER VALUE GIVEN.

7/6

H213—Ladies' Jap Silk Magyar Blouse, with lace yoke and cuffs, beautifully embroidered, **7/6**

Also different styles in Jap Silk Blouses, at **7/6**

Cheaper Qualities, **3/11** and **5/11**

H209—**Very Smart Blouse**, in Cream Delaine, with tucks over shoulders and beautifully embroidered front and collar, **3/11**

H600—Fancy Lace Blouse, similar to illustration. Very dressy Blouse, back fastening, Magyar style, long or short sleeves, **15/6**

Extra large sizes in Lace Blouses, large selection. **18/6, 21/-**

H214—Exquisite **Edelweiss and Guipure Lace Blouse**, with neat net yoke and cuffs, and trimmed with silk, **7/6**

H116—**Ladies' Coloured Silk Blouses**, in all the newest shades, rose, sky, helio, pink, and green, **7/6, 8/11, 10/6**, and **13/6**

H208—**Stylish Cream Delaine Blouse**, trimmed with silk embroidery, perfect fitting, **2/11**

13/6

10/6

H601—Ladies' Jap Silk Magyar Blouse, extra good quality, trimmed with pretty lace yoke and neatly tucked, **13/6**

Large variety of styles, short or long sleeves, back or front fastening. **14/6, 16/6, 18/6**

H115—Ladies' Black Merve or Taffeta Silk Blouse, with lace yoke and fancy silk braid and buttons, latest style, back fastening, **13/6**

Other styles, back or front fastening, in a large variety of styles, **7/6, 8/11, 10/6**

H602—Special Number—Ladies' Jap Silk Blouses, with fine Val. lace yokes and trimmed with heavy lace, very suitable for evening wear, **10/6**

Ladies' Jap Silk Blouses, with Peter Pan Collars, and daintily trimmed with lace or silk embroidery, **7/6** and **8/11**

OPPOSITE *Stylish clothes available from William Henderson & Sons of Liverpool, in 1912, with hems off the ankles and simple hats.*

with such sentiments. Dallas's catalogue remained wedded to the 'S' shape long after it had gone out of fashion; only maids were thought fit to wear calf-length skirts. The only concession to modernity was the addition of the hardly novel gramophone in 1913.

Britain experienced a period of unparalleled prosperity during 1913 and the first half of 1914. Retail sales soared with record returns. The *Drapers' Record* announced a boom in fitting new shopfronts throughout the country in March 1913 and a year later reported large outlays in Glasgow on the 'conversion of the old into the new.' Most ambitiously Harrods commenced the total reconstruction of Swan & Edgar's giant store in Regent Street and at the same time acquired Dickins & Jones across the street to fill the gap while work was in progress. In Sheffield John Walsh began remodelling their shopfront in June 1914, constructing a covered arcade to give a total frontage of over 500 feet. The interior

The temporary food hall of John Barker & Co of Kensington, after the fire, erected in December 1912.

was redesigned and the living-in accommodation for staff on the top floor converted into a sales area. A large house was purchased to provide improved staff quarters. Following a disastrous fire at Barkers of Kensington in November 1912, in which five girls lost their lives, the coroner criticised the management for its failure to provide adequate means of escape or practice for such an emergency and persuaded many stores to open hostels away from their premises. Modernisation of the shopping areas once again brought drapers and warehousemen into conflict with the law as open-plan displays inevitably resulted in an increase in shoplifting. The trade continued to complain of the inadequacy of sentencing and in 1913 condemned magistrates for lecturing shopkeepers for putting temptation in customers' way by failing to keep goods locked away in showcases. There was outrage that 'better class ladies', who complained of psychological disorders, were let off with a small fine and reprimand rather than being sent to prison. The new approach to shopping had other perils – the compulsive window shoppers who went from store to store viewing goods, but never making a purchase. In Glasgow during the spring of 1914, warehouses were hit by a wave of bogus women customers asking shop assistants to go to the trouble of cutting patterns and then leaving without placing an order for a dress or costume. At a time when it was becoming increasingly difficult to recruit staff, shopkeepers could not afford to allow such harassment of their assistants.

During July 1914 retailers continued to enjoy booming business, extensions were opened, and announcements of further new building published up to the beginning of August. The murder of Archduke Franz Ferdinand at the end of June in Sarajevo and the deteriorating situation in the Balkans did nothing to shake confidence. The sudden acceleration in international tension in the last week of July, leading to the declaration of war on 4 August, came as a shattering blow. During the following week sales of everything except food came to an abrupt halt. Many department stores were badly hit and summarily dismissed their staff. The men, particularly van drivers, enlisted in the armed forces at once, attracted by the higher rates of pay. The Home Office intervened to reduce the alarm, and called a meeting of storekeepers in London where it was agreed to halt the sackings and attempt to restore customer morale. There had been almost no planning for a major war. No thought had been given as to how the armed services would be kept supplied with either munitions or food and clothing, how the civilian population would be provisioned, or how the Government would treat the German and Austrian nationals, many of them refugees, living in Britain. In the first week of hostilities, drapers and clothiers were reluctant to respond to invitations from the War Office to supply the hastily assembled British Expeditionary Force because it would disturb existing business. Even the Army & Navy Stores rejected such an offer. Within days of the outbreak of war all employers were asked to supply the police with a list of aliens in their workforce. Since there were a large number of Germans and Austrian Jews in the clothing and furniture trades there was concern about their position. At first the Home Office gave permission for foreign nationals to remain at their posts, allowing stores to adopt a more relaxed attitude towards encouraging men to volunteer.

During the autumn the country was swept by xenophobia and stores were told to dismiss all their staff born in either Germany or Austro-Hungary. Manufacturers began a concentrated campaign to replace goods previously made in Germany with domestic products, particularly toys which had been imported in large quantities from Nuremberg. Small factories were hurriedly opened to make toy soldiers, guns, and china dolls for the Christmas market, and orders placed

On the outbreak of war on 4 August there was a real danger that the economy would be paralyzed by panic. The Government tried to allay people's fears by encouraging stores to adopt the slogan 'Business as usual.'

DALLAS'S LIMITED.   -   Business as usual.

Dallas's Limited desire to intimate that their business organisation is quite complete, and that notwithstanding the War and the European crisis, they are still able to despatch orders with the usual regularity.   Customers may have every confidence in sending forward their orders.   They will be despatched without delay, in the usual businesslike fashion.   The superiority of the British Navy has been proved; consequently trade routes are kept open; steamer sailings maintained, and mails despatched as usual.

Milton House, Glasgow,

August, 1914.

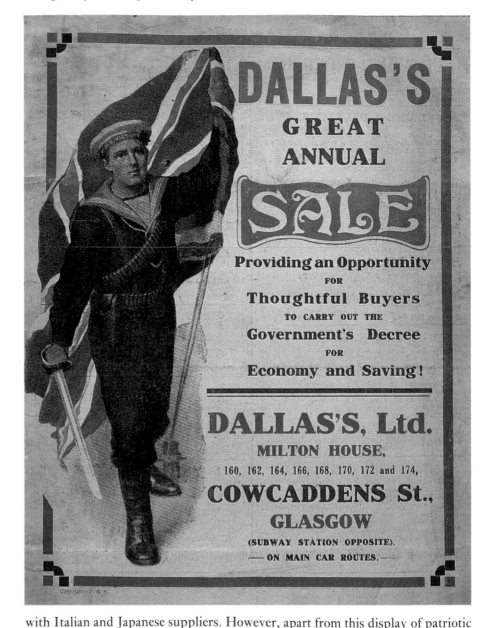

with Italian and Japanese suppliers. However, apart from this display of patriotic fervour, retailers were unsympathetic to emergency wartime measures that disturbed the normal pattern of their business. The London department stores were irritated by restrictions imposed in late October on shop and street lighting which they believed would favour provincial concerns. Such fears were groundless; sales during the Christmas season were better than had been expected and wholesalers were relieved to find themselves with little stock on their hands. When they came to re-order for the spring season there was no doubt that the conflict would not be over quickly, as so many had predicted, but would be long and bitterly contested. Already many drapery firms were engaged in making clothing for the front: uniforms, trench coats, gloves and warm woollens. Mawer & Collingham of Lincoln were making 500 pairs of khaki trousers a week for the War Office. Warehouses up and down the country were advertising foodstuffs, wines and spirits that could be sent in parcels to those on active service. The Army & Navy Stores listed eight standard parcels, ranging in price from five shillings to £1.

No. 4 DEPARTMENT.
USEFUL ARTICLES SUITABLE FOR PRESENTS FOR OFFICERS AND SOLDIERS AT THE FRONT.

Officers' Cap Covers.

Fawn Canton ......each 2/9
Oilskin .... ,, 2/3

Ground Sheets.

Silk Oilskin, weight only 6 ozs. ....each 8/6
Fawn Mull Waterproof Cloth, very light and strong, 84 by 54 in.,
weight 2lb.. ,, 13/9

The "Newmarket" Cape.

Military Cape and Ground Sheet combined, in
fawn cloth, sewn all through, and guaranteed
for all climates. Stock lengths 45 and 48
inches .... each 35/0

Military Coat.

Silk Oilskin, weight, 1¼ lb....................... 35/3
'Wester 6/6

Gentlemen's "Newmarket" Boots.

Good Field Service Waterproof boots, leather
soles, and with twill uppers. Weight 4 lb.
Pair 55/0

Combination Knife, Fork, and Spoon.

To detach the fork or spoon from the
knife, open it half-way and slide
that side of the handle downwards, when they will fall apart.
Complete 2/9

Pocket Filter.

In Metal Case. Complete 4/6

THE "OTICO" VACUUM BOTTLE.

All Otico Flasks are fitted with a pouring-out lip.
Manufactured and registered by the Society.
Will keep Hot Liquids hot for 24 hours, and Cold Liquids cold for
several days.

**Nickel-plated top and
bottom,** with leather-covered
body and sling strap.

1 pint size, 1 cup .... each 12/3
1 ,, 2 cups .... ,, 14/3
2 ,, 2 ,, ... ,, 18/3
1 ,, japanned body
with nickel top and
cup, not fitted with
pouring-out lip .... each 5/7
Refills, quart size. 6/6 ; pint
size .... each 4/9

**Electro-plated top and
bottom,** with leather-covered
body and sling strap.

1 pint size, 1 cup .... each 15/9
1 ,, 2 cups .... ,, 17/9
2 ,, 2 ,, ... ,, 23/3
Refills, pint size, 4/9 ; quart
size .... each 6/6

Jaeger Knitted Caps.   Knitted Body Belts

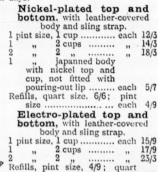

Each 2/0, 2/6, 5/0
White .... each 2/3
Jaeger .... ,, 2/

Khaki Air Pillow.

Waterproof. In cases, 18 in. by 13 in. Complete, 4/0

Military Coat.

In Fawn Cashmere Waterproof
Lined Fleece.
Infantry ... 89/6   Cavalry ... 97/0

Fitted Holdall.

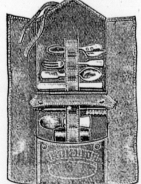

Containing military hair brush and
comb, shaving stick in metal case,
shaving brush, tooth brush, knife, fork,
spoon, and tin opener. Complete, 9/3.

Folding Collapsible Drinking Cup.

In Leather Case.
Electro-plated Cup .... each 5/10

Service Holdall.

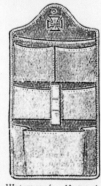

Waterproof. Unfitted.
Each 1/4

Telegraphic Address: ARMY, LONDON.
Telephone Number: VICTORIA 8500.

Army & Navy Co-operative Society, Ltd.,

105, VICTORIA STREET, WESTMINSTER, S.W.

LIST OF PARCELS SPECIALLY ARRANGED FOR THE EXPEDITIONARY FORCE.

Prices include Packing and Postage.

Members are requested when ordering to please quote the numbers of the Parcels.

EX. 1 - - - 20/-
(PACKED IN 2 PARCELS.)

- 1 tin Ox Tongue.
- 1 „ Oxford Sausages.
- 2 lbs. Rich Fruit Cake.
- 2 tins "Ideal" Milk.
- 2 „ Butter.
- 1 tin Turkey and Tongue Pâte.
- 1 pot Patum Peperum.
- 1 tin Marmalade.
- 1 „ Café au Lait.
- 1 lb. French Plums.
- 2 tins Potted Meat.
- 1 tin Mixed Chocolates.
- 12 Oxo Cubes.

EX. 3 - - - 12/6

- 1 tin Butter.
- 1 „ Milk (lever lid).
- 1 „ Chicken and Ham Pâte.
- 2 tins "Bivouac" Cocoa.
- 1 tin Café au Lait.
- 1 „ Rich Fruit Cake.
- 2 tins Sardines.
- 12 Oxo Cubes.
- 2 tins Oxford Sausages.
- 1 tin Neapolitan Chocolates.
- 3 tins Potted Meats.
- 1 tin Crème de Menthe.

EX. 5 - - - 7/6

- 1 tin Rich Fruit Cake.
- 1 „ "Bivouac" Cocoa.
- 1 „ Café au Lait.
- 1 „ Milk (lever lid).
- 1 „ Oxford Sausages.
- 1 „ Butter.
- 2 tins Potted Meat.
- 1 tin Camp Pie.
- 6 Ivelcon Cubes.
- 1 tin Everton Toffee.

EX. 2 - - - 15/-
(PACKED IN 2 PARCELS.)

- 2 tins Butter.
- 2 „ "Ideal" Milk.
- 2 „ "Bivouac" Cocoa.
- 1 lb. tin Cambridge Sausages.
- 1 lb tin Lambs' Sweetbreads and Tomato Sauce.
- 1 tin Chocolate Walnuts.
- 1 „ Puree Paté de Foies Gras.
- 1 „ Oxford Marmalade.
- 1 „ Genoa Cake.
- 12 Oxo Cubes.

EX. 4 - - - 10/-

- 1 tin Butter.
- 1 „ Milk (lever-lid)
- 1 „ Oxford Sausages.
- 1 „ Turkey and Tongue Pâte.
- 2 tins "Bivouac" Cocoa.
- 1 tin Almond Cake.
- 1 „ Sardines.
- 2 Cakes Chocolate Food.
- 2 tins Potted Meats.
- 6 Oxo Cubes.
- 1 box Cream Caramels.

EX. 6 - - - 5/-

- 1 tin Sultana Cake.
- 1 „ Milk (lever lid).
- 1 „ "Bivouac" Cocoa.
- 1 „ Butter.
- 1 „ Sardines.
- 2 tins Potted Meat.
- 1 tin Peppermint Bulls' Eyes.

EX. 7 - - - 8/6

- 1 bot. Port, Old Tawny, dry.
- 1 „ Scotch Whiskey (9 years old).

EX. 8 - - - 10/1

- 1 bot. Brandy, Pale, Choice Cognac.
- 1 „ Port, Old, full-bodied.

Other Selections can be arranged to meet Members' special requirements.

In the event of an article being out of stock, a substitute of similar character and value will be sent.

The Society cannot accept responsibility for non-delivery of, or damage to, these packages, its liability ceasing when the goods are handed the Postal Authorities.

N 503. 11705. 2 M. 27/4/15.

OPPOSITE AND RIGHT
The Army & Navy Stores advertised special food parcels for men at the Front almost from the outbreak of war, along with other useful gifts like 'Auto Strop' or '7 O'clock' safety razor sets.

Suitable Gifts for your Friends on Active Service.

The Morning Toilet in the Field—Shaving with AutoStrop and "7 o'clock" Razors.

Each AutoStrop or "7 o'clock" Safety Razor Set purchased from us contains a voucher which entitles you to have a Guinea AutoStrop Set or a Half-Guinea "7 o'clock" Set (according to which you purchase) sent as a <u>free gift</u> from yourself to the regimental or naval address of any friend on service

FREE OF ALL CHARGE
EXCEPT POSTAGE

The vouchers are available to purchasers of AutoStrop Safety Razor Sets between the dates of Oct. 26th and Dec. 31st, 1914, inclusive, and to purchasers of "7 o'clock" Safety Razor Sets at any time before the conclusion of the war.

AutoStrop Set complete, from 21/-.

We recommend these two razors as by far the most suitable presents for any man in camp or in barracks, in the field or on shipboard. They are absolutely the only two razors that can be stropped without taking the frame to pieces and putting the blade into a cumbersome machine. Each can be stropped instantly and satisfactorily without unscrewing a single part.

"7 o'clock" Set complete, 10/6.

The cheapest contained one tin of sultana cake, one tin of milk, one tin of Bivouac cocoa, one tin of butter, one tin of sardines, two tins of potted meat and one tin of peppermint bull's-eyes. Female fashions were changing in keeping with the important role of women in war work and in maintaining services to civilians at peacetime standards. The narrow skirt was rejected in favour of more comfortable short flared skirts which apparently afforded 'the employment once more of beautiful and delicate underwear.'

As in the two years immediately before the war, people had more than enough to spend on clothes and food parcels for their loved ones and on new clothes and household goods. There was an abundance of jobs and for those engaged in war work in manufacturing towns, any amount of overtime. Wages were rising fast, bringing goods of all kinds into the price range of less well-off families which had previously been beyond their grasp. In early June the *Drapers' Record* reported: 'Low-priced furs and other "extras" for the soldier's wife and for the

Part of Harrods' prewar fleet of delivery vans, an essential part of the service to the store's London customers. During the war the men joined the forces and the vans were commandeered, making local deliveries impossible.

wives of many industrial workers to whom the war has brought a period of steady prosperity constitute a demand on such a scale as to involve large slices of business. The cheapest class of drapery trader in some towns is having literally the time of his life. To a large extent the extra spending power of the industrial community goes upon substantial things, the purchase of which is more or less in the nature of laying up for a rainy day, and not upon mere finery with a very short life before it.' Although Fraser Sons & Co's profits in the last six months of 1914 collapsed to £700, they recovered to £1,300 in the first half of 1915. The Government, in urgent need of funds to finance the escalating cost of the war, was anxious to dampen demand by raising taxes and encouraging war savings. The retail trade, predictably, responded with a call to spend to relieve unemployment, condemning the hoarding of money as unpatriotic. Calls for economy and investment were favourably received by the better-off, who cut back on luxury goods and fashionable clothes supplied by the larger, more prestigious, department stores, particularly those in the West End of London. This withdrawal of custom was compounded by transport difficulties, with the railways given over to moving war materials, and horses and motor vehicles being commandeered for duty at the front. By mid-1915, local deliveries were becoming difficult and mail order, except to the armed services, almost impossible. In July 1915 Barkers of Kensington were forced to lay off staff in their household section and at Pontings where most of their mail order business was done.

A crisis in the manufacture of arms and equipment to prosecute the war on an unprecedented scale forced the Government to establish the Ministry of Munitions in May 1915 with wide powers to control production. Within a few months ninety-five per cent of the woollen industry in the Scottish borders was engaged in making uniforms and 'underwear and other comforts for the troops,' and the Ayrshire lace industry in producing mosquito nets for the Dardanelles campaign. Some firms reported ceaseless activity around the clock. In the face of such heavy demand from the Government, warehouses found stock hard to come by and prices exorbitant.

Despite the restricted supply and the mounting casualties at the front, a 'sense of fashion was kept alive.' There was a trend towards simpler, standard, ready-to-wear clothes which could be produced in long runs. Women's skirts became shorter and blouses were closer fitting, emphasising the long-suppressed bust. Coats took on a military style. Domestic design was encouraged by the imposition of 33.3 per cent import duty on foreign clothes in the emergency budget in September. An equivalent tax on hats solicited a storm of protest from the trade. A lull in Government orders in the late autumn allowed the stores to rebuild their stocks for the winter season. By the end of October the *Drapers' Record* was able to report that Christmas shoppers could expect 'a very excellent selection of appropriate lines.' There was a good supply of British-made fancy goods, particularly mechanical toys with a military flavour. Fears that the parsimony experienced earlier in the year would depress the Christmas market quickly proved groundless, with goods for shipment to the front dominating trade. The greatest obstacle to sales for most larger stores was not a lack of wares but of staff as more and more men enlisted following the Government's scheme to lift recruitment and more and more women found better paid munitions work. To hold on to their female employees, the warehouses agreed minimum wage levels and introduced a forty-eight-hour week. So successful was the Christmas period throughout Britain that there was little need to discount prices for the traditional New Year sales. The retail trade reported a bumper year. So confident were Pettigrew & Stephens in Glasgow that they commissioned a massive extension, almost completed at the outbreak of war, making it the largest store in Scotland. At the same time Fraser Sons & Co Ltd acquired a third stake in its warehouse premises in Buchanan Street from the brothers Hugh and John Fraser for £12,500.

Before the First World War many toys sold in Britain were imported from Germany. British companies started making toys shortly after the outbreak of hostilities, often with a military theme.

---

136   ARMY AND NAVY C. S., L.   [Nov.—Dec., 1914.

No. 12 DEPARTMENT.

TOY (BAZAAR) SECTION.—Ground Floor.

Boy Scout Equipment, Girl Guide Equipment, Flags, &c.

Prices and particulars upon application.

Soldiers. English make, in great variety.

Horse or Foot .... per box 0/10	Medical corps..each 2/6
Assorted.................................... 2/6, 3/6, 6/0, 12/0, 15/0	Artillery, R.F.A.......each 4/6, R.H.A. .... ,, 5/0

*The cover of McDonalds'
Christmas catalogue in
1916 showing, on the front,
a tree topped with the
French and English flags
and laden with fancy goods
and, on the back, hampers
of food and luxuries for
servicemen. In contrast to
the hardship at the front,
those who remained at home
enjoyed a rapidly advancing
standard of living.*

By the spring of 1916 warehouses and department stores were so well stocked
that 'no one could conclude that the nation is at war.' The only section of their
business to have suffered was the sale of expensive fashionable dresses for social
functions which had ceased following the King's call for austerity in public life.
This was more than compensated for by 'the high flying of the working class'
who were 'leaving off their custom to the smaller men and turning their attention
to the large warehouses, where the scope of selection is greater.' These new
customers preferred well-made better quality products, rarely seeking credit, but
choosing to pay in cash and take the discounts. Confidence in the industry was
dented in June when the Government imposed excess profits tax to cream off
the greatly increased returns that the majority of companies was earning as a
result of the war. This measure did nothing to depress demand which continued
to escalate. Stores in manufacturing towns experienced record sales during the
works' holiday periods in July and August as the lack of transport made it
difficult for families to travel to holiday resorts. Those who managed to get

away overpowered seaside shopkeepers with 'a shower of gold', returning with 'expensive souvenirs'. Determined to reap the benefits of the spending spree, stores placed their orders for the winter well in advance, building large stocks by mid September. Prices climbed inexorably throughout the autumn. In preparation for Christmas, manufacturers persisted in their attempts to produce fancy goods, leatherware and toys, previously imported from Germany, but were frustrated by the accelerating demand for munitions. In concert with the retailers, they petitioned the Government to defend their nascent industry by protecting their market through high tariffs, to no avail. Following numerous complaints from housewives, urgent but unsuccessful experiments were also conducted to find means of making synthetic fast dyes which had come from Germany before the war. It was not until November 1916 that the Chancellor of the Exchequer took steps to dampen spending by imposing double income tax. There was no noticeable effect on sales during the third Christmas season of the war. The New Year sales brought unprecedented turnover, with sales in Glasgow breaking all previous records.

After the United States entered the war in April 1917, the conflict intensified. The Germans, determined to score a victory before the arrival of American troops, tried to cut off food and raw materials to the United Kingdom through unrestricted U-boat warfare. Sinkings of Allied shipping soon outstripped new construction. The Government took emergency powers to control materials and industries, organising a programme of merchant shipbuilding. Control extended to the textile and clothing trades which were to give even higher priority to military requirements, particularly making uniforms for the rapidly expanding conscript army. In the absence of any measures to control prices, the scarcity of materials drove up the cost of goods even higher. By July it was reported that prices of cotton articles were 325 per cent higher than they had been in the months before the declaration of war in 1914. Such swift inflation, combined with exorbitant levels of taxation, made it hard for many stores to finance forward purchases. To have any chance of securing whatever goods might be available, part-paid orders had to be placed at least six months, if not eight, before delivery. In Scotland warehousemen were vociferous in their complaints against the banks for refusing to extend overdraft facilities, and responded by withdrawing credit from their customers and cancelling discounts for cash sales. In Glasgow in February 1918, Sir Andrew Pettigrew persuaded the leading warehouses, Pettigrew & Stephens, Copland & Lye, Daly & Co, Simpson Hunter & Young, and Fraser Sons & Co, to take such action. Higher prices and the absence of discount did not deter customers who continued to spend heavily in the confident expectation that inflation would continue to accelerate. So short had supplies become by early 1918 that Barkers of Kensington were forced to introduce a system of informal rationing for established clients, refusing to sell to newcomers.

The austerity of 1917 and reverses at the front following the German offensive at the end of March 1918, made for simpler, sombre designs, emphasising the slender silhouette of the female figure. Hemlines rose to calf length and evening dresses gave way to tea gowns. Since material was in short supply, new clothes had to be far more functional than in the past, easily cleaned and suitable for all occasions, including work. Colours were sober, in keeping with the nation's mood – claret, Russian green, mole, tan, putty, dark brown, and battleship grey. Materials were hard-wearing serges, gaberdines and tweeds. Mirroring patriotic fervour, Scottish tweedmakers improved their marketing, labelling all their products 'Made in Scotland', and educating customers in the quality of the cloth.

Women made up for the workaday drabness of their coats and dresses by indulging in frivolous underwear and fur coats. In the closing months of 1917 and into 1918, stores throughout Britain reported that turnover of finest lingerie was unparalleled. In Glasgow, during the summer sale of 1918, warehousemen were overwhelmed by the demand for silk petticoats and underskirts which were needed to wear with the slimmer style dresses. Despite Government efforts to hold back personal expenditure, spending continued unabated. Hugh Fraser told the annual meeting of Fraser Sons & Co in March 1918 that the company had had 'another highly prosperous year, all departments going up with leaps and bounds, making the largest turnover in the history of the company.' In September, with the outcome of the war still in the balance, the *Drapers' Record* commented, 'there is a carelessness in spending the like of which none of us has ever seen before.' Hostilities came to a sudden and unexpected end on 11 November when Germany requested an armistice. At home the country rejoiced.

Peace brought no end to the shortage of goods in the shops. Many items became even harder to come by as industry began the painful process of re-adjusting to normal trading. At the end of November 'not a blade of flannel was to be bought in Glasgow' and prices everywhere were still spiralling. Although there had been much discussion throughout the war about introducing effective measures to keep German goods out of Britain in the future, shopkeepers were too concerned about the day-to-day problems of stocking their shelves to care. Spending at Christmas 1918 reached another peak, with toys and luxury goods in great demand. Excess profits tax, which remained in force, cut deeply into the liquidity of department stores and there were mounting labour problems. In a riot in Glasgow in the first week of February 1919, several of the larger department stores had their windows broken and looted. Strikes in support of higher wages combined, with a shortage of shipping, to make goods scarcer still. By midsummer, men's underwear was almost out of stock. Faced with these obstacles to a return to prewar conditions, and uncertain of the future, some warehousemen decided to sell up, triggering a new round of takeovers. Harrods set the trend in 1919 by making their first investment outside the capital when they bought Kendal Milne & Co of Manchester, the leading department store in the north-west of England. Debenham & Freebody purchased another large West End store, Marshall & Snelgrove, in March 1919 and later in the year acquired the Knightsbridge business of Harvey Nichols. John Barker & Co took over Derry & Toms, their neighbours in the High Street, Kensington, in January 1920 for £600,000. Linked with Pontings which Barkers already owned, the purchase created a store group of an equivalent size to Harrods and Debenhams.

When prospects became more settled in the autumn of 1919, stores outside London planned further extensions. In Glasgow, Wylie & Lochhead bought the next-door premises in Buchanan Street from David Kemp & Son, who had decided to move to the more fashionable Sauchiehall Street. Anderson's Royal Polytechnic purchased additional property in Argyle Street and doubled its capital to pay for improvements. In 1920 J.& R. Allan of Edinburgh purchased the adjoining drapery and general warehouse business of Paterson & Smith to build an extension. These ambitious plans were almost immediately over-shadowed by accusations of profiteering and demands from shop assistants for substantial wage rises to keep pace with inflation and for a shorter working week. There was a bitter dispute at the Army & Navy Stores which ended with a settlement in the staff's favour. Although calls for rises of fifty per cent in Glasgow were conceded during December 1919, disturbances persisted into the New Year. The Scottish Retail Drapers' Association wanted the immediate formation of a

A Word from Harrods

*What should they know of England
Who only England know ?—Kipling.*

TO all our brave defenders, but especially to three thousand and more battle-weary men of Harrods, this House in these immortal hours tenders its admiration.

Those, alas, who sleep beneath the now quiet earth of foreign fields have wrought beyond all praise or gratitude.

Of the men and women who through these sombre years of trial and anxiety have carried on the business of this House so steadfastly we here record in public our appreciation.

Privately we shall attempt to mark in fashion practical our thanks and real sense of indebtedness.

In the meantime we share with overflowing hearts the joy and thankfu'ness of all humanity, finding new source of pride and inspiration in

*. . . . this little world,
This precious stone set in the silver sea,
This blessed plot, this realm, this earth, this England.*

Harrods Ltd

Woodman Burbidge Managing Director

Brompton Road   London S W 1

ABOVE LEFT
*A message from Harrods
on Armistice day, 1919*

ABOVE RIGHT
*The 1921 centenary sale
advertisement of
Hammonds of Hull.
Despite its confident tone,
goods were heavily
discounted due to the
economic uncertainty.*

1821   **100** YEARS   1921

A CENTURY AGO the business of HAMMONDS was commenced in a small shop near the North Bridge. Under the patronage of the inhabitants of Hull & the East Riding it has developed until it is now one of the largest & most important in the Provinces.

THE FINANCIAL YEAR which just closes HAS BEEN THE BIGGEST AND MOST SUCCESSFUL in the history of the firm and the Directors feel that to inaugurate the CENTENARY they would like to express their appreciation of the support received during the time the business has been under their control, in a practical form

IT HAS THEREFORE BEEN DECIDED THAT ON

TUESDAY & WEDNESDAY

NEXT 8 & 9 FEBRUARY

the WHOLE of their VALUABLE STOCKS *(with the exception of those goods where the prices are fixed by the Makers or by Trade Agreement and also the Food sold in the Restaurant)* will be offered for Sale at

ONE HALF THE MARKED PRICES

All the Stock is marked in plain figures at the usual cash prices, and whether the purchase is a piece of tape at 1d or a Suite of Furniture at £200, half the price will be charged. The Stock can be inspected now but no goods will be sold at half price except between 9 a m and 6 p m on the days mentioned

ALL GOODS MUST BE PAID FOR AT TIME OF PURCHASE. NO CREDIT CAN BE GIVEN on this occasion.

CELEBRATE THE CENTENARY BY MAKING A PURCHASE

HAMMONDS Ltd PARAGON SQUARE HULL

Trade Board for the retail drapery distribution trade to arbitrate in wage disputes. At the same time Copland & Lye was deemed by the newly established Government Profiteering Committee to have overcharged for a Donegal hat. This decision was later quashed, but in February 1920 Kendal Milne of Manchester was less fortunate and was forced to refund a customer. Stores throughout Britain faced similar charges in the coming months. These problems were compounded by big rises in local rates to pay for the raising of the school leaving age from fourteen to sixteen. By the autumn shopkeepers were deeply concerned about their prospects. The Germans had started dumping goods in Britain, particularly gloves and toys, threatening to undermine existing price levels and destroying the new industries established during the war. The miners' strike in October confirmed the gloomy outlook. Department stores began cancelling large orders placed earlier in the year, causing manufacturers to lay off staff. By January 1921 the Scottish woollen mills were reported to have virtually no orders to work on. Profits for Fraser Sons & Co, which had reached a peak of £21,988 in 1919, were halved.

The uncertainty of the first postwar years confused fashion designers. Some remained committed to the newer wartime look of simpler clothes with short hemlines for women, while others returned to Victorian and Edwardian styles in an effort to recapture a more secure and predictable world. For most stores the experience of 1921 only confirmed the impression that a return to 'normal' was still a long way off. Further industrial action by miners between April and June seriously disrupted production and transport, hitting spending, particularly in city-centre stores. Retailers responded by discounting heavily, abandoning agreements to fix prices and credit. Rather than buy highly priced stock left over from the previous season from wholesalers, many retailers bought direct from manufacturers who similarly slashed prices to retain their market. Despite these incentives, customers stayed away during the summer sales, notably in manufacturing centres like Glasgow, badly hit by the coal strike. Warehouses and department stores cancelled orders and ran down stocks, expecting worse times

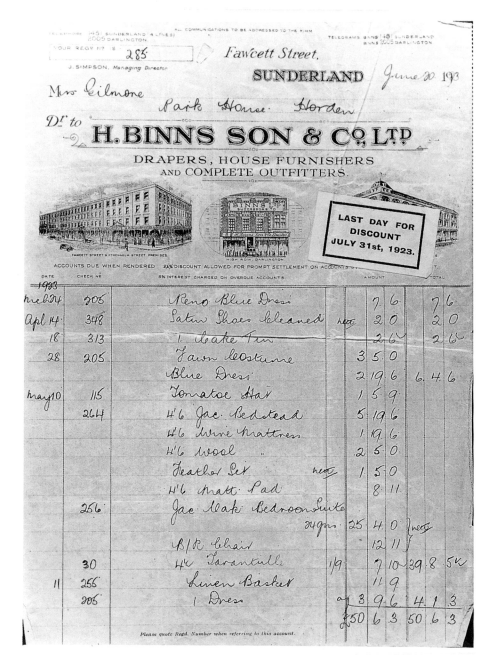

A 1923 invoice from Binns, advertising the last day for discounts at the end of the 'Shopping Week.' The items on this invoice range from a Reno blue dress to a wire mattress.

to come. To add to the problems, the Germans, whose dumping of certain products had been curtailed by the reparations stipulated in the peace treaty, resumed their activities, flooding Britain with cheap pianos as they had done before the war. Shopkeepers, realising that to remain competitive, costs must be reduced, pressed manufacturers and wholesalers to cover delivery charges and protested loudly at the high cost of road transport and telephones. With little sensitivity the Post Office had increased charges at the height of the coal strike crisis.

Matters remained unresolved into the spring of 1922, with most department stores reporting sharply reduced profits or even losses. Stewart & McDonald, the Glasgow retailers and wholesalers, recorded a total loss of £82,543, forcing the company to seek an amalgamation with another Glasgow concern, J. & W. Campbell in September. Much to the trade's relief, telephone charges were reduced by seventeen per cent in May and the railways lowered their rates in July. To meet such threats to their livelihood in a declining market, shopkeepers sought to create more effective organisations to represent their views. In June the Glasgow & West of Scotland Retail Drapers' Association merged with the Glasgow & West of Scotland Retail Garment Makers to form the Glasgow & West of Scotland Drapers, Outfitters etc. Association, and in September the Scottish Retail Drapers Federation joined the Scottish Retail Garment Makers & Millinery Trades Federation to form the Scottish Retail Drapers, Outfitters, Garmentmakers & Millinery Federation. They immediately lobbied for a cut in income tax, the abolition of corporation tax, and further reductions in post and parcel rates. The *Scottish Retail Drapery Journal* was launched in May 1923 to report on the issues of concern to the trade and 'the protection of common interest.'

The New Year of 1923 brought an upturn in sales stimulated by the announcement of the engagement of the King's second son, the Duke of York, to Elizabeth Bowes-Lyon. Trade was brisk and there was a general agreement that there were better times ahead. Cuts in income tax in the April budget gave prospects of a further boost, encouraging department stores to stage brilliant displays of the latest fashions for the summer sales. Styles were more certain, tubular dresses emphasising the slim boyish look. The *Drapers' Record* declared a year later: 'To follow the decrees of fashion in the spring months will not be easy for those who are built on generous lines, for the daughters of Eve are not to be allowed to have such things as hips and busts.' Slimming and exercise became popular and demand for sportswear, from golfing attire to swimwear, was strong.

Expectations of a sustained improvement were quelled as they had been in 1912 by the foul summer weather, particularly in Scotland. By the end of June Scottish warehousemen were worried by the lack of custom at the summer sales, and the likely effects of large-scale redundancies in the shipyard and engineering works at the beginning of the holiday period. The wholesale stores supplying smaller shops suffered more than the retail warehouses which could adjust their stocks rapidly in response to changes in customer preference. Middle-priced goods commanded a better market than more expensive lines. There was also evidence of a marked growth in mail orders, even in Glasgow where in the past customers had preferred to make purchases in person. In the midst of these difficulties, Pettigrew & Stephens opened an extension to their Glasgow store, incorporating a specialist men's department. Although shopkeepers were concerned that the general election in early December might disrupt sales even further, events proved them wrong. The central issue of the campaign was protection of domestic industries. Press criticism of department stores for showing preference to foreign manufacturers made shoppers more inquisitive about the origin of goods on view. Support for British products fuelled the Christmas market with customers spurning foreign goods, particularly German and Austrian toys.

Throughout these postwar years, Fraser Sons & Co achieved proportionately better returns than many of their competitors. After a setback in 1920, profits recovered during the next two years to reach £16,000 in 1922. Cheered by these results, Hugh Fraser determined to extend his warehouse by buying adjoining property. His brother John, who had always been a non-executive director, since 1909 living in the south of England, vetoed the proposal as he still personally owned one-third of the premises. The driving force behind the plan was Hugh Fraser's son, Hugh, who had come to work at the store in 1919 after spending a few months learning bookkeeping with the company's auditors. Born in 1903 he had been educated at Glasgow Academy and at Warriston School, near Moffat in the Borders. In a short time he became an accomplished window dresser and buyer, and it can be no coincidence that the company's fortunes revived after his arrival. In reporting on the company's trade in 1923, his father referred to the 'wet and cold' summer months, but was still able to announce a profit of over £15,000. This excellent result in a difficult year made the young Hugh more anxious than ever to press on with improvements to the premises. At the annual meeting Hugh Fraser senior proposed that his son should be a director of the company. The way was now open for young Hugh to realise his ambitions.

Since the conversion of Fraser Sons & Co into a limited liability company in 1909, the department store and warehouse trade had experienced a massive surge in turnover due in large measure to a rapid advance in wages, particularly during the war. Their great range of goods and opulent fittings had attracted custom away from local specialist shops. A broadening of their market, combined with a lack of demand for fashion wear during the war, had caused ready-to-wear clothes to increase in popularity. Fashion had changed almost out of recognition, with daring calf-length skirts which would have been thought vulgar a decade earlier. The layout of shopping areas had been transformed under the influence of Gordon Selfridge into open spaces with goods attractively displayed instead of locked away in drawers and cartons. In response to the construction of his vast new Oxford Street store many warehouses up and down the country had been reconstructed or extended to accommodate the new style of shopping and new departments. Despite the achievements, uncertainty remained. The labour disputes that followed immediately on the war reminded shopkeepers how vulnerable they were to any disruption in employment and in public confidence. The discounting that followed demonstrated the fragility of resale price policies and formal agreements to maintain price levels. Overall the boom in the last years of peace and of the war had brought unparalleled prosperity to the retail trade.

MAIDS' CAPS AND APRONS

G.P. 207.—Frilled Cap, finished Black Velvet, 2/9

G.P. 207a.—Afternoon Apron, good wearing, finished tucks and embroidery insertion, 3/6

G.P. 208.—Cap, of dainty Muslin, trimmed embroidery and beading, 2/1

G.P. 208a.—Tea Apron, of fine Muslin, finished wide hems and beading, 2/9

G.P. 209.—Muslin Cap, trimmed insertion, 2/1

G.P. 209a.—Strong Cambric Apron, finished fine embroidery, 3/6

G.P. 210.—Organdi Muslin Cap, 2/9

G.P. 210a.—Muslin Tea Apron, daintily trimmed fine lace, 3/3

G.P. 211.—Mob Cap, of Spot Muslin, 2/9

G.P. 211a.—Tea Apron, of fancy Spot Muslin, 2/11

G.P. 212.—Maids' Alpaca Afternoon Dress, of reliable quality, well cut and finished. Can be supplied with 1 in. collar band if desired. Colours: Black, Navy, Brown, or Grey, 27/6

G.P. 213.—Frilled Cap, of soft Muslin, 1/11

G.P. 213a.—Smart Tea Apron, of fancy Spot and Plain Muslin, 1/11½

G.P. 214.—Simple Muslin Cap, 1/6

G.P. 214a.—Afternoon Apron, of good quality Lawn, finished fine embroidery beading, 3/11

G.P. 215.—Alpaca Coat Frocks, loose at waist. Price 25/6

G.P. 216.—Maids' Morning Dresses of strong Washing Gingham, with Peter Pan collar or 1 in. collar band, in Blue, Grey, Butcher, or Steel. Price 12/11

Sizes	Waist.	Skirt Length.	Sizes	Waist.	Skirt Length.
..	26 in.	32 in.	..	28 in.	36 in.
,,	26 ,,	34 ,,	,,	30 ,,	38 ,,

ALL PRICES ARE SUBJECT TO MARKET FLUCTUATIONS

5 1924–1948
To be Developed by Local Men

Like many of his contemporaries, who were too young to have been conscripted during the war, Hugh Fraser junior believed that the postwar economic difficulties would soon be solved and trade would recover. Heartened by the family firm's seventy-fifth anniversary, he set to work urgently to bring the store up to date. Unable to alter the structure of the building because of his uncle John's opposition, he concentrated on the interior. His first improvement was to enlarge the tearoom and install a restaurant, facilities which were regarded as essential for the success of any department store. He personally designed the layout and the decor. He overhauled the gown department, recruiting 'an experienced party to take charge,' and appointed a new blouse and jumper buyer. He persuaded his father to give notice at the annual meeting that sooner or later arcades would have to be constructed at both the Buchanan Street and Argyle Street entrances if the company was to continue to prosper. Not all the young Hugh Fraser's reforms were to succeed. The 'experienced party' turned out to be rather less knowledgeable than she claimed and was dismissed. Admitting his mistake, he personally took charge of the gown department which rapidly returned to profitability. In selling gowns he recognised the need to make separate provision for women in service. A new maids department was fitted out on the second floor in space vacated by the furniture department which moved to the basement. All these initiatives could not prevent profits from retreating in a difficult market, but they remained well above prewar levels even allowing for inflation.

Hugh Fraser junior was not alone in thinking that better times lay ahead for the retail trades in 1924. The London West End department stores, which had fared better than they had expected the year before, launched massive sales campaigns in the New Year. Harrods' white sale included an elephant fourteen feet high by twenty feet long made entirely of Terry towelling, and many other attractions to draw the curious. The whole stunning display took six months to prepare and set a new standard in promotion. In 1925 Sir Woodman Burbidge, appreciating that the clientele of the store had been transformed by the war, opened an inexpensive department for gowns, coats and small sizes. Towards the close of 1923 Barkers had announced the reconstruction of their main store and that of Derry & Toms and an extension to Pontings, at a total cost of £3 million. Outside London, Mawer & Collingham of Lincoln extended their window frontage in 1924 and opened new showrooms for ladies' underwear and children's clothes. By the New Year of 1925 it was reported that record prices had recently been paid for shop premises with good frontages in Glasgow and Edinburgh. New shops and extensions were to be constructed in both centres, including large additions to both Copland & Lye's warehouse in Sauchiehall Street and Dallas's store in Cowcaddens, Glasgow. In Sunderland, Binns, under the direction of John Simpson, accelerated an expansion programme begun in 1922, remodelling its main store and those of two recent acquisitions, Arthur Sanders of Darlington and Thomas Jones & Co of Middlesbrough. James Howell of Cardiff opened a new block in Trinity Street in 1925, containing 'great

OPPOSITE *The sale of uniforms for domestic servants remained an important part of a department store's trade throughout the interwar years.*

HARRODS SEVENTY-FIFTH ANNIVERSARY

HORSMAN UN-
BREAKABLE
DOLL.
TY 85.
With " Ma-Ma "
voice. Soft, cuddle-
some body.
Price .. 11/9

OPPOSITE *Harrods celebrates its seventy-fifth anniversary, 1924.*

BELOW *A high-quality window display for one of Harrods' legendary 'White Sales' in 1930.*

furniture showrooms and decorative arts,' with a magnificent arcade 'giving direct access to the [company's] grocery, ironmongery, and jewellery shops, motor car showrooms, garage and builders' works.' The brochure, distributed at the opening, proclaimed that the store 'will clothe your wife and daughter and set them with jewellery ... feed you from their great grocery store ... furnish your house from cellar to attic, be it cottage or mansion ... in toys bring tears of joy ... and provide delightful entertainment.'

In providing this great variety of goods, department stores could call on an increasing range of ready-made clothes and other merchandise. To cater for women who lacked the fashionable boyish figure, the mass-produced rubber girdle was introduced from America and widely stocked, along with 'Norvic Crepe Binders' described as being 'invaluable in maternity'. Sir Bruce Bruce-Parker, a distinguished physician, roundly denounced these new garments as unhygienic. Also from America came dolls which 'will laugh or cry, walk and talk and wink, blink or roll their eyes from side to side, and flirt gaily as they toddle along.' Queen Mary was greatly taken with these ingenious dolls which went by such undistinguished names as Flossie Flirt or Soozie Smiles. The first radio broadcast by the British Broadcasting Corporation in November 1922 heralded the arrival in the shops of mass-produced wireless sets. Although the Conservatives had lost the election to Labour on the issue of protection, buying British remained an important issue, bolstered by the British Empire Exhibition that opened at Wembley in April 1924. The organisers took care to invite a large number of representatives of the retail trade to the opening of the biggest

Linens

China & Glass   Decorating

Soft Furnishing

Ladies' Hosiery & Gloves

Silks & Dress Fabrics   Cotton Fabrics

Laces

The departments of Walshs of Sheffield stylishly portrayed in a brochure of 1925 to mark the store's fiftieth anniversary.

OPPOSITE *In the aftermath of the war, customers were encouraged once again to 'Buy British' or Imperial goods. The concept of Empire featured heavily in advertising and promotions, as in this cover from the 1924 catalogue of Dallas's of Glasgow.*

OVERLEAF *During the mid-1930s a number of store groups were formed, including the Binns group in the north-east of England. This advertisement shows the stores which Binns owned by 1927.*

display of British goods since the Great Exhibition of 1851. Stirred into action, warehousemen made plans for 'British Shopping Weeks' on the model of those in 1911 – the Coronation year. This time Glasgow drapers lent their wholehearted support.

As at Frasers, across the country the promise of 1924 did not live up to expectations. The London West End stores were not happy with the returns and those provincial stores, like Binns, which did raise their profits seem to have done so as much by acquisition as by increased sales. There was widespread debate as to why this should be at a time when wages were still relatively high. One theory, particularly applicable to the south-east of England, was that many people had ceased to rent their homes and were buying them instead, so that disposable income previously spent in shops was now committed to mortgage repayment. It was thought that this problem was compounded by hire-purchase agreements to acquire the furnishings for the home. Whatever the reason, many families who owned large stores and other types of enterprise for that matter were so unnerved by faltering sales as to contemplate selling out. For department stores there were powerful motives for such action. During the war their value had risen far above the original cost of construction, and in the event of the death of a principal shareholder the business would inevitably have to be sold to meet death duties, which had been greatly increased during the war. There was no shortage of willing buyers, either one of the large London houses or a local storekeeper, like John Simpson of Binns of Sunderland, anxious to create a regional grouping capable of challenging metropolitan rivals. The pace was set, as it had been in 1909, by Gordon Selfridge. He had started buying stores in the suburbs during

What we Sell.

(1) Clothes for Under and Outer Wear for Men, Women and Children.
(2) Every description of House Furnishings, Furniture and Bedding.
(3) Every possible requirement in Household Linen.
(4) Any Article for use on the Table, as well as those used in the Decoration of the Home.
(5) All Sports and Games Requirements, as well as Toys and Games for the tiny tots.
(6) Travelling and Touring Requisites, both English and Foreign.
(7) Every Novelty as it is marketed.
(8) Jewellery, Silver Plate and Optical Requisites.
(9) Wireless Outfits and Shop Fittings.
(10) Pianos, Gramophones, and Musical Instruments.

The activities of the Removal Department extend beyo

VIEWS O

H. Binns

SUNDERLAND   -   DAI

Linthorpe Road, Middlesbrough.

Newport Road and Crescent, Middlesbrough.

Fawcett S

Depositories, The Green and Fenwick Street, Sunderland.

Aerial View, showing part of the Shops and Showrooms at Sunderland.

View showing John Street Extension, Sunderland.

Part of
Pre

Four Views of Middlesbrough Factories.

Part View of the Stables.

View of St

Isles. Contracts are accepted for any part of the World.

MISES OF
on & Co. L**td**
N - MIDDLESBROUGH

What we Do.

(1) Paint and Decorate a Cottage or a Mansion, Theatres, Picture Halls and Public Buildings.

(2) Furnish throughout a building of any size for any purpose.

(3) Manufacture Shop Fronts, Shop Fittings, Window Backgrounds, Library Fittings, Cases, etc.

(4) Manufacture High-class Furniture, Bedroom Suites, etc.

(5) Make Bedding under Hygienic conditions.

(6) Plumbing, Gas and Electrical Installations.

(7) Sanitary and Heating Engineering.

(8) Boot and Shoe Repairing in our own Factory.

(9) Clean, Dye and Renovate all classes of Goods.

m Street, Sunderland.

Fawcett Street and Borough Road, Sunderland.

High Row, Darlington.

Front View of the Warehouse, Villiers Street, Sunderland.

Demolishing Operations, prior to Re-building in Mechanics' Yard, Darlington.

Front of Premises acquired in Blackwellgate, Darlington, for the Extension of the Darlington Store.

lesbrough
asions

Front View of the Cabinet Factory, Sunderland.
(These buildings are to be considerably enlarged.)

Four Views of one of the Sunderland Factories.

the last year of the war, and by 1926 he controlled thirteen stores other than his Oxford Street flagship, as far north as Liverpool and as far west as Dublin.

The most ambitious grouping of stores was the brainchild of a city financier, Clarence Hatry, who in 1923 had seen his grandiose Commercial Corporation of London collapse in failure. Lacking any experience in the retail trade, he began negotiating in the summer of 1925 with a number of stores in London and elsewhere, including Pettigrew & Stephens of Glasgow, offering to acquire them through his Austin Friars Investment Trust. Sir Andrew Pettigrew, now an old man, agreed 'after much persuasion' to sell his beloved Pettigrew & Stephens on the understanding that the managing director, John Campbell, would succeed him as chairman and that he himself would be able 'to come in and out as he had been in the habit of doing'. Unknown to either Sir Andrew or the other directors, Clarence Hatry offered John Campbell most generous terms for his support; an annual salary of £6,000 a year as managing director, an additional £1,000 for his services as chairman, and 2.5 per cent of the profits – a further £1,000 in 1925. There was also the promise of a role in further acquisitions in Scotland. Hatry had sufficient pledges by the end of the year to launch the Drapery and General Investment Trust, with the Marquess of Winchester, who knew even less than he did about shopkeeping, as chairman. The other directors were representatives of the stores that were to be acquired by the Trust, including John Campbell. Hatry himself was not on the board. No sooner had the new company been established than Hatry looked for further purchases. His task was made easier in 1926 by the prolonged coal strike and the brief General Strike in May, which further disturbed confidence and depressed sales, particularly in manufacturing areas.

With John Campbell's help, Clarence Hatry approached three of Scotland's leading stores – Patrick Thomson Ltd of Edinburgh, D.M. Brown Ltd of Dundee and Watt & Grant of Aberdeen. Within a year all three had agreed to become members of a new group, Scottish Drapery Corporation, which was to include Pettigrew & Stephens. It was formed in December 1926 with John Campbell as chairman. The hiving off of the Scottish interests of the Drapery Trust, as it had been renamed, was part of a wider scheme to create other regional groupings and for the Trust's takeover from Harrods of the new Swan & Edgar store in Regent Street, which had been beset by difficulties. The announcement of these further deals caused raised eybrows in the press 'at the complicated financing' of the companies that made up the two groups, depending heavily as it did on debentures secured by mortgage over the stores themselves. Concerned that the Drapery Trust might make inroads in the north-east, John Simpson of Binns took steps to consolidate his position, planning the reconstruction of the Sunderland store and making successful bids for Gray Peverill & Co of West Hartlepool (1926) and Fowler & Brock Ltd of South Shields (1927). The company's expansion, financed by the simple device of mortgaging the property soon after purchase, was described at the time as 'one of the romances of the north.'

The advantages of these groupings were widely debated. There were reports in December 1926 that the Drapery Trust had established a central buying organisation which would not only cut out the wholesaler and deal direct with the manufacturers, but also secure hefty discounts for bulk orders. Such action struck at the roots of the informal price and credit agreements made through the trade associations. Many in the trade doubted if the claims for the economies to be achieved by this method of buying were justified. Despite the rumours there was little evidence that the Drapery Trust or the Scottish Drapery Corporation was bent on disturbing long-established buying practices. However, the dictates

Ready-to-wear garments came to dominate the fashion scene in the 1920s, making the latest styles much more available than before. This price list shows ready-to-wear coats in vogue at the time.

INEXPENSIVE COATS

JOAN

Graceful Coat in superior quality Wool Georgette, lined throughout crepe de chine. Well cut on becoming wrap-over lines, with roll collar and attractively shaped sleeve, smartly tucked. In shades of Beige, Fawn, Lido, Green, Rose Beige, Grey, Delphinium, Navy or Black. Sizes S.W., W. and F.W. 6½ Gns.

VALERIE

Perfectly cut on graceful slimming lines, this distinctive Coat is in a soft Wool and Artificial Silk material, lined throughout crepe de chine. Finished with softly gauged collar facings and strapping of reversed material. In shades of Biscuit, Dove, Blue, Fawn or Navy. Sizes S.W.,W. and F.W. 6½ Gns.

EVELYNE

Expressed in good quality Artificial Silk, this Coat has a becoming collar of Beige or Grey Foxaline, and is lined throughout crepe de chine. An exceptionally well-cut shape with wrap-over front terminating in slight flare at side and held with narrow tie of self material. In Black, Navy or Beige. Sizes S.W., W. and O.S. 6½ Gns.

of fashion were also changing the relationship between the retailer and the wholesaler. The popular short skirts and accompanying stockings made of artificial silk, recently renamed rayon to improve its image, were mostly ready-to-wear garments made in bulk. The short skirts and jumpers, which from 1926 were designed to reveal rather than suppress the figure, required far less underwear, just a 'princess petticoat with knickers combined' and 'a slip over belt and brassiere' – also made ready-to-wear. Stores without their own manufacturing facilities began buying such garments direct. Their appeal further depressed the traditional piece trade of wholesalers who failed to abandon the cotton and silk piece lines in favour of popular 'lighter and brighter types of fabric.'

For the retailer the cheapness of ready-to-wear simple clothing made for increased sales as women, with more money in their pockets than before the war, were willing to change their wardrobes more frequently. The craze for sport, sun bathing and the beach offered further opportunities for the ready-to-wear trade

Maule's Model · Villas ·

Entrance Hall – Villa – Murrayfield

During the 1920s many middle-class families became home owners for the first time. These houses and newly-built council houses were smaller than before, requiring more compact furnishings, but providing an obvious market for department stores. Maules of Edinburgh sought to attract new home owners by publishing this special catalogue.

OPPOSITE *Wylie & Lochhead, the Glasgow cabinet and furniture-makers, celebrated its centenary in 1929 with its 'first ever' sale.*

to expand their business. Men's and boys' wear was similarly transformed, with simpler, less formal, off-the-peg designs, fancy knitwear and baggy trousers. The fast expanding multiple chains were largely devoted to ready-to-wear garments and threatened to draw custom away from department stores and warehouses. Informality in dress was attacked for removing one of the principal bulwarks from civilised society – Correct Dress. Although the *Drapers' Record* did not share the Pope's criticism of short skirts and scanty underwear as immodest, believing them more 'hygienic', the paper condemned the man who abandoned his starched collar – 'If there are any cranky males ready to dine or dance in shorts or collarless shirts open at the neck we doubt whether they will find as partners self-respecting women.'

It was not only clothes that were affected by shifts in taste: the war had transformed home life and house design. Increasingly the middle-class drawing room, or the parlour of the less well off, was no longer forbidden territory to children, but in everyday use 'as a comfortable lounge'. The new owner-occupied houses and council houses built since 1919 were smaller than their predecessors. The heavy Georgian reproduction furniture, popular before the war, was replaced by lighter workaday Jacobean and contemporary functional styles in a wide range of sizes. Space-saving bedchairs and settees came into vogue. With domestic

CENTENARY SALE

Wylie & Lochhead Ltd.
45 Buchanan Street
Glasgow

D.H. Evans' store in Oxford Street acquired by Harrods in 1928.

servants harder to find, furnishings that required frequent polishing were replaced by more practical designs. Many of these new lines were mass-produced and supplied direct to department stores, squeezing the craft workshop of warehouses like Wylie & Lochhead in Glasgow, where higher labour costs resulted in high prices. Apparent as these changes were by 1927, the attention of the retail trade was focused on the takeover mania.

Throughout the year there were rumours and counter-rumours about possible acquisitions by Gordon Selfridge, the Drapery Trust, Harrods and other groups. After a tense struggle, Gordon Selfridge won control of the famous Whiteleys in Bayswater. He paid the fabulous sum of £10 million, rashly guaranteeing annual

dividends of twenty-five per cent for fifteen years. In May 1927 the city financier Sir Arthur Wheeler formed United Drapery Stores through his Charterhouse Investment Trust to take over seven London stores. The public issue of shares attracted little support and the underwriters were left with over ninety per cent of the stock on their hands. At the end of the year came the news that the Drapery Trust had been acquired by Debenhams. This was, in effect, however, a reverse takeover by the Drapery Trust: the Debenham family relinquished their interest in Debenhams and its associated stores in London, Marshall & Snelgrove and Harvey Nichols, to Clarence Hatry. Although the Scottish Drapery Corporation remained linked through cross-shareholding to the Trust, it operated independently and was separately quoted on the Stock Exchange. After the failure of Gordon Selfridge to win control of Anderson's Royal Polytechnic in Glasgow early in 1926, there were persistent reports over the next twelve months that the Scottish Drapery Corporation was in contention but their price was too low. Apart from this foray the board of the Scottish Drapery Corporation was preoccupied during 1927 with the difficult task of harmonising the finances of the four members of the Corporation and honouring the pledges made by Hatry at the time of purchase. Frantic speculation about the future of stores and the new conglomerates died down in 1928, but takeovers continued. In June Harrods acquired D.H. Evans' store in Oxford Street, with which they had a long informal connection, and at the close of the year the Scottish Drapery Corporation bought J. & R. Allan of South Bridge, Edinburgh. These deals were struck against a background of declining sales and stiffening competition as a reaction to the recovery in 1927 following the settlement of the coal strike. Throughout Britain stores had responded with heavily discounted summer and Christmas sales, where there was further confirmation of the shift in customer preference, noticeable since the war, away from expensive luxuries to 'popular priced useful goods'. Ostensibly because it had achieved its centenary, Wylie & Lochhead, the Glasgow cabinet and furniture makers, staged its 'first ever' sale in January 1929.

Hugh Fraser, the elder, died in late August 1927 after a long illness, leaving the family warehouse in the already capable hands of his son, Hugh, who was just twenty-five years old. So confident was he of his son's ability to manage the enterprise that he had altered his will in May to allow his trustees, immediately after his death, to transfer the whole of his holding in Fraser Sons & Co Ltd to the young Hugh. At the same time he dismissed as a trustee his brother John, with whom he had quarrelled over the proposed extension of the store. Instead he appointed his wife, Emily Florence McGowan, his son Hugh, his brother Matthew Pettigrew Fraser, a farmer in the Borders, and his nephew, Captain James Arthur Fraser Henderson, a Glasgow motor engineer, as trustees. His estate totalled £53,711, the bulk made up of his investment in Fraser Sons & Co Ltd. On taking command of the business, the young Hugh Fraser could draw satisfaction from the company's performance over the past two years when trading conditions had not been easy. The redecorated tearoom and new restaurant had proved a great success – 'with great numbers being turned away on Wednesdays for want of accommodation.' Still prevented from reconstructing the shop frontage, he and his father had rebuilt the interiors of the Buchanan Street windows and followed their competitors' lead in installing electric lighting to allow passersby at night to view the variety of goods on offer. Within a month of his father's death, Hugh Fraser convened a meeting of shareholders attended by his mother and his sister. After being elected chairman and paying tribute to his father, he proposed that his mother and cousin, Captain James A. Fraser Henderson, should become directors.

OPPOSITE *The sumptous arcade at the Army & Navy Stores, photographed in the 1920s.*

By mid-December, impatient with John Fraser's intransigence, the board opened negotiations for the purchase of his third share in the premises. While these took their protracted and painful course, Hugh Fraser busied himself with plans 'to bring our warehouse up to date, so that it may be in keeping with those of our rivals.' At the end of the year he enlarged the 'Small Ladies Department', which had been shown to be so popular in other stores. He concentrated his attention on new designs for the frontage, telling the annual meeting in the spring of 1928: 'Up to date it was sufficient to have a good family connection, but the rising generation of today do not shop in the centres which satisfy their parents, and we shall therefore – if progress is to be expected – have to make some capital outlay in the near future.' Coming to an agreement with his uncle took much longer than he expected. It was not until April 1929 that a price of £50,000 was settled for John Fraser's share in the building and his investment in the company. This was a large price, draining the company of liquidity and raising bank borrowings. Undaunted, Hugh Fraser pressed on with his plan for an arcade 'in artistic and dignified lines' on the Buchanan Street frontage, to cost £3,600. Completed towards the close of the year, the arcade soon vindicated Hugh Fraser's declared conviction that it would draw the crowds, raising turnover. Encouraged, the board approved early in 1930 the construction of a similar arcade in Argyle Street, which, along with other internal alterations, would make Frasers 'one of the finest warehouses in the city.' At the annual meeting in March 1930, Hugh Fraser confidently predicted that the company was 'now on the eve of great prosperity.'

The young Hugh Fraser putting the finishing touches to an exhibition display, possibly for the Empire Exhibition at Glasgow in 1938.

Throughout Glasgow and elsewhere in Britain during 1929, shopkeepers shared this optimism, based on evidence of an upturn in manufacturing industry after the disappointing performance since the war. In Glasgow Paisleys Ltd reconstructed their warehouse overlooking the Clyde. In Manchester, imaginatively, Kendal Milne – acquired by Harrods in 1919 - invited their customers to choose between four different architectural designs for their new store. The other large store in the city, Rylands, responded by announcing an even bigger new building of seven storeys. The *Drapers' Record*, by the end of June 1929, saw 'no reason for not taking a cheerful view of future prospects.'

There were further mergers; in February 1929 Scottish Drapery Corporation acquired John Falconer of Aberdeen; in April Binns took over James Coxon & Co of Newcastle-upon-Tyne, and in September, after much speculation, Lewis's Investment Trust bought Anderson's Royal Polytechnic in Glasgow. These mergers were greeted with much less enthusiasm than before – 'Everything and everybody are to be absorbed, merged, amalgamated, trustified, consolidated, federated, combined, associated, grouped, "chained", and generally boiled together until a lump emerges.' There was a concern that the individuality of department stores, which set them apart from multiple chains, would be destroyed. The merger movement was discredited in September when Clarence Hatry was arrested on charges of fraud. He was subsequently sentenced to fourteen years in prison in January 1930. Dealings in the preference shares of the Drapery Trust were suspended immediately the news broke, and Debenhams, under the leadership of Sir Frederick Richmond, took responsibility for salvaging the group which now comprised seventy stores. John Campbell was confirmed as chairman of the Scottish Drapery Corporation, answerable for the five stores in Scotland. The Wall Street crash in October 1929 finally pricked the bubble of confidence in the retail trades. There was a litany of complaints that customers were buying cheaper goods where margins were slim. This sudden reversal was aggravated in November by threats from the recently elected Labour Government to set up a Consumers' Council to investigate the price of clothing and drapery which, it was believed, were providing excessive profits for department stores. Worse still, the weather during the Christmas season was atrocious, keeping shoppers at home and, if they did venture out, causing them to patronise local shops rather than journeying into the city centres. As a way out of their difficulties the larger stores offered big price reductions in the New Year sales and attractive credit and hire-purchase terms. The annual conference of the National Federation of Credit Traders in July remarked on the advance in the use of credit since 1928 and the press warned shopkeepers not to 'tempt the careless or the improvident.'

During 1930 the world economy slumped. Manufacturing areas in the north of England and Scotland were badly hit and unemployment soared. In the face of declining household budgets, families were attracted to any schemes that would reduce the cost of goods. In the high street the new multiple grocery chains waged a fierce battle with the Co-ops, for long the enemy of the retail trade. Chain stores attempted to capture custom from their competitors by copying self-service techniques from America in selling ready-to-wear clothes. These shops were always 'brilliantly lit', the goods on display clearly priced in round numbers, and were equipped with machines for accounting and checking stock. Everywhere trading clubs and discount associations were established, especially by industrial firms, allowing members to buy goods direct from wholesalers or manufacturers. Independent grocers and shopkeepers joined, offering trading stamps as an inducement to their customers that could be exchanged for a range of goods depending on the number of stamps collected. The department stores

OPPOSITE *McDonalds' fabric department crowded with women customers in Glasgow in 1929, while the men waited in the smoking room.*

The hairdressing department at Harrods in 1930. The chairman, Sir Woodman Burbidge, complained bitterly at the time that it was becoming difficult for the store to maintain its excellent service because of rising costs.

Gentlemen choosing ties and accessories in the luxury of the Harrods menswear department in 1930.

retaliated with big advertising campaigns and further discounts. Those with sufficient resources and courage began another round of rebuilding and refurbishment both to attract business and reduce costs.

During 1930 Chiesmans of Lewisham began reconstructing their premises and Binns embarked on the modernisation of the old Coxon store in Newcastle. Lewis's installed an escalator in their Glasgow Royal Polytechnic to draw the crowds and gave notice that the whole store would be rebuilt to provide almost 380,000 square feet of shopping space, twice as much as in the old premises. Gordon Selfridge in December unveiled plans to make his Oxford Street store the biggest in the world, while Bernard George designed a magnificent Art-Nouveau temple for Derry & Toms in Kensington. These buildings represented a new departure in store design, using the recently developed pre-stressed concrete and other novel building techniques to provide open shopping floors uninterrupted by pillars. Not all the new building projects were opportune. In May 1931 Gamages, which had rebuilt its store in High Holborn in London, went bankrupt because the cost of construction had run forty per cent over estimate, reaching £5 million. Aware of such perils, Sir Woodman Burbidge had delayed the proposed reconstruction of Kendal Milne 'until trading conditions in Manchester are better,' turning his attention instead to grappling with the problem of cutting back overheads. In addressing the Management Research Group of Department Stores on a visit to Harrods in October 1930, he said: 'The item of expenses in all retail stores will want a lot of thought for the future, as there is no doubt that prices of goods are gradually getting back to prewar standards, and against the prewar standards the expenses have unfortunately grown tremendously in every detail. Our expenses before the war were equivalent to 15.84 per cent. Now as you know they were nearly 20 per cent last year.'

The impetus to reduce overheads was fuelled by the severe competition from other retailers. It was increasingly difficult for manufacturers to enforce resale price maintenance, and trade associations were almost powerless to police pricing agreements. John Lewis Ltd, early in 1931, deliberately flouted resale price maintenance by discounting proprietary brands and refusing to give way until supplies were cut off. They then purchased stock from wholesalers, which they again discounted, telling their customers what had happened. Such public action gave substance to the Labour Government's contention that the prices of clothes and drapery were kept artificially high by trade associations. The Lord Chancellor had set up a committee in April 1930 to examine restrictive practices. Before it reported, a new Consumers' Council Bill was introduced in Parliament in July of the following year to prevent profiteering in the retail trade by fixing maximum prices. To the relief of shopkeepers the Lord Chancellor's committee decided within a month that resale price maintenance was in the consumer's best interest and condemned price cutting as 'objectionable' and 'disruptive'. The proposed legislation was lost when the country and the Government were overwhelmed by the financial crisis in September which forced Britain off the gold standard and led to draconian cuts in public expenditure. Although the devaluation of the pound inevitably drove up the price of imports, the crisis led the new National Government to take powers in November to prevent dumping of cheap foreign goods. Department stores were immediately confronted by fifty per cent duty on many of the foreign fancy goods, which were staples of the Christmas trade – pottery, cutlery, cameras, electric lamps and radios.

With all the confidence of youth, Hugh Fraser assumed, like others, that these problems were transitory and that further expansion would yield handsome dividends. The buoyancy of his mood was no doubt due in large measure to his

marriage on 3 April 1931 at Queen's Cross Church, Aberdeen, to Katie Lewis, the youngest daughter of Sir Andrew Lewis, a shipbuilder in the town. He had met Katie the year his father died and proposed to her in 1929, but had been obliged by her parents to wait two years for the wedding. Soon after returning from his honeymoon in Monte Carlo, he began planning to modernise the store and to lease the upper four floors of Montague Burton's new chain of men's outfitters shop adjoining the family warehouse on the corner of Buchanan Street and Argyle Street. The first three floors were to contain additions to the fashion departments, and the top floor 'a restaurant and smoking room, affording a maximum of comfort and decorated in a modernist manner.' In announcing the scheme the month before the currency crisis, he told the press: 'I am tired of hearing people talk about the depression in trade. If I were not convinced of

ABOVE AND RIGHT
The supply of furniture and fittings for passenger liners represented an important part of the trade of Glasgow warehouses. Wylie & Lochhead made all the wooden fixtures and furniture in the saloon and nursery of the Queen Mary.

Glasgow's future, I would never contemplate extending on the scale mapped out.' The extension was officially opened by the Lord Provost, Sir Thomas Kelly, in a blaze of publicity in mid-November; mannequin parades of corsetry were staged during the whole of the following week. The inauguration was followed by a concerted advertising campaign in the local press. This fell on deaf ears after the decision in early December by Cunard & Co to suspend work on its giant liner, Ship No.534 - the *Queen Mary* - under construction at John Brown's Clydebank yard. By the time of the annual meeting in April 1932, Hugh Fraser's confidence had evaporated; he told the shareholders that 'when the lease of the building was contemplated the outlook for the trade was very different from what it is today, otherwise we fear we might not have taken on such a large extension.'

During the next two years the hull of the unfinished liner standing on the ways beside the Clyde became a symbol of the slump not just in Britain but throughout the world. For retailers it was a lean time; sales declined and price cutting was intense. As in the early 1920s many blamed the fall-off in business on the growth of property-owning amongst the middle class and consequent saving with building societies. In the opening months of 1932 Hugh Fraser's turnover collapsed and he only maintained his enterprise by extending the amount of credit he offered his customers. Unflinchingly he continued to seek for ways of increasing his trade, reorganising his household sections in the autumn

to take advantage of the rise in demand for furnishings. This was so successful that the sections were brought together into a much enlarged single department on the third floor, opened in May 1933. Despite the early promise, customers failed to patronise this new facility and results were disappointing. Still hoping for an upturn, Hugh Fraser added an 'inexpensive millinery section' later in the year. To provide the funds needed for these improvements and the greater volume of customer credit, the company's borrowings were raised from £29,080 to £76,000, using the warehouse premises as security. Although profits were depressed in the early 1930s, he never recorded a loss, unlike many of his competitors in Glasgow and elsewhere in Scotland. With no resources to battle against the foul economic conditions, some stores closed their doors, while others chose to sell out. In May 1934 Robert Maule & Sons, one of the most respected stores in Edinburgh with premises at the west end of Princes Street, was sold to Binns, and towards the end of the year the Scottish Drapery Corporation acquired Daly & Co of Sauchiehall Street, Glasgow.

The recovery came earlier in the south-east, with its new rapidly growing consumer industries, engaged for example in light electrical engineering, motor-car assembly and food processing, than in the north dominated by traditional heavy manufacturing and shipbuilding. The upturn in the south was evident by the beginning of 1934, encouraged by low interest rates and tax cuts. Confidence returned and shopkeepers who had survived the storm began yet another round

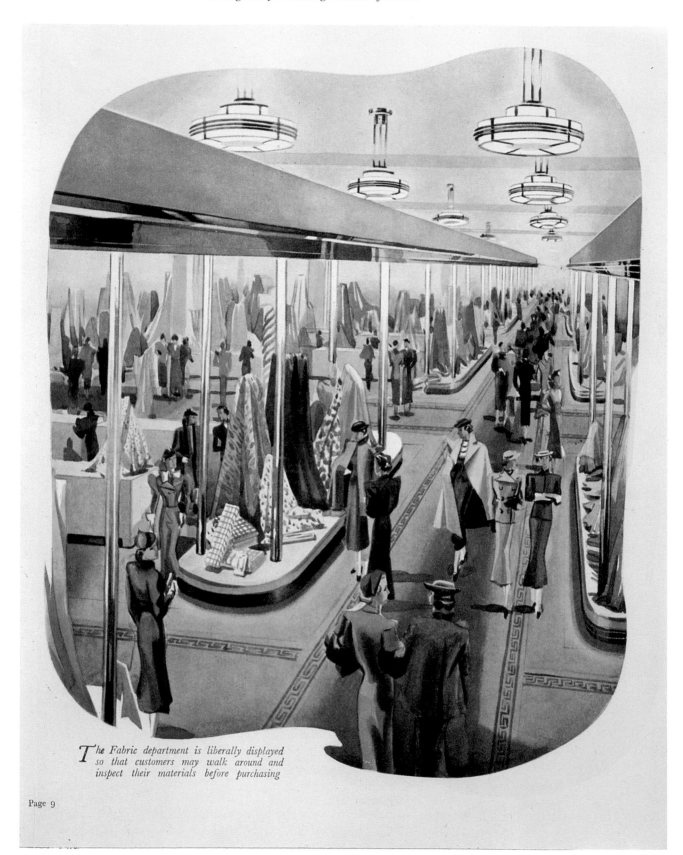

The Fabric department is liberally displayed so that customers may walk around and inspect their materials before purchasing

Page 9

OPPOSITE AND RIGHT
*D.H. Evans store was
completely rebuilt on a
single site in Oxford Street
between 1934 and 1937.
These pictures from the new
store brochure show the
textile hall and children's
area.*

*Peter Pan's Playground—a section of
the children's department complete
with fountain, pool and ornamental
trees, a delight to kiddies and
parents alike.*

of reconstruction. Harrods announced an ambitious plan to 'outdistance their competitors', by rebuilding the entire Oxford Street store of D.H. Evans on a single site at a cost of over £800,000 and were given the go-ahead for the reconstruction of Kendal Milne in Manchester. The decision, which reflected the resilience of middle-class incomes to the depression, even in the north of England and Scotland, was echoed elsewhere. In the spring of 1934 Brown Muff & Co purchased adjoining premises which allowed the consolidation of their store in Bradford on a single island site. Work on a large extension began in September and was finally completed two years later. The design and layout of these premises evinced the changes in shopping habits since the war, particularly the shift in the trade of department stores to the lower end of the market which had brought them into direct competition with the Co-ops and multiples. Special attention was given to sportswear, much in demand as the craze for exercise and sunbathing reached further down the social scale. There were experiments with innovative ideas in selling copied from America, particularly all-glass display cases and concession shops within a shop. Swan & Edgar opened their first shop inside the

During the mid-1930s
Britain was swept by a craze
for sports of all kinds.
These two views show the
Army & Navy Stores' boat
(above) and (left) sports
departments at the time.

The costume department of Mawer & Collingham of Lincoln, illustrating the open style of display with all-glass cases that had recently become popular.

store in July 1936 and Harrods quickly followed suit with a shop entirely devoted to women's stockings. Many of these concession shops within shops were opened to promote fashion wear which, with rapidly growing incomes, was enjoying a revival. With new cinemas opening up and down the country, styles were for the first time influenced by the stars of popular talking films. Newsreels shown before the main films, brought the Royal Family and major national events far more into the public eye offering further opportunities for clothes designers. There was disappointment in November 1935 that the Duchess of Gloucester wore a conventional dress at her wedding, but delight that her sister-in-law, the Duchess of York, chose to sport a new style of 'halo' hat that quickly became a best selling line.

Rising prosperity brought no respite in competition as it had done in prewar times. Shopping habits had changed fundamentally even amongst the better off who, with the advent of chain stores, discriminated in price to a much greater extent than before. The Scottish Drapers' conference in May 1936 was told by Dr J.A. Bowie, Principal of the School of Economics at Dundee, that multiple and specialist suburban shops were eating into the livelihood of the large city-

The amalgamated Glasgow stores of Arnott & Co and Robert Simpson, acquired by Hugh Fraser in 1936 as the foundation of his Group.

centre department stores. This message was reinforced by a store keeper who called for better staff training in salesmanship and stock control to counter the threat. Hugh Fraser was more than equal to the challenge, keeping his prices lower than those of his competitors and boasting that Frasers had 'one of the finest equipped departments for inexpensive coats, costumes, gowns and millinery in Scotland.' At the end of May, worried by the intrusion of multiples into Glasgow, he took the bold decision to buy Arnotts' warehouse across the road from his Argyle Street entrance. The purchase was financed by a loan of almost £60,000 from the Union Bank of Scotland. The existing partners retired and Arnott & Co was registered as a limited liability company with Hugh Fraser and his mother as directors. Immediately they set to work to modernise the store, opening up the second and third floors and installing an elevator and a new staircase. The first floor was enlarged and fitted out with 'quick serve' counters, and a bargain basement introduced. While this work was progressing, Hugh Fraser was negotiating through Arnotts for Robert Simpson & Sons around the corner in Jamaica Street, part of whose premises was required by Glasgow Corporation for road improvements. A successful deal, costing £46,000, was concluded at the end of September 1936. Further expansion followed in early November when the property adjoining the Buchanan Street front of Frasers' own store was purchased to make way for an extension. The property at 14–16 Buchanan Street, then leased to the woollen clothier Jaegar & Co, was immediately mortgaged for £32,000 to cover the price.

Within a few weeks Hugh Fraser learned that a London group was planning to acquire the drapery concern of Thomas Muirhead & Co of 200 Sauchiehall Street, Glasgow, which was founded in 1834 and catered for a better class of custom than either his family firm or Arnotts or Simpsons. Telling the press that he was 'not prepared to allow the whole of Glasgow to be the happy hunting ground of multiple firms and drapery combines,' he won control of the company for £36,500. Muirheads at once borrowed £75,000 secured over their property to finance the purchase and modernisation of the store. This was to be supervised by the newly recruited manager Elson Gamble, son of the manager of Anderson's Royal Polytechnic before Lewis's takeover. At breakneck speed all partitions, fixtures and pillars were swept away on the ground floor and 'a new frontage with a spacious arcade' constructed. The refurbished store was ready to be formally opened by the Lord Provost on 15 May 1937. In acknowledging the Lord Provost's tribute to his energy and enterprise, Hugh Fraser reaffirmed his commitment that Glasgow businesses should continue to be developed by local men. Following the example of other store groups, he had transferred Muirheads' property and those of his other stores to a new company, Fraser Estates Ltd, and registered Frasers (Glasgow) Bank Ltd to handle the Group's financial services.

At the annual meeting of Fraser Sons & Co Ltd in April, he had been triumphant, having no doubt that the year would 'go down as the most progressive in the history of the firm,' and naming his new group the 'House of Fraser'. He asked the shareholders to approve alterations to the articles of association, alterations which prevented the sales of the company's shares to anyone other than an existing shareholder without the chairman's consent. He also nominated his private secretary, Iris Picken, who had played a crucial role in all the negotiations, as a director of Fraser Sons & Co Ltd and its subsidiaries. If all this activity was not enough, he challenged the English multiples, particularly Marks & Spencer, by announcing plans to open a 'Nothing over 5 shillings' store in 14–16 Buchanan Street as soon as Jaegar's lease expired in September.

At the same time as the funds were put together for the modernisation of

RIGHT *D.H. Evans' new building in Oxford Street, 1937.*

OPPOSITE *The stores on the west side of Glasgow's Buchanan Street decked out for the Coronation of King George VI in May 1937.*

Muirheads, Hugh Fraser joined many of his contemporaries in the west of Scotland in advancing £1,000 to underwrite the Empire Exhibition to be staged in Glasgow in 1938. The Exhibition was to be at once a celebration of the renaissance of the Clyde's shipbuilding and engineering industries after the recession and the United Kingdom's imperial inheritance. Hugh Fraser sought to make the most of the commercial opportunities provided by the Exhibition. By the autumn of 1937 he had arranged for the stores of Arnotts and Robert Simpsons to be brought together under one roof by joining the two premises together. The amalgamated businesses were to trade as Arnott Simpson Ltd. The preliminary alterations were completed in February 1938 and work began on reconstructing the site between Jamaica Street and Argyle Street which adjoined the two stores. The new block was to be re-aligned to allow the pavement to be widened for the convenience of passers-by who hopefully would be attracted into the combined store. Elson Gamble was promoted to the post of general manager of the informally titled House of Fraser Group to co-ordinate the sales strategies of the four stores and to control stocks. The stores had to make weekly returns of turnover by department, which were scrupulously examined by Hugh Fraser, Elson Gamble and the company secretary, James Robertson.

Although Hugh Fraser made perhaps the most dynamic response to the changing conditions of the late 1930s in Glasgow, a few of his competitors adopted novel approaches. During the spring of 1938 Copland & Lye, following the lead of a few English stores in the previous year, installed a Viyella shop within their store. Most other warehouses in the city, however, did nothing to meet the competition from the multiples and chain stores head on as House of Fraser had done in fundamentally rethinking the layout and content of departments and deliberately focusing each outlet on a specific section of the market. Throughout Britain, the managements of department stores were accused of similar failings. A confidential report on London department stores, compiled by Frank Chitham in the summer of 1938, warned that unless urgent action was taken to reorganise buying and selling techniques and store layouts 'department stores will continue to give their better organized competitors an unnecessary start in the race for trade.'

Department stores had other more pressing worries by the late summer of 1938 as international tension mounted. In the spring there had been the hint of a slump in sales when war was rumoured. This had passed and the trade, faced with a decline in demand for adult clothes, had made a determined effort to extend fashion wear to schoolgirls and teenagers. The new King George VI and Queen Elizabeth, formerly Duke and Duchess of York, were asked to dress their eldest daughter, Princess Elizabeth, in more fashionable clothes to encourage sales. The year before, they had undertaken to ensure both Princess Elizabeth and her sister, Princess Margaret Rose, wore hats on public occasions to promote the British hat industry. When relations between Britain and Germany reached flashpoint during the Munich crisis in September, sales of most lines plummeted,

Changing fashions in the 1930s threatened the British hat industry and the Royal family promised to wear hats on public occasions to help maintain the tradition. This advertisement is for a stylish summer hat of the period from Binns of Edinburgh.

Binns *Limited*

SUCCESSORS TO ROBERT MAULE & SON LTD

TEL. 27041   EDINBURGH.

summer hats

ADÈLE. *Copy of Jean Patou in Fine Shantung Baku. From our model collection.* 49'6

Gas masks on display at the Army and Navy Stores.

except for bedding and clothes for schoolchildren because of the plans for their evacuation from the cities to the countryside. After the crisis had passed, most stores were left with huge quantities of blackout materials on their hands that had been purchased in anticipation of large sales to comply with the Air Raid Precaution (ARP) regulations. One consequence of Munich was an increased effort to sell British or Imperial goods and a widespread rejection of German clothes which, despite the tariff barriers, were continuing to be dumped in Britain.

Early in 1939 as war became increasingly likely, the Government turned its attention not just to more effective ARP measures but to the control, in the event of hostilities, of much of the country's industry and commerce, including retailing. The proposals for women to play a major role in munitions and ARP work soon affected fashion. Clothes became more functional, and mass-produced tailored trousers for women were widely advertised. During February girls wearing trousers on a Sunday in London's fashionable Hyde Park caused considerable excitement. Warehouses were called on during April to help directly in the preparations for war by releasing women staff for training as Air Raid Wardens and in the Women's Auxiliary Territorial Army. Hugh Fraser was enthusiastic in his support, offering additional paid holidays, including an extra week in the summer to go to camp. The following month the Government announced that retailing would not be treated as a 'reserved occupation' and all men working in shops would be available for conscription. The Ministry of Supply was formed in June with wide powers to control almost every part of the country's trade when war was declared. In planning for war the Government was determined that there would be no repetition of the boom in retail sales and the galloping inflation of the previous conflict.

When war was finally declared on Sunday 3 September 1939, there was less panic than there had been in 1914. Shops that had ordered large supplies of blackout material a year before found within hours that there was insufficient to meet demand. In Glasgow alone on the Friday before war, over eight miles of blackout was sold. Immediately the Ministry of Supply banned the import of textiles, except under licence, and took control of the manufacture of wool, silk, rayon, flax, hemp and jute, all needed for military purposes. Shopkeepers with stock worth more than £1,000 were instructed to take out expensive war risk insurance which, it was estimated, would push up prices. Recognising such increases might be abused, the Government issued a stern warning against profiteering. Stores were also advised to stock clothes that required no ironing

An advertisement for combinations published by D.H. Evans shortly before the National Government introduced its Limitation of Supplies Order (LIMISO). Customers are advised to 'lay in a stock'.

"Aberdeen's Foremost Fashion House"

UTILITY DRESSES

by three of the most Famous Designers

jersey de luxe

Jersey de luxe—Olive Green Fine Woollen makes this Two-piece with interesting yoke and bold patch pockets. It has smartly tailored Skirt with inverted pleat back and front. Woollen tailored blouse front in Tomato shade. Other styles and colours in stock. Sizes 36 to 38 hips. 15 Coupons.

Price 82/2

Jersey de luxe—An Iris Blue Handkerchief makes a vivid flash of colour in this Black Wool Dress with its unusual diagonally draped bodice. Pleats in front of skirt only. Size 38. There is a variety of other styles and colours. Size 36 to 44. 11 Coupons.

Price 60/-

Hollywood—A becoming Gown for the larger fittings. Made in Fine Wool with attractive scalloped design on bodice of same material. The skirt flares very slightly. Model sketched is in Cherry colour. Size 42 hips, but other styles and colours are in stock. Size 40 to 46. 11 Coupons.

Price 60/-

jersey de luxe

rembrant

Rembrant—This gay, youthful Dress by Rembrant is softly tailored in Fine Rayon Crepe. Front of bodice in lovely contrasting shades: Brown/Lime, Brown/Turquoise, and Black/Ice Blue. Sizes 36—38. 7 Coupons.

Price 53/.7

hollywood

WATT & GRANT, LTD.   UNION ST.   ABERDEEN

As part of the austerity measures the Government introduced Utility 'U' furniture and clothes designed by leading designers to be made simply and economically and to be hard-wearing. These dresses, advertised by Watt & Grant of Aberdeen, would have been available throughout the country.

Binns' store in Sunderland damaged by bombing in 1941. Department stores with their large city centre premises were prime targets and many were destroyed.

and could be easily washed, as women would be heavily committed at work or on ARP duty. This led to the design of what clothing manufacturers called 'Utility Models', including the all-in-one 'Siren suit' for women that was advertised for the first time by Goorwitch of Oxford Street in the third week in September. At the end of the month paper and string were restricted, making it impossible for shops to continue wrapping goods. Stores appealed to customers to return paper bags and unwanted string. Small boys were employed after school to join bits of string to make up balls for the counters. Paper used for parcels delivered to customers' homes was recovered to be used again. The restrictions in supply of goods, combined with the drive for national savings, drove down sales and, as in 1914 the large stores dismissed staff. Drapers blamed sagging demand on the trend, since the outbreak of hostilities, for a woman to wear 'clothes for comfort', rather than dressing 'according to fashion' and taking 'care of her appearance and accessories.' During October the Government imposed compulsory six o'clock closing on all shops, 'except for one late night a week when they could stay open for a further hour and a half.' In the midst of these difficulties Hugh

Fraser celebrated the ninetieth anniversary of the family business, Fraser Sons & Co.

At the beginning of the Christmas season, Sir John Simon, the Chancellor of the Exchequer, added to the miseries of shopkeepers by warning the nation to save as much as possible and not waste money on new clothes. After an outcry from the trade he, half-heartedly, attempted to make amends in the week before Christmas by calling for a resumption in expenditure. His recantation was short-lived for, by the end of January, he was again demanding greater savings to the fury of the *Drapers' Record* which questioned, 'Is the Government out to throttle home trade?' The Government, committed to a policy of curbing wartime inflation, was in no mood to relax its grip on domestic expenditure at a time when the country was in urgent need of foreign exchange to buy materials from the United States. Manufacturers were encouraged to export as much as possible. In April 1940 textile houses were instructed to limit their supplies to the home market to seventy-five per cent of sales in 1939 for most materials and twenty-five per cent for linen. To depress domestic demand further and raise additional funds for the war effort, Sir John Simon in his spring budget introduced a purchase tax which was to be imposed on all clothing. Its implementation was delayed by the formation of the National Government with Winston Churchill as Prime Minister in May 1940. In the meantime, early in the following month, after the collapse of France, the Limitation of Supplies Order (LIMISO) was passed, which reduced a whole range of goods available to the public, including underwear, gloves, corsets and stockings. Shopkeepers demanded that multiples should not receive an unfair allocation of the merchandise available. To prevent retailers taking advantage of the scarcity of goods, all prices were to be controlled. The rate of purchase tax was fixed at the end of July at 33.3 per cent on all goods except food, with an additional 16.3 per cent on luxuries. The department stores were appalled, accusing the Government of having gone too far in suppressing civilian demand. With his confidence undiminished, Hugh Fraser took over the fashion house of Kings Ltd at 249 Sauchiehall Street in the week that purchase tax became law. This acquisition was financed by loans secured against the property from the National Bank of Scotland. His introduction to the National Bank of Scotland had followed a chance meeting in April 1939 with Alex Stirling, the manager of the Renfield Street Branch, in a Glasgow coffee shop, which quickly developed into a close business friendship. Within a month all the Group's accounts had been transferred from the Union Bank to the National Bank, which was prepared to offer higher borrowing limits to permit further expansion.

By the time purchase tax began to be charged on 21 October 1940, the Blitz was at its height with nightly raids on London and other major cities. During September, Oxford Street was bombed causing over £2 million worth of damage to the John Lewis Partnership's new store. Throughout the country shops began to close at five o'clock to allow the staff to get home before the raids started. As fighter squadrons of the Royal Air Force fought heroically to prevent the Germans gaining superiority of the skies over Britain, department stores promoted 'Spitfire weeks' and the Government requisitioned all silk for parachutes. In the Atlantic the German U-boats were taking a heavy toll of British shipping, threatening the country's supplies of raw materials. At the end of November the Board of Trade cut the LIMISO drastically for most goods. There were anomalies; garters, previously excluded, were now included in the corsets class. More seriously, retailers, dubbing the Board of Trade 'the Board to Strangle Trade', objected that as the LIMISO was calculated on value rather than quantity, manufacturers could evade the regulations by reducing the quality of their products. There were reports early in December that the Government was planning to overcome this problem by introducing clothes rationing on the pattern that had been in force in Germany since the outbreak of war and had been much ridiculed in the British press. The dearth of goods forced some stores to merge their businesses for the duration of the emergency. During December Hugh Fraser took the bold decision to extend his business beyond Glasgow by acquiring the Edinburgh store of Peter Allan. This purchase was financed by loans secured against the property from the National Bank of Scotland. Having set foot on the national stage Hugh Fraser, in January 1941, accepted the presidency of the Scottish Appeal for Warehousemen Clerks and Drapers' Schools.

The already serious situation deteriorated even further for all shopkeepers in the spring of 1941. There were complaints that some smaller shops were not receiving adequate allocations of goods, and talk of standardising clothing and furnishings. As a first step to respond to this grievance in May 1941, the Retail Advisory Committee was established under the chairmanship of the Glasgow member of parliament, W. Craik Henderson, 'to examine the present problems of the retail trade in goods other than food, having regard to the immediate needs of the conduct of the war and to the position after the war.' The Committee immediately got down to work, collecting a mass of evidence from all the trade associations involved in the distribution and sale of goods and conducting a statistical survey of retail outlets. They had hardly begun their enquiries when on 1 June clothing and footwear were rationed. Everybody was issued with forty coupons for the next year which were to be handed in whenever an article was purchased. There were set numbers of coupons required for every item, nine for an 'unlined mackintosh or cape, eleven for a dress, gown, frock, one-piece shelter suit and like garment, and six for a nightdress.' Some articles were exempt, including boilersuits, knickers, shorts and trunks that did not measure more than twenty-three inches from the waist, and at first all clothing for infants less than four years old. These complex regulations, combined with the requirement to complete returns for the Retail Advisory Committee and the administration of the LIMISO, placed a heavy burden on shop staff at a time when all shopgirls between the age of twenty-one and twenty-five were being called up for military service.

Despite these obstacles, Hugh Fraser remained determined to enlarge his business, buying the drapery warehouse of Gordon & Stanfield in Perth at the end of June 1941. Any hope he may have had that the worst might be over was soon dashed. In September the Special Quota of Cloth and Apparel Order was introduced setting the quantity of materials to be used in a range of 'Utility' clothes. These were to be sold at nationally fixed prices and marked with the CC41 symbol. The Utility scheme, which also covered furniture, involved a maze of detailed regulations, imposing yet another strain on already overworked shop staff. In London the West End stores were forced, because of the nightly air raids, to send home such staff as they had before four o'clock from October to February. Still Hugh Fraser was not to be diverted, consolidating his position in Sauchiehall Street in Glasgow at the end of October through the purchase of the old-established firm of house furnishers, Muir Simpson Ltd. A fortnight later he secured a foothold in Dundee when he bought the drapery business of Alexander Ewing & Co. With so many businesses now under his control, he decided at the end of November to form a new company as a vehicle for acquisition, House of Fraser Limited, with himself and his secretary, now Mrs Iris Estcourt, as directors, and the National Bank of Scotland as bankers. Hugh

A servicewoman being fitted with sensible shoes at Harrods during the war.

Soldiers choosing Valentine cards at Brown Muffs of Bradford during the war.

Fraser was now a national figure in the drapery business, publicly recognised by his election earlier in the year as the deputy appeal president of the Linen and Woollen Drapers' Institution and Cottage Homes. He became the first Scottish president in April 1942, quickly winning the confidence and respect of senior members of the trade in England. His photograph, always cigarette in hand, began to appear regularly in the trade press.

Believing that conditions could only get worse, the Retail Advisory Committee reported at the outset of 1942, that many small shops had closed since the beginning of the war and advocated further concentration. Shopkeepers, understandably, were not convinced and repeated their demand for the equitable distribution of available goods, particularly the new Utility styles. It had taken some weeks for Utility goods to be designed and manufactured. When Utility underwear first went on the market in November 1941, sales were brisk. More substantial garments were not ready until the New Year of 1942 and were similarly well received. In February the well-known fashion designer Norman Hartnell agreed to design Utility frocks for the ready-to-wear manufacturers Berkertex. The clothing ration was cut by twenty-two per cent in March adding to drapers' difficulties. Answering the howls of protest from the trade, the Government agreed in April that Utility clothes would be exempt from purchase tax. This welcome news was soon dampened by further petty regulations – for example, forbidding decoration on nightwear and underwear except corsets and brassieres, and fixing the number of buttons, dimensions and finish of menswear. Throughout the rest of the year there was a constant stream of new regulations and amendments from the Board of Trade, some bewildering in their detail – for example, from 14 June 1942 the item 'women's non-woollen legless knickers' at two coupons was amended to 'women's non-woollen knickers and panties with side lengths not exceeding $18\frac{1}{2}$ inches.' An elaborate scheme for compensating shopkeepers who withdrew from business because of the restrictions was proposed in July, but rejected. As president of the Cottage Homes, Hugh Fraser's response to the problems of the trade was to campaign hard to raise a record £20,000 to help 'the old folk of our trade' whose need he believed was greater than ever. He was regularly in London at meetings and with his wife attending fund-raising functions. He did not, however, neglect his business. In April he helped organise a motor-pool for delivery services between six of Glasgow's largest stores. When, at the beginning of November, there was an opportunity to effect further concentration in Glasgow, he snapped up the offer of Dallas's store in Cowcaddens with its, at one time, large mail-order trade to West Africa, and its sister enterprise, the once famous Colosseum store of Walter Wilson in Jamaica Street. These companies had been badly hit by the recession and the war.

Although the war in North Africa began to turn slowly in the Allies' favour after the Battle of El Alamein in November 1942, supply problems became even more acute. Over the next two and a half years leading up to the final victory, there was a progressive tightening of the regulations and reduction in the ration. Retailers were frustrated by the extent of the bureaucratic interference in their business, complaining regularly to the Board of Trade through their various trade associations. There was particular annoyance at the flood in sales after successive distributions of coupons, followed by long periods of little activity. In February 1943 Hugh Fraser became a spokesman for the trade when he was elected a vice-president of the Scottish Retail Drapers' Association. Despite this additional responsibility, he continued to spearhead the appeal for the Cottage Homes. The strain told on his health, already damaged by very heavy smoking, and towards the end of November he had a mild heart attack at the age of only forty. To help

*Harrods with its windows
still boarded up as part of
the air raid precautions
ready to celebrate VE-Day
in 1945.*

in the overall management of the Group, Cecil C.S. Harker, the manager of
Thomas Muirhead & Co and previously the dress buyer at Frasers' own store,
was appointed assistant general manager of the whole Group, to work under
Elson Gamble. He had an extensive knowledge of the department store business,
having worked before he joined Frasers in Harrods, Barkers, Selfridges and
Lewis's. Hugh Fraser's illness and the uncertainty of 1944 prevented any further
expansion of his Group until January 1945 when D.& A. Prentice of Greenock
on the lower Clyde was acquired.

By the beginning of 1944, with the Second Front in prospect, the Government
had begun to consider the shape of retailing in the immediate postwar years. To
the dismay of shopkeepers, the Board of Trade had made it known that there
was little hope of any relaxation in the controls for some years to come. This
did not prevent shopkeepers, town councils and the trade press from making
preparations for the redevelopment of bombed city centres. There were many
ambitious proposals based on the imaginative use of reinforced concrete and steel
that had become popular since the late 1930s. Developing concepts pioneered in
Britain just before the war, designs were bold and functional. Shops were to be
grouped in precincts, serviced by arterial ring roads and adequately provided
with car parking. Hugh Fraser contemplated some reconstruction of his shops,
buying properties in Glasgow to allow for the extension of both Muirheads
in Sauchiehall Street and Dallas's in Cowcaddens. After the victory celebration on

VE day, 8 May 1945, when all shops were closed, the Government promised an early end to the petty restrictions of clothes styles, regulating, for example, the size of pockets and the use of pleats and tucks. Any hope of further slackening of the ration and increase in supplies was soon dashed by the abrupt termination in August of American support for Britain through lease-lend. The newly elected Labour Government was plunged into a serious economic crisis. The whole of the country's manufacturing industry was mobilised in a massive export drive to earn badly needed foreign exchange, and supplies to the home market were even more stringently rationed. To prevent shopkeepers making excessive returns from 'Non-Utility' goods, price controls were imposed from October.

Before the coming of peace Hugh Fraser had lobbied hard that Scottish warehousemen needed a single organisation to speak to Government about their distinctive problems, particularly if the complex web of rules and regulations was to continue for the foreseeable future. His work as appeals president of the Cottage Homes had brought him into regular contact with Government and he had taken every opportunity to put the Scottish case. As vice-president of the Scottish Retail Drapers' Association (SRDA) he had been the moving spirit behind the formation of a joint committee with the Wholesale Textile Association (Scottish branch) in June 1944 and a year later the amalgamation of the Allied Trades Association of Edinburgh and South East Scotland with the SRDA. In April 1946 he was elected the first president of the combined associations, which continued under the title SRDA, and at once launched a hard-hitting campaign against Government plans to reduce retailers' profit margins by cutting the controlled prices. He organised a well-attended rally of Scottish shopkeepers in July, attacking the Secretary of the Board of Trade and calling for open discussions of pricing policy. He condemned the fixing of prices of Non-U goods as unnecessarily heavy handed. Despite the onslaught the Labour Government refused to listen, even though Hugh Dalton, the Chancellor of the Exchequer, had publicly promised Hugh Fraser in 1943 that retailers would always be consulted. When a further cut in margins was announced just before Christmas 1946, on the grounds that retailers' turnover had risen by thirty per cent following an easing of the ration earlier in the year, Hugh Fraser led the Scottish delegation to the Board of Trade to explain that in Scotland trade had only recovered by twenty-two per cent. In the spring of the following year he attacked the apparently meaningless bureaucracy and form filling of the whole control system. He was outraged by loopholes in legislation that allowed chain stores from the south to buy shops in Scotland, evict the tenants whatever the terms of their leases and redevelop the properties for their own purposes without having to pay any tax on capital gained.

Hugh Fraser's firm commitment to the Scottish cause made him the preferred buyer for drapery concerns that were put on the market by families who lacked either the resources or the courage to keep going. At the end of December 1945 he advanced into east central Scotland by buying Logie & Co of Stirling, adding a further store in the town, McLachlan & Brown, the following summer. He enlarged his representation in Edinburgh in March 1946 when he took over William Small's warehouse on the prestigious shopping thoroughfare of Princes Street. He consolidated his position in Perth at the end of 1946 through the acquisition of D.A. Wallace. In April 1947 he purchased Anderson's Arcade, a block of shops, considered to be one of the most valuable properties in Princes Street, rather than seeing it pass to English owners. All these acquisitions were made by House of Fraser Ltd, financed by a bond of cash credit advanced from the Standard Property Investment Co of Edinburgh of over $£\frac{1}{2}$ million secured over the premises; this replaced all existing loans.

The management of the Group remained relaxed and decentralised. The stores continued to trade under their own names and little was done to disturb their style and customer profile. The only central buying undertaken was for Non-U fashionwear, organised by Miss Pudaloff from Glasgow. Apart from Hugh Fraser's instincts, and later those of Elson Gamble, in managing drapery concerns and warehouses, there was no grand design for the integration of the Group into a powerful unified buying or selling force north of the border. Against the background of wartime controls, such ambitions would, anyway, have been inappropriate. Fraser's success was undeniable, with profit after tax and charges climbing as a consequence of all the acquisitions from just under £56,000 to almost $£\frac{1}{4}$ million by 1947 without any increase in the company's share capital or widening of its ownership. This improvement was not due simply to the aggregate of the profits of the stores that had been acquired, but to tight control of management and finance exercised through the monthly review of turnover, stock and wages by Hugh Fraser and his central management team, Elson Gamble, Alfred Spence, who had recently replaced Cecil Harker as assistant general manager, and Robert Keenan, who had succeeded James Robertson as secretary in 1940. Any problem was investigated immediately to minimise loss of profit. With this track record and the need to raise further capital to modernise and enlarge the Group's stores and make further acquisitions, Hugh Fraser decided towards the close of 1947 to go public, selling equity to individuals and institutions, hopefully in Scotland.

In less than twenty-five years Hugh Fraser had transformed the family's small department store at the foot of Buchanan Street into a major Scottish warehouse group. He had at first modernised and extended the original store to improve its competitiveness with the leading stores in Glasgow. He had then deliberately set out to create a Scottish group with the simple objectives of keeping out the English and achieving a spread of businesses that would give him access to customers across the social scale, but particularly at the bottom end where sales had grown most swiftly since the First World War. In Glasgow he had won control of Walter Wilson's Colosseum, one of the leading warehouses in the city in the 1890s, and in Edinburgh he had two major stores to his credit. He had youth and experience on his side, where many managers and owners were old and only too ready to leave the trade. He had also become a national figure in the drapery world, not just as a Scottish spokesman, but as the leader of its charitable endeavours. In so doing he had gained the ear of Government and the respect of his colleagues in the trade, as a steadfast advocate of department stores, however great the opposition from the multiples. He had met the challenges of retailing in the interwar years and during the Second World War itself and emerged victorious and considerably richer.

6 1948–1966
Scottish Retail Drapery King

A cartoon of Hugh Fraser with his ubiquitous cigarette.

OPPOSITE ABOVE AND BELOW *The dress department of an Aldershot store in the early 1950s with the flaired 'New Look' dresses prominently displayed and accessories that were available again after the lifting of the wartime restrictions.*

The retailing landscape, hedged about with the maze of government regulations and controls that Hugh Fraser surveyed in 1948, was very different from the unfettered world in which he had grown up during the aftermath of the First World War. He admitted frankly to the company's annual meeting in July, 'In my many years' experience of the drapery trade I have never known a time when it was more difficult to assess future business prospects.' Nevertheless he remained convinced that the obstacles, however great, could be overcome. To remain competitive, shopkeepers had to be skilled in working to best advantage within the rules, using whatever resources they could lay their hands on to respond to the changing needs of the market. The more imaginative squeezed a little room for manoeuvre out of the special clothes ration made to women in the armed forces and munitions workers when they were demobbed. Many of these women were barely out of their teens and keen to make up for their youth lost in the wartime austerity. 'Junior Miss' sections were opened in department stores to capture the custom of young women from the multiples. These often incorporated novel features, particularly bars where the customers sat at a bar on high stools to buy hats, shoes and accessories. Department stores that had made such radical innovations were well prepared for the revolution in women's fashions that came in the spring of 1947 when Christian Dior unveiled his 'New Look' which emphasised the female figure, lifting bosoms and pinching waists. 'New Look' clothes, with their coquettish air, rapidly became the rage amongst the young, breathing new life into the demand for undergarments and corsets which many women needed to achieve a shapely figure.

Hugh Fraser had learned from the experience of bringing his family's own store in Glasgow up to date in the 1920s that the Group could only remain competitive if the stores were refurbished to reflect contemporary tastes and aspirations. This could not be achieved without additional funds, and these could no longer be raised by the simple expedient of mortgaging property. With advice from the distinguished Glasgow accountant, Sir Ian Bolton, founder of Glasgow Industrial Finance Ltd, Hugh Fraser was persuaded to convert his Group, of which he owned ninety-five per cent of the equity, into a public company. Like nearly every other contemporary business decision this required permission from the government. When this was forthcoming in mid-December 1947, the assets of Fraser Sons & Co Ltd and all the other associated companies were transferred to House of Fraser Ltd, which was to become the public company. Two days before Christmas Mrs Iris Estcourt resigned from the board, and Hugh Fraser's management team, Elson Gamble, Alfred Spence and Robert Keenan, were appointed directors. On 29 December House of Fraser Ltd officially became a public company, issuing £250,000 of ordinary shares divided into 5-shilling units and 350,000 £1 preference shares. The flotation of the shares did not take place until after a Stock Exchange listing was assured early in the New Year. Afterwards Hugh Fraser still held a little less than half the equity through Fraser Sons & Co Ltd, now in liquidation, which was transferred in August to

The coffee bar at Brown Muff's store in Bradford opened in the 1950s to attract younger customers with money to spend on 'New Look' clothes.

a new private company, Scottish & Universal Investments Ltd, popularity known as SUITS. This company was to become a vehicle for Hugh Fraser's other Scottish ambitions beyond the confines of retailing.

Deeply conscious of their new responsibilities to outside shareholders, the directors were more vigilant than ever in their scrutiny of monthly trading figures, investigating in March excessive outlays on wages during the previous month at Smalls of Edinburgh and the stores at Dundee, Greenock and Stirling. In May Alfred Spence was despatched to enquire why Muir Simpson's stocks were abnormally high. At the same time the assistant secretary, Miss Irene MacGregor, was instructed to prepare a more detailed monthly analysis of oncost expenditure. When this first became available in June Hugh Fraser demanded to know why salaries were up 1.1 per cent on the previous year and advertising costs 0.5 per cent higher. He was also concerned that the Group's foray into central buying for fashionwear might be the cause of the overstocking of these goods. Throughout the year he was persistent in his queries, endlessly comparing one store's performance against another, reserving his harshest criticism for the conduct of the original Buchanan Street store. Although Elson Gamble and Alfred Spence earned his praise for their vigilance in maintaining the board's tight financial grip on costs and in driving up turnover, they found the going tough. In August they were offered relief when the counting house manager, F.E. Patron, was promoted to be assistant general manager and Alfred Spence became a general manager on

The Dingle Anniversary

T HERE is magic in numbers and in seven more than most — Seven League Boots, Seven Pillars of Wisdom, Seven Seas, Seven Wonders of the World, and the beginning of our Seventh Year in our New Store, Seventy Seven since we first began, and if we talked till seventy times seven we could not begin to tell you how excited we are about this very special Anniversary, an Anniversary which symbolises by its number both the individuality that has made Dingles a name to conjure with, and the long tradition of service on which you have come to depend.

Because Anniversaries are coupled with an invitation, we are inviting you at this time to pay us a special visit. Our Buyers will be making a particular effort to show a unique range of goods so that wherever you look you will find merchandise that is distinctive and yet of unassailable quality.

Explore Departments that perhaps you know little of, revisit familiar haunts with new eyes — talk to us as we go about the Store, ask to see those background activities which are so little known but which contribute so greatly to your enjoyment of our Service.

We want to know you and you to know us, for it is our proud boast that we alone in the West Country have a Store large enough to house all your shopping needs under one roof yet small enough to know and serve you personally.

1947

1937

1880

E. Dingle & Co. LIMITED

ROYAL PARADE — PLYMOUTH — Telephone 66611

Normal shopping hours: 9—5.30.   Wednesday 9—1.

equal terms with Elson Gamble. From the moment that Glasgow Industrial Finance Ltd became involved in the flotation of the company, they had made it clear that institutional shareholders would expect there to be at least one non-executive director. Reluctantly Hugh Fraser in August agreed to the appointment of James D. Cochrane, manager of the Standard Property Investment Co of Edinburgh which held mortgages for more than £500,000 secured over the companies' properties. At his first board meeting Hugh Fraser created a committee of executive directors 'for the purpose of reviewing the monthly trading results in detail,' which would submit formal reports to the board.

Hugh Fraser's obsessive concern at even the slightest upward movement in costs during 1948 was due entirely to the distortions in the market resulting from government policy towards domestic retailing. Early in the year more goods were released for home consumption, but neither the clothes ration was raised nor was the punitive level of purchase tax lowered. The spring Budget offered no comfort, purchase tax on some items was in fact increased. The trade was so incensed at the increase in the rate for Non-U children's clothes that the Chancellor of the Exchequer – the normally unrelenting Sir Stafford Cripps – was forced to cancel it. By the end of April retailers throughout the country were complaining that they had the goods to sell, but people lacked sufficient coupons to buy. The sternest critic of the government was Hugh Fraser who, as president of the Scottish Retail Drapers' Association for a second year, constantly railed against Harold Wilson, the newly appointed president of the Board of Trade. When the ration was increased in mid-May he was amongst the first to condemn the concessions as too little and too late and hit the headlines by storming out of a meeting with the Board of Trade whom he publicly berated as 'completely out of touch'. His words hit home, wringing further concessions from the Board of Trade. Harold Wilson gave way with ill grace, declaring that the high price of goods, as much as rationing, was responsible for sluggish sales. Hugh Fraser hit back hard, censuring the Government's tight money policy and demanding a reduction in purchase tax. He also raised the spectre of the nationalisation of the large stores. After disastrous summer sales with goods returned to wholesalers and the cancellation of orders for new goods, Harold Wilson finally admitted that the money supply was too restrictive. However, he remained an advocate of the Utility scheme as guaranteeing good quality and fair prices. Clothes rationing had now ceased to be a constraint on purchase and, after further delay, was abolished with a flourish in March 1949. Retailers were not deceived, particularly when purchase tax was not altered in the Budget and tax on credit sales remained in force. Worse was to follow when Harold Wilson suddenly slashed gross margins on Utility clothing by five per cent at the beginning of August and then left for a holiday in France. Hugh Fraser descended like a lion from the north on a protest meeting held by the National Chamber of Trade. He had no time for the tame motion of complaint, declaring, 'I'm afraid we are more revolutionary than you in the south.' He struck precisely the right note, winning the backing of the meeting for a call for a vigorous campaign directed at the Prime Minister, Clement Atlee. Despite the strength of the opposition, Harold Wilson at the Board of Trade remained implacable.

His increasing role as a national spokesman and leader of the trade did not dull Hugh Fraser's competitive spirit. Throughout 1948 he and his management team took every opportunity to win custom. They assigned high priority to establishing an in-house hire-purchase company, Retail and General Discounting Limited, which it was hoped would compensate for the shortage of cash. This venture rapidly matched expectations and brought the added advantage of bigger margins as hire-purchase sales were rarely discounted. Promotions at individual stores were flamboyant, designed to attract press notices and the crowds. On 18 September 1948 the Glasgow store Arnott Simpsons celebrated the centenary of the foundation of Arnott & Co (see page 278). To mark the occasion £1 vouchers were given away to customers at five-minute intervals throughout the day. As the news spread, people flocked to the store to make small purchases in the hope of receiving a gift. Next month Seton Cotterill, a London and New York designer, opened a shop within Fraser's original store in Buchanan Street, exhibiting clothes in 'classic rather than revolutionary tendencies'. The success of these initiatives was a prelude to a more ambitious campaign in the autumn of 1949 to commemorate Frasers' hundred years in business. The anniversary events were launched on 7 September when Hugh Fraser welcomed the Duchess of Buccleuch to the Buchanan Street store to open a market bazaar in aid of the Scottish Association of Girl Guides. The following day the Scottish newspapers carried articles on the history and development of the Group, advertising the ten-day Centenary Celebration Sale at all the stores with gift vouchers of £1 and ten shillings. There were special features at each store – mannequin parades and the opening of new departments, particularly household, piece goods, linens and soft furnishings. As a further incentive to women customers, large quantities of nylon stockings, which had been in short supply since the outbreak of war, were available each day for those who had the patience to queue. To the annoyance of Sir Richard Burbidge, Frasers' centenary advertising bore a remarkable resemblance to that of Harrods, which was also celebrating its hundredth anniversary.

Dickins & Jones' pattern department. With money tight in the early 1950s, home dressmaking was popular.

*The store of McLaren &
Son, gentlemen's outfitters
of Glasgow, the first business
to be purchased by Hugh
Fraser after House of
Fraser became a public
company early in 1948.*

These aggressive promotions drew customers from as far away as the north of England and bolstered turnover just at the moment when Harold Wilson was driving down retailers' margins.

Frustrated in his attempts to rebuild some of his stores by shortage of materials and by planning regulations, Hugh Fraser continued to search for new recruits to the Group. In May 1948 he made his first acquisitions since going public, when he purchased two Glasgow businesses, wholesale clothiers Brown Smith & Co, and gentlemen's outfitters McLaren & Son. D. Hourston & Sons of Ayr was acquired in May of the next year, and pursuing the well-tried course, the property was immediately mortgaged, in this case for £75,000, to cover the cost and help pay for improvements. It was Hugh Fraser's declared intention to provide a department store in this Clyde coast resort that 'would hold its own with the best Glasgow stores'. The renamed open-plan store, designed to appeal to the whole family, was completed in time for the Christmas sales. Although a new McLarens branch in Edinburgh was opened in July 1950 by Hugh Fraser's son, Hugh IV, still a schoolboy, and a 'Modern Homes Centre' incorporated in Arnott Simpsons store in the autumn, further takeovers were delayed by the continuing pressure from the Labour Government to squeeze retailers' margins even harder and a refusal to cut purchase tax. These problems were compounded for Hugh Fraser early in the morning of 3 February 1951 when half of Arnott Simpsons store in Glasgow was completely gutted by fire with a total loss of £140,000. With remarkable speed the remaining half of the store was refurbished and re-opened for business within ten weeks.

The Labour Government lost its grip after the general election in February 1951 left it with a slim majority. Sensing controls could not last much longer, Hugh Fraser made a successful bid of £337,000 in April for McDonalds Ltd which owned the department store on the other side of Buchanan Street from Frasers, where Hugh Fraser I had started his career as a lace buyer. As part of this deal House of Fraser acquired its first business outside Scotland, E.J. Clarke of Harrogate, the fashionable Yorkshire spa town. As if confirming Hugh Fraser's confidence in the future, Harold Wilson resigned as president of the Board of Trade just days after the takeover of McDonalds. His successor, Sir Hartley Shawcross, offered a more realistic approach to retailers' margins at a time when prices were rising sharply and there were demands from shop assistants for substantial wage rises to keep pace with inflation, but the Labour Government was rapidly coming to the end of its life, collapsing finally in October. During the ensuing election campaign some elements in the Labour party raised accusations of profiteering against retailers, encouraging shoppers to go on strike. Sensing a political ploy Hugh Fraser, as president of the Scottish Retail Drapers' Association, refused to be drawn and, unusually, remained silent. The Conservative victory brought relief, not only to shopkeepers but to the whole business community. Despite the restrictions on retail margins between 1948 and 1951 Hugh Fraser and his management team, through the combination of their flair for selling and rigid financial discipline, succeeded in maintaining the Group's profits until 1950 when Harold Wilson's policies were most savage. These years were tinged with personal sadness for Hugh Fraser; his only sister, Emily, died in January 1949 after a serious operation. Her only son, a brilliant student at Oxford, was killed in a road accident in France not long after. These twin tradgedies left him deeply shocked and he threw himself into his work to escape his grief, often working from sixteen to eighteen hours a day to the concern of his colleagues.

Encouraged by the change of government in 1951, Hugh Fraser looked for ways of financing further acquistions to the Group. Part of the attraction of his bid for McDonalds, a publicly quoted company, had been that it offered cash as an alternative to shares in House of Fraser. This deal exhausted the Group's cash reserves which were hard pressed by the need to finance the high rates of purchase tax. Hugh Fraser's first reaction was to issue further share capital, but this was abandoned when the financial markets turned down. Instead he turned to his original method of raising finance through the Group's property portfolio which was increasing rapidly in value due to an unprecedented boom in the property market. After the election he invited the London firm of valuers Healey & Baker to put a price on all the stores. They quoted a figure in excess of £2 million and suggested that the existing mortgages with the Standard Property Investment Co should be redeemed and some of the properties sold and leased back on a very long lease at a rent of '4.75 - 5 per cent of the cash realised.' This technique was used extensively by multiples at the time to redevelop old stores, since the banks were prohibited by government regulations from lending for such purposes. Hugh Fraser was delighted with this proposal and by early March Healey & Baker had negotiated the sale of fourteen properties to the Legal & General Assurance Society Ltd for £1.6 million and four, including Fraser's own Buchanan Street store, to the Prudential Assurance Company for £698,000.

No sooner had these negotiations been completed than Hugh Fraser bought two further Glasgow stores, Wood & Selby and Duncans, both at St George's Cross to the west of the city, which he pledged to make 'one of Glasgow's main shopping centres'. The stores were to be amalgamated and converted into a walk

HF 11/14/6

FESTIVAL OF BRITAIN 1951

A Message from the General Manager

Today, Their Majesties The King and Queen with the Royal Family are attending a Service of Dedication at St. Paul's Cathedral and tomorrow H.M. The King will officially open the Festival of Britain Exhibition on the south bank of the Thames.

This Ancient City of London, the capital city of these islands, is the main centre of the Festival to which many thousands of visitors will come in the next five months. They will come from abroad, from the Commonwealth and foreign lands, from all parts of the world, both Old and New, but by far the greater number will come from the provinces and from our own homeland—for brief one day visits and for their holidays.

These few months bring opportunity to London, to Oxford Street and to D. H. Evans. How are we going to take that opportunity ?

Firstly, to attract attention to our wonderful building which is still London's most modern shop, by additional floral decorations to beautify our Oxford Street frontage, a galaxy of flags to fly gaily from our flag masts, and, at night, to mellow the building with floodlights, not only from the canopy but also at the sixth and seventh floor levels ; and, in due course, large illuminated name signs will be erected to proclaim to the world that here is D. H. Evans.

Secondly, whilst it is one thing to please the eye, we must make visitors want to come in. Therefore our window displays must beat our previous best—selling windows with a Festival flavour—and our internal displays must back those efforts. Here the Display Department have their opportunity, and the co-operation of all Departments will be needed to carry out our plans.

Finally, and the most important, everyone of us can play a part by giving to each and every customer a degree of courtesy which you would extend to any visitor in your own home. Let the Festival symbolise for D. H. Evans COURTESY, that extra effort in courtesy, to all visitors, British or Overseas, in the shop or on the telephone, amongst ourselves and in all our dealings with the world at large so that we may all emerge at the close of the Festival period with a stronger habit of courtesy than when we began.

To help us to remember our object every woman and girl on·our staff will be given a red rose to wear to remind us all of what we are trying to achieve—that little extra in courtesy. The red rose will be our emblem for the Festival. Red roses will be in the windows and on our displays, and to customers who ask we shall reply that they stand for the courtesy with which D. H. Evans greets the Festival.

If we can do this, we shall indeed have achieved something worth while in spreading the spirit of goodwill in this Festival year.

3rd May 1951

round 'modern home store selling everything from a pastry cutter to a bedroom suite.' At the same time he announced the modernisation of McDonalds, 'with a striking new layout'. Work also began on fitting up a perfumery department at the original Fraser store, 'set in a semi-circle of contemporary counters, mirrored doors, fine wood alcoves and modern lighting,' and stocking reportedly the widest range of brands in the country. By now the outlook for department stores had changed radically. In January the Board of Trade abolished profit margins on the majority of goods and replaced them with maximum permitted selling prices. In his March Budget Rab Butler cleared away 118 regulations and replaced them with the simpler 'D' scheme. Hugh Fraser, speaking as president of the Scottish Retail Drapers' Association, likened this reform to the action of Louis XIV when commercial life in France had been stifled by government control. He recounted that the king asked businesses what could he do for them – 'Leave us alone', he was told. Hugh Fraser sympathised with this advice, calling on the Conservatives to: 'Let us get on with our businesses. Then, as now, what could not the doers do if they were not hindered by talkers and planners.' The trade's only cause for complaint was the maintenance of purchase tax with all its anomalies.

In the course of his negotiations with Healey & Baker, Hugh Fraser learned that George M. Wright, the chairman of Debenhams, was keen to sell the company's majority stake in the Scottish Drapery Corporation to help finance the modernisation of stores south of the border. The Scottish Drapery Corporation owned some of the most prestigious stores in Scotland – Pettigrew & Stephens Ltd and Daly & Sons Ltd in Glasgow; Patrick Thomson Ltd, J. & R. Allan Ltd and J. D. Blair & Son Ltd in Edinburgh; D. M. Brown Ltd of Dundee; Reid & Pearsons Ltd and Watt & Grant Ltd in Aberdeen; and J.S. Shannon Ltd in Greenock. Hugh Fraser could not help but be interested in a group of stores that would extend his market amongst the better off and which in other hands would be a powerful adversary. His initial cash offer of £3 per ordinary share was accepted almost unanimously. The total price of just under £3 million was to be financed partly out of the cash raised through the sale of the Group's existing premises and partly by selling off all the Scottish Drapery Corporation's stores, with the exception of Pettigrew & Stephens and Patrick Thomson, to Legal & General Assurance to realise a further £2 million. The new stores were at once assimilated into the House of Fraser Group, reporting directly to the directors.

Sensing that Hugh Fraser had more or less exhausted the potential for further expansion in Scotland, the press began to speculate about a determined foray south of the border to add to his toehold in Harrogate. During September there were rumours, never substantiated, about an imminent link up with Hide & Co of Kingston-on-Thames and its chain of Barnett-Hutton ladies' costume shops. Instead Hugh Fraser and his team plunged into the task of organising a bigger and better 103rd birthday sale embracing all the stores now in the Group. At every store there were well-publicised massive reductions on a limited number of select items, Axminster carpets, fur coats, children's clothes, bed quilts and tea sets. Once again £1 and ten-shilling vouchers were distributed to draw the crowds. Throughout Scotland newspapers carried stories about women queuing for almost twenty-four hours to secure the bargains, providing House of Fraser with extensive free advertising. After the sales came fashion weeks, with plain slim styles which it was hoped would characterise the opening years of the reign of the young Queen Elizabeth who had succeeded to the throne on the death of her father, King George VI, in April. Separates – a full skirt, easy to slip out of, and four or five different coloured blouses – were heavily promoted 'for the astute

OPPOSITE *Message from the general manager of D.H. Evans of London advising staff, on 3 May 1951, that each customer will receive a red rose to inaugurate the Festival of Britain. The Festival symbolized the end of wartime austerity and a new era of prosperity.*

business girl or woman.' The New Year sales were equally dazzling, helping to lift profits to new heights.

With a successful sales season behind him, Hugh Fraser was now ready to make his next move. Perhaps predictably, he had since the autumn been stalking Binns Ltd which had stores in Scotland, north-east England and Dumfries and Carlisle. He had won the support of one of the directors, A.I. Cameron, who was dissatisfied with the conservative style of management of John G. Simpson – then aged eighty-four. On 20 February 1953 Hugh Fraser and Robert Keenan travelled to Sunderland to make a formal offer of £4.25 million, later raised to £4.6 million. John Simpson and his fellow directors were determined to retain their independence, doing everything in their power to spoil Fraser's chances – proposing the capitalisation of the sums at the credit of the share premium account and promising a large dividend. These strategies were reported immediately by A.I. Cameron to Hugh Fraser who was not to be out-manoeuvered. Having failed to win the support of the other directors he then made an offer direct to shareholders and sought a High Court injunction to prevent the company carrying out its intentions. When this was refused he withdrew the offer to buy the preference shares and made an unconditional bid for the ordinary shares which carried voting control of the company. Hurriedly Binns' directors arranged for the group's premises to be revalued to show that the underlying asset value was greater than House of Fraser's bid. Time, however, was running out for the directors. By the beginning of April Hugh Fraser had secured some forty-seven per cent of the ordinary shares which, with the promise of the shares held by A.I. Cameron and his father, Neil, would give him voting control. Horrified at the seeming duplicity of one of their colleagues, John Simpson insisted upon Cameron's resignation from the board, but had no alternative but to accept the offer.

On 4 April 1953 Binns' directors formally admitted defeat and a week later Hugh Fraser and Robert Keenan joined the board. After all the formalities had been completed at the end of May, all Binns' directors resigned with the exception of John G. Simpson, and were replaced by the other members of Hugh Fraser's management team – Elson Gamble and Alfred Spence. In taking over Binns, Hugh Fraser, for the first time, acquired a group with a strong corporate identity. When he had made his acquisitions before the war, John Simpson had renamed the shops Binns, obliterating the old company names and traditions. The stores, as they were developed and modernised, were similar in appearance and layout. The rebuilt original Sunderland store, which had been destroyed by German bombs in 1941, was but the latest example of the characteristic Binns style. These new premises, costing more than £500,000, were opened at the height of the takeover battle. Hugh Fraser had no intention of changing the names or public presentation of Binns' stores and the existing managers, including three of the former directors, A.H. Gardiner, T.C. Hunter, and K.T. Marley, continued in post. The company had to remain in being as House of Fraser did not control the preference shares which made up the bulk of the authorised capital – £1.2 million out of a total share capital of £1.36 million. Throughout the takeover struggle there had been questions from financial commentators as to where Hugh Fraser would find the cash to fund the offer. These were answered in October 1953 when, to the fury of the preference shareholders, it became known that he had sold five of Binns' stores to the Prudential Assurance Company and Co-operative Insurance Society Ltd for £2.6 million and leased them back to House of Fraser.

Although articles regularly appeared in the press comparing him with other takeover tycoons, Charles Clore and Isaac Wolfson, who were engaged in building large retailing empires by acquisition, Hugh Fraser was not prepared to become involved in a scramble for stores even in Scotland. At the annual meeting in June 1953 he was quick to deny reports suggesting he was poised to make a raid on a London West End store, preferring to promote and consolidate 'the trading group as it is.' With the economy expanding and wages rising, and Queen Elizabeth II's forthcoming Coronation in June promising to focus attention on *haute couture* fashions, Hugh Fraser enlarged the Group's commitment to

Brights of Bournemouth (opposite) and Schofields of Leeds (above) decorated for the Coronation of Queen Elizabeth II in 1953. The Coronation provided a golden opportunity for the British fashion industry.

fashionwear. He opened a new fashion floor in the original Frasers' Buchanan Street store on 22 April with clothes to suit every pocket. The floor was sumptuously fitted with oatmeal and burgundy carpets, wide open cabinet wardrobes, and illuminated with dainty lampshades and concealed lighting. The Coronation displays in all the stores were dominated by the latest summer styles. Towards the end of May Hugh Fraser invited Norman Hartnell, the designer of the Queen's Coronation gown and the Coronation dresses of the other members of the Royal family, to Glasgow to display his famous Berkertex gowns at a fashion parade in the Kelvin Hall. The collection, with flying panels, generous cuts and full underskirts, emphasised the end of wartime controls on materials and a return to a more liberal world. The gowns were to be sold in shops within stores at Pettigrew & Stephens in Glasgow, D.M. Brown in Dundee, and Falconers of Aberdeen. There were other attractions directed particularly at children. Tommy Morgan, the Glasgow music-hall star, visited Arnott Simpsons to give away Coronation souvenirs, including miniature looking-glasses with portraits of the Queen. On 11 June Elizabeth Allan, one of the first British television stars, visited the hardware department of Pettigrew & Stephens to autograph her book *Ironing*. Yet again there was a highly publicised birthday sale in the autumn with massive discounts and the now customary gift vouchers.

These selling techniques were beginning to be outmoded as the manufacturers of branded goods and the multiples, particularly Marks & Spencers and Littlewoods, began to sharpen their image following the end of control. In March 1952, to the fury of drapers, Lever Brothers started offering free wool in exchange for tokens collected from their Persil brand. Shopkeepers complained that prices should be reduced to promote sales instead of offering free gifts. The multiples and larger stores, however, quickly saw the advantage of extending or rein-

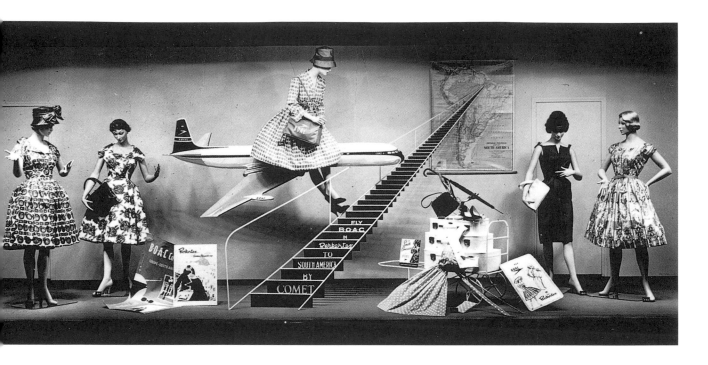

With rising prosperity department stores vied with each other in the novelty of their window displays.

troducing their 'own labels' in combination with the new British Standards Institute (B.S.I.) mark to guarantee quality and foster customer loyalty. Many 'own labels' had been allowed to lapse when the wartime Utility schemes were introduced. Marks & Spencers' own label, St Michael, registered in 1928, led the field. In the early 1950s members of the company were regularly invited to address meetings of retailers to explain their rigorous systems for controlling the quality of the goods that bore the St Michael name. Harrods, in the spring of 1954, revamped their 'own label' which had been such a feature of their prewar catalogues. Sales of branded goods increased rapidly, particularly in American-style self-service chain stores which often negotiated exclusive distribution rights with manufacturers. With their bright lights and relaxed atmosphere the self-service chains deliberately sought to encourage impulse buying amongst the young for informal casual clothes – the fashionable jeans, blouses and shirts. Their lower staff costs, combined with central buying, gave them a price advantage over department stores. Inexorably they pushed up their share of the retail market every year. The Board of Trade estimated in March 1953 that since 1950 spending on women's and children's clothes in multiples had risen by a staggering forty-two per cent while it had fallen by one per cent in department stores, three per cent in Co-operative Societies and five per cent in smaller shops. Concerned by this threat to their livelihood the department stores sought to introduce some element of self-service. In May 1952 Lewis's installed a 'self service' fashion shop within their Liverpool store and two years later the first wholly self-service store, Landport Drapery Bazaar, was opened in Portsmouth.

Hugh Fraser was well aware of these developments, announcing in July 1953 that he intended to open a chain of grocery stores beginning with a new shop alongside Wood & Selby's store at St George's Cross in Glasgow. During a visit to New York eighteen months later to promote British goods for the Dollar Export Council at the National Retail Dry Goods Association of America, he declared that his strategy was now to build suburban stores, like those he had recently visited in America, because of the traffic congestion in Britain's larger towns. These proposals were largely idle speculation, seized on by the news-thirsty press. Hugh Fraser remained steadfast to the world of retailing he knew and loved, the central department store – an Aladdin's cave of quality goods to suit every pocket and beguile even the most reluctant shopper. He believed passionately that by playing to their ability to merchandise in depth, department stores could defeat the multiples, drawing in the crowds with well-advertised special events and by glittering window displays, such as those he had seen in America. He was convinced that part of the explanation for the current success of the multiples was that the wartime Utility schemes with their standard ranges of goods had robbed department stores of their individuality. For eighteen months after the acquisition of Binns he and his management team worked hard to restore the distinctive identity to each store within the Group by defining the customer profile of each store – popular, medium-priced or exclusive – and giving the buyers more freedom to buy stock suited to their own local conditions. Integral to this policy were further renovations. In the spring of 1954 Smalls of Edinburgh was brought up to date as a fashion store, widely publicised through an official opening by Norman Hartnell. As incomes rose, every store was perceptibly to trade-up within its customer base to raise expectations and awareness. Ambitious new stores were planned for Arnott Simpsons in Glasgow and Binns in Middlesbrough to replace a store burned down in 1942. Construction of the Glasgow store was delayed when Glasgow Corporation refused to sell the corner plot that linked the two parts of the site. As a temporary expedient, Hugh Fraser erected a one-storey building at break-neck speed on the site left vacant by the fire. In Ayr further major improvements were made to Hourstons, including the addition of a new basement department to display heavy electrical and hardware goods, such as washing machines, cleaners, refrigerators, cookers and garden implements. Muirheads, the house furnishers in Glasgow's Sauchiehall Street, was modernised with the 'ground floor devoted to impulse buying, particularly by office girls going to the fourth floor for lunch in the new restaurant that could seat 500 people.'

Although he had invested outside Scotland, Hugh Fraser's business aspirations remained essentially Scottish. By the new year of 1955 he was ready to consider further acquisitions, raising the necessary finance through a loan of £1.25 million from the Standard Property Investment Co on the security of Pettigrew & Stephens and Patrick Thomsons. It was ironic that he chose to borrow from Standard since shortly after the Binns takeover in 1953 their representative on the board had been replaced by William McLellan of the Legal & General Assurance Co. Within weeks he had negotiated the purchase of Forresters (Outfitters) Ltd of London Road in the east of Glasgow, which was owned by an old friend, T. R. Patterson, the honorary president of the Scottish Retail Drapers' Association. In the early autumn Hugh Fraser extended his interests in Aberdeen through the purchase of the drapery firms of Isaac Benzie Ltd and Watt & Milne Ltd. Throughout the closing months of the year there was mounting speculation that he might be preparing an attack on Debenhams which was in the process of raising additional capital. There was even a suggestion at a meeting of Debenhams' shareholders on Christmas Eve that Hugh Fraser should join the board.

Not long after, his attention was distracted away from retailing to other Scottish ventures. Despite his temperance upbringing he was persuaded in February 1956 by the American drinks concern, Schenley Industries Inc, to acquire on his own account the Scotch whisky distilling interests of Seager Evans, which included the well-known 'Long John' blend. This deal was financed by Schenleys who agreed to take the investment off his hands as soon as possible. Three months later Hugh Fraser received an urgent plea for help from the beleaguered Scottish Motor Traction Co (SMT) which was the subject of a hostile bid from Charles Clore's Sears Holdings. The local press was incensed that Scotland's leading distributors of Vauxhall cars and Bedford vans should be controlled from England. Hugh Fraser agreed to make a counter bid through House of Fraser on condition that the Treasury would allow him to create 'A' ordinary shares with very limited voting rights to pay for the deal. Directly permission was received the Group's authorised capital was increased to £5 million and a bonus issue, one-for-one, made to all the existing ordinary shareholders. The House of Fraser offer was precisely the same as Sears Holdings, one 'A' share in exchange for every SMT ordinary share. It never had any real chance of success and Charles Clore won after only a brief tussle. Disappointed, Hugh Fraser returned to retailing, buying two Glasgow menswear shops, John Kirksop & Son Ltd in November 1956 and Carswell (The Modern Man's Shop) Ltd in May 1959. Kirksops was purchased for cash, but Carswells was paid for in the 'A' ordinary shares – the first time Hugh Fraser had been successful in using this technique. He was still keen to extend his interests into other sections of the Scottish economy, becoming personally involved early in 1957 in an acrimonious fight to gain control of the Border knitwear company of Lyle & Scott. Although he secured more than fifty per cent of the ordinary shares, he was forced to withdraw after a lengthy court case which went all the way to the House of Lords.

This bruising struggle and the failure to acquire SMT left their mark on Hugh Fraser. His health suffered and he was told to give up his chain-smoking which had so frequently been mentioned in the press. As a result, by the time of his silver wedding in April 1957, he had begun to put on weight, losing his gaunt eagle features. He was increasingly accompanied by his son, Hugh, now aged nineteen and working for the family firm as his father's chosen successor. He started work in McDonalds in Buchanan Street. On being asked on his first day by one of the cashiers what his name was, he replied 'Hugh Fraser'. She laughingly rejoined, 'With a sense of humour like that you should go far.' During the spring of 1957 his father regularly defended the advantages of amalgamations which he was convinced had contributed to the rise in the standard of living since the war. He turned on his critics who called him a 'Big Bad Wolf', asserting – not altogether truthfully – that he had only acquired shops he had been invited to buy and had never set out deliberately to take over a business without the support of at least some of the shareholders. He told the annual meeting of the Scottish Retail Drapers' Association in April that 'the only takeover he was interested in was the one his son Hugh would do to the business.' To groom him for his awesome responsibilities, Hugh junior, at his own suggestion, was given overall responsibility for the stores in Scotland during the autumn of 1957. In the Binns group Hugh Fraser had already reappointed three of the former directors, T.C. Hunter, A.H. Gardiner and Kenneth Marley, to the board to help in the direction of the stores in the north of England. These men, including his son, were like the original members of the management team, Elson Gamble, Alfred Spence and Robert Keenan, his talented lieutenants. Hugh Fraser was still firmly in command of strategy, from merchandising to new acquisitions.

In July 1957 he finally responded to conjecture in the press of a major acquisition in the West End of London when he unveiled a bid of £11 million (made up of a mixture of 'A' shares and cash) for John Barker & Co Ltd of Kensington, owners of Barkers, Derry & Toms and Pontings in Kensington, Gosling & Sons Ltd in Richmond and a Barker store at Eastbourne (see page

The magnificent sweep of the frontage of the Kensington store of John Barker & Co, acquired by House of Fraser in 1957.

286). Hugh Fraser had for long been an admirer of the company's eighty-year-old chairman, Trevor Bowen, who had joined Barkers in 1914 from J. Lyons of Cornerhouse fame to manage their food hall. He succeeded Sir Sydney Skinner as chairman of Barkers in 1941. Plans for completing the new main Barker store, left half finished at the outbreak of war, were confirmed in 1951, but not begun for another four years. Rebuilding depressed profits, making the company vulnerable to a predator since its properties were worth considerably more than their book value in the balance sheet. Trevor Bowen, recognising in Hugh Fraser a shopkeeper like himself, had no hesitation in recommending the offer which comprised ten shillings in cash and four House of Fraser 'A' shares for each ordinary share in John Barkers. The city, increasingly critical of the use of restricted or non-voting shares in takeover bids, was less convinced. Despite reports of other possible suitors, none emerged and John Barker & Co joined House of Fraser on 16 August 1957. As in other acquisitions, the existing directors resigned and were replaced by Hugh Fraser and his management team. Fittingly Trevor Bowen was appointed to the honorary position of president of the company. Immediately Hugh Fraser left for a holiday at Monte Carlo, his favourite summer resort, encouraging reporters to believe that other bids were in the pipeline – 'I consider I am only a boy yet, and I have a long way to go.'

He had no sooner found his way to the gaming tables than his concentration

The central well of Wylie & Lochhead's recently refurbished store in Glasgow's Buchanan Street, taken over by House of Fraser in 1957.

was distracted by Sir Robert Hobart, a stranger with a proposal to make. Sir Robert had inherited from his mother, Violet Wylie, a large shareholding in the family business, Wylie & Lochhead, the famous Glasgow furnishing company. After a career in the Royal Navy, he decided in 1950 to make a career with the company and was co-opted on to the board as a major shareholder. Since the war Wylie & Lochhead had made great efforts to bring their product range up to date, manufacturing fitted kitchen units and stocking the latest range of white electrical goods, domestic refrigerators and washing machines. Five years later Isaac Wolfson offered to buy the business as part of his wider ambitions to enter the furnishing trade. His approach was rejected, but he went on to acquire the well-known London furnishing concern, Waring & Gillow, which became a subsidiary of his Great Universal Stores group. During 1956 Wylie & Lochhead launched an ambitious plan to upgrade their Glasgow store and opened a new shop in Edinburgh, whetting Isaac Wolfson's appetite even more. He made a fresh approach in February 1957 which was followed almost immediately by an enquiry from Booker Bros McConnell & Co which was hurriedly diversifying away from its original interests in sugar. Sensing that time was fast running out, J.D. Stewart, the managing director of Wylie & Lochhead, advised that Sir Robert should seek an urgent meeting with Hugh Fraser. He arrived in Monte Carlo in the nick of time. Hugh Fraser, reluctant to see one of his principal rivals occupy a prime site opposite his own family store in Buchanan Street, hurried home. On 5 September 1957 Isaac Wolfson renewed his attack with a formal offer to the directors before appealing directly to the shareholders, but Hugh Fraser's bid valuing the company at over £1 million was on the table. The directors recommended a merger with House of Fraser and Isaac Wolfson withdrew without a contest. During the negotiations Hugh Fraser was impressed by the flair of Sir Robert Hobart whom he immediately appointed his personal assistant and representative in London.

The main staircase at Binns' new store at Middlesbrough, considered to be the most up-to-date store in the country when it opened in 1957.

OVERLEAF *Views of Binns' Middlesbrough store*

Despite his respect for Trevor Bowen, Hugh Fraser was convinced that the Barker stores could be better managed. When the new Binns store at Middlesbrough had been opened on 23 March, the retail world had been given a taste of his concept of a modern department store capable of defeating the chain stores. Heralded as 'the most up-to-date store in the country' it was reminiscent of shops in suburban America, with open-plan floors and goods displayed in perspex cases on glass shelving. The walls were decorated with murals painted by local art students in colours chosen to match the carpeting, which was different on all six floors. Merchandise was grouped logically. All the ladies' fashion was on the first floor, which included a 'Miss 1957' department designed 'to cater for the girl leaving school at age fifteen or sixteen who felt fully grown up and was no longer interested in the children's department, up to the 20-year-old girl who considered a "teenager" department was too young for her.' On the second floor was a children's section with a girls' shop running the whole length of the building. The floors were serviced by a battery of three lifts and an elliptical staircase which gave shoppers a clear view of each floor. Hugh Fraser and his management team hoped to inject new merchandising ideas into the John Barker stores and at the same time define precisely the character of each store as they had done with Binns. They concentrated their efforts at first on the three Kensington stores whose image had become blurred, restoring their individuality which represented the 'three distinctive grades of trading from the "popular" Pontings through the comprehensive medium-priced Barkers to the more exclusive Derry & Toms, which catered especially for the Royal Borough of Kensington, while the other two drew in customers from the suburbs and Home Counties.' An important part of this strategy was to give the buyers in the individual stores more independence.

Throughout the autumn Alfred Spence, who had been appointed general manager and resident director in London, worked tirelessly to refashion Derry & Toms and the Barker main store which was nearing completion. Both stores remained open throughout the exercise, nicknamed 'Operation Leapfrog' as each area was transformed bit by bit behind screens out of sight of customers. The new Barker food hall opened in mid-November, a treasure trove of gastronomic delight, entirely matching Hugh Fraser's concept of merchandising in depth. The other West End stores were outraged when Barkers started their New Year sales, just two days after Christmas, ignoring the traditional holiday period. In February 1958 Derry & Toms inaugurated their revamped furniture department, claimed to be 'Europe's finest', well-stocked with the best in contemporary designs. Pontings used the slogans 'The House for Value' and 'Value in Store' for their New Year sales. At the same time Hugh Fraser sold Barkers' chain of thirty Zeeta cake shops and restaurants to help pay for these developments. Derry & Toms was completely modernised by March and Barkers' main store by mid-May. The press was full of praise for the quality and imagination of the layouts and displays.

The colossal task of welding John Barkers into the House of Fraser Group did not deter Hugh Fraser from considering further expansion. In November 1957 there were reports, later vigorously denied, that he had set his sights on Harrods, the best-known London department store. At the New Year he was invited by Colonel Evelyn Arthur, the grandson of James Arthur who had established Arthur & Fraser with Hugh Fraser in 1849, to acquire Arthur & Co. This Glasgow-based textile manufacturing and wholesale business had been established in 1856 when the retail branch of Arthur & Fraser had been hived off. The company now had a textile factory in Leeds and wholesale warehouses

A Barkers delivery van advertising the New Year sale in 1958 which stole a march on the other London stores.

BELOW *A party on a special shopping excursion arriving at Kensington underground station for the Barkers' sales.*

The Army & Navy Stores'
television department in the
late 1950s. Hugh Fraser
was concerned that hire
purchase of electrical goods
would damage sales of
clothes.

in Glasgow, Edinburgh, Newcastle, Cardiff and London. The large Glasgow warehouse at the corner of Queen Street and Ingram Street, which had been bombed during the war, was in the course of reconstruction – one of the largest developments of its kind in Scotland since 1945. Worried about the likely effect of death duties, the directors were keen to find a buyer. Hugh Fraser believed there was considerable potential in Arthur & Co's 'White Heather' branded clothes in the south of England where branded supplies were coming to dominate the market. He willingly agreed to offer £1 million. The reunion merger was announced on 17 January. Colonel Evelyn Arthur retired as chairman and was replaced by Hugh Fraser's friend, T.R. Patterson, who had joined the group after the acquisition of his family business, Forrester (Outfitters) Ltd. The other directors of Arthur & Co, unlike those of most other companies that had been taken over, remained at their posts. In midsummer Hugh Fraser further extended his geographical spread in Scotland by buying Benzie & Miller, owners of a small group of department stores in the north-east of Scotland with shops at Fraserburgh, Banff, Inverness and Peterhead.

As financial commentators had predicted, the House of Fraser's profits for 1957, announced in June 1958, were depressed by the acquisition of John Barkers. Some had the temerity to suggest that Hugh Fraser had got a bad bargain. Confident that the reorganisation of Barkers would soon yield handsome returns, he went on to the offensive, circulating with the annual report a coloured brochure, 'Getting to Know', which traced the development of the Group over the last twenty-one years. Defying commentators who called for a period of consolidation, he told shareholders that expansion would go on. Towards the end of October he reflected more generally on the future at the annual meeting of the Scottish Retail Drapers' Association of which he was still president. He believed that credit trading would increase future demand for vacuum cleaners, televisions, refrigerators and washing machines to the detriment of the textile trade. He urged drapers to counter this threat as they had done in the past by creating greater dress consciousness amongst women. This was already happening, but not in the way that he anticipated. During the autumn of 1957 fashion had moved decisively from the 'New Look' of the postwar years to short narrow skirts with amply cut colourful tops. Younger men rejected the formal attire of their schooldays in favour of very casual wear. Such clothes soon became popular with the new generation tired of the conventionality of British society. In seeking to reshape attitudes and perceptions, the dress of young people was designed as much to shock as to become. An article in the *Scotsman* newspaper in December 1958 complained: 'young men's fashions currently have staggered into bedlam. All grades of society are affected. Working-class boys invest in black leather jackets and jeans, although the dirtiest work some of them ever do is lounging in a tenement backcourt punishing a guitar.' Young men and women preferred to buy such clothes in chain stores, new boutiques or street markets, rather than department stores, which smacked of the establishment. With the economy growing strongly under Harold MacMillan's Conservative Government, these developments had little immediate impact on department stores. Hugh Fraser announced plans in November to rebuild Binns' store in Sunderland, and in the opening months of 1957 was pressing Glasgow Corporation to consent to the total reconstruction of Arnott Simpsons.

'New Look' dresses in one of Derry & Toms' window displays during London Fashion Week, 1959.

Hugh Fraser celebrated his fortieth jubilee in the trade in February 1959 with a glittering party in the Central Hotel in Glasgow. There were over 800 guests from the House of Fraser stores from Elgin to Eastbourne. Shortly afterwards a

Dickins & Jones' store in Regent Street which formed part of the Harrods group in 1959.

quarterly house journal, *In Company*, was launched to give the 20,000 people who now worked for the Group a sense of belonging to a long established family firm. One of the well-wishers for the success of the new magazine was Sir Richard Burbidge, the chairman of Harrods, who hoped it would be 'as strong a force in linking your Group together as is the *Harrodian Gazette* in our case.' Speculation that Harrods might fall to a predator had intensified in 1958 when it was announced that the company's stores in London and the provinces had been revalued at £20 million compared with an issued capital of £8 million. Determined to mark his jubilee in a spectacular fashion, Hugh Fraser began to stalk Harrods in the late spring of 1959 sensing that a bid from another store group might be

in the offing. At the end of May he sold some of Barkers' properties on the north side of Kensington High Street for £1.5 million in a highly publicised deal, telling reporters 'and, my friends, I have plans to use the money.' When on Friday 12 June he confounded his critics by declaring a more than fifty per cent increase in profits for the previous year, there were widespread rumours that he was poised to launch a bid in a few days. During the following week he held informal discussions with Sir Richard Burbidge who undertook to consult his fellow directors formally on Monday 22 June. In the meantime the Conservative Government inaugurated a three-year programme to improve tourism in the Highlands and Islands and to his delight appointed Hugh Fraser as its director. The day after this announcement was made he admitted publicly that he was engaged in talks with Harrods. There was conjecture in the press that there were other contenders, possibly Debenhams and Great Universal Stores. For any store group, Harrods was a rich prize; not only did it own the fabulous domed emporium in Knightsbridge, but it also controlled Dickins & Jones in Regent Street and D.H. Evans in Oxford Street, Kendal Milne & Co in Manchester, John Walsh Ltd in Sheffield, Rackhams of Birmingham, William Henderson & Sons Ltd of Liverpool, and J.F. Rockhey Ltd of Torquay and Newton Abbott. Rackhams, which had been acquired as recently as 1955, was being rebuilt as part of the massive redevelopment of central Birmingham following the devastation of wartime bombing.

When the Harrods board and their advisers met on Monday they had two offers on the table – one from House of Fraser and one from Debenhams. The bid from Debenhams was for four ten shilling ordinary shares for each Harrods ordinary share, valuing the company at £34.2 million, and that from House of Fraser 2½ 'A' ordinary shares plus £1 in cash for each Harrods ordinary share, valuing the company at £32.6 million. Sir Richard backed the Debenhams proposal. Hugh Fraser, who had travelled from Scotland overnight and spent the day at the opening of the Barkers sales, was disappointed, accusing Sir Richard and John Bedford, chairman of Debenhams, of unfair practice. With the simple statement, 'I fight on', he returned by air to Glasgow to consult his management team about where to pitch the price of his offer. He also began buying shares. The newspapers on the Tuesday morning gave the impression that the battle was over and House of Fraser had lost. They underestimated Hugh Fraser's tenacity and skill. He was back in London again on Wednesday, ostensibly to attend the annual lunch of the Automobile Association of which he was honorary treasurer, but also for urgent talks with his financial advisers in his suite at the Savoy Hotel. At every turn he attempted to throw sand in the eyes of the press, telling reporters that the best news he brought from Scotland was that his bull had won first prize at the Highland Show. On the same day United Drapery Stores, owners of both the John Collier and Alexander tailors shops, came forward with a further offer, valuing the company at £36 million, but still Hugh Fraser refused to up his price. His next move came on Friday when he surprised the City by enfranchising all the restricted voting 'A' shares in House of Fraser, effectively renouncing the Fraser family control of the company to secure his prize – 'we are now becoming a shareholding democracy with unit trusts and so on, and I think it is only right that shareholders in any business, should the occasion arise, should have a vote at the shareholders' meeting.' This not only diffused city criticism of the use of restricted voting shares in takeovers, but also raised the value of his original bid as the voting shares traded at a higher price than the 'A' shares. Hugh Fraser kept the City waiting until Tuesday evening of 7 July before announcing his revised offer of sixty shillings in cash and 2¼ ordinary shares in House of Fraser for every Harrods £1 ordinary share, valuing the company at between £36 and £37 million. He now waited patiently for events to unfold, busying himself about his new responsibilities in the Highlands and the affairs of the Group, but continuing to buy Harrods shares. Hotly denying that House of Fraser was a one-man board, he told the House of Fraser annual meeting that the Group would continue to expand with or without Harrods.

It was now Debenhams' turn to delay and be reticent. For the next three weeks they steadfastly refused to be pushed into raising the stakes, but on 28 July with encouragement from the Harrods board, they matched Hugh Fraser's bid but offered less cash. Immediately United Drapery Stores withdrew, selling their block of at least fifteen per cent of Harrods ordinary shares to Hugh Fraser after Debenhams had turned them down because they were priced above the value of the bid. Knowing that Harrods had a large number of small investors who would be attracted by a certain amount of cash in return for their shares, Hugh Fraser raised this element in his offer from sixty shillings to sixty-six shillings and eightpence on 6 August. Over the next fortnight the struggle between House of Fraser and Debenhams grew increasingly bitter with each side accusing the other of acting unscrupulously. Sir Richard Burbidge and the Harrods board still favoured Debenhams and tried hard to persuade the shareholders to accept their offer. However most shareholders, as Hugh Fraser had rightly predicted, wanted a mixture of cash and shares for their stock. Despite a revised bid from Debenhams on 19 August which raised the number of shares to be exchanged, House of Fraser was gaining ground. Shareholders were struck by Hugh Fraser's aggressive and determined style which, thanks to the efforts of Sir Robert Hobart, was widely reported. By 23 August he judged it safe to leave for his summer holiday at Monte Carlo, telling reporters, not entirely truthfully, as he boarded his plane, 'that House of Fraser had won control of Harrods.' Debenhams admitted defeat the following day and Sir Richard Burbidge accepted House of Fraser's terms. In announcing the acquisition in the Group's new house magazine, *In Company*, Hugh Fraser made it clear that his purpose in buying Harrods was as much for its top-of-the-market provincial stores as for the Knightsbridge shop itself – 'our group will now enjoy an unrivalled geographical and social spread in the major cities of the country.' At the first Harrods board meeting after the takeover on 7 September, Hugh Fraser became chairman and House of Fraser directors all joined the board. Sir Richard Burbidge was the only one of the previous directors to remain, but the post of Executive Director responsible for the store was taken by Alfred Spence who moved over from Barkers.

Following the well-established strategy, Hugh Fraser's team at once began to define the identity of the stores in the Harrods group, introducing their concept of merchandising in depth. Drawing on their extensive experience in commissioning new stores, they reshaped the layout of the new Rackhams store in Birmingham, which was under construction. When it was opened officially on 29 November the layout bore a distinct resemblance to that which had proved so successful at Binns' Middlesbrough store. The architecture of the building, settled by Harrods well before the takeover, was in its way as bold and imaginative as that of a great nineteenth century emporium, designed to point the way to a modern classless postwar Europe. In keeping with this spirit the window displays and entrances made none afraid to enter whether to buy or simply to browse – 'Rackhams extends a welcome to all men. Chairmen or clerks, somebodies or nobodies – all VIPs to us!' Hugh Fraser was equally keen to use the example of Harrods to stimulate his other stores to 'trade-up' in line with rising prosperity.

Hugh Fraser and his son standing confidently outside Harrods after winning the takeover battle in 1959.

This ambition was realised in the design of the new Arnott Simpsons store in Glasgow, with an equally bold functional exterior, finally approved by the Corporation in January 1960. When the first phase of the development was opened in April 1961, the general manager remarked 'merchandise will now be better quality and there will now be general trading on a higher level.' The promotional booklet to mark the occasion stressed how fashionable all the merchandise was and how well trained the staff. Less than a year after the takeover of Harrods disaster struck when one of its stores, Hendersons in Liverpool, was destroyed by fire on 22 June 1960 with the loss of eleven lives. Even after the fire had got hold, the staff and firemen had found it difficult to persuade shoppers to leave. Hugh Fraser and his son, deeply concerned for the safety of their customers and staff, drove from Glasgow as soon as they heard the news. Their exemplary prompt action prevented any possible criticism of the new owners of the Harrods Group. Sir Richard Burbidge did not find Hugh Fraser's style to his liking and left Harrods in August 1960 to join a multiple, British Home Stores. This was a prelude to sweeping changes in the management structure of the Harrods group, bringing it firmly within House of Fraser.

By this time the winds of change were blowing fiercely through the world of retailing. In early October 1959 Kennards of Croydon and Owen Owen of Birkenhead simultaneously opened self-service supermarkets that sold both groceries and draperies. By the end of the month Tesco had followed suit offering shirts, towels, tablecloths and umbrellas. Hugh Fraser responded by reviving his idea for suburban shopping centres with generous parking provision. Opening hours, which had been firmly fixed since before the First World War, were

The new Arnott Simpson store in Glasgow with its bold functional design.

becoming more relaxed. In the Gallowgate area of Glasgow Sunday trading was flourishing with 'buses bringing shoppers from as much as fifty miles away' and in many towns throughout Britain shops were staying open late in the evening in direct contravention of the law. The trade called for the liberalising of the Shops Act which was designed to protect shop assistants from conditions of employment that would no longer be tolerated.

Resale price maintenance was also breaking down, due in part to the action of House of Fraser's Binns store in Newcastle-upon-Tyne in granting 2.5 per cent discounts on all the goods they sold to monthly account customers who paid promptly. Bainbridges, Lewis's Newcastle store, protested that they were being 'knowingly undersold' and in January 1960 introduced 2.5 per cent discounts on certain price-maintained or recommended goods. The retail trade was dismayed that manufacturers did not step in to endorse their prices until mid-February. Most worrying for department stores was the opening of American-style discount

houses in low-priced premises where customers selected their goods, even furniture and large electrical appliances, and carried them home themselves. It was
confidently predicted in the *Drapers' Record* in July 1960 that the retailing
revolution that had swept the United States in the wake of such stores would
transform British shopping during the next decade. To remain competitive,
shops would require to provide credit and adequate parking, stay open late in
the evening, and rethink their commitment to personal service. Hugh Fraser
believed that the Group's new stores could more than meet this challenge –
'Designed for adaptability and built for an age when we, as a people, increasingly
seek to control our own destiny, and when having achieved a near degree of
material equality, we shall be last upon asserting our own individuality, especially
during the longer hours of leisure that automation and mechanisation will provide
for us. With perhaps a lesser attachment to possessions and so with a greater
frequency in changing them, the department store, as House of Fraser recognises,
given the right managerial, merchandising, and aggressive promotional policies
is poised to make a significant contribution as a dynamic force in a decade when
pure materialism will give way to a new concept of morality – based on an
appreciation of quality craftmanship and individuality.'

The realisation of such ambitions demanded a period of consolidation. Hugh
Fraser told the annual meeting in August 1960 that the Group was 'not planning
any more takeovers', quashing rumours that he had designs on Debenhams. The
Group was organised into four divisions – a Scottish group, a Binns group, a
Barker group, and a Harrods group. Hugh Fraser junior was promoted to be
assistant managing director. A.I. Moffat joined the main board to represent
Barkers, following the transfer of Alfred Spence to take command of Harrods.
In determining his future strategy, Hugh Fraser could no longer call on the wise
counsel of his mother, who died in June 1960 at the age of ninety-two. She had
encouraged him to develop and expand the family business at the outset of his
career and until the day of her death whenever he was in Glasgow he called on
her twice a day at her home in the West End to discuss progress. The Fraser
Foundation was established in her memory by the family to support good causes
in the West of Scotland, particularly health care. Before his mother's death Hugh
Fraser had decided to expand his personal investment company, Scottish and
Universal Investments Ltd, which now held a fifteen per cent stake in House of
Fraser. SUITS was converted into a public company in January 1960 with sale
of £2 million worth of shares. Shortly afterwards, SUITS won control of the
borders knitwear firms of D. Ballantyne Brothers of Peebles, Braemar Knitwear
and Turner Rutherford, with the object of promoting their branded goods in
House of Fraser. Public recognition of Hugh Fraser's achievements came in the
1961 New Year honours when he was created a baronet for his public and
charitable services. He was delighted with this honour, particularly as after his
death it would pass to his son. His joy was clouded early in April when Robert
Keenan, the company secretary and a key member of his management team since
1948, died suddenly. More than any other person he had been responsible for
enforcing Hugh Fraser's strict financial control over the Group through the
collection and comparison of the monthly statistics. He was succeeded by the
deputy secretary, Walter Keymer.

True to Sir Hugh's word House of Fraser made few acquisitions over the next
four years. During 1960 the Edinburgh caterers, J.W. Mackie & Sons, with
premises next to Smalls in Princes Street, were acquired to underpin the Group's
now extensive restaurant business. This was followed in 1961 by the purchase
of the Glasgow confectioners, Alexander Manson Ltd. The Group's Scottish

coverage was strengthened by the takeover in 1961 of Fraser & Love of Paisley, and Darling & Co of Edinburgh; in 1962 of Simpson Hunter Ltd of Glasgow; and in 1964 of Robert Cochran & Son Ltd of Paisley. Like many other acquisitions, the purchase of Robert Cochrans was negotiated over dinner. The price was worked out on the back of a paper napkin, endorsed by Hugh Fraser and pasted into the minute book. During these years the financial press and the City became less enchanted with the Group, the share price languished in an otherwise buoyant market. After the absorption of Harrods in the 1960 financial year, turnover rose only gradually in comparison with the meteoric rise of the previous five years. Profits were even more disappointing, climbing to £5.4 million in 1960 and then falling to around £5.1 million until 1963. The work of rebuilding and refurbishing stores continued in an effort to lift business, incorporating novel self-selection areas to reduce labour costs. Sir Hugh told the annual conference of the Scottish Retail Drapers' Association in April 1962 that to survive retailers had to raise their productivity as wages accounted for seventy per cent of their overheads. During that year work began on rebuilding Hendersons' store in Liverpool. Hourstons of Ayr was doubled in size and Benzies of Elgin revamped. One of the chief causes of the Group's problems was its large exposure in northern England and Scotland where the local economies were badly affected by the Conservative Government's deflationary stance in 1961 and 1962. The future of the Scottish economy concerned Sir Hugh greatly and he threw himself into his task of developing tourism in the Highlands to compensate for the decline of the country's traditional heavy industries. In January 1961 he also accepted the chairmanship of Associated Fisheries Ltd and quickly became a vociferous protagonist of the Scottish fishing industry. These additional responsibilities and an increasing public role left him less time to devote to House of Fraser. He was, however, reluctant to relax his grip on the Group and devolve power to his son, telling journalists in 1961 that 'in due course he will overtake me, but he will never take me over.'

Hugh Fraser, a young man, saw that the Group badly needed to update its merchandising to reflect changing fashions, distancing itself from the Norman Hartnell styles that had served his father so well in the previous decade. In London department stores were already experimenting with new approaches to merchandising. Selfridges, building on Lewis's Young Idea boutiques and targeting girls between seventeen and twenty-two, opened Miss Selfridge's, the first of a planned chain of fashion stores. The name was borrowed from the Miss Bonwit sign in a Bonwit Teller window in New York. The philosophy behind the shops was to establish a fashion image for young women with money to spend, which would set them apart from their counterparts in jeans and sweaters. Hugh Fraser, learning quickly from such examples, persuaded his father to allow him to convert the original Fraser store into a high-class fashion shop during 1962 and to close the other departments. His marriage in April of that year to Patricia Bowie from a Glasgow family gave him greater confidence and very gradually he succeeded in introducing some of his ideas into other stores. Watt & Grant of Aberdeen was refitted incorporating a Frank Usher boutique and a Vanity Fair lingerie boutique. There was a setback in July 1963 when Pettigrew & Stephens was badly damaged by fire with the death of one person.

Although House of Fraser had played a significant role in questioning the future of resale price maintenance, Sir Hugh and his management team were slow to foresee the consequences for large groups like their own of its abolition, which came eventually in 1964. Two years before, Debenhams had introduced central buying for some lines, allowing them to negotiate large discounts from

OPPOSITE *Dressing a window at William Henderson of Liverpool, a member of Harrods group, in 1959.*

suppliers – critical if, as could be expected, a price war with the multiples followed abolition. At the same time they began to push their own brands in opposition to those offered by the large chains, particularly Marks & Spencer. Such strategies were anathema to Sir Hugh who believed passionately that the individuality of each store and the independence of its buyers was an essential ingredient of department stores. As a halfway house he gave his backing to the Scottish Retail Drapers' Association's central bulk-buying scheme set up in the autumn of 1963 to act as a clearing house for orders from any member, irrespective of size. There was no compulsion for House of Fraser buyers to use this service and few did. There was a tentative move towards branding during the summer of 1964 with the opening of 'White Stag' ski shops within the Group's stores. On the whole, times were against Debenhams as much as House of Fraser. Department stores, however modern and up to date, were not in keeping with the attitudes of the 'Swinging Sixties'. The trends in clothes evident in the late 1950s continued travelling in an opposite direction from Sir Hugh's prediction,

Hugh Fraser and his wife help their daughters open the Young World shop in Buchanan Street, Glasgow, in 1964.

The Chelsea Look glumly displayed at Aberdeen in 1964.

away from quality and craftmanship towards a cheap throw-away society that was excited by disposable paper bras and panties.

Sir Hugh, like many of his generation, found these changes difficult to accept, continuing to dress conservatively and correctly in the manner of his youth. Although he maintained a hectic daily schedule travelling long distances almost every week, the strain was telling on his health. After his attempts to give up smoking, he was again rarely photographed without a cigarette in his hand. He was elevated to the peerage in Sir Alec Douglas-Hume's dissolution honours in October 1964, taking the title Lord Fraser of Allander after the stream that ran through the grounds of his home at Milngavie to the north of Glasgow. During that month he won control through SUITS of the *Glasgow Herald* after a bitter duel with the newspaper magnate, Lord Thomson. In March the following year he suffered a massive heart attack in his suite at the Savoy Hotel in London. He was confined there for some weeks, taking great care to prevent news of his illness reaching the press. The responsibility of managing House of Fraser from day to day fell to his son, Hugh Fraser. He won permission in June to convert Simpson Hunter's fashion shop in Buchanan Street into a Young World shop devoted entirely to children's wear. Officially opened by his two-year-old daughter,

Patricia, in mid-September, the new shop combined displays with amusements for its young customers. Two months earlier Hugh Fraser had been confirmed as his father's successor at the annual meeting when he was appointed deputy chairman. By the spring of the following year his influence was felt throughout the Group with fashion shows of the latest Chelsea look from London to Aberdeen. On 9 March Barkers staged a Youthquake before an audience of 1,300 young people when six models danced along the catwalk to pop music, wearing clothes designed by Britain's 'new young designers'. A His and Her Chelsea Boutique was added to the Fraser Buchanan Street store and another Young World shop opened in Aberdeen. These initiatives could do no more than hold sales level at a time when Harold Wilson's Labour Government was pursuing massively deflationary policies to cure the country's balance of payments problems.

In midsummer 1966 Lord Fraser's health was noticeably failing. He died on the night of 6 November at the age of sixty-three. His loss was mourned throughout Britain, but especially in Scotland. In less than twenty years he had made House of Fraser a household name. In creating the Group his motive had always been to maintain and preserve the traditions and identity of the stores he acquired. He offered protection and security for the future to the companies he took over, sharpening their management and presentation. Despite his growing business commitments, he gave freely of his time to charities and other organisations connected with the drapery trade, particularly the Cottage Homes, the Scottish Retail Drapers' Association and latterly to the Retail Trades Education Council. He never forgot the debt he owed to those who worked for him, showing his appreciation by countless acts of kindness. Like many of his contemporaries in the world of business, he was directly responsible for the construction and management of the Group, evincing fierce loyalty from his staff. He always conceived of House of Fraser as a family, with himself as a patriarch watching over its development and caring for its many members. There was nothing overbearing about the way he exercised his authority, preferring to encourage and admonish with gentle Scottish candour rather than with the heavy hand of a dictator. Like a good father he was fearless in defending his family in the outside world, reserving his most severe criticism for government policies which he regarded as misguided and half-baked. Speaking on Scottish Television, Elson Gamble paid this tribute to his friend and leader over thirty years: 'We all know and he proved that he was a brilliant man, but what perhaps impressed me most of all was his tremendous courage and determination in good times and bad. He had this wonderful ability, almost genius, to inspire the loyalty and affection of his colleagues and, indeed, of all the members of his staff. Above all, I and many people who knew him will remember his kindliness of heart. I know many, many people will feel they have lost a true friend.'

7 1966–1976
No Easy Path

A month after Lord Fraser's death, the board of House of Fraser assembled, still in a state of shock, at the Buchanan Street office. All the directors were present and they unanimously elected Hugh Fraser chairman assuring him of 'their confidence in his ability to carry on the great family tradition and ... that he could rely on the same feelings of loyalty and affection that had been so willingly and happily given to his father.' Hugh Fraser's first action was to pay tribute to his father by renouncing the peerage, declaring, 'my father was a man unique in character and achievement and I feel that the greatest mark of respect I could accord him is that, certainly during my lifetime, he should be remembered as the one and only Lord Fraser of Allander.' He was obliged, however, to accede to the baronetcy, becoming known as Sir Hugh Fraser. He had no doubt of the problems and responsibilities that he was shouldering in accepting not only the chairmanship of House of Fraser but also that of his father's investment company Scottish & Universal Investment Trust (SUITS).

At the annual meeting in July 1966 his father, Lord Fraser, had warned shareholders of the difficulties that lay ahead in the retail trade due to gathering inflation and the imposition in the spring Budget of selective employment tax, a poll tax on services, designed to push labour out of services into manufacture. Lord Fraser had also delivered a stern reprimand to local authorities in Scotland for raising the rateable value of department stores, forecasting widespread closures and possibly the removal of the House of Fraser headquarters to England. Shortly before his death the sale of the once famous Colosseum store in Glasgow had been agreed because of falling sales and rising rates. Well aware of his need of expert advice in tackling these serious obstacles, the young Sir Hugh immediately appointed two of his father's closest advisers to the House of Fraser board, James Cathcart Stewart and John B. Kinross. James Cathcart Stewart was a partner in the House of Fraser's auditors, the Glasgow accountants Wilson Stirling & Co, and a director of Dalmore Whyte & MacKay, the whisky blenders and distillers. He was to assume the reponsibilities of House of Fraser finance director. John B. Kinross was a brilliant London financier and deputy chairman of the Industrial and Commercial Finance Corporation. Sir Hugh also asked Elson Gamble to become deputy chairman in his stead and invited Robert Midgley, who was a director of Harrods, to join the board. Confident that the much strengthened board would have the courage to take difficult decisions, Sir Hugh announced the Group's first half-year's results, cheering shareholders and the stock market by reporting increased turnover despite the Government's deflationary policy, but cautioning that a period of 'rationalisation' rather than expansion was in prospect.

Within weeks Sir Hugh and the board were negotiating the Group's first major disposal – the winding up of Arthur & Co, the Glasgow-based wholesalers, which had been acquired less than eight years before. Wholesaling sat uneasily alongside House of Fraser's principal activity of retailing, and the young Sir Hugh did not share his father's attachment to the firm in which the first Hugh Fraser had

Sir Hugh Fraser at Harrods' Way In boutique in 1967.

House of Fraser (formerly Walshs), Sheffield.

embarked on his career. The sale of the firm's Glasgow warehouse and its entire stock was finalised just before Christmas. At the same time other unwanted property and ground within the Group were sold to realise cash for redevelopment, including Barkers' sports ground to the All England Tennis & Croquet Club. Early in the new year of 1967 the attention of the board was diverted by a surprising offer of amalgamation from an American store group, Federated Department Stores Inc. Some of the directors, particularly Alfred Spence, welcomed the proposal, but by May Sir Hugh had concluded that 'it would be proper for the company to proceed independently.'

As much the youngest member of the board he had a clear vision of how he wished to meet the challenge of changing fashions and shopping habits. Goslings' store in Richmond, which had been badly damaged by fire in 1962, was to be reconstructed as an out of town branch of Dickins & Jones, serving 'as the prototype for further extensions of a similar nature' in the suburbs. More dramatic was the creation of Way In at a cost of £120,000 on the fourth floor of Harrods. The brainchild of one of the directors, Gordon Anthony, three years before, it had been blocked by Lord Fraser. Opened on 7 June 1967 by Sir Hugh, in a lilac shirt, corduroy suit and floral tie, and his wife in a trouser suit, Way In was designed to revolutionise the sale of fashion wear in department stores. No longer were men and women to be segregated into separate departments. The salesgirls wore popular very brief dresses. Mobile units built on the modular systems allowed displays to be changed frequently. The layout was planned for the lowest cost maintenance and rapid service. The *Drapers' Record*, under a headline 'Way In is way out', declared: 'Traditional retailers with a lifetime of in–built concepts about how to serve the customer will never have seen anything like it.' Sir Hugh explained that Way In was an example of his new concept of store shopping whereby 'goods are grouped according to the activities they serve – thus sea and seaside needs might be served by a "beach boutique" selling clothes, boats, picnic and camping kit and sporting gear, so saving customers from trailing round several departments.'

Bold and enterprising as these ideas were, the financial markets looked for further evidence that the new chairman could manage the Group effectively when, within two days of the Way In opening, Sir Hugh reported only a small growth in turnover for the year as a whole and profits drifting downwards. Despite his firm belief in the future of department stores, he counselled against optimism – 'omens in the short term are not auspicious' and explained that the board was urgently seeking to cut costs by closing uneconomic stores and modernising others. Work was already under way on a new store for Walshs in Sheffield and a futuristic design, reminiscent of American suburban stores, approved for the new Dickins & Jones branch in Richmond. Other improvements included the opening of the 'Hi-Street West Eight' boutique for young fashions at Barkers of Kensington which was currently trading at a loss. Early in the New Year of 1968 Sir Hugh called for Saturday shopping in the West End of London in the firm opinion that it would lift turnover and profitability as had happened in provincial towns and cities. At the same time it was announced that Harrods was to have more boutiques. In February André Courrèges, the innovator of the mini skirt, opened a new salon on the first floor. By the summer the board was sufficiently convinced of the profitability of the Way In boutique to approve the opening of another at Kendal Milne, Harrods' Manchester store.

As part of the cost-cutting exercise the outstanding preference shares in Harrods, Dickins & Jones, Barkers, and Binns were exchanged toward the close of 1967 for unsecured loan stock or preference shares in House of Fraser. At a stroke this did away with the necessity of publishing annual reports and holding annual meetings for the preference shareholders of these subsidiaries, saving over £100,000 a year. In February 1968 the Edinburgh catering and confectionary business of J.W. Mackie & Sons Ltd, which was peripheral to the Group's main activities, was sold to D.S. Crawford Ltd, a subsidiary of United Biscuits, for £135,000. The firm's premises behind Princes Street were to be used for an

Promoting D.H. Evans
'Fashion-Wise' in 1966.

extension to Smalls. The board also agreed to sell Watt & Milne's store in Aberdeen and to merge Pontings' business with that of Barkers' with a view to disposing of the premises. Altogether, between July 1967 and July 1968, eight small stores were closed, mostly in Scotland, and all the subsidiary companies liquidated with the exception of the principal operating companies.

Learning from the example of Debenhams, which was moving towards almost total central buying, the board made efforts to foster similar developments in House of Fraser, but without either massive disruption or the loss of individual buyers' freedom. By the summer of 1968, forty per cent of the merchandise of the Binns group was bought centrally and thirty per cent of that of the stores in Scotland. Cost control and the co-ordination of buying was improved by the installation of computers at the divisional headquarters. The financial markets responded positively to Sir Hugh's determined policy of retrenchment and his longer term objective of shifting the balance of the group away from Scotland and the north, badly hit by the recession, towards the more prosperous south. With sales topping £100 million for the first time and profits rising for the year to January 1968, the shares were marked higher after the annual meeting at the end of July. At the meeting William McLellan stood down as a director and was replaced by the company secretary, Walter Keymer.

Heartened, Sir Hugh and his board intensified their campaign, enlarging the scope of central buying and modernising stores. In January 1969 they made their first acquisition since Lord Fraser's death when the old-established store of Guy & Smith of Grimsby on the North Yorkshire coast was purchased for £680,000. The new building for Smalls in Princes Street, Edinburgh, was approved in April, and the following month Impact, another boutique for young customers, was opened at McDonalds in Glasgow. Further Way In shops in other stores were planned after the successful commissioning of the first outside Harrods at

Kendal Milne. The innovator of Way In, Gordon Anthony, was appointed a director of House of Fraser in February 1969 to oversee the development of his creation elsewhere. Although margins continued to be squeezed by the Labour Government's efforts to hold down domestic consumption, Sir Hugh confirmed in August that the board 'would examine carefully any possibilities of expansion through acquisition.' Within days he was in discussion with Louis Michaels, the chairman of J.J. Allen Ltd, which owned a group of quality stores in London, Leicester and the south and west of England. Their shops included Allens' own store in Bournemouth, Brights of Bristol, Cavendish House of Cheltenham, and Morgan Squire of Leicester, places where prospects for growth were good and where House of Fraser was not represented. Allens also owned the Chanelle and Maryon chain of fashion shops. By mid October 1969 a price of £5.3 million had been agreed and the following month J.J. Allen joined the Group. At the same time House of Fraser took control, for £1.4 million, of Robertson, Ledlie, Ferguson & Co Ltd with stores in Belfast and Cork. The cash required for these acquisitions was raised by selling and leasing back various properties valued at just over £3 million.

Not content simply with adding new outlets to the Group, Sir Hugh began to explore the possibility of an ambitious connection with Boots Ltd, the high street chemists, which had diversified into retailing other merchandise, particularly at their larger city-centre stores. He offered Boots the opportunity to create shops within House of Fraser stores, selling pharmaceuticals, toiletries and perfumeries. Nothing came of the proposal as neither side could agree terms, but Sir Hugh came to like and admire Boots' deputy chairman, Lord Redmayne, a former Conservative chief whip. Lord Redmayne had been a friend of his father, and Lord Fraser had suggested that he might become a member of Harrods' board. Towards the end of February 1970 Sir Hugh invited him to join House of Fraser. Lord Redmayne accepted and he was appointed a director on 5 March 1970 especially charged with 'organising the study of the continuing growth and development of the company.' Ten days later Alfred Spence, one of Lord Fraser's most trusted lieutenants, died in his early fifties, robbing Sir Hugh of the expert advice of an experienced warehouseman who, alone with Elson Gamble, understood the internal logic of the Group. Although he was replaced in April by Kenneth Marley, a director of the Binns group, Sir Hugh turned increasingly for advice, not to his deputy chairman, Elson Gamble, but to Lord Redmayne. Within two months Gordon Anthony was also dead, less than eighteen months after he joined the board. He was succeeded at Harrods by Robert Midgely, who had been managing Barkers.

Although retailing continued to be unsettled by the twin effects of deflationary policies and the selective employment tax, Sir Hugh was confident, echoing his father's sentiments in forecasting that increased spending power 'would lead to a demand from customers for higher quality goods, greater individuality in design, and higher standards of retail service.' He was not just whistling in the dark for there were signs that popular taste was moving away from the gauche styles of the 1960s and rediscovering designs and fashions of the past. Laura Ashley began selling Victorian-style dresses, made of printed cotton fabrics that would have been considered outmoded at the beginning of the decade. Her first shop in Pelham Street, Kensington, opened in 1968, was an instant success. Other designers looked back to the 1920s and 1930s, creating, in reaction to the mini, elegant midi-length and maxi-skirts for the increasingly large number of women who were now working. Many stores, including House of Fraser, over-reacted to this shift in fashion, buying in large quantities of midi-skirts for the

Cavendish House, Cheltenham, one of the stores of J.J. Allen Ltd which was acquired by House of Fraser in 1969.

1970 season. Ridiculed as 'Instant Age', sales of the new longer-length fashions failed to materialise and stores were left with stock on their hands. Despite this setback, the uniformity of the mid-1960s styles had been broken, fragmenting the fashion industry and holding out the possibility to department stores of rebuilding their traditional market for quality clothing.

The impression that attitudes were changing was confirmed in June 1970 when the Conservatives won a surprise victory at the general election, committed to taking the country into the European Economic Community (EEC) and to trying to reduce retail prices in an attempt to head off wage increases. These two objectives were oddly enough related because entry into the EEC required the replacement of the existing differential purchase tax and the much disliked selective employment tax by across-the-board value added tax (VAT). Convinced that a reform in indirect taxation would stimulate sales, the directors of House of Fraser redoubled their efforts to rationalise the Group extending central buying to about fifty per cent of purchases in all the stores except Harrods. In Glasgow proposed developments presaged the closure of two more House of Fraser stores, Dallas's in Cowcaddens and Pettigrew & Stephens in Sauchiehall Street. The threatened sale of these two large city centre stores permitted the board to pursue their policy of enlarging the Group's representation in suburban west of Scotland. An ideal opportunity presented itself in midsummer when Selincourt & Sons Ltd of London put their loss-making Scottish companies, T. Baird & Son Ltd and Alexander Henderson Ltd, on the market. Bairds owned seventeen out-of-town shops in places such as Wishaw, Airdrie, Coatbridge, Hamilton, Motherwell, Shotts, Whifflet, the new town of East Kilbride, and the Glasgow housing scheme at Drumchapel. Hendersons had a recently enlarged shop in Sauchiehall Street, an ideal home for Pettigrew & Stephens when its existing premises were demolished. House of Fraser paid £165,000 for Bairds and £152,000 for Hendersons. Announcing the deal, Sir Hugh made it plain that the rates burden made it prohibitively expensive for the Group to continue operating its seven large Glasgow stores. A new House of Fraser store was to be incorporated within a shopping complex on the Pettigrew & Stephens site. Incorporating the latest ideas, the development contained a mix of retail outlets grouped round a central covered piazza, with a car park on the roof. When the Glasgow Corporation refused to approve the proposed building early in 1971, House of Fraser consolidated their position by acquiring the site of the adjoining Copland & Lye store which had closed. In London a more ambitious redeployment of resources towards the suburbs was planned, with the construction of further satellite stores under the control of Dickins & Jones and D.H. Evans. A buyer was found for Pontings' premises, which closed at the end of February 1971, and the prestigious Derry & Toms was informally put up for sale. Residual parts of both businesses were to be amalgamated with Barkers. Bill Crossan, who was responsible for the direction of the stores in Scotland, became a director of House of Fraser in January 1971 with the job of pushing ahead with the re-organisation of the Group.

By now Sir Hugh had a clear vision for the future of his group which was very different from his father's. Writing in 1971 he declared, 'We are going to see immense changes and developments in department stores, which more and more I envisage modelling themselves on chain store groups. Self selection, for instance, will be vastly on the increase, not only because staff costs are so high but also because we have found that so many women prefer to take time over choosing their own purchases.' He forecast 'more and more central buying and greater scrutiny of the return on every square foot of space.' He believed passionately in 'new and effective shop fittings – not of the old-fashioned battleship variety which would last for a hundred years but of the new light disposable kind that can be scrapped and renewed as visual tastes change.' His faith in the future was confirmed by the 1971 budget which brought the hoped-for reformation of indirect taxation which was to be phased out over two years while VAT was introduced. In midsummer, following the findings of a committee on consumer credit, hire purchase controls were abolished. Later in the year limits on bank borrowings were also removed. As the Government intended, retail sales, particularly for durable goods, rose sharply, benefiting the department stores more than the multiple chains.

Sir Hugh and the House of Fraser board, confident that their strategy would yield handsome returns in the coming boom, began to search for new acquisitions to improve the Group's geographical spread. In early May they made a bid for E. Dingle & Co Ltd, the south west of England group, with stores at Plymouth, Newton Abbot, Falmouth, Truro, Newquay, Bath, Penzance and Helston (see page 309). After a brief tussle a price of £6.15 million was agreed and Dingles joined House of Fraser at the end of July 1971, strengthening the Group's presence in the south-west of England. Although Dingles was to continue to function as a separate group, its activities were to be harmonised with those of J.J. Allen Ltd wherever possible. At the same time House of Fraser was engaged in joint discussions with Waterford Glass to buy Switzer & Co Ltd, the well-known Dublin department store, for £4 million. After the offer had been accepted

OPPOSITE ABOVE
The Plymouth store of E. Dingle & Co, which joined House of Fraser in 1971.

OPPOSITE BELOW
Switzer & Co, the Harrods of Dublin.

Waterford Glass held sixty per cent of the shares and House of Fraser forty per cent. In the midst of these negotiations James Cathcart Stewart decided that he could now step down as finance director and his place on the board was taken by the company secretary, Walter Keymer.

At the end of 1971 the Group reported bumper half-year profits, more than matching expectations. With the Government committed to tax reforms and reductions, Sir Hugh, like others in the retail trade, looked forward to even better results in the coming year. The City was impressed with his apparently determined efforts to restructure his father's Group. On 30 November 1971 the closure in eighteen months time of Derry & Toms, with its legendary roof garden, and the sale of the site for £4 million, was made public. The staff accepted the decision as inevitable. One of the waitresses in the restaurant commented, 'We used to get the Duchess type of person. Ladies with accounts who used to have things sent home. There are few of them left, a lot of them have moved out of the area altogether. The young people have invaded Kensington High Street and they want boutiques and gear shops. In the restaurant people don't want the four-course meals any more, only snacks.' Sir Hugh was only too conscious of the threat such changes in customer preference posed for his Group. He explained to Graham Turner of the *Sunday Telegraph* in the week before Christmas, that despite record profits 'not everything in the Group looks quite so rosy.' He believed that there were still 'too many stores in cities like Glasgow and Aberdeen; too many stores in areas affected by high unemployment; too little management both at the top and in the middle; and too little control over the Group's operations, both on the financial front and in the field of buying where at the moment, it scarcely uses its considerable muscle.' In charting the future direction of House of Fraser he adhered to his father's policy of trading up, steering well clear of the fashionable hypermarket. Making it clear that he was now in undisputed command of the whole enterprise, he unveiled his plans to reorganise the management by 'appointing a top level trouble-shooter personally responsible to himself, making a high-level appointment on the buying side and trying to make sure there's much better co-ordination through the Group by regular meetings of all the managing and merchandise directors of the regional store groups.' He also predicted several significant acquisitions during the coming year. He concluded with a thinly disguised attack on his father's methods: 'In the past we've done too much by the seat of our pants and it's wrong for a group of our size.'

These ambitious plans began to take shape early in the New Year. On 31 January 1972 Elson Gamble, the deputy chairman and close colleague of Sir Hugh's father, retired and John B. Kinross resigned from the board. Sir Hugh was fullsome in his praise of their help in the five years since his father's death, appointing Elson Gamble honorary deputy chairman in recognition of his thirty-six years of loyal service. Sir Hugh asked Bill Crossan to act as his 'personal assistant' and Lord Redmayne was promoted to be deputy chairman. Immediately Lord Redmayne embarked on an appraisal of all the Group's general managers, issuing detailed questionnaires to judge their capabilities. Changes came thick and fast over the next few weeks. Retail management was reorganised into six groups, Harrods (London), Harrods (Provincial), Barkers, Dingles, Binns, and Northern Management. E. Dingle incorporated all the J.J. Allen stores in the west country and those elsewhere were transferred to Harrods (Provincial). Northern Management controlled all the stores in Scotland except for Binns in Edinburgh. As Sir Hugh had suggested, there were to be regular meetings between groups to discuss policy, central buying, and promotion. As part of these

OPPOSITE *Harrods Provincial was formed in 1972 to bring these quality stores into one grouping within House of Fraser.*

Six Shopping Specials.

Daily Service Monday to Saturday

Rackhams, *Birmingham.*

Kendal Milne, *Manchester.*

Morgan Squire, *Leicester.*

Walshs, *Sheffield.*

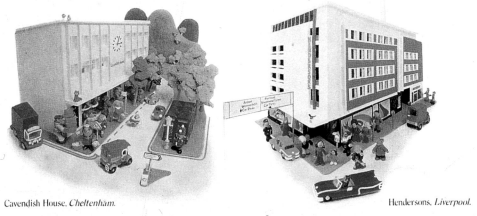

Cavendish House, *Cheltenham.*

Hendersons, *Liverpool.*

Harrods Provincial Ltd.

reforms Winston Brimacombe, the chairman of Dingles and J.J. Allen, joined the House of Fraser board to represent their interest. The customer credit structure of the Group was overhauled. With the exception of Harrods, no new monthly accounts were to be opened, but instead customers were to be offered interest-bearing option or budget accounts on the pattern of commercial credit cards, which were becoming increasingly widely used following the abolition of credit controls. Advertising budgets were cut back, staffing levels reduced, and delivery services limited.

No sooner had these reforms been effected than Sir Hugh and Bill Crossan were once more on the takeover trail. During April 1972 House of Fraser bid just under £5 million for James Howell & Co Ltd, 'the Harrods of Cardiff' (see page 332), in what Sir Hugh thought to be an amicable understanding. At the last moment, Thomas Stevens (Property) Ltd, a subsidiary of the fast-moving Slater Walker group, stepped in with a much higher offer, endorsing the existing management's progressive policies. Refusing to become involved in a contest, Sir Hugh withdrew and at once offered £8 million for Hammonds Ltd of Hull. He was convinced that the opening of the Humber bridge would bring increased prosperity to the area in much the same way as the Severn Bridge had boosted the economy of Cardiff and South Wales. The company's store had been severely blitzed in the war and rebuilt in 1952. For the last ten years Hammonds had been planning a major extension with associated car parks and small shops, for which permission had only recently been secured. A satellite store, similar to Dickins & Jones at Richmond, had been constructed in 1970 at Bridlington for £500,000. The directors accepted the offer without protest and Hammonds joined House of Fraser at the end of May. By this time Sir Hugh was also casting his eye over Army & Navy Stores Ltd, which owned prime sites in Victoria Street in London and was being stalked by Amalgamated Investment and Property Ltd.

The Group was not alone in seeking to improve its position. Big chains like ASDA, Sainsburys, Carrefour, Woolworth, and Fine Fare, were beginning to use their experience in moving bulk to sell clothing for the first time. To accommodate new merchandise, large new stores were constructed away from traditional shopping centres where vehicle access was difficult. B.P. Fagan, soft goods controller of ASDA, explained the attraction of drapery: 'Clothing offers an attractive profit situation for the more food-orientated superstore operation whose margins are generally lower.' To escape from their cut-price image, these stores began trading up, making much of buying British. In the high street itself, and presenting a greater threat to department stores, specialist menswear chains, like Austin Reed, Moss Bros, and Gieves & Hawkes, were extending their presence to most of Britain's major cities, revolutionising male attire with brightly coloured shirts and ties. Laura Ashley had similar ambitions to open her popular shops throughout the country. The Dorothy Perkins chain ceased to offer a limited range of merchandise, mostly underwear, to appeal to the widest possible market. Instead, following the example of Miss Selfridge, they targeted the fifteen to thirty age group and extended the number of lines. The shop fittings were redesigned to entice these younger customers, with emphasis on light easily moved units, allowing displays to be changed quickly. In children's clothes, Mothercare was pioneering a chain of baby and infant shops. Terence Conran's new Habitat stores were developing exciting novel concepts in household furnishings, china, glass and kitchen goods. All these new stores were carefully sited after intensive market research. Their interiors were often radically different from those to be found in more traditional shops. Their success and that of independent boutiques had severely dented Harrods' Way In stores, forcing Robert Midgely, the managing director, to rethink their image and extend their range of goods.

The urgent task for Sir Hugh and his new management team was to accelerate the process of rationalising House of Fraser in the face of renewed competition from these outlets and the established multiples which were fast trading up. The end-of-year results, announced in July, showed a forty-five per cent rise in profit to over £10 million, confounding the pessimists who believed that Sir Hugh could not sustain his record growth into 1972. Shortly afterwards it was agreed to abandon Lord Fraser's policy of allowing stores to continue trading under their original names. As a first step six stores in Scotland changed their names to Arnott on 31 July 1972 - J.& R. Allan of Edinburgh, D.M. Brown of Dundee, Isaac Benzie of Aberdeen, Benzies of Peterhead, and Muirheads and Arnott Simpsons in Glasgow. They were to trade as an integrated group with common merchandise. Later in the summer the board decided to call the 'top-end stores' Frasers, experimentally renaming Falconers in Aberdeen. The plans for a shopping centre development on the Pettigrew & Stephens and Copland & Lye site in Glasgow's Sauchiehall Street, in association with Scottish Amicable, was approved and was to include a 165,000-square-foot department store for the Group.

With Britain's entry into the EEC scheduled for 1 January 1973, Sir Hugh began to search for a suitable acquisition in a European city. He identified the Illums department store in Copenhagen 'because the Danes are very like the British, they all speak English and this helps in the negotiations.' A.C. Illum, which employed 800 people, had recently been modernised and claimed to be the largest department store in Scandinavia. In mid-August the Illum family accepted an offer which valued the business at just over £11 million. Norman H. Powell was sent out from Scotland in September to take over as chairman and spearhead further expansion elsewhere in Europe. The Group's merchandising strategy, particularly the introduction of house brands, was sharpened in September when George Burke, the managing director of Switzer & Co, was appointed merchandise director of House of Fraser. At the same time Bill Crossan's central role in the organisation was confirmed with his promotion to be assistant managing director. Walter Keymer became financial director, and John Aiton replaced him as company secretary. Financial control was greatly improved by the installation of a large computer at Harrods to handle customers' and suppliers' accounts for the whole Group. Within a month House of Fraser had been offered the Cardiff store of James Howell & Co Ltd, which it had failed to buy in April. The new owners, Anglo Continental Investment and Finance, who had bought the property interests of Slater Walker, were keen to sell and House of Fraser acquired this prestigious Welsh store for £5.5 million.

The boom in the economy during 1972, stimulated by the Government's reflationary stance, caused property values to soar. The House of Fraser board was well aware that, even though many stores had been sold and leased back, the underlying asset value of the Group's properties were becoming alarmingly out of step with the book value in the balance sheet. House of Fraser commissioned outside consultants to revalue the leasehold and freehold properties. This massive exercise was completed by November and showed that the properties were worth £94 million compared to a book value of £32 million. House of Fraser was now as vulnerable to a determined predator as Harrods had been in 1959. Although profits for the first half declared at the same time were still buoyant, the financial markets were nervous about the likely effects of the deflationary pay and prices freeze imposed by the Government on 6 November. The shares were marked down, increasing the danger of a bid from a company keen to realise some, if not all, of House of Fraser's properties. The board could do nothing but sit tight. Lord Redmayne threw himself into negotiations with the Government on pay and prices in shops and stores, as chairman of the Retail Consortium – the mouthpiece of the trade.

Throughout January 1973 House of Fraser shares drifted lower. At the very end of the month Sir Hugh's worst fears were confirmed when he received an informal approach from Richard Dobson, chairman of British American Tobacco (BAT), offering to buy House of Fraser at a price of around £2 a share, 60 pence above the market price. Sir Hugh at once called an emergency board meeting. Rallying behind him, the directors decided that unless the price was over £2.20 there could be no basis for discussion. They recognised that an amicable merger would head off any hostile bid, but agreed that to avoid capital gains tax the offer should be composed largely of BAT shares. While the other directors waited tensely at Harrods, Sir Hugh, Lord Redmayne, Bill Crossan and Walter Keymer hurried off to the Group's merchant bankers. Negotations continued throughout the afternoon. BAT accepted the price, but baulked at giving so much in shares as this would have given Scottish & Universal Investment Trust (SUITS) a five per cent stake in the company. SUITS, which was chaired by Sir Hugh and in which the Fraser family had a forty-seven per cent stake, had raised its investment in House of Fraser from fifteen per cent at the time of Lord Fraser's death to over twenty-five per cent. Unable to reach agreement, negotiations were broken off. Throughout the first week of February the press was alive with reports of a possible bid, hotly refuted by Sir Hugh. When details of the talks leaked out, neither side denied them and discussions were resumed. Towards the end of the month Richard Dobson brought a halt to speculation with a statement that no formal bid would be made.

All too conscious of their vulnerable situation, the directors returned to the job of streamlining the Group's activities. In the background to the abortive negotiations with BAT and to the management changes earlier in the year was a desire by Sir Hugh to devolve much of the responsibility for the day-to-day direction of the Group. The strain of the last six years was beginning to tell. He was smoking as heavily as his father. His marriage had broken up and his wife and three daughters were living in Canada. Having devoted all his energies and time since he left school to helping his father and then managing House of Fraser and SUITS, he wanted more time to spend with his children in the summer and with his girlfriend, Aileen Ross, the international show jumper. At the end of February 1973 he promoted Bill Crossan to be managing director of House of Fraser, a post he had held, like his father, along with the chairmanship.

By this time George Burke had matured his merchandising plans for the Group, selecting Allander as the house brand name with the Fraser clan's stag's head motif. Over the next six months he devoted his attention to the design of packaging for Allander products and to introducing uniform carrier bags and other wrappings for the Group as a whole. Buying was further centralised with the appointment of Group buyers for certain lines. Efforts were made to reduce stocks by persuading more key suppliers to open shops within House of Fraser stores. With the Government controlling prices even more firmly, Bill Crossan and Walter Keymer tightened the board's financial grip by standardising account-ing procedures and introducing annual budgets for each store. He revived Lord Fraser's original policy of encouraging stores to compete with each other. Apart from their purely financial performance, Sir Hugh and Lord Redmayne were to record their impressions of every store they visited for comparison at the end of the year. Overall, their ambition was to make House of Fraser the leading store

Army & Navy,
Bromley.

in every town in which it traded by modernising its premises and improving the quality of service. This reorganisation was made all the more necessary by the steady decline in sales from the spring as the Government's deflationary measures began to take effect. The annual accounts in June revealed that the Group's properties were valued at three times their book value, leading to further speculation about the likelihood of a takeover. Several companies were said to have held unofficial talks with Sir Hugh, including Imperial Tobacco, United Drapery Stores and the Rank Organisation, but none had proceeded beyond preliminary soundings.

Sir Hugh was not prepared to allow his desire to sell his interest in the Group to stand in the way of the acquisition of other stores either in Britain or in Europe. During July he was approached by Amalgamated Investment and Property (AIP), owners of thirty per cent of Army & Navy Stores, to enquire if House of Fraser would be willing to join in a combined bid. A package was quickly assembled whereby AIP and International Caledonian Assets, in which Sir Hugh had a large stake, would buy the property in Victoria Street and House of Fraser acquire Army & Navy's goodwill, stocks and out-of-town stores at Aldershot, Bromley, Camberley, Chichester, Dorchester, Guildford, Leamington Spa, and Wolverhampton (see page 272). Having only recently obtained planning permission, after a difficult struggle, for the development of its Victoria Street site at a cost of £11 million, the Army & Navy board held out for a high price. At the beginning of August they accepted an offer that valued Army & Navy at

£40 million with reassurances that the company's existing trading policies would be maintained. Although financial commentators were agreed that the deal was a good outcome for Army & Navy, it drove down House of Fraser's share price to even lower levels. The economic climate began to deteriorate seriously during the autumn. The Conservative Government was in open conflict with the trade unions over the next round of its statutory prices and incomes policy. The outbreak of war between Israel and the Arab states in October led to a massive increase in oil prices and a sharp reduction in output, directly fuelling inflation throughout the developed world. In mid-October the National Union of Mineworkers rejected their pay offer and, along with the power workers, began industrial action in the following month. The outlook for the whole of British commerce and industry was bleak.

Sir Hugh still hankered after a less arduous life. He told the press that throughout the summer his mother had pleaded with him to reduce his commitments. The worsening trading conditions convinced him that he should withdraw from the direction of House of Fraser as soon as possible. Boots had already been considering forming a joint venture company with House of Fraser to expand into Europe, where in many countries regulations forbade chains of chemist shops. In the knowledge that Sir Hugh would welcome an approach the chairman of Boots, Dr Gordon Hobday, asked Lord Redmayne, a non-executive director of the company, to act as an intermediary in negotiations leading to a full merger. Gordon Hobday and his senior executives had recently been prevented from merging with Glaxo, the pharmaceutical company, and were now looking for ways of expanding the retail side of their business through the extension of their range of merchandise. They had two choices – either to enlarge their existing shops or to merge with a retail company with complementary experience. By 6 November a price of £1.85 per share, composed of Boots ordinary shares, loan stock and cash had been settled and Sir Hugh had pledged the support of SUITS. The other House of Fraser directors had little alternative but to concur. Sir Hugh made no secret of his personal reasons for supporting the merger – 'I feel I've proved myself ... I've been up to *here* with House of Fraser. It's been taking up ninety-nine per cent of my time and I haven't had a Saturday off for nearly two years.' He explained that he would relinquish the chairmanship of House of Fraser as soon as the deal went through and concentrate his efforts on developing SUITS.

This admission did little to help Boots' case which, to outside commentators, including the company's institutional shareholders, smacked of expediency rather than a considered view. A year before, the proposed merger would have been approved without question, but in the worsening economic and political environment of November 1973, large-scale amalgamations were regarded with suspicion. A week after the merger between Boots and House of Fraser was made public, Edward Heath's Conservative Government declared a state of emergency because of the crisis in supplies of fuel. Interest rates were raised by 1.75 per cent in an effort to reduce spending. Almost inevitably the bid was referred to the Monopolies and Mergers Commission on 27 November. In the meantime, Sir Hugh had gone on holiday to the West Indies, marrying his fiancee, Aileen Ross, in St Vincent, Barbados. He returned at the end of the month determined to give himself more free time.

With the fuel crisis at its height, Sir Hugh had little alternative but to plunge back into his business interests until the inquiry was completed. Lord Redmayne was delegated to prepare the Group's submission in consultation with Bill Crossan and the secretary, while Sir Hugh devoted his time to the continuing direction of the enterprise. The most serious problem that faced the board was the implications of Phase III of the Government's prices and incomes policy. The Commission's regulation bore a distinct resemblance to the wartime controls, setting permitted profit margins for retailers. The Group was finding it almost impossible to operate within the set ceiling and in early December prices were reduced. As a result it became all the more necessary to control costs and achieve higher turnover if profits were to be maintained. The death of Walter Keymer, the financial director, on 4 December was a serious loss at a time when his knowledge and experience were sorely needed. Any hope that turnover might be increased by extending credit was dashed in December when the Government reintroduced hire-purchase controls and took other measures to discourage bank lending. The Group's capital expenditure programme was immediately restricted to essential work, and projections for increases in turnover revised downwards to five per cent, which was less than the current rate of inflation. Every manager was instructed to monitor his expenditure very carefully and revise his budget in line with this estimate. George Burke, the merchandise director, persevered with his plans to rationalise group buying, restricting the number of suppliers and seeking improved terms. In the grave circumstances, which confronted every business in Britain, the management of cash became crucial.

The political crisis escalated rapidly in January 1974, and in head-on confrontation with the miners Edward Heath, late in the day, called a general election for the end of the following month. The Labour party, committed to even harsher price restraint, won by a narrow margin. The incoming Prime Minister, Harold Wilson, recalling his time at the Board of Trade in the postwar Labour Government, set up a new Department of Prices and Consumer Protection under Shirley Williams with statutory powers to control prices and retailers' margins. Within days, in an almost copybook replay of Harold Wilson's actions in 1949/50, she told the Retail Consortium that she would impose a cut of two per cent on their gross margins and tighten the already strict regulations. The Retail Consortium, whose members were already severely affected by the economic crisis, were outraged, protesting that if, as was likely, firms could not reduce costs, net profits would be cut by as much as twenty per cent. The Department was unmoved and the proposals were made public in the last week of March.

The Labour election victory could not have come at a worse time for House of Fraser. The Boots' management at once re-examined their future strategy in the light of the prospect of sharply reduced returns from domestic retailing for some time to come. As Harold Wilson intended, they chose to concentrate their efforts on export markets and abandon their ambitions to enlarge their position on British high streets. Instead they decided to rename their fancy goods departments, and revamp them as fashion departments, concentrating on a narrow range of merchandise complementary to the rest of their business. They immediately approached House of Fraser seeking to re-negotiate the terms of their offer for the company, if not cancel it altogether. Sir Hugh refused to alter the terms of the merger, leaving the board of Boots no alternative but to seek permission from the City's Takeover and Mergers Panel to call off the deal on the grounds that the economic climate had deteriorated rapidly since November. The Panel replied that the deal could only be cancelled if House of Fraser agreed. Surprised by this advice, Boots made a public statement on 4 March that they were not willing to proceed. Since the merger required the increase of Boots capital which had to be approved by a meeting of shareholders, Dr Gordon Hobday made it clear that he would instruct them to vote against it. The House of Fraser share price slumped. Sir Hugh, stunned by this turn of events, quickly sought an alternative buyer for SUITS' stake in House of Fraser. Within days he had signed a conditional agreement with the United States store group, Broadway Hale, to acquire a twenty per cent stake from SUITS for £20 million in cash should the Boots bid fail. This firm offer, which valued House of Fraser slightly above the Boots bid, gave much needed support to the flagging share price. Although publication of the Monopolies and Mergers Commission report was delayed until October by a printing strike, Shirley Williams announced the findings in May that recommended that the merger should be disallowed, chiefly because Boots no longer wished to proceed. SUITS concluded the agreement with Broadway Hale, now named Carter Hawley Hale Inc, using the cash realised to pay off borrowings and for new investment. Instead of resigning as chairman of House of Fraser as he had intended, Sir Hugh agreed to stay on, restructuring the management of SUITS to reduce his involvement in that company.

The collapse of the planned merger with Boots was a bitter personal blow to Sir Hugh. He had openly declared his intention of breaking his links with House of Fraser and now he was forced to go back on his word. He was particularly disillusioned with the Conservative party whom he blamed for having referred the bid to the Monopolies Commission in the first place. In a fit of pique he joined the Scottish National Party, which had won seven seats at the general election. Subsequent press interviews suggested that he had not thought through the consequences of this new commitment very clearly. He reiterated his unhappiness with his hectic business life and his determination to take more time off. Sadly for Sir Hugh, Boots' very public withdrawal from the bid severely damaged the reputation and standing of his deputy chairman, Lord Redmayne. Some members of the board accused him of acting entirely out of self-interest in promoting the deal, believing that one outcome would have been his promotion to the vacant chairmanship. Lord Redmayne, who had worked very hard since he joined the board to improve the management and performance of House of Fraser, was deeply wounded by these allegations. In a letter to Sir Hugh as chairman on 3 July 1974, he laid out his position, stating that he was not party to Boots' decision to abandon the bid.

There was no time for such recriminations when the economic environment for retailers was becoming increasingly hostile. Inflation was rampant and consumer spending was in retreat. Sir Hugh told shareholders, 'It is no easy path which lies ahead of us but we shall tread it with fortitude.' The greatest cause for concern was the impact of the new prices code in a declining market. With margins controlled, House of Fraser was obliged to reverse policies and trade down at the expense of profit. The board redoubled its endeavours to pare costs to the bone and raise turnover through more effective promotions of merchandise. In August Norman H. Powell joined the board as promotional director for the Group. Sir Hugh proposed in October the formation of a management committee under the chairmanship of Bill Crossan which would scrutinise the monthly statistical returns from the stores in advance of main board meetings in a further move to tighten financial control. The first meeting was not held until February 1975. The worldwide recession, consequent on the sharp rise in oil prices also had an adverse effect on the Group's investment in A.C. Illum of Copenhagen which had been a drain on resources since its acquisition in November 1972. Despite the foul trading conditions Sir Hugh did not lose sight of the long-term objective of making House of Fraser the leading store in every large British town, buying a twenty-seven per cent stake in Brown Muff & Co Ltd, arguably the best department store in Bradford (see page 297), between April and July 1977. Not every store that was offered to the Group was purchased. Proposals to acquire

(see page 297)

OPPOSITE ABOVE
Rackham, (formerly Brown Muff) Bradford.

OPPOSITE BELOW
R.H.O. Hills, Blackpool.

The newly refurbished stores of McDonalds and Wylie & Lochhead in Buchanan Street, Glasgow, which were renamed Frasers when the original store across the street was closed.

Browns of Chester and the Lewisham-based Chiesmans Ltd group of stores (see page 302) were rejected as too expensive. During the autumn of 1974 negotiations were opened with Tootals, the textile company, to take over their Hide group of thirteen stores, including R.H.O. Hills of Blackpool, Hides of Kingston-on-Thames, Dunnings of Maidstone, and Seccombes of Cardiff. In November the premises of Bainbridges, the main store in Newcastle-upon-Tyne, were bought from the John Lewis Partnership for £1 million.

The management committee quickly extended its brief to include a review of the operations of the Group as a whole, recommending in April 1975 the amalgamation of the operations of the Army & Navy and John Barker groups

and the separation of Harrods Provincial group from Harrods. The committee worked hard to upgrade the Group's overall efficiency by constantly honing the management at every level from the top to the bottom. The protracted negotiations with Tootals to buy the Hide Group were completed in May 1975 at a price of £2.5 million. Two months later Argyle Securities, the owners of the Chiesman group, approached House of Fraser once more, naming a price of £3.25 million which was accepted. These acquisitions enhanced the geographical spread of House of Fraser, shifting the balance firmly away from Scotland and the north. Testimony to the difficulty of trading in Scotland was the decision in January 1975 to close the original Frasers store in Buchanan Street. The business was amalgamated with the newly revamped McDonalds and Wylie & Lochhead store across the street, which was renamed Frasers.

The owners of both the Hide and Chiesman groups had been keen to sell because of the continuing difficulties in the retail trade, stemming from persistent inflation, decline in consumer spending, stringent price control and competition from newer dynamic shopping chains like Dixons, Habitat and Mothercare. Recognising the challenge from these new specialist stores, which laid great emphasis on the design of both their premises and merchandise, the chairman, Bob Thornton, had transformed Debenhams in the previous two years, introducing a new unified image for the sixty-nine department stores in that group with a stylish 'd' logo. Debenhams' Harvey Nichols' store in Knightsbridge was revamped to appeal to a younger clientele rather than its traditional older customers who were 'beginning to hang on to their pennies as economic circumstances got tighter.' It was not just the long-established stores which were vulnerable. In August 1975 Biba, which just two years previously had moved into the old Derry & Toms building in Kensington High Street, collapsed. Refitted to evoke the 1930s when the store had been constructed, Biba misjudged the market – 'a lovely idea that became a white elephant.' Throughout 1975 and 1976, Bill Crossan and House of Fraser's management committee, found the going hard. Their determined efforts to control costs kept margins within the permitted limits and maintained profits. Staffing levels were reduced by twenty per cent through voluntary redundancies and early retirements. In May 1976 the management committee's function was clarified when it became responsible for the day-to-day administration, leaving the main board to concentrate on corporate planning and policy. Like other retailing companies strapped in the straightjacket of price restraint, House of Fraser was out of favour with financial markets and the shares remained very depressed.

Although Carter Hawley Hale had suggested that they might enlarge their stake in House of Fraser after their purchase of the SUITS twenty per cent interest in the company, they were deterred by the recession in the United Kingdom from buying more shares. In June 1975 Edward Carter and Prentice C. Hale joined the House of Fraser board to represent their investment. Sir Hugh and his family, however, began to buy House of Fraser shares on their own account. The annual accounts for 1974, published in May 1975, showed that his own stake had almost doubled to 1.1 million shares and that his beneficial investment in the company as a trustee had risen from 1.7 million to 2.3 million. These purchases were remarked on in the press, particularly when it was rumoured that he bought and sold House of Fraser stocks to fund his adventures in gaming houses. He had been introduced to gambling at the tables by his father and enjoyed the thrill of playing for very high stakes. Since the failure of the Boots bid he had started gambling heavily to the alarm of his friends. The City institutions were very critical of his actions which created erratic movements in the share price. Sir Hugh was also under attack for the incorrect balance sheet entry of a loan of £4.3 million from SUITS to Amalgamated Caledonian. This company was involved in the redevelopment of the Army & Navy site in Victoria, which had run into difficulties. The loan had become unsecured and was wrongly entered in SUITS published accounts as 'cash at bankers and on hand.' The auditors were forced to resign and Sir Hugh was later fined for contravening the Companies Act. He was severely censured after a Stock Exchange inquiry.

In the ten years since Lord Fraser's death, House of Fraser had been transformed from being managed directly by the chairman and a small band of able lieutenants into a modern corporation. The process had been painful and inevitable, particularly after the fuel crisis of 1973 and government measures to halt inflation. Sir Hugh, advised by his father's friends and admirers, had realised from the outset that the Group had to change rapidly to meet the new conditions and expectations of the late 1960s and early 1970s. He had tried hard to introduce new shopping ideas in conditions that were more difficult than those his father had experienced in the 1930s. Unlike his father, he had not been afraid to close unprofitable stores in the north and had greatly strengthened the Group's presence in the more prosperous south of England. He had sacrificed his youth in proving that he was a worthy successor to his father. Having almost achieved his goal, he was finally prevented from reducing his commitments by the swift recession in the autumn and spring of 1973. Like many of his generation brought up in the stable and increasingly affluent postwar years, he was defeated by the uncertainties of the 1970s and the return with a vengeance of government control. Fortunately, Bill Crossan was able to pick up the baton from Sir Hugh, establishing an executive management committee capable of imposing the financial discipline demanded by price control. Like many other businesses in Britain, House of Fraser had survived this difficult decade by becoming more professional and perceptive in tailoring its resources to the needs of consumers who could now take their custom to a greater range of different types of shops than ever before.

8 1976–1985
Retailing out of the Recession

The obstacles that lay in the path of every shopkeeper in Britain in 1977 were as formidable as those the House of Fraser board had struggled with throughout the previous decade. Interest rates were at record levels and price control remained an essential component in the Labour Government's anti-inflation strategy. There was a glimmer of hope on the horizon. The resignation of Harold Wilson as Prime Minister in April of the previous year and his replacement by the avuncular James Callaghan had signalled a change in the Government's appearance, if not in its approach. Although stiff action had to be taken in the autumn of 1976 to protect the value of sterling, including making sweeping cuts in public expenditure and a large loan from the International Monetary Fund, the economy began to recover early in the following year as North Sea oil started to flow. The retail trade was boosted by the Queen's Silver Jubilee celebrations which took place throughout the summer with spectacular visits to the country's principal cities. To mark the occasion many retailers, including House of Fraser, enthusiastically supported another Buy British campaign, reminiscent of that at the time of the Coronation of the Queen's grandfather in 1911.

Frasers store in Buchanan Street decorated for the Queen's Silver Jubilee.

Fashion, always quick to respond to the popular mood, broke away from the restrained sombre styles of the early 1970s with 'Big Look' peasant styles and Punk. Unlike the fashions of previous generations, however, these styles were not universally popular and it was impossible for stores to use them as vehicles for raising sales in a depressed market. The only way forward was for retailers to continue to improve their merchandising techniques and in so doing refit their premises to reflect accurately the changing tastes and attitudes of customers. To justify large capital outlays, ideal customer profile had to be clearly identified and nurtured. The success of the Miss Selfridge chain was witness to the importance of such careful planning combined with sensitive management. There was now little doubt that refurbishment was not a long-term investment to be written off over a decade or more, but a continuous rolling programme from which there was no escape if customers' loyalty was to be retained. Writing in 1978 John Stephenson, managing director of Conran Associates who designed the Habitat Stores, declared 'the maximum life for the fittings of a women's fashion store is five years.' He challenged the major 'retail chains to take a long hard look at their image.'

Having devised effective procedures for working within the Price Commission's regulations, the House of Fraser board was well placed to take up the challenge. At the first joint meeting between the board and management committee in January 1977, plans to rationalise the Group's suppliers were endorsed, measures were approved to raise the profile of the Allander brand, promotional activities

Sir Hugh Fraser (left) and Lord Redmayne (right) chatting to staff at a wine and cheese party at Brown Muff of Bradford in 1977.

reviewed, and staff training and career structure discussed. With the worst of the economic crisis behind them, the directors were able to take a more confident view of the proposals for refurbishment. These included an ambitious scheme to improve the image of Barkers by closing the bargain basement, building a new main entrance and introducing more concession shops. Behind this scheme for Barkers was a determination to recapture the essential ingredients in a department store to entertain and enchant. The policy of seeking to make House of Fraser the best store in every major British town was to continue to be pursued vigorously. Early in 1977 a successful bid was made for Brown Muff & Co Ltd of Bradford (see page 293), in which the Group already held a twenty-seven per cent stake.

The efforts of Bill Crossan and his senior managers to improve the Group's competitive strength during 1977 were conducted against a background of increasingly hostile press reports about Sir Hugh Fraser himself. These centred on the charges brought under the Companies Act against him and his fellow directors on the SUITS board for the mis-classification of a loan, but also made regular mention of his private life, particularly his gambling. Sickened by this public exposure when he was more than anxious to reduce his business commitments, he met R.W. (Tiny) Rowland, managing director of Lonrho, the international trading company, which was seeking to extend its interests in the United Kingdom. He was immediately impressed: 'He reminds me very much of my late father. If he makes up his mind to do something he does it.' Sir Hugh, who had declared his intention during the abortive Boots merger negotiations of bowing out of House of Fraser, surprisingly reversed this decision and instead offered Lonrho his personal stake in SUITS of some twenty-six per cent. Lonrho accepted to the dismay of other SUITS directors, some of whom had worked with Lord Fraser in building the company from scratch. By this time SUITS had brought its investment in House of Fraser back up to 10.29 per cent, following the sale of its twenty per cent holding to the American Carter Hawley Hale Stores Inc in 1974. Although Tiny Rowland became chairman of SUITS, he gave assurances that he would be out of the country so often that Sir Hugh would in practice take the chair at most meetings. As a major shareholder in SUITS Tiny Rowland naturally was interested in the future direction of House of Fraser. He and Sir Hugh discussed a bold strategy to deepen the connection with Carter Hawley Hale, buy the moribund Woolworth chain in the United Kingdom, and acquire National Car Parks Ltd to improve public access to the 1500 stores in the enlarged group. This grand plan came to nothing, partly because Carter Hawley Hale were looking for a buyer for their twenty per cent stake in House of Fraser. On learning this news Sir Hugh suggested that Lonrho might be interested.

In September Lonrho purchased 23.5 million of Carter Hawley Hale's House of Fraser shares, a 19.5 per cent investment, with an option over their remaining holding of 1.16 per cent. Tiny Rowland wrote at once to House of Fraser directors to assure them that Lonrho regarded the shareholding as a long-term investment and had no immediate plans to increase it. He explained that Lonrho would only seek to be represented on the House of Fraser board if the Carter Hawley Hale directors stood down. In the event, Edward W. Carter and Prentice C. Hale resigned in November, but were persuaded to maintain their connection with House of Fraser by acting as alternates for Philip M. Hawley who remained on the board. They were replaced by Tiny Rowland, who became non-executive deputy chairman, and Lord Duncan-Sandys, the Lonrho chairman, who became a non-executive director. Earlier in the year Robert Midgely had been appointed joint deputy chairman with Lord Redmayne, who announced his decision to retire in January 1978.

While these high-level transactions were taking place, the House of Fraser management committee pressed on with the urgent task of improving the performance of the business. Merchandising strategies were refined with the development of a technique described as concentration – an area within a store 'specifically designed in terms of decor and merchandise to sell a particular look projected by a certain manufacturer and the merchandise selected by the manufacturer himself.' This concept was introduced at Kendal Milne's Manchester store in 1978 in the refurbished first-floor fashion department named, appropriately, 'Collections.' The floor contained eleven concentrations of well-known fashion houses – 'Feminella, Mono, John Marks, Marcel Fenez, Frank Usher, Designit, Jersey Masters, Peter Barron, Louis Feraud and the Designer Room.' Each had its own selling team, till and fitting room to emphasize its unique identity. Critical to the success of such innovations was the effectiveness of the Group's data processing when margins were so tightly drawn by the Price Commission. After an intense enquiry over the summer, better systems were adopted for the Group's new central computing facility at Swindon. It was hoped that this would make for superior control of stocks which had increased uncomfortably in the first half of the year.

Another pressing issue was the optimum method of financing the enlarged capital expenditure programme. The finance director, George Willoughby, and Peter Humphries, who had joined the board as a non-executive director in the autumn of 1976, favoured raising additional share capital. This plan was soon abandoned when the stock market turned down in favour, in the immediate future, of increased medium term bank borrowing. The programme of releasing cash for new investment by disposing of less economic stores and unwanted sites continued. In June the old Dalys store at 199 Sauchiehall Street was sold and Dalys transferred its business up the street to a new store in the recently completed shopping complex on the site of Pettigrew & Stephens and Copland & Lye. Smalls in Princes Street in Edinburgh, property in Perth, Seccombes of Cardiff, Brown Muff's Doncaster store, and Binns' stores in Newcastle and Liverpool were put on the market at the same time. Some of the funds raised helped to meet the cost of fitting out the new Brown Muff store, renamed Rackhams, at Altrincham, the prosperous fast-growing Cheshire residential town. With no sign of any immediate recovery in trading conditions, further offers for the sale of companies to the Group were received. Astral Sports & Leisure Ltd, which operated concessions in House of Fraser and other stores, was rescued when it got into difficulties in 1978. Debenhams' proposal to hand over the celebrated but troubled Harvey Nichols of Knightsbridge was rejected. In midsummer the Group took over the whole of the share capital of Highland Tourist (Cairngorm Development) Ltd, which owned the conference centre at Aviemore on Speyside. Since the time of its development in the early 1960s under the guidance of Lord Fraser, House of Fraser had held a one-third stake in the company. The decision to take control of Aviemore and rescue Astral reflected a general conviction that over the next twenty years leisure and sports activities would assume an increasingly important place in people's lives.

In April 1978 Lonrho made a bid for SUITS, which was supported by Sir Hugh Fraser, but was contested by the other directors. The bid came at an inopportune time for the Labour Government which was piloting devolution legislation for Scotland and Wales through Parliament in an effort to appease nationalist feelings. It was referred to the Monopolies and Mergers Commission for investigation in May, partly because, by acquiring the SUITS holding in House of Fraser, Lonrho would then hold an almost thirty per cent stake in the Group. The Monopolies and Mergers Commission inquiry dragged on for a year with rumours of tension in the House of Fraser boardroom, publicly denied in March 1979. The following month Tiny Rowland gave an undertaking to the House of Fraser board that he had no intention of making an offer for the outstanding share capital of the Group. The Monopolies and Mergers Commission finally gave their approval for the bid in June 1979 and SUITS joined Lonrho shortly thereafter.

During this time the House of Fraser management had little time to worry about the ultimate ownership of their company. The Budget in April 1978 was mildly expansionary holding out the possibility that retailing might at last be less hazardous. Without relaxing its vigilance, the management committee brought forward additional projects for refurbishment and extension particularly in the south, including developments at Bristol and Lewisham. David Evans & Co of Swansea was taken over in July for £2.8 million. With a little more room for manoeuvre the warehouse provision for the whole Group was overhauled and rationalised. The expansionary mood touched the entire retail trade. Spending climbed, with strong demand for durable goods, like colour televisions and freezers.

These optimistic expectations of the spring of 1978 were soon dashed. By the autumn the House of Fraser board was so worried by the losses at their Danish store, A.C. Illum of Copenhagen, as to put it on the market. Illums, operating within even more restrictive Government controls than those in the United Kingdom, had never performed satisfactorily since its purchase seven years before. When no buyer could be found, the store was brought under the direct control of House of Fraser. At home the opening months of 1979 were dominated by a series of strikes leading to large wage settlements that effectively destroyed the Prices and Incomes policy of the last seven years. The strikes disrupted power supplies and local services, damaging every industrial and commercial sector. Development plans for the Group as a whole were temporarily put on one side. With the swift return of grim trading conditions, combined with the troubles in Northern Ireland, Robertson Ledlie Ferguson & Co, with stores in Belfast and Cork, was sold. In the midst of these difficulties the new computer centre at Swindon failed to perform to specification.

The Labour Government collapsed in March 1979 and Margaret Thatcher and the Conservatives were swept into power in one of the most decisive elections since the war. The new Government acted quickly to change the tenor of economic policy; taxes were cut and the Prices and Incomes board abolished, but VAT was increased to fifteen per cent and interest rates raised to even higher levels to hold back monetary growth and reduce inflation. These policies spelt great hardship for British industry and commerce which, as a result of the tight controls of their margins by the Price Commission, were ill-equipped to survive a sudden fall in demand. Many enterprises simply went to the wall. Throughout Britain shops closed and competition between the larger stores became severe. Even Marks & Spencer was forced to announce an £11 million package of price cuts in early September to strengthen its position in the tougher times ahead. Bill Crossan and his management committee were deeply concerned about the effect of this worsening economic environment on the future of the Group, and discussed how to proceed. If they cut prices to win business, losses would inevitably result unless costs could be reduced dramatically. In July an expenses committee was established to bring costs more firmly under control. The instal-

The store of A. C. Illum in Copenhagen, a mecca of shopping in Scandinavia.

lation of point of sale and point of receipt computer terminals linked to the central computer at Swindon were accelerated in the expectation of better oversight of purchasing. It was hoped that this system would lead to further reductions in investment in stocks and stock losses, improvements in credit control, and the introduction of an in-house credit card for the Group as a whole. Such gains were vital if House of Fraser was to match the prices of other store groups which were making similar investments. To exploit the ever increasing popularity of own label goods, particularly those of Marks & Spencer, the Allander range was extended and consolidated to include some 1,300 items. 'Allander story sections' were opened in several stores offering a fashion range of co-ordinated merchandise. As far as was practical, Allander goods were manufactured domestically, confirming the Group's commitment to the Buying

British campaign. The board, however, was not so disheartened as to refuse acquisitions in towns where the Group was still unrepresented. Taylors of Basildon was purchased later in 1979 and the old-established business of Mawer and Collingham Ltd of Lincoln early in 1980. A new Dickins & Jones store was also to be opened at Milton Keynes in one of the largest all-weather shopping developments in Europe.

In July 1979, Lonrho exercised its option to buy the remaining shares from Carter Hawley Hale. Shortly afterwards Terry Robinson, Tiny Rowland's alternate as a director, proposed a higher interim dividend than that suggested by the board, but was defeated. Later in the year Tiny Rowland had at least two meetings with Sir Hugh Fraser to discuss the level of the final dividend and the size and composition of the board, as Lonrho wished Terry Robinson and Paul Spicer (Lord Duncan-Sandys' alternate) to become full directors. At the same time Kenneth Marley from the Binns group, who retired in June 1978, was replaced by Ron Head and Murdoch McMaster. In January 1980 John Aiton retired as company secretary and director and was succeeded by David K. Milligan, the secretary of Harrods. Tiny Rowland was surprised and annoyed that the additional Lonrho nominees had not been appointed. During February House of Fraser executive directors turned their attention to the final dividend. After taking advice from the company's stockbrokers and merchant bankers, a figure of four pence was agreed. Lonrho believed the dividend should be higher, and relations between their representatives on the board and the other House of Fraser directors soon became highly charged. After a series of difficult board meetings, where the Lonrho directors opposed approval of the annual report and accounts, Tiny Rowland decided to take the matters of the dividend and the composition of the board to the shareholders. Lonrho sent out circulars criticising the record of the House of Fraser management and their 'meanness' to shareholders and calling for the appointment of additional outside directors. Shareholders were urged to vote against the re-election of the four directors retiring in rotation that year. Sir Hugh reacted sharply: 'Mr Rowland seems to forget that House of Fraser is run by a board of directors and not by one man, which seems to be the case at Lonrho.' The executive directors sought the advice of the company's institutional shareholders through their merchant bankers, S.G. Warburg, and their stockbrokers, Cazenoves. The institutional shareholders promised to support Sir Hugh Fraser and the board at the annual meeting on 19 June 1980. At the meeting Sir Hugh spelled out the number of proxies House of Fraser held and all the directors were re-elected on a show of hands. In the knowledge that they would now be defeated, Lonrho did not put their resolutions to the vote. Following the meeting the institutional shareholders urged the appointment of a non-executive chairman. The House of Fraser executive directors resisted and as a compromise it was agreed to appoint two new outside non-executive directors with broad management experience.

The executive directors were alarmed that these disputes were sapping the energy of the senior management to grapple with the rapidly deteriorating situation in the marketplace. Many shopping chains were reported during 1980 to be carrying at least half of the VAT increases of the previous year at the expense of profits instead of passing it on to customers. In London, where conditions were most severe, Whiteleys, Swan & Edgar, and Bournes all closed. Debenhams, with stores throughout the country, 'traded down amid a blaze of banners and bonanzas.' In the prevailing conditions high-volume discount stores like ASDA, Comet in electrical goods, and MFI for furniture, appeared to be gaining ground rapidly at the expense of the department stores. By the end of the year Marks & Spencer was forecasting 'a very grim decade' and Ian MacLaurin, the managing director of Tesco, predicted 'the highest rate of bankruptcies you've ever seen in the retail trade.'

In April 1980 the House of Fraser board was warned that February had been a bad month, that 'extreme difficulty' was experienced in March, and that presently 'we are barely holding our own.' The following month in an effort to stimulate sales Bill Crossan won permission for twelve months interest-free credit for purchases of more than £100 during June and July, and six months for purchases of over £75. He underlined the 'extremely serious trade position' by circulating figures which showed that the already tight margins had been squeezed by another two per cent in the last month. Bank borrowing was also rising fast and there was an urgent need to reduce stocks.

On 4 August 1980 Sir Hugh wrote to Tiny Rowland, who was out of the country, enclosing an agenda for the next day's board meeting which proposed, in accordance with the board's undertaking with the institutional shareholders, that Professor Roland Smith, Professor of Marketing at the University of Manchester Institute of Science and Technology, and Ernest Sharp, formerly joint managing director of Grand Metropolitan, should join the board at once. Professor Smith, already a director of a number of companies, was described as 'one of the few people in Britain who combine high academic respectability with business credibility.' At the meeting Sir Hugh went further, explaining that, if elected, Professor Smith would become sole deputy chairman and the other deputy chairmen, including Tiny Rowland, would demit office. When the nominations were confirmed, despite the opposition of the Lonrho directors, Sir Hugh announced the formation of an executive committee to take charge of the day-to-day management of the business. Lonrho was not to be represented on the committee. Tiny Rowland was incensed, threatening legal action against those responsible.

The executive committee rapidly set about devising a strategy for the recovery of the Group's flagging fortunes. Professor Roland Smith, as a marketing expert, understood the need to identify precisely customer expectations: 'Our customers believe that our stores, our product ranges and our services are attractive. They believe we are keenly competitive on price and that we promote our products with excitement ... As well as producing profits, we believe our stores are part of the quality of life within local communities. Our management structure places great emphasis upon customer needs in regional locations. One of our major stores – Harrods – is regarded by most international retailers and consumers as the finest and most prestigious store in the world.' If these contentions were only partly correct it was the job of the executive committee to make them true for every store in the Group. Urgent reviews were undertaken into the Group's operational structure, and property portfolio. By the end of October George Willoughby had worked out a scheme for the reorganisation of the Group by the creation of House of Fraser (Stores) Ltd which would be responsible for operating the department stores through separate management divisions rather than the present subsidiary companies. All the subsidiary companies, with the exception of House of Fraser (Northern) Ltd which would be renamed House of Fraser Stores Ltd, would be liquidated with very large savings in both administrative costs and tax. Despite the fears of some directors that these changes would affect the character of individual stores, they were implemented. There were similar worries about the likely outcome of action to extend and give more coherence to central buying which some thought would impose a 'uniformly grey' pattern. Fundamental to the efficient running of central buying was computerised stock

OPPOSITE AND BELOW
Details of the decorative tiles in Harrods' food hall.

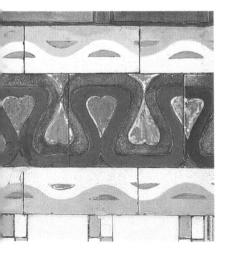

control, and efficient warehousing and transport. Additional impetus was given to the installation of point of sale and point of receipt terminals with the allocation of £12.5 million over and above the £4.5 million already spent on the new computer systems to complete the network by 1985. New warehouses were planned by the Dingle group in the south-west and the Army & Navy and Chiesman stores in the south-east as part of a five-year rationalisation programme.

In scrutinising House of Fraser stores themselves, the executive committee defined more clearly the objectives in making new investments and their relationship to overall marketing policy. Rebuilding and refurbishment were placed on a three- to five-year rolling cycle instead of the existing year on year arrangements. London, where trade had been badly hit in the previous three years, was given immediate attention. The huge Barkers store in Kensington, which had never earned adequate returns, was to be totally redeveloped, with a reduced trading area for House of Fraser, a small multiple store, several shop units and offices. Aleck Craddock, who assumed direct responsibility for Harrods on Robert Midgely's retirement in January 1981, busied himself in putting together the 'Harrod's Major Project' which would increase the sales area on the fourth floor by an additional 40,000 square feet and allow for the expansion of the food hall, resulting in an estimated £2 million increase in returns. While feasibility studies were carried out, work went ahead in fitting new escalators on the west side of the store to enhance traffic flows and the density of existing trading operations. Outside London new stores and extensions were planned over the next three years for Bromley, Perth, Maidstone, Chichester, Carlisle, Aberdeen, Lewisham, Kirkcaldy and Paisley, often as part of major town-centre redevelopments. Altogether these investments were to cost considerably more than the £56.5 million spent on acquiring and developing stores in the previous three years.

As the executive committee was energetically setting the agenda for the future of House of Fraser, the Lonrho directors, excluded from these discussions, continually questioned decisions, whether they were presented to the board for approval or not. Before the formation of the executive committee Sir Hugh and his senior colleagues had considered the future of several stores which produced poor returns. They had decided either to dispose of D.H. Evans in Oxford Street as a going concern or sell the property and lease it back. When Tiny Rowland found out from a press report in September that the Group was negotiating a sale and lease-back agreement with the Legal & General Insurance for both D.H. Evans and the Rackhams store in Birmingham, he wrote to Sir Hugh stating that Lonrho was opposed to any such arrangement. After further correspondence and two board meetings the lease-back was approved on 4 November 1980, and shareholders were informed by circular the following day. Lonrho responded with its own circular attacking the sale and lease-backs and demanded an extraordinary general meeting to consider a resolution preventing the directors from going ahead. A date for the extraordinary general meeting was set for 20 January 1981 with both sides sending out documents explaining their positions. The lobbying was intense. Tiny Rowland accused the City institutions of not wanting him to succeed as it was their job 'to pick up cheap property assets.' He also questioned how long Sir Hugh could remain as chairman: 'Both Professor Roland Smith and Mr Ernest Sharp have their eye on his job.' Ernest Sharp, ignoring these allegations, spoke strongly in favour of the lease-backs, describing them as 'a damn good deal and we are certain that Mr Rowland would be doing it if he owned House of Fraser.' Professor Smith called on shareholders to see 'Lonrho off heavily this time.' Sir Hugh regarded Lonrho's interference in the Group as 'intolerable, tasteless and obstructive.' There was a growing conviction amongst

The charcuterie in Harrods' magnificently refurbished and extended food hall.

D.H. Evans store in Oxford Street, which was at the centre of a disagreement between House of Fraser and Lonrho, in 1981.

the institutions that Lonrho's harassment of the House of Fraser board had gone far enough and if they were serious in their intentions they should make a full bid. One pension fund manager complained angrily: 'Tiny and Sir Hugh have been using House of Fraser as a personal battling ground for too long. In my view they should both now go.'

The dispute took an unexpected course when, on the eve of the meeting, Tiny Rowland wrote to Sir Hugh asking if the fact that his cheques for gambling tokens had been dishonoured meant that he was insolvent and therefore statutorily debarred from holding office as a company director. He requested the post-ponement of the extraordinary general meeting. Nevertheless, the meeting took place and Lonrho's resolution was defeated. Later in the day Tiny Rowland repeated his concern to the board. Sir Hugh explained that he had a long standing arrangement with his bankers not to honour his cheques in an attempt to curb his urge to gamble. He reported that he had tendered his resignation to 'his colleagues on the board' but that this had been refused. Immediately afterwards Tiny Rowland invited Sir Hugh to meet him privately at some time in the near future. The executive directors urged Sir Hugh to take one of them with him, but, in the event, he went alone two days later on 22 January 1981 to meet Tiny Rowland at the Marine Hotel in Troon. In what was described as one of the most bizarre episodes in British business history, Sir Hugh and Tiny Rowland were reconciled and pledged that they would work together in the future. Together they called for the immediate removal of Professor Smith. Lonrho at once cancelled an advertisement offering their House of Fraser shares for sale at open tender, which was to have appeared in the press the following day.

Shocked by this dramatic turn of events, the other House of Fraser directors called Sir Hugh to account on 23 January. When he made it clear that he would from now on support Lonrho in any further disputes, the executive directors finally lost confidence in his ability to act as their chairman. A board meeting was called for 28 January to review Sir Hugh's position. The day before, Lonrho wrote to Sir Hugh making a formal offer for House of Fraser at 150 pence per share on condition that the composition of the board remained unaltered. The board at their meeting the following day rejected the offer and George Willoughby moved that Sir Hugh should no longer hold the position of their chairman. After this resolution had been passed, Professor Smith was elected chairman. Only the Lonrho representatives supported Sir Hugh. George Willoughby echoed the feelings of all the directors with long service to the company, when he said later: 'It gave me no personal satisfaction. It was a very emotional meeting for us all.' For the time being Sir Hugh remained an executive director. After the meeting Sir Hugh was unabashed, looking forward to 'going along in the same ship with Tiny Rowland.'

Professor Smith was determined to fight, telling the press that he regretted Sir Hugh had chosen to align himself with Lonrho, but 'our loyalties must remain to the company and its shareholders and not to one man.' Referring to the Lonrho offer as miserable and half-priced, he formed a bid committee to co-ordinate the Group's defence campaign. The terms of the Lonrho offer were distributed to shareholders on 16 February. Within days Tiny Rowland was taunting Professor Smith to come out and defend himself: 'He's far too long in the corner with his crowd of seconds.' Vilifying the new chairman 'as an odd-day-a-week employee,' he declared, 'We have lost confidence in the financial acumen of the board, we want to take over or sell.' Tiny Rowland had underestimated his opponent who was not to be panicked by such tactics. On 26 February Professor Smith struck back with a hard-hitting circular titled 'Your SUPERVALUE shares – Hold on – they're worth much more – LONRHO MUST BE STOPPED.' The main thrust of the House of Fraser's defence was that the underlying asset value of the Group's properties was greatly understated not only in the balance sheet but also in a hurriedly commissioned revaluation: 'A study of six properties with redevelopment potential shows a significant surplus for House of Fraser which would more than double their new valuation.' He stated that it was the board's policy to unlock the hidden supervalue contained in group properties for the benefit of shareholders. Professor Smith carried the attack into Tiny Rowland's camp by raising the same questions about Lonrho's performance and management expertise as he had raised about House of Fraser's: 'House of Fraser is a financial asset to Lonrho and is needed by Lonrho to remedy its own structural financial weakness aggravated by very heavy borrowings.' Summarising House of Fraser's defence, the circular declared that the offer price was 'less than half the asset value of your company at 302 pence per share,' ignored 'the record profits earned in the last half year,' took 'no account of your Company's ability to realise its earning potential,' was 'a tiny premium over the market price of your shares,' and 'ignored the unique value of Harrods.' The day after this circular was published, 27 February, the Secretary of State for Trade and Industry, worried that Lonrho might launch a dawn raid on House of Fraser, referred the bid to the Monopolies and Mergers Commission with an instruction that the report should be published in six months.

Any expectation that there would now be a cooling in the hostile relations between the two companies was soon quashed. At a tense board meeting on 26 March Tiny Rowland and Terry Robinson requested confidential financial and other information over and above that supplied for the meeting. When they refused to declare whether Lonrho would renew its bid or not if the Monopolies and Mergers Commission found in their favour, the board, after taking legal advice, had no alternative but to assume that under the terms of the City takeover code Lonrho was still in contention for House of Fraser. It was agreed that this being so the Lonrho directors' interests and those of Sir Hugh conflicted with those of the company and they should only be supplied with information necessary for them to discharge their duties as members of the House of Fraser board during the course of the inquiry. Following this decision Sir Hugh resigned as chairman of Harrods, which he had recently assumed after the retirement of Robert Midgely, on the grounds he would not be in receipt of sufficient information to discharge his duties.

Only too aware that they would have to work hard to achieve the promises held out in their defence, the management committee returned to the urgent task of revitalising the Group. Bill Crossan announced an increased emphasis on fashion which was expected to receive a fillip from the Royal Wedding of the Prince of Wales to Lady Diana Spencer in April. Aleck Craddock, who had been appointed chairman and managing director of Harrods, completed his plans for the store and the Group agreed to participate in a large town-centre development in Perth. Lonrho maintained its relentless questioning of any projects that required board approval. When, for example, Aleck Craddock presented his 'Harrods Major Project 1981–4' for approval, Sir Hugh and the Lonrho representatives doubted whether it would achieve the estimated return. Bill Crossan and David Milligan were disappointed with Sir Hugh's attitude to the scheme which repeated many of the arguments voiced against Way In in 1969 that he himself had dispelled. In September Lonrho questioned the decision to invest in new buildings in Scotland, particularly the scheme in Perth, suggesting that the policy of having the best store in every major town was misguided. Professor Smith, making it clear that investment anywhere in Britain had a very low return in the prevailing economic conditions, called for the board to take a long-term view. During August House of Fraser lost the opportunity to buy the Scotcade company because the negotiations had been leaked to the satirical magazine *Private Eye* immediately after details had been circulated in the board papers.

After the deadline for the publication of the Monopolies and Mergers Commission's report passed in August, the board meetings grew more and more acrimonious. Professor Smith and George Willoughby were unable to obtain the support of Lonrho's Paul Spicer in September for a letter to the staff congratulating them on the excellent results for the first half year. His excuse was that he lacked the necessary information to make such a judgment. The Monopolies and Mergers Commission reported, with one dissenting voice, on 9 December 1981 that there was 'a very real and substantial risk that the efficiency of House of Fraser would deteriorate seriously as a result of the merger, and that it would be detrimental to the public interest that it should be exposed by the merger to such a risk.' This conclusion was based largely on the almost inevitable departure, after the bitterness of the months preceding the bid, of all the House of Fraser executive directors if the merger came about. A delighted Professor Smith immediately wrote to shareholders to inform them, 'We shall be seeking to ensure that Lonrho will not frustrate the efforts we are making to develop the business in the interests of *all* our shareholders.' The press was not so enthusiastic, believing that the report's conclusions were flawed and that there were no real obstacles to Lonrho's bid. Tiny Rowland, encouraged by this support, warned, 'This is not over yet. We have a large stake in House of Fraser and we are not going away.'

Within a week of the publication of the report Lonrho at the Government's insistence, gave an undertaking that it would not, either alone or with others, seek to increase its shareholding to more than thirty per cent. The Government for its part indicated that it would be willing to release Lonrho from this commitment if circumstances changed. Welcome as the outcome of the inquiry was to the House of Fraser executive directors, it did nothing to ease the tensions in the boardroom, particularly as Tiny Rowland had been widely reported in the press as saying it would be weeks rather than months before Lonrho renewed its offer. Considering that a 'bid situation' still existed, Professor Smith refused, again on legal advice, to make further information available to the Lonrho representatives and Sir Hugh. Lonrho approached the Secretary of State for Trade and Industry on 26 January 1982 asking that they should be released from their undertaking. After consulting the Office of Fair Trading, this request was turned down.

In the circumstances the executive committee decided that Sir Hugh Fraser should no longer continue to hold an executive position in the company. When he was informed on 25 February Sir Hugh resigned from the board on the grounds he wished 'to pursue' his own line of business, to the genuine regret of those directors who had worked with him in happier times before the failure of the merger with Boots. He had recently acquired Paisleys, an old-established Glasgow drapery business. In a welter of publicity the new store was renamed 'Sir Hugh', the first of a projected chain in the West of Scotland. Despite all the adverse publicity that had dogged him over the last eight years, Sir Hugh remained an immensely popular figure in Glasgow and the west of Scotland. Like his father before him, he gave freely of his time and talents in helping those much less fortunate than himself. Through the family trust he gave generously to medical research in Scotland. In 1981 he provided an endowment of over £1.5 million that allowed the National Trust for Scotland to acquire the Island of Iona for the nation as a memorial to his father. He also gave his Mugdock estate

The glorious island of Iona, the cradle of Christianity in Scotland, purchased for the nation as a memorial to Lord Fraser.

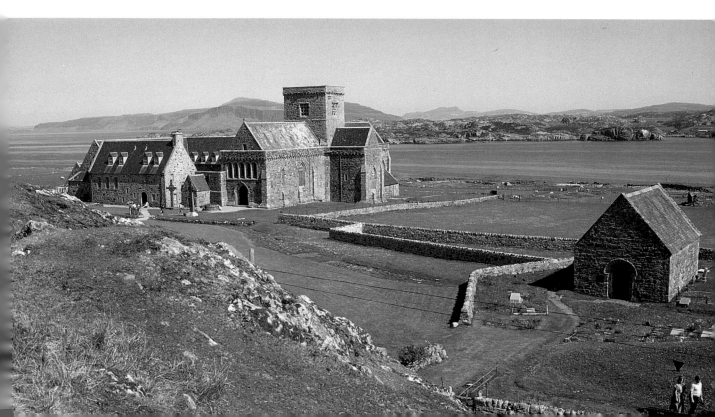

to the north of Glasgow to form the Mugdock Country Park with its striking ruins and panoramic vistas south across the city. To the end of his life in May 1987, even though changed by fatal illness, he remained a striking personality. A friend wrote on learning of his death: 'No one had a clue just how generous Hugh was. He gave huge sums to cancer relief and other good causes and never looked for any credit. He was a good man, much maligned sometimes but a kinder man than anyone understood.'

The Monopolies and Mergers Commission's inquiry had made heavy demands on the time of Professor Smith and his senior executives, which they could ill afford. The Conservative Government's much-vaunted economic miracle had not materialised and the arduous conditions in the high street persisted. The Kendal Milne furniture store in Manchester was sold, along with surplus properties in Bournemouth, Bristol and Aberdeen. During the autumn of 1981 a firm of outside management consultants specialising in the retail trade, Management Horizons, were brought in to survey the operations of Rackhams of Birmingham, and in January 1982, those of Army & Navy in Victoria. These and other investigations showed House of Fraser's space productivity was poor. Professor

The Army & Navy Victoria Street frontage today.

Smith wondered if the upper floors of the larger stores, where performance was markedly worse than on the ground and first floors, could be converted to sports and leisure centres. Drawing on his experience of similar problems in the 1960s, Bill Crossan was unconvinced, suggesting that the solution must be to adopt new merchandising techniques. Management Horizons suggested the introduction of Lifestyle departments throughout the Group to sell well-designed clothes and furnishings as aspects of one total image. There was a general concensus that this approach to merchandising would come to characterise retailing in the 1990s. House of Fraser targeted for Lifestyle women customers aged between twenty and thirty-five, a market which was being successfully exploited by the Burton group through Dorothy Perkins and Peter Robinson. Management Horizons developed the concept and took the name from an experiment initiated by the manager of Frasers' Buchanan Street store who, during 1982, combined the basement houseware department with the ground-floor Impact Boutique in a new department on the fourth floor as a young person's Habitat. Named Impact Lifestyle, it was an immediate success, achieving higher margins than existing departments and suggesting to Management Horizons that it might provide a solution for under-utilised floors in other stores. Prototype departments were opened in Dundee and Inverness later in the year with similar results. Lifestyle departments for stores in England were planned for 1983. However, Lifestyle could do nothing in the short term to bring relief to the hard-pressed Group.

The reorganisation of the trading groups proceeded as fast as was practical. The eleven Chiesman stores in south-east England were integrated with the Army & Navy group, and the D. H. Evans stores in Oxford Street and Wood Green amalgamated with the Dingles group, yielding considerable savings through the merger of accounting operations. With sales drifting relentlessly downwards during the spring, drastic steps were taken to reduce stocks and to rationalise and concentrate supplies in an endeavour to maintain constant prices. Merchandising strategy was overhauled following the appointment of Peter Brimacombe as merchandising director in April. The emphasis was shifted towards fashion and leisurewear. Budgets for store promotions and advertising were increased 'with significant contributions from our suppliers.' A merchandising bulletin was launched in October 1982 where Peter Brimacombe could expound his views and solicit information from House of Fraser staff. In the first bulletin he rehearsed his fears that merchandise in all the large high street stores was beginning to look remarkably similar and competition was confined almost entirely to price. With Lifestyle in mind, he called the staff to concentrate 'their efforts on merchandise ranges and concepts that are more innovative, distinctive and different from the store next door, making this the main reason to attract customers within our doors rather than over-reliance on price appeal.'

By this time the economic indicators were pointing firmly upwards, giving added incentive both to improvements in merchandising, and to the modernisation of House of Fraser stores up and down the country. Directly planning permission was received work began at Barkers and at Harrods. The go-ahead was given to the refurbishment of Frasers' store in Edinburgh at an eventual cost of some £6 million. With the installation of the computer network ahead of schedule, preparations were brought forward for the phased introduction of a Frasercard to counter similar innovations by other high street stores. The promise of sustained prosperity was rapidly changing the shape of retailing. New specialist shops were opened in every sector of the trade, including that of food where the multiples had made the largest inroads since the war. Long-established drapery chains were transformed by new management or owners to sell increasingly fashionable designer clothes for younger customers whose disposable incomes could be expected to rise fastest. The inspiration for many of these changes came from Sir Terence Conran, the founder of Habitat. In 1982 he became chairman of the Hepworths clothing group and purchased the unprofitable Kendal's chain of women's-wear shops. Taking as an example the popular Benetton franchise stores in Europe, he rethought the image, changed the name to Next and chose to focus on stylish clothes for women over twenty-five. The furnishings and fittings were designed to be both eye-catching and flexible, displaying the co-ordinated ranges of fashion to best advantage. Under the dynamic leadership of George Davies, the results were impressive, with sales jumping from £7 million to £40 million in less than twelve months. At the same time Habitat acquired Mothercare, the babywear and maternity chain. Sir Terence declared his intention of making it a springboard for a chain of young fashion shops.

With property ownership at the heart of the Conservative Government's ethos, more and more store groups, like Marks & Spencer, which had previously concentrated on clothes, began to sell furnishings and household goods, blurring any remaining distinction between multiples and department stores. Laura Ashley, which had already taken this route in 1972, extended its range of furnishings setting new standards in design. There was a belief that if customers enjoyed buying clothes in a specialist store, they would also enjoy buying furniture and furnishings with the same image. As Peter Brimacombe had rightly predicted, for such customers, competition between stores was becoming less a matter of price and more a matter of quality and lifestyle. These concepts quickly made an impact on developers and planners engaged in creating large town-centre shopping complexes and pedestrian precincts. If the customer profile for the development was properly defined, retail units could be leased to shops with complementary merchandise in the correct price range. In November 1979 the Forum des Halles opened in Paris directed specifically at the top end of the

Next in Buchanan Street, Glasgow, one of the shops in the chain built up by George Davies.

The spectacular Forum des Halles shopping complex in Paris.

market. The futuristic architecture and the sophisticated quality of the shops attracted over 200,000 shoppers on the first day. Such thinking underlay House of Fraser's redevelopment of Barkers. Part and parcel of this more careful approach to retail development was a dramatic improvement in the standard of shop design, fitting and presentation, taking advantage of the many new materials that were now available. Encouraged by the success of Conran Associates, specialist shop design consultancies were established to provide retailers, in the words of Richard Birtchnell of Burton's Top Shop, with 'a unique and unmistaken identity – a fresh statement – that will stand the test of time and also be ahead of the competition.'

Some retailers, like Great Universal Stores, saw an opportunity in these increasingly homogeneous shopping concepts to revive mail order. Publishing an almost identical glossy catalogue under six titles, including Burlington and Peter Craig, Littlewoods captured five per cent of sales of women's clothing by the late 1970s. Unable to ignore such success, retailers, whose main business was on the high street, followed suit. Most chose to enhance their image and merchandising strategy through the publication of free magazines for customers. Towards the close of 1981 Harrods introduced a twice-yearly mail-order magazine. All these profound changes in retailing required the undivided attention of the House of Fraser board if the Group was to benefit from the upturn in the economy.

However, Lonrho's inexorable scrutiny of the decisions of the executive committee continued. Their representatives demanded additional information on almost every issue, questioning the wisdom of a joint venture with Mitsukoshi,

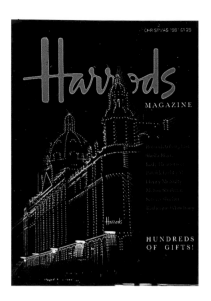

Harrods' new mail order magazine, 1981.

the largest store group in Japan, to sell Harrods' merchandise, and seeking clarification on depreciation policy. Paul Spicer and Terry Robinson also doubted plans to extend the range of financial services offered to Harrods' customers in co-operation with the Bank of America, even though there was agreement amongst observers of the retail scene that this was a logical development for store groups. In late May 1982 Lonrho tabled two resolutions to be put to the annual meeting the following month. The first related to the allotment of unissued shares and the second requested that the directors give the shareholders 'the opportunity to consider any offer made for their shares.' A special committee was established by the board to deal with the matter. After a further flurry of circulars both resolutions were defeated at the annual meeting. On 16 September 1982 Lonrho announced that 'it would not wish in the present circumstances to renew its bid for House of Fraser,' but asked that its request to be released from the undertaking to the Government should lie on the table to await further developments. On the same day Lonrho notified the House of Fraser board that it intended to requisition an extraordinary general meeting to consider resolutions relating to the de-merger of Harrods and the removal of Professor Smith both as a director and as chairman. Tiny Rowland's case for demerger rested on the large contribution Harrods was making to the Group's profitability which was then deployed not to improve Harrods' facilities but those of other House of Fraser stores. Fundamental to the proposed demerger was an expectation that the name Harrods, symbolising style and quality, could be used under lucrative licence agreements throughout the world. House of Fraser complained that the executive directors had never heard any of these arguments from the two Lonrho rep-resentatives on the board and asked that the request for the extraordinary general meeting be withdrawn so that 'this important matter may be discussed in a reasoned manner and without the rancour of personal attacks on the company chairman.'

When this suggestion was ignored, the situation in the boardroom became very fraught. Professor Smith immediately commissioned an exhaustive investigation of the demerger suggestion to be carried out by a special working party. He was well aware that if it was to be defeated, the board would not only have to show that it did not make good financial sense, but also have a detailed corporate plan to put in its place. His position was weakened by the announcement before the end of September of a pre-tax loss of £387,000 for the first six months of the year. Confident that this was merely a temporary setback, the senior executives and outside consultants worked at breakneck speed to assemble all the necessary facts and figures on which various projections could be based. Shareholders were yet again bombarded with circulars. The extraordinary meeting was held over two days – 4 and 5 November – to allow the polls to be counted. At the meeting the second resolution relating to Professor Smith was not put to the vote, because it was clear that it enjoyed little support. Tiny Rowland, however, cautioned, 'He shouldn't be too cocky. After all he'll have to fight another day.' The first resolution was passed requiring the board to formulate proposals for the de-merger of Harrods into a separate public company and to convene another extraordinary general meeting within ninety days to consider the matter. Throughout the proceedings Professor Smith stressed that he could see no merit in demerger – 'I will not be persuaded by a foolscap sheet of paper. I want the facts and I want the figures.' He made his disapproval of Lonrho's actions very plain: 'If this is your idea of a game would you please play it somewhere else in future. We have work to do and we want to get on with our proper job of making profits for the shareholders. Get your tanks off our lawn.' He strongly suspected

that Lonrho was 'trying to make House of Fraser unmanageable. That sticks out a mile even to a simple mind like mine.'

The resolution could not have come at a worse time for House of Fraser, right at the beginning of the Christmas season – the principal trading period of the retailing year. Lonrho rejected a plea for the timetable to be relaxed to take pressure off the Group's over-worked senior staff. The draft 360-page report by a special working party was completed on Christmas Eve, and circulated for comment to the Group's main shareholders, who had formed a case committee. It reached no conclusion but simply stated the facts. This consultative process with the case committee would inevitably be time-consuming and on 20 January 1983 the board was told that the ninety-day deadline was impractical. Lonrho's response was hostile and their representatives on the board tirelessly cajoled the other directors until the report was presented on 31 March.

At this meeting the only item on the agenda was consideration of papers prepared by the working party on demerger, collectively known as the 'Red

Book.' Five papers on the subject were introduced by George Willoughby, the chairman of the working party, and all the directors were invited to comment. Aleck Craddock, the chairman and managing director of Harrods, had no doubt that demerger offered no attractions. It would increase organisational costs, make Harrods very exposed to takeover (Sears Holdings plc had already indicated their interest), and leave the store vulnerable to short-term fluctuations, such as foreign exchange movements which could interrupt the flow of foreign visitors. Without Dickins & Jones, Harrods would not have been able to expand in London beyond its Knightsbridge site. The store would suffer from the loss of referrals from other House of Fraser stores, incur higher credit-card charges and, most importantly, be unable to draw on the central services provided by the Group – essential for profitable trading.

The Lonrho directors objected to the whole tenor of these arguments. Ernest Sharp rejoined by pointing out that even when House of Fraser acquired Harrods in 1959 it was already part of a group. He also drew attention to the serious tax implications of demerger which would place a heavy burden on an independent Harrods in unrecovered Advance Corporation Tax and stated that the management and staff were 'uniformly' against the plan. Professor Smith then proposed that a resolution be put to the extraordinary general meeting accepting 'the recommendation of the board of directors to shareholders that Harrods should remain within the House of Fraser Group,' and expressing 'confidence in the board'. Paul Spicer of Lonrho retorted, 'of course we have confidence in the board,' and asked that the resolution be drafted so as not to confuse the position. The board supported Professor Smith's proposal and Paul Spicer was told that Lonrho could put their own resolution relating simply to demerger proposals.

There followed an intense campaign to persuade shareholders to support the board's position. Professor Smith wrote to them on 12 April 1983 outlining the case against demerger and criticising 'the destructive influence of Lonrho,' 'leading to yet another public debate which is unsettling to our employees and damaging to our business ... It is difficult to over-emphasize the fundamental importance of Harrods to our Group. The suggested separation does not involve spinning off an unrelated business but wrenching apart two complementary parts of an integrated retailing group'. Lonrho replied with their own circular, using both House of Fraser and Harrods' logos, putting their case: 'Protect Harrods and Secure Its Future For Your Benefit – Allow Harrods – the star performer – to fulfil its true potential without being the guarantor and cash generator for the rest of the group'. At the meeting on 6 May the resolution was passed, but Lonrho demanded a further meeting to vote on the demerger question alone, arguing that the resolution had clouded the minds of shareholders with its reference to confidence in the board. A further meeting was fixed for 30 June, with yet another round of intense canvassing of the shareholders by both camps.

While House of Fraser had been locked in this bitter dispute with Lonrho, a takeover battle had been raging for United Drapery Stores (UDS), owners of the Allders department stores, the John Collier chain of men's outfitters and the Richard chain of women's-wear shops. The original bid had been put together in January by a consortium called Bassingshaw, including Heron International and the newly revitalised Burton Group. Ralph Halpern of Burtons was interested in the John Collier and Richard shops which he believed he could 'quickly' turn round into profitable operations. The Hanson Trust soon after began building a stake in UDS, leading to a full bid at the beginning of April. Late in the day on 30 April, House of Fraser signalled that if Hanson's bid was successful House of

Fraser would like to acquire the Allders stores as part of their continuing commitment to extend the Group's national coverage. Although Hanson was in control of UDS early the following month, nothing came of the approach from House of Fraser because the attention of the board was now firmly focused on the next extraordinary general meeting at the end of June.

House of Fraser had taken legal opinion as to how best to achieve a tax efficient demerger of Harrods well before the first meeting on 12 April. The board had been advised that this would require a special resolution to be passed under the Companies Act of 1948 to effect a scheme of arrangement supervised by the High Court. This procedure would protect the interest of all shareholders, giving them the right to make their views known directly in the courts. Accordingly two resolutions were tabled for the meeting: an ordinary resolution by Lonrho approving 'the proposal to demerge Harrods,' which required a simple majority to be passed, and a special resolution authorising a scheme of arrangement to transfer all the ordinary share capital of Harrods to a new company which would issue shares *pro rata* to existing House of Fraser shareholders. This special resolution required at least a seventy-five per cent majority to succeed. Professor Smith and George Willoughby met Tiny Rowland and other Lonrho directors on 3 June 1983. They were told that an understanding could be reached if Tiny Rowland became deputy chairman of House of Fraser, if the Lonrho representation on the board was doubled, and if there was a commitment to look again in depth at the proposal to demerge Harrods. Convinced that these terms would be almost tantamount to a takeover, Professor Smith was more determined than ever to thwart Lonrho's ambitions. He wrote to the shareholders on 22 June quoting an article in a financial journal: 'Hobbies are all very well but obsessions are something else, and the continued pre-occupations with House of Fraser of certain Lonrho directors would seem to have gone far enough'.

The extraordinary general meeting took place in Glasgow in a glare of publicity. In a strongly worded speech, Professor Smith outlined the board's position, countering criticism that the special resolution was a 'smart thing to do' by stressing that it was the only thing to do – 'to demonstrate that the support necessary for the implementation of a demerger is not there'. He was adamant that House of Fraser would continue to pursue its new trading strategy and demanded that the board 'should be given a reasonable opportunity to prove that it is the right strategy'. The special resolution was carried with 67,541,696 voting in support and 64,055,974 against, falling far short of the seventy-five per cent of votes required under the Companies Act. The ordinary resolution was carried with 68,182,818 voting for and 63,445,416 voting against. Professor Smith, refusing to be moved by this setback, wrote again to shareholders on 7 July telling them that 'there can be no effective demerger of Harrods and your Board regards the demerger debate as over'. Lonrho refused to accept this decision and took advertising space in major newspapers, demanding that the board honour the majority view and 'put forward detailed proposals for the demerger, or give way to Directors who will'.

Time-consuming as the fight against demerger was, the board was able to use it as a vehicle for defining policy precisely for the rest of the decade. The existing objectives spelled out since 1980 were confirmed: 'increase sales per square foot of store space, maintain or improve gross margins so as to increase gross profits per square foot of floor space, increase the rate of stockturn and thus increase the return on capital invested in stocks, control operating costs, and increase net profits after charging each store an economic market rental'. Out of the application of these aims in the past two years had emerged a new strategy involving the major refurbishment of stores, the re-allocation of selling space between different categories of goods, more selective and competitive pricing and a number of new merchandising programmes designed to broaden the appeal of the Group's stores and goods. Early in 1983 this strategy began to be implemented in a coherent fashion throughout the Group. Professor Smith told shareholders, 'what we are proposing with our new trading strategy is to de-mature the House of Fraser store business – refresh it – re-position it in marketing terms and make much higher profits as a result'. Initial appraisals based on information supplied for the compilation of the Red Book were made for every store in the Group and a rolling programme of detailed external market and financial evaluations started. It was calculated that this would take Management Horizons a year to complete.

The first outcome of these investigations was a decision to create a younger fashion image for Dickins & Jones' store in London giving emphasis to high-margin departments where profits were assured. D.H. Evans was also to be re-launched, with a Lifestyle department, bringing some of the grandeur back to shopping. A timetable was set for the opening of other Lifestyle departments in Birmingham, Bromley, and Camberley. A national launch of Lifestyle took place on 5 July 1983 in London, with the slogan 'It's what you wear. It's how you live'. Buying for Lifestyle demanded an energetic and innovative approach to ensure exclusivity and greater centralisation to prevent margins being eroded by overstocking. The Lifestyle approach was echoed in November by Sir Terence Conran when he purchased the Richard Shops from the Hanson Trust, as part of the break up of UDS, with the intention of presenting fashion merchandise in the Habitat image. Burtons announced plans to begin selling clothes for all the family, launching an experimental store in Poole. Marks & Spencer responded by rethinking their whole range to incorporate exciting new designs. The mood of the retail sector was buoyant. During the Christmas season branches of some chain stores ran out of stock before the holiday. The consumer boom encouraged developers to revive schemes for shopping centres that had been abandoned during the depression of the late 1970s. Many of these were very ambitious in concept with large covered central shopping malls, striking architecture, and an emphasis on the spectacular. Their novelty, combined with generous provision of fast-food eating areas and high standards of service, were designed to attract both customers and tenants. The shop units continued to be of different sizes to suit all comers, but with an increasing number of smaller areas for specialist outlets. Concerns like Dash, the leisurewear company, and Benetton, the Italian-owned franchise organisation, that operated in Britain principally through concessions within department stores, began reserving these units.

There was no reduction in the tension in the boardroom of House of Fraser over the summer of 1983, with Lonrho requesting and receiving a stream of statistics and other information relating to the performance of the Group. The confrontation between Professor Smith and Lonrho deepened with further rancour, particularly after his insistence that the logos of House of Fraser and Harrods could not be used without the board's express permission. Terry Robinson and Paul Spicer retaliated by criticising Professor Smith's use of a company house in Kensington, stating it 'was becoming a matter of national interest'. Ernest Sharp had little doubt that this was another deliberate tactic to make House of Fraser unmanageable. During August 1983 House of Fraser's executive directors became suspicious that 'certain shareholders had acquired their holdings recently to act in concert with Lonrho' and requested an investigation by the Department of Trade and Industry. The inspector extended his report in December following allegations by Lonrho about the existence of a

OPPOSITE ABOVE *Lifestyle at Binns promoted on a Tyne & Wear bus.*

OPPOSITE BELOW *The new Lifestyle department at Howells of Cardiff in 1983.*

'concert party' comprising a number of institutions and other persons connected with House of Fraser and alleged to be opposed to Lonrho. The previous month the Lonrho representatives on the board commenced proceedings against House of Fraser to prevent 'the Group approving or sanctioning capital expenditure or entering contracts without first providing the board with all the necessary information to enable the board to give due and proper consideration to such expenditure'. The Court of Session in Edinburgh declined to grant an interim interdict on 23 November. After the hearing George Willoughby commented, with obvious relief, 'Had this interdict been granted Lord Duncan-Sandys and Mr Rowland would have effectively posessed veto powers that would have enabled them to argue in the Courts on every decision House of Fraser wished to take where money was involved in modernising any of House of Fraser's stores'. In December 1983 the board and the country was shocked by the IRA bombing outside Harrods at the height of the Christmas sales. Although the whole board at its first meeting in the New Year of 1984 congratulated the staff on their exemplary behaviour, the shadow of the outrage did nothing to lessen the acrimony at the meeting.

By mid-March 1984 Professor Smith and his executives had completed the next stage of their analysis of future strategy. Management Horizons and Allied International Designers (AID) were invited to make a full presentation to the board, refining the corporate objective. The presentation showed how a modest increase in each store's revenue could produce a marked improvement in net profit. This could only be accomplished by winning new customers and raising the spending of existing customers. It was claimed that already the statistics compiled by Management Horizons were helping the Group re-position stores to appeal to the largest spread of the population. AID recommended the use of standard design concepts which would not only be cost effective but also create a unified image for House of Fraser. These conclusions were accepted and the executive committee began adjusting their detailed plans accordingly. One of the directors, Murdoch McMaster, was given overall responsibility for implementing a £100 million refurbishment programme. A leaping stag with a more progressive image replaced the old stag's head logo, which had served the Group since the adoption of limited liability by Fraser Sons & Co in 1909. Trade was at last running ahead of budget and the outlook seemed more optimistic than for some time. There was, however, no time to lose if House of Fraser was to benefit from the upturn. Their competitors were jumping unashamedly on the 'Lifestyle' bandwagon. Massive investment programmes were announced throughout the stores sector, including the expenditure of £60 million in the coming year alone in revamping the Burton group. Sir Terence Conran launched 'Now' as a young person's fashion boutique within Mothercare shops and pressed on with the refurbishment of his Richards chain, declaring that decisions about merchandise would only be taken after the environment had been upgraded. The competition in the high street was intense. Even Marks & Spencer was finding the going very tough, lacking the necessary technology to collect vital sales data as rapidly as their rivals.

On 16 May 1984 Lonrho demanded resolutions to be put at the next House of Fraser annual meeting to increase the maximum number of directors from eighteen to twenty-five and to appoint twelve named individuals to the board, six of whom were directors of Lonrho. The stated purpose of the resolution was to ensure that the issue of the demerger of Harrods was fairly put to the shareholders. Professor Smith reacted angrily: 'This is a takeover of House of Fraser without using money. Lonrho are trying the first cashless takeover in

Britain'. Recognising the strength of this argument, the Secretary of State once more referred the matter to the Monopolies and Mergers Commission on 31 May. During the following month Mohamed Al Fayed, who had been a director of Lonrho until 1974, approached Tiny Rowland with an offer to buy Lonrho's stake in House of Fraser. Tiny Rowland replied in friendly terms on 3 July – 'I am so pleased that you are taking an interest in House of Fraser and hope it will continue'. The next day Lonrho gave an interim undertaking to the Secretary of State to withdraw the resolutions relating to the enlargement of the board and only request the appointment of two additional directors, Terry Robinson and Paul Spicer who had previously acted as alternates. In the meantime John Griffiths, the inspector of the Department of Trade and Industry, reported that he could find no evidence of a concert party operating on either side to acquire shares during the previous year. The report, however, cast doubts on the reliability of Tiny Rowland as a witness. In retaliation Tiny Rowland issued his own shadow report which questioned the suitability of John Griffiths to act as inspector in the case.

Although the resolutions relating to the board were withdrawn in accordance with their undertaking, Lonrho submitted two additional resolutions for the annual meeting which required House of Fraser not to do anything that would prejudice a demerger. The board wrote to shareholders on 3 September urging them to defeat the four remaining Lonrho resolutions and to support the re-election of Professor Smith and Ernest Sharp. The circular contained a personal letter from Bill Crossan paying tribute to Professor Smith who had borne 'the brunt of Lonrho's attempt to further its own factional interests to the detriment of the company's interests,' and complimenting him on his 'determined efforts to implement a new trading strategy that would exploit to the full the resource of the company'. Lonrho replied with its own circular which compared House of Fraser's performance unfavourably with Bentalls, Debenhams, Marks & Spencer and the John Lewis Partnership and dubbed the results as 'dismal'. At the annual meeting on 28 September the shareholders endorsed the re-election of Professor Smith with a massive majority of 57 million votes because Lonrho lent this resolution their support for the technical reason that the Monopolies and Mergers Commission was still in progress. However, even though they opposed the re-election of Ernest Sharp, he retained his seat. Lonrho's nominations of both Terry Robinson and Paul Spicer were defeated, but the additional resolutions relating to demerger were carried by a small majority. Tiny Rowland wrote at once to shareholders telling them that Lonrho would 'continue to advocate demerger, which is such an attractive idea, and while support increases we should maintain the policies towards House of Fraser, which we have been pursuing until now'. In the boardroom the questioning of every aspect of the Group's management continued, with Terry Robinson demanding more time at the meeting of 25 October to consider stock levels and stock turn.

Just six days later, on 31 October 1984, Tiny Rowland went to breakfast with Mohamed Al Fayed at his home at 60 Park Lane when he agreed to sell Lonrho's stake in House of Fraser to Alfayed Investment and Trust (UK) Ltd (AIT) for 300 pence a share within two days. Tiny Rowland claimed in March 1988 that his reason for taking this decision was that legal advice suggested that the Minister could force the sale of the stake if the Commission's findings went against Lonrho. During the following week Lonrho purchased another seven million shares – a 6.4 per cent stake – in House of Fraser, but told the Monopolies and Mergers Commission on 7 November that it had no intention of bidding for the Group. After at first refusing to leave the board, Lord Duncan-Sandys and Tiny Rowland resigned as directors on 22 November with effect from the end of the year, and on 3 January 1985 Mohamed Al Fayed and his brother Ali Fayed were appointed directors. On 4 March AIT made a cash offer for House of Fraser at a price of 400 pence per share, valuing the Group at £615 million. The board considered the offer 'to be fair and reasonable' and undertook 'in absence of unforeseen circumstances, to recommend the offer to House of Fraser ordinary shareholders'. Under the Takeover Panel rules AIT was barred from buying any further shares for another seven days.

On learning this news Norman Tebbit, the Secretary of State for Trade and Industry, in his own words 'exceptionally accelerated publication of the Monopolies and Mergers Commission's report to 7 March'. This concluded 'that the merger situation which will be created if arrangements in contemplation or proposed for the acquisition of House of Fraser plc by Lonrho plc are carried into effect may be expected not to operate against the public interest'. Consequently Sir Jasper Hollom, the chairman of the City Takeover Panel, told Lonrho's stockbrokers, Capel Cure Myers, the next day that Lonrho could immediately make a full bid 'subject to the pre-condition of a clearance being received from the Secretary of State'. The City held its breath but there was no offer from Lonrho. On 11 March AIT was free to re-enter the market. At first their brokers, Kleinwort Grieveson, could find no sellers, but at 11.00am Tiny Rowland offered his crucial 6.4 per cent stake, believing that the bid would be referred to the Monopolies and Mergers Commission within days causing the share price to fall sharply. Once this transaction became known shares were traded quickly and by the close of dealing AIT held 51.03 per cent of the capital. Three days later, to Tiny Rowland's disappointment, Norman Tebbit announced that the matter would not be referred to the Monopolies and Mergers Committee and consequently AIT's offer became unconditional. Writing to everyone who worked for the Group on 23 March Professor Smith assured them that there would be 'no change in the existing management and employee structure of House of Fraser, and that no redundancies will arise as a result of the bid'. In characteristic mood, he quipped that for Lonrho it was 'a bit like arriving at the platform to find that your train has just gone'.

House of Fraser had weathered the most turbulent decade in its history, exposed not only to the harsh climate of a recession but, when the upturn came, to a gale of criticism of its plans and policies from Lonrho. With steely courage, Professor Smith had resisted Tiny Rowland's relentless attrition and turned it to advantage in shaping future strategy. With his marketing expertise he was able to give definition to the latent talents in House of Fraser. Bill Crossan and the other executive directors responded by building on the foundations laid by Sir Hugh Fraser since 1966 to regenerate the Group in the 1980s. Lifestyle and the massive refurbishment programme were poised to transform House of Fraser, which would continue to combine the quality of tradition with the best of modern merchandising. Hedged about with difficulties, House of Fraser had deployed all its skill to retail out of the recession.

9 1985–1990

The Store is King

By 1985 shoppers were in no doubt that the high street of every town and city in Britain was being transformed by the new approach to retailing pioneered by such men as Sir Terence Conran of Habitat-Mothercare, George Davies of Next, and Ralph Halpern of Burtons. Everywhere old established stores were being renovated to remain competitive. With disposable incomes rising quickly under Mrs Thatcher's second Conservative Government, customers could not only afford more, but were becoming more and more discerning. In changing the image of British Home Stores, the managing director, Dennis Cassidy, declared during the year: 'the customers of the 80s are much more demanding, articulate and better off. They are not prepared to adopt the standards people had to accept twenty years ago. If we are to succeed we have to give them a warm exciting environment in which to shop.'

House of Fraser, under the chairmanship of Professor Roland Smith, was engaged in implementing a massive refurbishment programme of its stores throughout the United Kingdom, costing over £100 million. Directed by Murdoch McMaster, this ambitious scheme sought to effect the concepts expounded by Management Horizons in their penetrating enquiry into the Group. The overall goal was to ensure that each store sold its merchandise with authority, dominated its market, and had departmental layouts which accurately reflected local tastes and patterns of expenditure. To this almost clinical analysis of future strategy, the Fayeds brought their own vision of the craft of retailing, a commitment to quality and unstinting service to customers.

Adjusting to these even more exacting objectives, Professor Smith and his team forged ahead with their plans, freed from the daily encounters with Lonrho. When in late May 1985 Ralph Halpern's Burton group announced a bid for Debenhams plc in co-operation with Sir Terence Conran, the board became concerned that their carefully prepared efforts might well be thwarted by these two giants of modern retailing. Professor Smith and Ernest Sharp counter-attacked at once by buying Debenhams shares in the market. Their object was not simply to frustrate the Burton bid but to bring about a community of interests between House of Fraser and Debenhams. It was proposed that the two companies should share merchandising and distribution facilities and also financial services through Welbeck Finance, Debenham's very successful in-house credit company. The Fayeds also had their eyes on Debenham's flagship store, Harvey Nichols of Knightsbridge, and the world-famous Hamleys' toy shop in Regent Street. Ralph Halpern's plan for Debenhams was the radical introduction of the galleria concept whereby an atrium would be constructed in the centre of each store, with the departments, mostly operated through concessions, ranged around it in tiered galleries. Although some doubted the wisdom of such an approach, based as it was on American and Japanese experience, Burtons' bid gradually found favour with the financial press and institutions during the summer. Professor Smith and the Fayeds, however, continued to build House of Fraser's stake in Debenhams in what was reputedly 'one of the biggest operations of its kind ever

257

seen in the stock market.' By early August, when the bid became unconditional, House of Fraser held twenty-six per cent of Debenhams. Acknowledging defeat the Fayeds accepted the Burton offer, but continued desultory negotiations with Ralph Halpern for parts of the group. When these failed, they identified other businesses which could contribute to their ultimate objective of enhancing the quality of House of Fraser's stores.

Towards the end of 1985 Turnbull & Asser (Holdings) Ltd, which precisely matched this criterion, was acquired. Through its subsidiaries Turnbull & Asser, Hawes & Curtis and James Drew, with shops in London's exclusive Jermyn Street, Burlington Arcade, and Burlington Gardens, the company provided an exclusive range of men's and ladies' wear for discerning customers throughout the world. Turnbull & Asser shirts were reckoned to be the best in the world. Although the firm had boutiques in the principal cities of North America, Australia, and Japan, there was scope for opening shops in stores like Harrods. At the same time House of Fraser took over Kurt Geiger Holdings Ltd, which traded as Kurt Geiger, Bruno Magli and Carvela shoes, importing and retailing quality Italian shoes and accessories for ladies. Kurt Geiger and Carvela operated a number of concession shops within House of Fraser and other stores. As part of the long-held commitment to extend the Group's geographical representation, the sixty per cent of the share capital of Switzer & Co, the Dublin based stores group, which House of Fraser did not own, was purchased from Waterford Glass plc. Switzers was the principal store in Dublin, with branches at Limerick, Cork and Galway.

While these deals were being negotiated, work continued with relentless energy and at breathtaking speed on the major refurbishment of the Rackhams' store in Birmingham, Frasers in Aberdeen, Kendal Milne in Manchester, Binns in Grimsby, Cavendish House in Cheltenham, and Dingles in Plymouth. In implementing these major projects and many smaller improvements, the goal was the achievement of a distinctive appearance for the Group's stores, devised by Allied International Designers. Recognising that property-owning was now firmly established as a desirable social objective, concept departments for linens and soft furnishings were designed and fitted in over twenty stores. Murdoch McMaster, who had become joint managing director of House of Fraser (Stores) Ltd on Bill Crossan's retirement in September, was constantly on the move, checking on progress and the standard of the workmanship. Rackhams of Birmingham was ready to be re-opened in May 1986, just twelve months after work had started, establishing the store as 'the flagship of House of Fraser outside the capital.' Prominent place was given in the publicity literature to the range of financial services now offered by the Group in conjunction with the recently privatised TSB. Brought together under the Fraser Finance banner, these services ranged from the already well established Frasercard and through Fraser Cover providing all types of insurance, Frasermove, a complete house-moving service, Frasercash, providing cash to customers, Fraserloan, a loan service, to Frasercredit, a credit facility. It was now widely believed that a major retailing group could not remain competitive unless it provided such financial services. Having failed to capture Welbeck Finance, House of Fraser had had to move fast to make alternative arrangements.

During 1986 the first phase of the total redevelopment of Barkers' building in Kensington High Street into the Barkers Centre was completed. Originally the board had planned to sell the newly created office accommodation and street level retail outlets, only retaining the much reduced Barkers' store. The Fayeds reversed this decision, preferring to retain the property and improve the quality

OPPOSITE *The new shopping arcade and atrium at the Barkers Centre in 1987.*

ABOVE AND LEFT *The House of Fraser store at the Metro Centre at Newcastle, with its eye-catching atrium.*

of the reconstruction to exploit the full grandeur of the Art-Deco building. Murdoch McMaster had decided that the new Barkers required individual treatment, engaging the New York designer, Andre Ruellen. The concept of including what was in effect a new House of Fraser store within a much larger shopping complex was advanced a stage further in 1986 with the opening of the Metro Centre in Newcastle-upon-Tyne. The Centre, the brainchild of John Hall, was conceived as Britain's first regional shopping centre, situated on reclaimed land with motorway access, south of the River Tyne in Gateshead. John Hall's ambition was to create a novel shopping environment, at least in Britain, where customers, both young and old, would both be entertained and enthralled. The overall design was based on the galleria concept on two floors with over two hundred retail units, of which seven were to be large focal anchor stores. John Hall had persuaded the board to take one of these units for House of Fraser. Again designed by Andre Ruellen of New York, the House of Fraser store, straddled both floors of the centre with stunning effect. Marks & Spencer was another of the anchor stores, the first time they had been enticed out of a town centre. The artful use of glass and walkways endowed the whole centre with a compelling identity and sense of excitement. From its inauguration it set new standards in British retailing and was quickly copied by others elsewhere, particularly in similarly depressed areas.

The completion of these two distinctive new House of Fraser stores coincided with Professor Smith's decision to relinquish the chairmanship of the Group at the beginning of June. He was succeeded by Ali Fayed. Already the Fayeds had shown a close interest in House of Fraser stores and a keen awareness of the changing expectations of British shoppers. Deciding that the Group was in need of an injection of fresh retailing ideas, they appointed as their chief executive Brian Walsh, who had transformed the Australian David Jones' store group. Convinced that the changes in the British high street amounted to little more than catching up with the rest of the world and in no sense a revolution, he brought new perspectives to House of Fraser. He quickly concluded that it was a mistake to seek uniformity between the Group's stores, rather it would be better to stress their individuality and long associations with their local communities. Reinforcing the opinion of Management Horizons, he thought that at least twenty per cent of the stock should also reflect the diversity of the country's geography and experience – 'You've got such a rich variety of accents and cultures within this island, and it would be a pity to lose that, to have a bland sameness everywhere.' By adopting this approach, he believed that House of Fraser could steal a march on the multiples whose stores, by their very nature, have standard appearances and layouts. He declared – 'the great thing is that all other shops in the high street look the same. You can make a department store very distinctive. They are part of show business.' The refurbishment programme was adjusted and extended to reflect this new thinking by building on the eye-catching individual design and layouts already achieved at the Metro Centre and the Barkers Centre. This second wave of refurbishment included the total refitting of Arnotts in Glasgow, House of Fraser in Sheffield, Howells in Cardiff, Binns in Hull, D.H. Evans in Oxford Street, Jollys in Bath, and the Army & Navy Stores in Victoria, Bromley, Guildford and Basildon. Small units in unprofitable locations continued to be sold and the nine You shops recently opened in southern England to sell cosmetics and accessories, closed. With Aleck Craddock's Harrods Major Project now complete, a further massive upgrading of the Group's leading store was unveiled by Mohamed Al-Fayed in August 1987. Estimated to cost £200 million, his ambition was to restore Harrods to the way it looked in 1912,

The refurbished Binns store in Hull in 1983.

OPPOSITE *Ladies' shoe department and an Astral Sports & Leisure concession shop in a House of Fraser store.*

uncovering original decorations buried beneath later alterations and installing fabulous fittings. The store was to be transformed into a 'palace of romance, fantasy and history,' serviced by the most sophisticated of modern computer controlled warehouses constructed at Osterley. Throughout, the emphasis was concentrated on the department store as a treasure house of merchandise.

As well as the issue of presentation, Brian Walsh tackled the difficult problem of the Group's approach to merchandising and selling. From his knowledge of selling in Australia and America, he realised that British department stores attracted more traffic than elsewhere in the world, but achieved far lower sales per head. Considering that the staff were 'not ready to sell here', he made determined efforts to improve attitudes. 'Service is just being nice to people. You think of a time when you had really good service; all it came down to was that the person was nice to you. If you have that you can get away with anything. If you haven't got it, you'd better find something else to do.' Part and parcel of this drive to raise sales was a further deepening of merchandising by making staff, through improved training, much more aware and knowledgeable about the goods they had to offer customers. When he arrived Walsh claimed that sales were being lost by stores being out of stock of best selling lines and that this obstacle could be simply overcome by the accurate logging of individual sales on the newly completed electronic point of sales system and their daily central analysis. With this information, stock levels at each store could be rapidly adjusted to reflect demand. This action, essential if House of Fraser was to remain competitive with its high street rivals, demanded further investment in rapidly advancing new technology. Paul Livesy was recruited as director of Information Systems

and given the task of providing the systems and the technology to resolve these problems. A charismatic figure, Brian Walsh inspired awe and respect at all levels, renewing in less than a year the Group's sense of purpose and urgency. However, after little more than twelve months in post he decided, for family reasons, to return to Australia in October 1987. He died suddenly eighteen months later of a brain tumour.

On the departure of Brian Walsh, both Mohamed Al Fayed and Ali Fayed became much more closely involved in the management of the business. Mohamed Al Fayed became executive chairman of Harrods, assisted at first by Michael Ellis Jones and later by Paul Taylor, who transferred from Dickins & Jones. Ali Fayed appointed George Willoughby as deputy chairman of House of Fraser plc and Murdoch McMaster as sole managing director of House of Fraser (Stores). Robb Hampson, a fellow Australian whom Brian Walsh brought to Harrods, became merchandise director of House of Fraser (Stores). Unfortunately, before the new team had time to become established, Murdoch McMaster retired early in May 1988 to return to Scotland. He was succeeded by Robb Hampson.

Continuing where Brian Walsh had left off, Robb Hampson engaged new design teams, particularly from America, to create exciting new interiors in existing stores and plan completely new stores at Thurrock in Essex, off the M25; at Meadowhall, a regional centre near Sheffield on the Metro model; and at the Schofields Centre in Leeds. During 1988 House of Fraser acquired Schofields store in Leeds which, at the time, was trading in temporary accommodation at the Briggate, while its original site in the Headrow was redeveloped as the Schofield Centre (see page 359). It was soon decided not to close the

Artists' impressions of two new House of Fraser stores to be developed at Meadowhall near Sheffield (opposite), and at Thurrock in Essex (right).

temporary store when the Centre was complete in 1990, but to refurbish and expand it, continuing trading but under the Rackhams' name. In taking this initiative and in planning other new stores, Robb Hampson redefined House of Fraser's corporate mission with the objective of making the Group's stores the best in Europe. A fresh strategy was devised for the whole Group towards advertising and visual merchandising, and also to staff culture, disseminated through training sessions and manuals. The thrust of the new approach was to trade up, summed up in the simple phrase 'Expect the Best', with the purpose of wooing more customers into House of Fraser stores through the quality and distinction of their service. The education of the Group's 20,000 employees in these concepts and goals had startling results, raising not only customers' perceptions of House of Fraser stores but also their spending. This was vital at a time when competition was accelerating from a revitalised Debenhams and from Sir Terence Conran's Habitat which had merged with B*h*S (formerly British Home Stores) in 1985. Both these groups, like House of Fraser, were committed to large capital investment programmes to capture custom. Conran's attempt to transform B*h*S was similar to the onslaught of Brian Walsh and Robb Hampson on House of Fraser – 'You have to change the culture right the way through store. It is incredibly difficult to get rid of the "Are You Being Served" mentality ... We are going back to the micro situation of more personal retailing rather than the macro vision of the 1950s of bowling people over with sheer size.'

Any expectation that Professor Smith and the directors of House of Fraser may have had that in recommending the takeover by Alfayed Investment Trust they would be relieved of the remorseless criticism of their policies by Lonrho were soon dashed. Disappointed that he had failed to gain control of House of Fraser, just when the Monopolies and Mergers Commission had finally given its consent, Tiny Rowland almost immediately publicly condemned the takeover, despite the fact that it was his sale of shares to the Fayeds which had made it possible. At first he directed his attack solely against the Fayeds themselves with allegations about their background and the source of their wealth, but he soon began to question their management of House of Fraser in exactly the same way he had done in the past. In the absence of any other information, he criticised the level of bank borrowings required to sustain the greatly enlarged capital expenditure programme. His aspersions were largely financial and made in the context of a public company governed by the short term considerations of shareholders. He offered no comment on the merits or otherwise of the new investment. House of Fraser retorted by indicating that they were operating 'well within the financial covenants required by the new Bank Loan Agreements' and that as a private company they could afford to take a longer view. The board stressed the extent of both Ali Fayed and Mohamed Al Fayed's involvement in the Group – their regular attendance at the head offices of both House of Fraser and Harrods and frequent visits to the stores throughout the country.

The questions raised by Lonrho and the persistence with which they were addressed, finally obliged Paul Channon, Secretary of State for Trade and Industry, to appoint inspectors in April 1987 to enquire into the circumstances surrounding the takeover. This report was completed in July 1988, but was not published as its findings were referred to the Serious Fraud Office for further detailed investigation. Throughout the year and into 1989, Tiny Rowland and Lonrho maintained their pressure on the Fayed brothers and House of Fraser, distributing documents containing various allegations and criticisms to all House of Fraser senior staff, causing concern and confusion. In late March 1989 a copy of the DTI report came into Tiny Rowland's hands and extracts were published

OPPOSITE *The recently refurbished banking hall (above) and menswear department (below) in Harrods.*

Harrods, illuminated for the Christmas season in the 1980s.

in a special, mid-week issue of the Lonrho-owned *Observer* newspaper. The DTI and House of Fraser immediately took legal action to have the newspaper withdrawn from circulation. Over the following days, Tiny Rowland tried, unsuccessfully, to have the embargo lifted by the courts and force the secretary of state for Trade and Industry to publish the report. At the same time he was challenging the decision not to refer the acquisition to the Monopolies and Mergers Commission. Such a reference was necessary if Tiny Rowland was to achieve his objective of having the Fayeds forced to divest themselves of their interest in the House of Fraser. These two issues were eventually settled in the House of Lords in May 1989 when it was unanimously agreed that the Secretary of State had acted correctly in not referring the matter to the Monopolies and Mergers Commission and in deferring the publication of the DTI report. It was now four years since the Fayed family had acquired House of Fraser and at last the debate about their ownership had been resolved.

Against this disquietening background, Robb Hampson and his team have had to conduct the business in a highly competitive and rapidly changing marketplace. New shopping complexes specifically targeted at certain income and social groups have been constructed, or are planned, for nearly every town and city in Britain. They incorporate, on the Newcastle Metro Centre model, large and small retail units. With their all-weather protection and dramatic environment, they have the potential radically to change established shopping patterns in any locality. For this reason the main retail groups cannot afford to refuse to participate. On the high street itself, specialist shops which have carved out a specific niche, like the Body Shop, Tie Rack and the Sock Shop, have grown rapidly in numbers since 1985. There has also been a revival in independent retailing as disposable incomes have grown. Many of these find their custom amongst the better-off, traditionally the market of the department store. In the face of these developments, the Storehouse Group (Habitat, Mothercare and B*h*S) and Next faltered in 1988, losing their appeal as their original customer base has grown older. Even Marks & Spencer was forced to rethink its approach to merchandising and store layout, shifting the emphasis towards fashion wear and making furnishings integral to their shopping experience. The key to the future of retailing in Britain will be government success in curbing inflation and maintaining the upward movement in the wealth of the population. If it is successful, then retailing, particularly at the quality end of the market, will be buoyant as it is, for example, in prosperous European countries like Germany, and Switzerland. Whatever the outcome, continued investment by retail groups is essential for future prosperity. The challenge for House of Fraser in the 1990s is to ensure that the idea of total shopping within a store of many departments containing a galaxy of well presented merchandise, reigns supreme. To achieve this objective the Group has plans for further improvements and another new store, to open in Tunbridge Wells in 1991. But these are the practical implementations of the Group's vision for the future; a vision which, strangely, has altered little over the years despite the enormous social, cultural and economic changes which have taken place. It is a vision cherished by four generations of the Fraser family and of all those other families whose stores have long been household names   Harrods, Barkers, Binns and so many more. To encapsulate their vision the Group has coined a watchword for the nineties which Lord Fraser, with his passionate belief in the supremacy of the department store, would wholeheartedly have supported:

'The Store is King'.

OVERLEAF
*Detail of Harrods'
dome and portico.*

Selected Store Histories

The narrative account of the development of House of Fraser includes little information about the evolution of the individual businesses which now comprise the Group. The following brief histories, in describing the growth of a selection of the principal stores, clearly demonstrate that, despite diversity of geographical location and original ownership, a number of common circumstances have often led to the emergence of the department store. Most operated low-price ready-money policies from the outset; growth was generally fuelled by the vision and drive of a talented proprietor or manager; the trade always diversified piecemeal by the gradual provision of additional services and purveyance of new lines; and the construction of palatial buildings was only made possible by the slow and deliberate acquisition of adjoining businesses and plots of land. The histories of all of House of Fraser's old-established stores reflect these same characteristics, which are also shared by nearly every department store in the country.

The Store is situated within Five Minutes' Walk of Victoria Station, *from which Omnibuses run to all parts of London.*
The St. James's Park Station *is within Three Minutes' Walk of, and is almost opposite to, the* Store.

Army & Navy Stores Ltd, Victoria, London

The Army & Navy Co-operative Society Ltd was formed in 1871 by a group of army and navy officers for 'the supply of articles of domestic consumption and general use to its members at the lowest remunerative rates.' It was based on the model of two earlier middle-class co-operatives, the Civil Service Supply Association and Civil Service Co-operative Society. Membership was open to 'officers, non-commissioned officers and petty officers, serving, or who have served, in the army, navy, militia or yeomanry, the widows of officers, the secretaries or other recognised officers of the military and naval clubs and representatives of regimental and naval messes and canteens.' Members were entitled to deal at the store, share in profits and have certain goods delivered free. Annual membership tickets were issued. The initial capital of £15,000 was divided into 15,000 £1 shares.

A portion of the distillery premises owned by Vickers & Co in Victoria Street, Westminster, were leased and the traders advertising in the price lists of the other civil service societies were approached with a view to securing supplies. The store opened on 15 February 1872 for the sale of groceries, and during the following weeks further departments were established for stationery, drapery, perfumery, fancy goods and tailoring. Over 10,000 price lists were posted. During the first five months sales amounted to £38,787, the profit was over £6,000, and continued to increase steadily. By early 1873 the warehouse was regularly overcrowded and the directors rented an adjoining house to which the stationery, turnery, chemist and tailoring departments were removed. In addition, the issue of free membership tickets with share purchases was abandoned. At the end of 1873 a gun department was established and premises acquired in Johnson Place, nearby, for warehousing, packing and a carpenter's shop. By early 1875 the Society was also running a banking department by holding members' money on deposit for interest. By then more space was again urgently required in Victoria and negotiations were concluded with Vickers for the lease of additional premises with an option to purchase. To finance this expansion, the company's capital was increased from £30,000 to £60,000 by the issue of further shares. In May 1875 a Paris agency was opened.

By 1876 the Johnson Place premises had become too cramped for the Society's growing manufacturing activities. New workshops were acquired at Ranelagh Road, Pimlico, where a separate manufacturing department was established for tailoring, shirt-making, printing and, from 1877, the production of portmanteaus. In 1877 a Leipzig office was opened. That year a new category of membership, unaffected by share ownership, was introduced, known as life membership. Meanwhile the option to purchase the Victoria premises had been taken up and a new building was completed in 1878, where a refreshment room was opened. By 1878 annual sales were enormous and a general price reduction was implemented in order to diminish the unexpectedly large profits which had accumulated. Co-operatives, like Army & Navy, carried to extreme the early department stores' tactics of bulk buying and ready-money sales and were able to sell even cheaper because they offered no services – customers were even expected to make out their own orders. Consequently, middle-class shoppers flocked to the Stores, as the Society's warehouse became known, amazed by the real cost of merchandise which they had been accustomed to buying at high mark-ups. Those who could not visit the Stores in person bought through mail order. A few enterprising shops, like Harrods, deliberately adopted the co-operatives' low-price policy and benefited from their popularity. Other retailers were incensed by what they saw as unfair competition and, by lobbying, secured the appointment of a parliamentary select committee on co-operative stores to investigate their complaints. The committee concluded that there was no evidence to justify the closure of the Stores.

Despite these setbacks, the Society's business grew rapidly during the early 1880s and, in September 1881, Vickers was given notice to quit the remaining premises which it occupied. Alterations were not completed until the end of 1882 when the Society's warehouse premises were moved from Tooley Street to a more convenient location in Westminster. In 1882 the Army & Navy Auxiliary Co-operative Society Ltd was formed to supply fresh provisions, boots, furniture and estate agency services. Located in adjoining buildings, the Society shared the same management and membership as the Army & Navy Co-operative Society, and in 1919 the two organisations were merged. In 1882 a purchasing agency was established in New York and a Thomas Cook ticket office briefly installed in Victoria Street. Meanwhile the manufacturing activities had grown enormously and could no longer be accommodated in the Ranelagh Road property. Consequently in 1884 workshop premises were acquired in Johnson Street nearby. In 1888 office space in Howick Place was converted for retail use and the wine and gun departments transferred there from the Victoria Street block which was connected to the new showrooms by a gangway.

Problems in satisfying the requirements of the military and naval messes prompted the establishment of an agency in Plymouth in 1890 and plans were also laid for the creation of a depot in Bombay for the convenience of members in India. During the latter half of 1890 one of the Society's directors travelled to India to organise the depot, and premises were quickly found in Apollo Street,

Membership tickets.

New premises under construction at Bombay in 1893.

Bombay, to be supplied with merchandise from Britain. In 1891 a second Indian depot was opened at Karachi, to serve regiments quartered in the Punjab and Scind, and the following year larger premises were leased in Esplanade Road, Bombay, although they were not ready for occupation until the end of 1894. Both depots were profitable from the outset, but experienced trading difficulties during the late 1890s caused by the frontier campaign and the low prices charged at local bazaars. Nonetheless, it was decided to open a new store at Calcutta and a site was acquired at Chowringhee in 1900. That year the Karachi depot was closed as the area had ceased to be used for military purposes.

Meanwhile, in London, the Stores were continually extended and improved. In 1894 a preserved provisions factory was erected in Coburg Row, and in 1897 adjoining premises were acquired at 107 Victoria Street and occupied in 1899. By this time the Society was issuing an enormous illustrated price list each year, running to more than 1,000 pages, had introduced a telephone ordering service and considerably reduced the cost of mail-order delivery. During the Boer War the Stores sent groceries, wine and tobacco to South African ports where they were sold by local agents on a commission basis. In 1900 a large warehouse was erected in Westminster for making up export and country orders and storing groceries. The following year the shirt and collar factory was moved out of Ranelagh Road to allow the further extension of the printing department. During the late 1900s trade became less buoyant and efforts were made to attract custom by advertising on railway stations and omnibuses. Harrods was seen as the principal competitor and the directors frequently instigated comparisons of prices and delivery times.

During the First World War the Stores, which encouraged employees to join up, suffered from acute staff shortages as well as from the diminished spending power of its customers, although some new business was forthcoming in the form

This advertisement appeared in the Stores' price lists throughout the late 1920s.

ON ARRIVAL IN THE EAST

ON disembarking at Bombay, Members will find the Society's representative there to meet them, ready to make arrangements for travellers and do everything possible to assist with their baggage, railway tickets, and accommodation. This is the first service that the Society is able to render its members on arrival in India, but one that is of immense assistance to all new-comers to the East.

of army bedding and clothing contracts from the War Office. The end of the war brought little relief and in December 1919 the Stores were paralysed by a major and much publicised strike of its shop staff. Trade remained depressed throughout the early 1920s and efforts were made to widen membership by issuing subscribers' tickets free of charge. In 1922 the Victoria Street front was improved by the introduction of floodlighting and display windows. Later the railings and porches were removed as part of the general reconstruction programme and glass shopfronts were introduced on the Howick Place side. The shop's name was abbreviated to the Army & Navy Stores in an effort to throw off its traditional image, although it was not until 1934 that the company's official name was changed to the Army & Navy Stores Ltd. A persistent trade depression brought difficult trading conditions throughout the 1930s. During the Second World War part of the store was requisitioned for the production of camouflage netting and helmets. Merchandise was in short supply and the production of the large annual price list was discontinued. During the blitz the Turnham Green and Portsmouth premises suffered serious bomb damage and the Plymouth depot was entirely destroyed. After the war, following Indian independence in 1947, most of the British military and government officials left India, and the Army & Navy's depots there were gradually wound down. The last Indian store, in Bombay, continued to operate until 1952.

Thereafter the company determined to extend its business in the United Kingdom and, rejecting three takeover proposals in early 1952, launched a massive advertising campaign and embarked upon the acquisition of a network of small provincial stores. In March 1953 the company purchased Genge & Co Ltd, a small department store in Dorchester, and in November also acquired William Harvey of Guildford Ltd. The Guildford store was later expanded and refurbished with the erection of a new five-storey building. In March 1955 J.D. Morant Ltd of Chichester also joined the group. Morants had been destroyed by enemy action during the war and relocated in rambling premises opposite Chichester cathedral. Five years later, in 1960, the company's provincial expansion was resumed with the acquisition of the furnishing store of Thomas Clarkson Ltd of Wolverhampton. The following year Thomas White Ltd of Aldershot was purchased and in 1963 Burgis & Colbourne Ltd of Leamington Spa. The company had also acquired a site in Camberley, where a new Harveys store was built in 1964. That year extensions were opened at Guildford, Chichester, Dorchester and Wolverhampton. In 1968 the company purchased, from the receiver, the Bromley stores of Harrison Gibson Ltd. Most of these stores retained their original names but a group buying policy was adopted and the company began to advertise and promote its stores under the 'A & N' banner.

During the early 1960s the board had begun to consider the redevelopment of its extensive premises in Victoria Street. It was, however, many years before planning permission was secured and it was not until 1973 that work began on the construction of a new store. In 1973 Army & Navy Stores was taken over by House of Fraser and combined, as Army & Navy Division, with the John Barker stores at Kensington and Eastbourne. In 1977 the new Victoria Street store, heavily promoted as 'London's dazzling new store', was completed. Built on four open-plan floors, it comprised over 147,000 square feet of selling space and featured a modern frontage of bronze tinted glass. Subsequently the amount of sales space in the Howick Place building was reduced, to allow for the phased development of the London administrative and buying offices of House of Fraser. Between 1984 and 1986 the store was partially refurbished and remains the focus of the Victoria Street shopping area.

OPPOSITE *Customer lift and attendant in the 1930s.*

Arnott & Co Ltd, Glasgow

Around 1850 John Arnott established a drapery and general warehouse at 19 Jamaica Street, Glasgow, as a branch of a business already represented in Cork, Belfast and Dublin. Trading as Arnott, Cannock & Co, the shop sold dress materials, towellings, sheetings, linens, blankets, quilts and counterpanes. Jamaica Street was an excellent location close to the recently rebuilt Glasgow Bridge, the main railway station and the principal steamer quay. The warehouse quickly developed a reputation for its adventurous salesmanship, offering ready-made coats, trousers and boys' clothing as early as 1851, and for advertising frequently and boldly. In September 1860 the partnership between Arnott & Cannock was dissolved. Thomas Arnott, half-brother of Sir John Arnott, the Dublin merchant, assumed control of the Glasgow business, which traded thereafter as Arnott & Co.

In 1864 Arnott obtained title to the premises at 19 Jamaica Street from the trustees of the City of Glasgow Bank, and the showrooms were greatly improved and extended. By 1870 stocks were purchased abroad on a regular basis and Irish poplins were supplied by Arnott & Co's Dublin factory for sale at 'ten per cent under the usual prices.' In 1872 the firm was describing its warehouse as 'the largest retail drapery establishment in the city,' selling dry goods of all kinds, ranging from shawls and parasols to carpets and haberdashery. In 1874 new costume galleries were opened and premises were acquired in Adam's Court Lane. At the end of 1881 Arnott embarked on an extensive refurbishment programme. The new warehouse, opened in March 1882, was described in the local press as 'one of the finest and most commodious in the city.' The shop front, 'featuring two huge plate glass windows,' caused particular interest. Each window, twenty feet in breadth, was divided into three panes – 'these spans are considered to be perhaps the largest ever attempted in warehouse architecture.' An attractive mosaic pavement in the main entrance was decorated with the store's name and inside separate counters had been arranged for perfumery, lace, gloves and a new fancy goods department. Three years later, in 1885, the store became the first warehouse in Scotland to install an automatic cash carrier, the Lamson cash railway.

Thomas Arnott died at Stranraer in July 1883 leaving an estate worth £59,642. Sir John Arnott subsequently exercised his option, under the terms of the co-partnership agreement, to acquire his half-brother's share in the business at a price of £45,532, secured against the Jamaica Street property. A few years later, in December 1891, Arnott & Co Ltd was incorporated as a private limited liability company with a capital of £80,000, divided into 12,000 £5 ordinary shares and 4,000 per cent preference shares of £5 each. Sir John retained a majority shareholding receiving a sum of £99,000 for the property, stock and goodwill of the business. The directors of the new company comprised Sir John Arnott, Thomas Leburn Arnott, Robert Brown and John Alexander Arnott, a Bristol shipowner. Brown, who became managing director, had entered the firm as an office boy at its foundation. During 1903 the warehouse was remodelled and a new paper-pattern department added. Three years later the store frontage was extensively altered creating a new entrance and additional window area.

Arnotts traded successfully for many decades but, during the depressed inter-war years, the company began to experience severe cash-flow problems. Profits diminished during the early 1930s and in 1936 the store recorded a loss of £272. In May 1936 Arnott & Co Ltd was acquired by Fraser Sons & Co Ltd. The existing directors were replaced and the company wound up. A new company,

OPPOSITE *The store frontage during the 1890s.*

Page from a brochure produced for the opening of the new Arnott Simpsons store in 1964.

'Tots' to 'teens' and in betweens

Most parents know that it's quality that counts in Children's wear . . . that it pays to buy an article that can be relied upon to stand up to all the hard knocks of a child's school time and play hours. At the New Arnott Simpsons you'll find just that quality, and furthermore, at prices that will be an agreeable surprise to you.

Every "Junior" is catered for, from the crib stage to his or her "first job" outfit, and as one can imagine, in a new store, the whole atmosphere of the departments is such that it will be a real pleasure both for you and the children to shop there.

Special emphasis has been put on the school clothing section, representing as it does, such a major part of a child's life. Blazers, shorts, gym tunics, blouses, etc., in regulation styles, and the general school shades are available in a complete size range.

There's a real touch of fashion in the children's dress department . . . stylings are imaginative and appealing to the young . . . the colours a riot of every hue.

Arnott Simpson realise that today more than ever before, there's a demand for children's casual clothing . . . practical, well-styled garments

at the new Arnott Simpsons

Arnott & Co Ltd, was incorporated the following month with Hugh Fraser and his family as principal shareholders. By September 1936 Fraser had also negotiated the acquisition of the neighbouring store of Robert Simpson & Sons Ltd. Established by Robert Simpson as a shawl warehouse in Trongate in the 1820s, the store had removed to Jamaica Street in 1851. In February 1938 Arnott & Co Ltd was renamed Arnott Simpson Ltd, a company which was liquidated in 1949 along with a number of subsidiaries owned by Frasers in Glasgow and Edinburgh. During the early 1960s Arnott Simpsons was rebuilt. The final phase of the new store opened in April 1963 boasting 140,000 square feet of sales space on six trading floors, more than double the size of the previous building, including a new food hall and a fine helicoidal staircase. The store continued to trade successfully during the following decades and in 1987 was totally refurbished at a cost of £6 million, including the installation of an additional twelve escalators.

Stylishly dressed models in the menswear department today.

John Barker & Co Ltd, Kensington, London

John Barker was born at Loose in Kent on 6 April 1840, the son of Joseph Barker, a carpenter and brewer. He was educated privately and in 1853 began a three-year apprenticeship to a Maidstone draper. He gained further experience in drapery shops in Folkestone and Dover before moving to London, in 1858, to join Spencer, Turner & Boldero, furnishers and drapers of Marylebone. After a few years in London Barker was offered a position at William Whiteley's new emporium in Westbourne Grove. He proved a talented salesman and was promoted to departmental manager at an annual salary of £300. Within a year he had doubled sales at the store and, although his salary was also doubled, his expectation of a partnership was disappointed. Whiteley, loath to relinquish sole control, instead offered Barker £1,000 per annum in compensation. Barker was, however, an ambitious man and left Whiteley in late 1870 to open a small linen drapery shop on his own account in nearby Kensington. His partner, James Whitehead, a wealthy City merchant who had also begun his career as a draper's apprentice, provided capital and credit without overly interfering in the running of the business. Whitehead remained the principal investor throughout the early years with an initial stake of around £6,000 to Barker's £240. Both received interest on their invested capital and Barker, as managing partner, also drew an annual salary of £250. Barker had left a remunerative position for a speculative venture but, as part owner, was now able to implement and adapt the adventurous modes of retailing which he had experienced at Whiteleys. By dealing directly with manufacturers and selling for cash he was able to keep prices low and to achieve a rapid turnover. Overheads were kept to a minimum and Barker and his family lived over the shop with the staff for several years.

Barker's initial premises at 91 and 93 (then 43 and 44) Kensington High Street, recently rebuilt under the Kensington improvement scheme, quickly proved inadequate and, by the end of 1870, Barker had annexed 26 and 28 Ball Street where he installed millinery, dressmaking and underclothing departments. In 1871 he moved into 87 Kensington High Street, setting up men's mercery and tailoring and juvenile clothing departments. At that time he employed over thirty staff, including his younger brother, Francis. The following year he acquired the stock and premises of a draper at 89 Kensington High Street and 24 Ball Street, where he installed book, stationery, fancy goods and mantle departments which were, in 1873, extended into a newly acquired parcel of land behind 85 and 87 Kensington High Street. In 1880 Barker also took over 77 Kensington High Street, 14 and 16 Ball Street and the stock of a firm of ironmongers. This acquisition led to the development of furniture, carpet, china and glass departments. Later the same year he purchased 75 Kensington High Street, the stock in trade of a grocer, and houses at 12 and 14 Ball Street, redeveloping the latter site to accommodate attractive showrooms for groceries, provisions, wine and spirits and cigars.

From the outset Barker had envisaged the creation of a vast store selling a huge range of goods, and accordingly took every opportunity to acquire the leases and freeholds of adjoining premises. By 1880 he was trading in fifteen shops and boasted an annual turnover of £150,000, almost four times the invested capital, and an annual profit of £8,500. The expansion of the business continued unabated with the acquisition of 95 and 97 Kensington High Street, on the corner of King Street, for silk and dress goods, mantles and millinery in 1885, and the purchase of the former London and County Bank and two shop premises at 67–71 Kensington High Street, for the cabinet, upholstery and drug dispensing departments, in 1888. The following year 63 and 65 Kensington High Street, 2, 4 and 6 Young Street and 6 Ball Street were purchased and immediately pulled down to make way for a handsome six-storey building, with a high mansard roof, offering some 30,000 square feet of floor space. This new wing was completed in December 1889. Invitations to the grand opening promised 'music, decorations and electricity' and attractions included the string band of the Scots Guards, sword dancing by Highland pipers and a lift or 'American elevator'. More than 1,200 guests attended the event. The new wing was primarily devoted to the extension of the furnishing, upholstery and carpet departments and was principally stocked with purchases made at the recent Paris Exhibition. By 1892 John Barker & Co was operating one of the largest emporia in London with over forty-two departments, including building and plumbing and refreshment catering departments, along with allied workshops. The store employed over 1,000 staff and the huge delivery service despatched some 2,000 parcels daily.

In 1888 a company had been formally established to run the new druggists department with Barker and Whitehead as equal partners. However, in 1893, after a disagreement, Barker acquired Whitehead's share in the business, using capital provided by his son-in-law's father, Sir Walter Gilbey of Bishop's Stortford. To satisfy a condition of the loan the firm was floated as a public company, John Barker & Co Ltd, with an authorised capital of £330,000 and £150,000 45 per cent mortgage debenture stock. Over the previous seven years the firm had averaged annual net profits of around £28,350. As vendor, Barker received £402,017, comprising £282,017 in cash and the remainder in shares and debenture stock in the new company, including the entire issue of management shares. Barker became chairman and the new directors included Barker's brother, Francis, and H.H. Johnstone, who had long been partners and now became managing directors, Barker's son-in-law, Tresham Gilbey of Bishop's Stortford, and J.G. Barnes, former manager of Parr's Banking Company, Kensington branch. The incorporated business was divided into five sections – finance, purchases, audit and salaries, stationery and advertising, and horse vans and deliveries, with a committee of directors appointed to each. The transition from private ownership to public company was not, however, an easy one and the board was to be continually divided by disagreements large and small.

In early 1894 the new company bought the premises and stock of Seaman & Little, a shop which had previously divided the warehouse in half requiring customers to venture outside to reach certain departments. The acquisition of the new shop, incorporated in the main warehouse within five days, was celebrated with a huge sale. During the first day four departments alone took more than £4,000. The company then owned thirty-three shops, including sixteen fronting High Street. The store itself comprised sixty-four departments and employed 1,500 staff. By 1895, save for two shops (numbers 73 and 85), the company owned every property between King Street and Young Street. The growth of the business continued with the opening of new jewellery and watch, and bicycle departments in 1895, the rebuilding of the Ball Street property in 1897, to house office staff, and the acquisition of numbers 48$\frac{1}{2}$, 52, 54 and 56 on the north side of Kensington High Street in 1898. In 1900, 73 Kensington High Street was finally acquired and negotiations successfully concluded with London County Council for the provision of a building lease for a site with a 440-foot frontage on to the north side of Kensington High Street and two new side streets. Soon afterwards plans were laid for a large warehouse with flats above, along the lines of Harrods' recent development in Knightsbridge, and work began on rebuilding 42–60 Kensington High Street. Later the depository facilities in Cromwell

John Barker (1840–1914), the store's founder.

The grocery department window in around 1898.

Crescent (acquired 1895) were also reconstructed.

In 1905 the new furnishing building was completed and Sydney Skinner, who had joined the firm in 1889, was appointed a director to manage the reorganisation attendant upon the expansion into larger premises. It was largely through Skinner's influence that John Barker & Co Ltd continued its expansion in April 1907 with the acquisition of Ponting Brothers, a large drapery store a block further west along Kensington High Street, at a price of £84,000. The business, founded in 1873, had remained a profitable concern until 1906 when an ambitious scheme to diversify the trade foundered and the company went into liquidation. Pontings' old stock was largely cleared in a massive sale but the business continued to trade under its old name and with its own buying team. During the following years attention focused on the redevelopment of Pontings' premises.

In November 1912 the east section of the main block was devastated by fire and 130,000 £1 ordinary shares were issued to finance the rebuilding. Temporary premises were quickly found on the opposite side of the street, and reconstruction, to include a subway between the showrooms on the north and south sides of Kensington High Street, began in 1913 undertaken by the company's own building department. The work was, however, scarcely complete when, in December 1914, John Barker died. Awarded a baronetcy in 1908 he had been actively involved in the management of the business to the end, despite sitting as a Liberal member of parliament for Penrhyn and Falmouth between 1906 and 1910. Barker was succeeded as chairman by Sydney Skinner, who was immediately

In 1921 Barkers opened a small tearoom and roof garden.

faced with the problems consequent upon the outbreak of the First World War. Despite some new orders from the army and Red Cross, trade, by 1915, was diminishing leaving the business over-stocked and over-borrowed. Unprofitable departments were closed, wages were reduced and the delivery service was curtailed, particularly after the sale of 100 horses to the War Office.

The end of the war brought some relief and in January 1920 the policy of expansion was resumed with the acquisition of Derry & Toms, a large drapery store established in 1853, occupying the block between Barkers and Pontings. A purchase price of £603,084 was agreed and met by bank loans and a new share issue. Derry & Toms, like Pontings, was to continue as a separate concern and it was agreed that 'Barkers should be conducted on high-class lines and Pontings and Derry & Toms cater for the multitude or good middle-class lines.' During the next two years Derry & Toms' turnover doubled. Meanwhile Barkers' store on the south side of High Street was reorganised by carving a grand central entrance out of the window frontage and providing a magnificent staircase and lift service to every floor.

The difficult postwar years demanded a flexible approach and during the early

1920s intensive advertising was coupled with the introduction of new lines, such as ready-to-wear clothing and branded 'Kenbar' products, and an emphasis on such departments as furniture, household goods and provisions. The latter was, in fact, flourishing under the control of Trevor Bowen, an experienced confectioner, who joined the business from J. Lyons & Co Ltd in 1914 and handled the army supply contracts during the war. In 1919 Bowen and other managers visited the major American stores to acquire new retailing techniques and to buy unusual stock.

In 1922 Sydney Skinner was knighted and Bowen was promoted to departmental manager. That year Pontings was extensively refurbished. Both Pontings and Derry & Toms were, however, beginning to show trading losses. Both were massively over-stocked and a gulf was emerging between managers and buyers. These difficulties were compounded in succeeding months by rapidly falling prices. In 1924 experimental piano and gramophone shops were opened in Liverpool, Birmingham and Manchester; these were not, however, a success and were closed within two years. In 1925 Zeeta Co Ltd, a chain of high-class catering shops created by Bowen and Skinner as a separate business in 1919, was acquired by Barkers for £120,000. That year Bowen was appointed a director. Between 1922 and 1930 the area of property owned by the company doubled with acquisitions on both sides of High Street. In 1926 a large furniture store was built on a site belonging to the Crown and adjoining the existing building, opposite the main block, at 26–40 Kensington High Street. The company had occupied temporary premises here since the fire of 1912 and took a long lease in

Giant cheeses bought, as a publicity stunt, at the Empire Exhibition in 1924.

1919. Work on the store, known as the Ladymere Building, had begun in 1924. The eight floors were attractively fitted out with specimen rooms and, on the first and mezzanine floors, a men's shop was installed. The new store was linked with the main block by a subway at lower ground floor level.

In 1927 the company reached agreement with the Crown, the principal local landowner, for an exchange of properties which would allow the consolidation and rebuilding of Barkers and Derry & Toms. Plans were laid for a phased redevelopment of both stores during the 1930s, setting Barkers back by thirty feet to reduce the acute congestion in Kensington High Street. The project was to be financed entirely from reserves. The first stage involved the closure of Ball Street, which was built over between 1927 and 1929, and the erection of new administrative offices and household showrooms. Meanwhile Pontings was developed southwards along Wrights Lane.

Architect Bernard George was commissioned to produce designs for both stores, and work on Derry & Toms began immediately, greatly disturbing the trade. The new Derry & Toms store was opened in March 1933 amidst a fanfare of press publicity – 'a beautiful store to sell beautiful things.' Arranged on six floors it was a bold and simple departure in store design, with a fine stone facade of columns and friezes and restrained interior, marble and bronze Art-Deco panels providing the only decorative features. An American designer was engaged to plan the floor layouts and Derry & Toms was consequently one of the first London stores to adopt the horizontal system. Each floor was totally open plan, whilst the absence of well-holes and central staircases reduced the risk of fire. On the fifth floor there was an elegant restaurant, The Rainbow Room, and a fashion theatre. The entire store was beautifully appointed with blue and gold carpets, concealed lighting and attractive display areas. In 1936 work began, at the instigation of Trevor Bowen, on the famous roof gardens. Opened in May 1938, the gardens comprised a sun pavilion and three discrete areas – an English woodland garden, a Spanish garden and a Tudor garden. Meanwhile the demolition team had moved in on Barkers where a new frontage was to be linked with the earlier Ball Street building. Construction began at the western end and was only two-thirds complete when war was declared.

Despite some bomb damage to Derry & Toms and extreme staff shortages, profits were maintained throughout the war. This success was in a large measure due to the company's cash purchasing policy and prudent acquisition of large stocks of merchandise during the late 1930s. Sir Sydney Skinner died in 1941 and was succeeded as chairman by Trevor Bowen. Despite postwar shortages and controls Bowen determined to expand the business. In 1947 he acquired Gosling & Sons Ltd of Richmond, a small drapery business established during the 1790s, and in mid-1951 explored the possibility of acquiring the enormous Selfridge business in Oxford Street. The latter was in fact taken over by Lewis's Investment Trust and Bowen subsequently bought a vacant site in Terminus Road, Eastbourne, where, in September 1953, he opened a new store with thirty departments. It was not, however, until April 1955 that work was resumed on the Barker building in Kensington and the new store there was opened in September 1958. Inside the store was designed along the same open-plan lines as Derry & Toms, although the exterior, with its curved frontage, continuous canopy and projecting tower staircases, presented a striking contrast.

Before the construction of the new building was completed, the business had changed hands. In July 1957 House of Fraser made an offer for the entire share capital offering ten shillings cash and four Fraser 'A' five-shilling shares for each Barker £1 ordinary share. The board recommended acceptance and the offer became unconditional in August. Bowen remained honorary president of the company until his death in 1965, but was replaced as chairman by Hugh Fraser. Under House of Fraser's ownership, the business was gradually streamlined. Between 1959 and 1962 the Zeeta stores were gradually disposed of along with surplus property on the north side of Kensington High Street and in Young Street. In 1965 John Barker (Construction and Development) Ltd was formed to continue the company's old-established building and decorating department. In 1968 Gosling & Sons of Richmond ceased to trade and the store was demolished prior to redevelopment.

By 1970 it had become evident that it would not be economical to maintain all three of the Kensington stores. In February 1971 Pontings was closed and within forty hours the entire store had been installed in the lower ground floor of the Barkers building where it became known as 'Pontings Bargain Basement'. The new showrooms included menswear, fabric, linens and furnishing departments, and a self-service restaurant. The mail-order business was continued as before and the entire Pontings site was sold. The same year, agreement was also reached for the sale of Derry & Toms, although the store was not closed until January 1973. Meanwhile, in late 1972, work began on the refurbishment of Barkers in order to capture the trade of the closed stores.

In 1975 House of Fraser also acquired Army & Navy Stores Ltd and Barkers became the flagship of a new Army & Navy Division. In 1976 the food hall was revamped and a new china and glass department and restaurant opened. The following year automatic lifts were installed and the Pontings basement, which was out of keeping with the new store image, closed. Further modernisation work was undertaken in 1978 with the construction of a new main entrance on the corner of Derry Street and the opening of a new fashion area on the first floor and electrical and hardware departments on the lower ground floor.

By the early 1980s it had become clear that the store's sales area, in excess of 600,000 square feet, was too large for the existing trade. In 1982 the number of sales floors was reduced from seven to four and architects were commissioned to refurbish and redevelop Barkers as a compact store of 140,000 square feet alongside a new arcade of nine boutiques. The remaining part of the building was to comprise around 200,000 square feet of office space, with a spectacular barrel vaulted atrium, the largest in Europe, overlooking garden terraces. The new department store was completed by November 1986 and the shopping arcade opened in October 1987.

Binns Ltd, Sunderland

George Binns was born in Lancashire in 1781. In 1811 he acquired Thomas Ellerby's small linen and woollen drapery shop at 176 High Street, Bishop's Wearmouth, a town adjacent to Sunderland which was already prospering as a successful port for the import of coal. His strict Quaker upbringing endowed his approach to business with an honesty and fairness so that he soon earned a reputation for quality merchandise and integrity in every transaction. He was aided in the shop by his eldest son, Henry, and also, between 1817 and 1824, by his nephew, David Binns. David undertook much of the buying in Manchester and travelled on horseback to local colliery villages in order to increase sales of drapery goods. When George died in 1836 he was succeeded by Henry, then in his mid-twenties, and thereafter the store traded as Henry Binns. Henry shared his father's high moral standards and was an active member of the anti-slavery lobby. He instituted a policy of selling only 'goods manufactured from cotton

TO THE FRIENDS OF THE SLAVE.
H. BINNS

HAS pleasure in announcing, that he is now in a position to supply the following descriptions of Goods, manufactured from Cotton warranted to be free-labour grown, viz., Prints, Shirting Calicoes, (white and grey) Hosiery, Tapes, and Sewing Cottons.

An opportunity is thus afforded to such as consider it a duty to discountenance the atrocities of the slave system, so far to withhold their support from it, it being obvious that every shilling spent in the labour produce, displaces a similar amount which is wrung from the blood and sinews of the slave; and that in proportion as the British public carry out this principle, will the increased demand induce a larger growth of free Cotton, thus giving the most effectual blow to a traffic so opposed to the interests of religion and humanity.

173, High-street, Bishopwearmouth.

Advertisement concerning Binns' support for the anti-slavery lobby.

BELOW *A street hoarding advertising the store during the 1920s.*

warranted to be free labour grown,' thereby allowing his customers to strike an 'effectual blow to the traffic so opposed to the service of religion and humanity.' In 1844, Henry left the shop at 176 High Street and removed the drapery business to premises at 173 High Street where he employed three shop assistants. When Henry retired and moved to Croydon, Surrey, in 1865, control of the business passed to his son, Joseph John, trading under the title of H. Binns, Son & Co. In 1878 the shop boasted sales in excess of £17,500 and a profit of £3,500.

During the early 1880s the westward shift of the town centre prompted the acquisition of new premises and in October 1884 the shop was installed in two houses at 38 and 39 Fawcett Street close to the town hall and post office. The old frontage was demolished and replaced by a brick and stone facade with a large central doorway paved with marble mosaic. Inside the partition walls were removed to create a large open showroom with long lines of ash and mahogany counters. On the first floor there were mantle and millinery departments and fitting rooms and on the second floor there were workshops, the whole building being centrally heated by hot water pipes. In 1897 the business was floated as a limited liability company, H. Binns, Son & Co Ltd, with a share capital of £10,000. Joseph Binns, then almost sixty years of age, became chairman of the new company, and John Simpson, who had recently joined the firm, was appointed director and general manager. By that time the store employed thirty staff and was still trading on two floors with a window frontage of fifty feet. Simpson was a talented warehousemen with experience in stores in Scotland, London and Bath, and under his management sales grew rapidly.

In 1899 the premises at 38 and 39 Fawcett Street were bought outright. By 1905 additional shops had been leased at 40 and 42 Fawcett Street and 3 Athenaeum Street and two years later all the showrooms were extensively remodelled in a way which encouraged casual browsing. In 1909 a third director was appointed, Neil Cameron, manager of the household furnishings department. Expansion continued during the following years, with the acquisition of premises at 36 Fawcett Street in 1910, where a new man's shop was opened, 35 Fawcett Street in 1912 and 33 Fawcett Street in 1913. In 1914 the business of McDonald & Co was taken over as a going concern and Mr McDonald was appointed

A store delivery van in around 1920.

A tram in Fawcett Street, Sunderland, sporting a 'Shop at Binns' poster.

manager of the new furniture department. This growth was funded by successive share issues and, by 1914, the capital of the company stood at £65,000.

In 1915, 34 Fawcett Street was extended and altered, and three years later 32 Fawcett Street was acquired, to accommodate the household departments, and linked, at first-floor level, to the showrooms at number 33. At this time the store was borrowing heavily in order to take advantage of purchase discounts and, between 1918 and 1920, further share issues were made increasing the company's capital to £310,000. In 1918 Harry Bennett, manager of the outfitting department, was appointed as a fourth director. During the following three years premises were acquired at 37 Fawcett Street and a number of the existing showrooms were extended, adding a further storey to 41 Fawcett Street. Simpson had studied large stores in the United States and was determined to create a modern

department store in Sunderland, along American lines. By 1921 the store was trading on both sides of Fawcett Street, boasting a sales area of seven acres and a turnover in excess of £760,000 per annum. The store supplied 'everything that is required for human comfort and welfare except perishable goods,' and also offered lounges and a tearoom (where a band played regularly), a post office, telephone rooms and a hairdressing salon. The company owned extensive cabinet-making and upholstery workrooms and undertook removals. In the store merchandise was displayed in the most modern fashion, using revolving showcases and model furnished rooms. Simpson advertised aggressively, taking full pages in local newspapers, adopting such slogans as 'Shop at Binns for everything' and 'You always get satisfaction at Binns'.

In March 1922 Joseph Binns died and was succeeded as chairman by John Simpson who was determined to extend the scope of the business. In August 1922 H. Binns, Son & Co Ltd negotiated the purchase, from the liquidator, of Arthur Sanders Ltd which owned a drapery shop in High Row, Darlington. Adjoining premises were quickly acquired in High Row and Blackwellgate and the store, trading under the Binns name, was extended and refurbished. A new oak and bronze frontage was executed by Binns' own workmen and plans were laid for the inclusion of new carpet and bedding departments alongside tea and rest rooms and telephone facilities. In October 1923 the company also acquired Thomas Jones' huge store in Middlesbrough with a frontage of 465 feet and a fine central location. Again the store was extended and remodelled and began to trade under the Binns name. During the first year turnover doubled. In January 1925 the company suffered a slight setback when the Darlington store was destroyed by fire. Temporary premises were, however, quickly found and rebuilding began the following year.

The shell of the Darlington store following the fire in 1925.

Meanwhile Simpson intensified the group's advertising effort. In 1924 Binns took the novel step of securing advertising space in all London and North Eastern Railway carriages. The following year the group advertised extensively on local buses and trams and in railway stations, instituting 'shopping week' promotions. Later, mannequin parades were held. These promotions were highly successful and, despite the keen recession of the early 1920s, the group's turnover had risen to over £1 million pounds by 1925. In April 1926 the company acquired Gray Peverill & Co Ltd, which owned a four-storey clothing and furnishing store in West Hartlepool. The store was later renamed and remodelled. Expansion continued with the acquisition of Fowler & Brock Ltd of South Shields and adjoining property in July 1927 and a substantial site in Borough Road, Sunderland, for the erection of a new six-storey building later the same year. The new Sunderland store was opened in 1928 and James Coxon & Co Ltd of Newcastle-upon-Tyne was acquired in May 1929. By the late 1920s the Binns name was well known all over north England and the company was securing furnishing contracts as far afield as Edinburgh and Southampton. The improvement and extension of all the stores and the acquisition of local warehouse properties continued and, during the early 1930s, the geographical coverage of the group was greatly extended by the acquisition of Robinson Brothers Ltd, with stores in Carlisle and Dumfries, in 1933 and of Robert Maule & Co Ltd of Edinburgh in 1934. Sales were sluggish during the depressed years of the early 1930s, and in 1935 the company organised a series of eighty-five special trains to take customers on shopping excursions to Binns stores. A free lunch or tea was provided for those making purchases worth over £2. By 1935 the company had a capital of over £1 million, and employed 5,000 staff, with each of the principal stores accommodating around sixty departments.

The group continued to trade strongly until the outbreak of the war in 1939 when several stores were requisitioned and air-raid shelters built in basement areas. In March 1941 the Dumfries store was destroyed by fire. A few weeks later most of the Fawcett Street premises in Sunderland were lost after a heavy bombing raid. Within three days the Sunderland store was operating again from the converted motor store in Holmside but many staff had had to be laid off and additional premises were sorely needed. On 27 March 1942 the group was dealt yet another blow when the Middlesbrough store was also destroyed by fire. Three months later a second Middlesbrough fire followed the first and the entire stock was lost. A rebuilding licence for the Sunderland store was not secured until 1949 and rebuilding of the basement and ground floor on the west side of Fawcett Street began in November 1949. Meanwhile John G. Simpson had replaced his father as chairman. The new Sunderland store, with five storeys and a fine Portland stone facade, opened in March 1953. It incorporated the most modern shop fittings and equipment and specialised in women's wear with a hairdressing salon and restaurant on the upper floors. Meanwhile the board was fighting a bitter battle to ward off a takeover bid from House of Fraser. In April 1953, however, House of Fraser finally secured a majority shareholding.

In 1954 planning permission was received to build a new store in Middlesbrough which was opened in March 1957. Heralded as the most modern store in the country, it comprised six open-plan floors and an attractive elliptical staircase. In Sunderland reconstruction work began on the corner of Borough Road and Fawcett Street, a site which was to be connected by subway to the existing fashion building. The new store, with twenty-five acres of sales space on four floors, was completed in October 1962 and incorporated the most modern lighting and display equipment and a handsome self-supporting staircase. Entire floors were devoted to both carpets and furniture and there were also large china and glass, fabric and electronic equipment departments, along with a sizeable self-service food hall. The fashion building on the other side of Fawcett Street was simultaneously refurbished in the same style. In 1968 a Binns credit card was introduced. In 1972 the Sunderland store received a massive face-lift and traded successfully for the next fifteen years. However, by the late 1980s, the store's customer base had diminished, and in April 1989 the furniture building was vacated and unprofitable departments, such as the food hall, closed down. Meanwhile many of the store's in the Binns Division were trading strongly and between 1984 and 1986 those at Hull, Darlington and Grimsby were totally refurbished.

Brown Muff & Co Ltd, Bradford

In March 1814, William Brown advertised the forthcoming sale by auction of his saddler's shop in New (later Market) Street in Bradford. It is said that he had to give up his business owing to ill-health – he died two years later – and that his wife, Elizabeth, opened her little shop at 11 Market Street in order to provide for their family. Elizabeth Brown's uncle and brother were drapers, and she began trading at 'Mrs Brown's' as a clothes broker, specialising in fustian goods and ready-made underclothing, as well as housing a circulating library in her tiny bow-windowed shop. By 1828 she was conducting the business in partnership with her son, Henry, as Brown & Son, linen drapers and clothes brokers, at 11 and 12 Market Street.

Elizabeth Brown retired in 1834, and her son continued trading on his own as Henry Brown & Co. He married Betsy Muff that year, and in 1835 he employed Betsy's fifteen-year-old brother, Thomas Muff, in the shop. Elizabeth Brown

A customer bill illustrating the main store in 1888.

CORNER OF MARKET STREET & NEW IVEGATE, BRADFORD.
ESTABLISHED 1814.
WHOLESALE & RETAIL
DRAPERS.
SILK MERCERS
& OUTFITTERS.

Carpet & Bedstead Furnishing Warehousemen.

Mr J. W. Kay   1st Oct 1888

Bo. of Brown, Muff & Co

died in 1845, the same year that Thomas joined Henry as a partner in Brown & Muff, linen and wool drapers, tailors, hosiers and hatters. Market Street was renumbered in 1850, and the shop's address became numbers 54 and 56. Business grew enormously during the following decade and by the 1880s Brown & Muff was one of the largest drapery stores in Bradford, with an extensive retail and wholesale trade.

In 1870 the Corporation's street improvement plan called for the demolition of Brown & Muff's store and in 1871 an impressive five-storey building was completed on the corner of Market Street and Ivegate. New carpet and furnishing departments were opened, but the retail business conducted on the ground floor was small compared to Brown & Muff's large wholesale business. Henry Brown retired from the business in 1871, and died seven years later with no surviving children. He was a well-known and respected figure in Bradford, sitting on the boards of several local educational and charitable institutions. Brown played an important role in securing Bradford's charter of incorporation in 1874 and, serving as an alderman for fourteen years, he was three times elected Lord Mayor. When he retired from business in 1871, a partnership agreement was drawn up between Thomas Muff, his three sons, Henry, Charles and Frederic, and four other colleagues, trading as Brown Muff & Co.

In 1878 the store was badly damaged by fire, causing between £40,000 and £50,000 worth of damage to the building and stock. Temporary premises were opened at 29 Bridge Street and an enormous sale of water-damaged stock held. When trading resumed in the old building, the firm began selling iron bedsteads, perambulators and travelling trunks as well as drapery and furnishings. Thomas Muff retired in 1889 and the business was continued by the other proprietors, with Henry Muff as senior partner. In 1905 the partnership was converted to a private limited company, Brown Muff & Co Ltd, with Henry, Charles and Frederic Muff and George and Richard Walker as shareholders. Four years later, the Muffs reverted to an older form of their surname, Maufe, but it was decided to leave the name of the business unaltered.

Philip Maufe, Frederic's son, joined the store as an office junior in 1906 and Frederic became chairman of the company upon Charles Maufe's retirement in 1913. The business prospered during the prewar years, paying a dividend of $12\frac{1}{2}$ per cent to the ordinary shareholders at the end of every financial year from 1906 until 1914. The outbreak of the First World War inevitably led to a disruption of trade, but the company continued to expand. In 1916, premises on the corner of Ivegate and Tyrrel Street were acquired for £29,000, and in March 1918 major alterations to the store were begun at a cost of over £20,000. In 1921 the premises were mortgaged, as security for the company's increased lending, and the money invested in further expansion. In March of the following year a warehouse in Nesfield Street was purchased and in April 1926 premises at the corner of Bank and Market Streets were acquired for incorporation into the main store. A new beauty parlour opened in 1927, when the theatre on the fourth floor was converted into a 'baby park' to provide a further attraction for women shoppers.

Bradford's traditional industries were severely affected by the depression of the early 1930s, and high unemployment resulted in a falling off in spending in the town's stores. In September 1931 Brown Muff announced that the company's directors, as well as buyers, staff, and workroom employees, would have to accept cuts in salaries and wages, and in January 1932 customers were informed that discounts on monthly accounts were to be reduced from 5 per cent to $2\frac{1}{2}$ per cent, while the number of departments offering trade discounts was reduced. In September 1932 Brown Muff's property was mortgaged for £124,998, but by

The elegant and spacious ladies' costume department during the 1910s.

August 1934 conditions had so improved that the company was able to borrow £20,500 to purchase the last corner of their island site, the old Midland Bank building. Taking advantage of the favourable state of the money markets, Brown Muff proceeded, in 1936, to issue £200,000 of debenture stock, doubling the authorised share capital of the company, in order to discharge oustanding loans secured on the property. This issue required the registration of Brown Muff as a public company, but the business remained under the control of the Maufe family. Replacing the old trade slogan 'Quality and value' with 'The cheapest that is good and the best that money can buy', and advertising heavily in the local press, Brown Muff emerged from the depression with booming sales and renewed optimism.

During the interwar years, Brown Muff's image as a high-class store, catering in the main for the 'carriage trade', was replaced by one of a more popular establishment. This trend was confirmed during the Second World War, when the introduction of coupon rationing encouraged people to pay greater attention to value for money. After the war, Brown Muff continued to seek to attract a wider range of income groups to the store, concentrating on building an image for fair dealing and for offering good, reliable articles at reasonable prices. This policy proved extremely successful and the company estimated that the real value

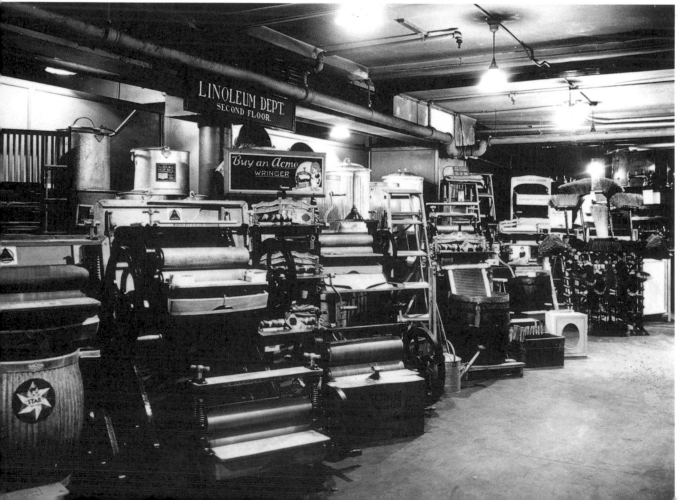

OPPOSITE ABOVE
The men's hairdressing department during the 1930s.

OPPOSITE BELOW
The household equipment department during the 1930s.

of sales increased by fifty per cent between 1937 and 1950. In 1956 the company failed to reach agreement with the Corporation to lease a prime corner site on Market Street, but acquired the lease to Howard House, on the corner of Bank Street and Broadway, on which was built a new five-storey extension to the main store. Two years later, preference and ordinary shares were made available to the public, thereby raising capital for more improvements to the business at a time when the redevelopment of central Bradford seemed likely to attract greater numbers of shoppers to the area. A new building, adjoining an existing warehouse and workroom block in Leeds Road, was completed in 1959 and the garage, maintenance workshop and stockrooms were transferred there from the old premises in Nesfield Street. The following year, 1960, was the best in the company's history, with turnover and profits reaching record levels.

In September 1961, Brown Muff acquired Eastbrook House, adjoining the Leeds Road premises, with a view to further development. That same month, the business and premises of Amblers, a fashion store in Skipton's High Street, as well as vacant land lying behind, were purchased. A new store was opened on the site in 1963 and was later connected with the Carla Beck snack bar premises, acquired in 1962, to create the town's leading store. Also in 1963, Brown Muff began to trade in Bingley, with the purchase and renovation of Pratt's men's and women's wear store.

Brown Muff's policy of extending the area of their operations continued during the 1970s. The selling space and the frontage of the Skipton store were doubled in 1973, and in February 1975 a new two-storey furniture centre was opened in Doncaster's Arndale Centre. In 1976, major alterations to the facade and the interior of the main store in Market Street were completed, and plans announced to open a sizeable new store in a three-storey building in Altrincham. Brown Muff's success and annual turnover of around £5 million had by then attracted the attention of House of Fraser. By May 1975 House of Fraser had acquired a 27.2 per cent holding of the company's ordinary shares, and in the spring of 1977 launched a successful bid for control. The following year the Bradford store was renamed Rackhams. Meanwhile construction work proceeded on the new branch in Altrincham which opened as a Rackhams store in late 1978.

A store delivery van in 1946.

CAVENDISH HOUSE,
PROMENADE, CHELTENHAM;
No. 44, WIGMORE STREET, LONDON
AND HARROGATE, YORKSHIRE.

DEBENHAM, POOLEY, & SMITH
BEG to announce they have OPENED their NEW and EXTENSIVE PREMISES, and are now offering for Sale a STOCK unrivalled in extent, and selected with the greatest care from the British and Foreign Markets, consisting of every novelty in

Silks, Cachmeres. Shawls, Mantles, Cloaks, Lace, and Embroidery ;

HOSIERY, FLANNELS, AND BLANKETS;
MOREEN, DAMASK, AND CHINTZ FURNITURE ;
SHEETINGS, DAMASK TABLE CLOTHS,
And Linen Drapery of every description ;
COBOURG AND ORLEANS CLOTHS ;
A large LOT of FRENCH MERINOES, EXCEEDINGLY CHEAP:

Cavendish House & Co Ltd, Cheltenham

During the late 1770s William Franks established a small drapery shop at 44 Wigmore Street, close to Cavendish Square in London. The business later traded as Flint's and was subsequently acquired by Thomas Clark. In December 1813 Clark, in return for a capital investment of £500, assumed young William Debenham as an equal partner, and thereafter the firm traded as Clark & Debenham. The shop, renamed Cavendish House, carried drapery, silks, haberdashery, millinery, hosiery, lace and family mourning goods and adopted a ready-money system. As the trade grew the partners determined to expand the business by opening provincial branches in such spa towns as Cheltenham and Harrogate which were were beginning to rival the earlier popularity of Bath.

By 1823 Clark & Debenham had opened a small drapery business at 3 Promenade Rooms, Cheltenham, selling a selection of silks, muslins, shawls, gloves, lace and fancy goods. The business was conducted along the same lines of low prices and ready money as its London counterpart. The Promenade was then a new thoroughfare stretching into meadows on the edge of the town, but the opening of Sherborne Spa in 1818, town improvements, such as the laying out of new walks and drives and the introduction of gas-lighting, and faster transport links with London, encouraged the growth of a large residential and visiting population. The new shop flourished. In 1837 Clark retired from the business and Debenham assumed two of his most trusted staff, William Pooley and John Smith, as partners, trading in both London and Cheltenham as Debenham, Pooley & Smith. By 1840 the management of the Cheltenham branch appears to have been given to young Clement Freebody, Debenham's brother-in-law, who took up residence in Cheltenham, initially living over the shop with his staff. Around 1843 another branch shop was launched in Harrogate.

In October 1844 the opening of extended and refurbished premises in Cheltenham was heralded by a massive sale of drapery and other goods. By December 1844 another showroom had been taken for the display of evening dresses, which included facilities for 'showing the effects of every colour by candlelight.' Pooley and Smith retired from the business in 1851 when Debenham took his son, William, and Clement Freebody into partnership, trading as Debenham, Son & Freebody. Later that year the Cheltenham premises were extensively altered and enlarged. By 1872 the store occupied a huge site, stretching from the Promenade to Regent Street, with attractive showrooms offering more than twenty departments and extensive workrooms to the rear. Soon afterwards the firm also acquired Stamford House, at the end of Rodney Terrace, a substantial mansion built in the early 1820s. At this time all three shops, in London, Cheltenham and Harrogate, were trading in similar goods and issued a joint catalogue, called the *Fashion Book*, which was the basis of an extensive mail-order trade.

In 1876, when Freebody retired, a new partnership, Debenham & Hewitt, was formed. George Hewitt appears to have worked at the Cheltenham store as a draper's assistant during the early 1860s but details of his subsequent career are not known. By 1883 George Hewitt was sole owner of the Cheltenham business, Frank and William Debenham having withdrawn to manage the London store as a separate concern. In July 1883 Cavendish House Ltd was registered as a private limited company to acquire the Cheltenham business with a capital of £35,000. George Hewitt, chairman of the new company, took most of the shares and the remainder were largely split between John Cooper, an accountant and secretary of the company, Charles Williams, manager of the general departments, and Albert Nichols, manager of the furnishing section. By the 1880s the store had established large cabinet-making works in Regent Street, and in 1886 also erected a fire-proof warehouse adjoining Stamford House for the development of a depository business. In 1888, upon Hewitt's retirement, the first company was liquidated and reconstructed as Cavendish House Co Ltd, a public company with a capital of £85,000. The entire share capital was taken up. Colonel J.C. Griffiths became chairman and Cooper, Williams and Nichols initially remained managing directors. Both Hewitt and Debenham had modest shareholdings which were gradually sold off over the following years.

The cover of the 1946 winter sale catalogue.

By 1890 the store boasted a frontage of 143 feet and a floor space of 20,000 square feet. Agents were employed in Paris to purchase the latest fashion novelties and an afternoon tearoom was opened. The capital provided by the public flotation of the business allowed the implementation of an extensive refurbishment programme. In 1891 an attractive frontage of plate glass, with a frieze of richly coloured leaded windows, was erected, and in 1898 electric lighting was installed throughout the store. The business thrived with turnover and profits rising steadily despite a general trade depression. In 1903 an established silk mercery business at Brunswick House, 3 Promenade Villas, was purchased on favourable terms. The acquisition was financed by the issue, in November 1903, of £20,000 of debentures. The purchased stock was quickly sold off at a discount to facilitate alterations, and carpet showrooms were installed in the new premises. During 1904 the company also purchased 56 Regent Street which was used for the bedding department, and in 1907 the furniture showrooms were greatly improved by the addition of suites of furnished rooms. Refurbishment continued during the years immediately before the First World War with the addition of a new millinery salon, a ladies' waiting room and lavatories and a corset department. In 1920 a gentlemen's outfitter and music shop were acquired with capital raised by the issue of a further £30,000 of debentures, and in 1928 a site in Regent's Mews, formerly a livery stable, was acquired and opened as showrooms.

In July 1928 the company was taken over by Standard Industrial Trust of Broad Street Place, London, which also owned Morgan Squire Ltd, a Leicester department store. Three years later the Cheltenham premises were entirely refurbished, creating a large store of over 163,000 square feet, with a 287-foot frontage on Promenade. In 1957 the company opened a branch store in Oxford Street, London, but it proved impossible to manage effectively from a distance and the venture was closed within three months. In 1961 a controlling interest in both Cavendish House and Morgan Squire was acquired by Swears & Wells (1926) Ltd. The following year the Cavendish House shares again changed hands passing to J.J. Allen Ltd, a Bournemouth-based store group. J.J. Allen invested heavily in the development of the store, initiating a three-phase refurbishment programme rebuilding the facade to a depth of sixty feet, installing escalators and enlarging several departments. In 1970 J.J. Allen Ltd was acquired by House of Fraser, and in 1972 a new food hall was opened. The store which initially traded as part of Harrods Provincial Group later joined Midland Division of House of Fraser. In 1985 Cavendish House was partially refurbished, with the creation of a new restaurant and fashion floor and the installation of a bridge linking the store to an adjacent new shopping development.

The new food hall in 1972.

The Pavement 1887.

The store and adjoining shops on The Pavement in 1887.

Chiesmans Ltd, Lewisham, London

The store was founded by two brothers, Frank and Harry Chiesman, who acquired the small drapery shop of Cross Brothers at 59 High Street, Lewisham, in September 1884. Their father, Walter, accountant to a London wholesale firm, provided half of the capital but advised that The Pavement, where the shop was situated, was on the wrong side of the street to catch passing trade. The partners were, however, determined and hard working and used their complementary skills to great advantage. Frank had been apprenticed in Gorringes and Harry at Whiteleys and both had also served in stores in Paris. The original shop had a frontage of some eighteen feet where heavy goods were displayed on one side and fancy goods on the other, with a recess for showing millinery at one end. The early years were difficult and in May 1885 a note was entered in the private ledger: 'We have only been in business as fancy drapers for eight months and so far as we can ascertain our profits will not reach per annum £130.' Seven years later the annual profit had risen to £865 and the partners had begun to acquire adjoining properties in order to expand the business. As each shop was acquired, a separate department was installed – carpets at numbers 41 and 43, ironmongery at numbers 33 and 35, and furniture at number 45. A single frontage was later erected to unite the rambling showrooms.

The store, known locally as Paris House, advertised aggressively as cash drapers and specialised in sales of remnants and job lots. Gradually the business diversified away from drapery to the sale of new lines, such as stationery, toys, furniture and boots and shoes. In 1899 waiting rooms and tearooms were opened. By 1908 the store occupied 41–59 High Street and comprised premises across a dividing lane which were joined to the main building by a new subway. By 1910 Chiesman Brothers was advertising as 'the most commodious, convenient, comfortable and economical shopping centre in Kent.' As the store's trade in furnishings and removals increased, a number of properties were acquired to use as furniture depositories. These included the Old Road Institute in Lee in 1900, a site in High Street (where stables were also erected) in 1901, and the East London Industrial School in 1920. Growth was checked by the outbreak of the First World War. After the war the founder's sons, who had been on service overseas, also entered the business. Frank's eldest son, Stewart, had trained at Bon Marché in Brixton and specialised in fashions and staff management; his brother, Russell, who had worked in a Stretford store had special knowledge of furnishings and transport, and Harry's son, Harold, formerly of Derry & Toms, showed a flair for advertising and publicity.

In 1921 the construction of a new store was begun, its design being influenced by Frank Chiesman's experience of American stores. In 1929 a private company, Chiesmans Ltd, was established. That year a tower and arcade were added to the original building, and the basements of 37–41 High Street extensively altered. The acquisition of adjoining premises on the south side of the main store continued and in 1932 the furniture and china departments were also rebuilt. The store then had a frontage of 250 feet with two handsome buildings on either side of a dividing roadway.

In 1933 a second store was acquired in Maidstone from the liquidator of a bankrupt firm. The store, renamed Chiesmans and refurbished in a manner which encouraged browsing, enjoyed a good site and was soon made highly profitable. In 1929 Frank Chiesman died, followed by his brother, Harry, in 1940. In 1947 another branch store was purchased in Canterbury but was disposed

The store's new display windows in 1910.

of within a few years. In 1953 Chiesmans acquired Bon Marché, a general drapery store in Gravesend, from the retiring proprietor. In 1957 a public company was formed, Chiesmans Ltd, although a major part of the shares remained under family ownership. During the next two years the new company was offered and acquired stores in Newport, Isle of Wight, and Tunbridge Wells, Kent, by retiring proprietors anxious to retain a link with a family firm. In 1959 Chiesmans also took over Burnes of Ilford, John Lewis of Upton Park and Leonards of Rochester. In 1960 the principal store in Lewisham was greatly extended by the construction of a back building, comprising a new fabric hall and self-service restaurant, adding an extra 30,000 square feet of sales space. In 1976 the company was acquired by House of Fraser and began to trade as part of the Army & Navy Division. In late 1979 a new fashion floor was completed and in 1981 a walkway was opened, crossing High Street and joining the store to a busy shopping precinct.

Dickins & Jones Ltd, Regent Street, London

During the 1790s Thomas Dickins' father, a coal merchant of Market Weighton near York, apprenticed his son to Richard Hodgkinson, a Worksop draper. Dickins was, however, keen to improve his prospects and during the late 1790s Hodgkinson secured for him a situation in a suitable house in London. At his new place of employment Dickins befriended William Smith. By around 1803 the pair had saved sufficient capital to open a linen drapery establishment on their own account at 54 Oxford Street, where they adopted a golden lion as their trade sign. Little is known of the business in its early years but around 1827 Dickins & Smith were joined by a third partner, Joseph Stevens, and thereafter the firm traded as Dickins, Smith & Stevens. As the business grew it became clear that larger and more prestigious premises were required.

The Regent Street frontage, decorated for the Coronation, in 1902.

In 1813 an Act of Parliament, instigated by the Prince Regent, had been passed to provide for the building of a new street intended to create a magnificent carriageway from Carlton House to the new royal park in Marylebone. From the outset, John Nash, architect of the scheme, envisaged the section between Piccadilly and Oxford Circus as a high-class shopping promenade. Huge pavements, covered arcades and elegant ground-floor showrooms were incorporated in the design, and domestic traders, hawkers and taverns were all prohibited. In 1835 Dickins, Smith & Stevens moved into 232 Regent Street, the central portion of a symmetrical block built by Samuel Baxter. The facade was an imposing one featuring four large columns and the golden lion brought from the Oxford Street premises. Situated opposite Hanover Street, the warehouse grandly adopted the title Hanover House. By 1835 Dickins, Smith & Stevens had built up an extensive connection based on the sale of quality goods at reasonable prices. Their insistence on cash and no abatement of price must have been unusual in Regent Street where huge mark-ups were the rule and customers expected to haggle. During the mid-1840s Dickins loaned his eldest son, Thomas, a large sum of money to purchase a Manchester silk manufactory, and this family connection may well have been an important factor in the gradual diversification of the store's trade away from its original specialisation in linen drapery. Thomas consequently retired from the business, which was already trading as Dickins, Stevens & Dickins, and around this time Charles John, Dickins' second son, joined the firm, living over the showrooms with ten other young shopmen.

In 1856 Thomas Dickins senior, died leaving a huge estate. Charles John and Henry Francis, his two younger sons, took over the shop and created Dickins & Jones by assuming John Prichard Jones as a partner. The new management was more ambitious than the old. Regent Street was in its heyday. The nascent omnibus and underground systems were bringing more shoppers to the West End than ever before and the purchasing power of the new suburban middle classes was becoming more profitable than the old carriage trade. In 1869 the store occupied adjoining premises at 234 Regent Street and, by 1890, 236 Regent Street and 29-31 Argyll Street had also been added. The separate houses were converted into a single, commodious warehouse.

The 1890s proved to be a period of tremendous growth. Traditional linen lines were augmented by the sale of lace, dresses, furs, mantles, wedding trousseaux, mourning apparel, underclothing, gloves, umbrellas and a huge variety of oriental and other giftwares. The showrooms were beautifully arranged and noted for their fine displays of lace goods. In 1895 an afternoon tearoom was opened, 'where a choice tea is made fresh at a small charge for each visitor.' The staff numbered around 200, most of whom lived-in in Argyll Street lodgings. The store, which supplied royalty and the aristocracy at home and abroad, had acquired a remarkable reputation for the quality of its goods and services. Indeed, Dickins & Jones held appointments to the Princess of Wales, the King of Spain, the Queen of the Netherlands and King Louis Philippe of France. For the convenience of customers the firm also operated one of the largest-mail order businesses in London, circulating catalogues and patterns post-free on application. By 1895 special premises in Argyll Street had been allocated to the growing postal department which also offered free delivery to central and sub-urban London.

The growth of the business was reflected in sharply rising profits which increased from £20,106 in 1894 to £63,434 in 1900. In 1900 the firm was incorporated as a limited liability company, Dickins & Jones Ltd, with a share capital of £600,000. The vendors, Charles John Dickins, Henry Francis Dickins, John Prichard Jones and their sons, Charles Thomas, Frederick Albert and Vernon William Dickins, all remained directors and retained a high proportion of the issued shares. Family control was not, therefore, impaired although, as an incentive, a small number of shares were given to heads of departments. The premises at that time comprised 232–244 Regent Street, with an extensive frontage on both Argyll Street and Little Argyll Street and various stable premises.

The 1900s witnessed a new kind of growth as Dickins & Jones began to take over other successful firms including Lewis & Allenby of Conduit Street, silk mercer; Allison's of Regent Street; Balls & Flint of Regent Street, baby linen retailer; Redmayne of Bond Street, tailor; and George Hitchcock of St Paul's Churchyard, silk mercer. This spate of acquisitions, masterminded by John Prichard Jones, store manager, extended the activities of the company and introduced, in particular, a new emphasis on silk. The Regent Street business was built up during these years by a policy of special sales and judicious advertising. A coffee shop was introduced on the third floor. By the 1910s it had become apparent that Dickins' sons were not interested in carrying on the business and Harrod's Stores Ltd, encouraged by John Prichard Jones, acquired a controlling interest in Dickins & Jones in July 1914. Richard Burbidge, managing director of Harrods and a brilliant businessman, assumed control although the store continued to trade as a separate entity. Within weeks Britain was at war. In August 1914 the Government commandeered all the store's delivery horses and huge numbers of staff joined up, making it difficult to maintain standards of service. All male employees at the front were, however, assured of their jobs upon return and received a retaining wage and Christmas food parcels from the firm.

In 1919 the entire island site was finally secured and, between 1920 and 1922, the old building was pulled down and work began on a new store designed by Messrs Henry Tanner. The cost of the redevelopment was enormous at a time when trade was difficult and the value of stocks was collapsing. In 1923 £1 million of mortgage debenture stock was issued, on the security of the company's property, in order to repay outstanding loans. The new store, handsome and spacious, included a library, tearooms and restaurant and comprised a total sales area of 167,000 square feet. Later hairdressing and theatre ticket departments were opened together with a whole floor devoted to inexpensive fashion. The building was not, however, completed until 1939 when the Argyll Street extension was opened. The beautiful Dome Restaurant, where tea dances were held daily, became a particularly popular rendezvous.

The outbreak of the Second World War was, however, a major setback for it heralded a long period of controls and shortages. Again many of the male staff

52 · CHRISTMAS PRESENTS.

No. 42. **New Apron**, trimmed good embroidery, with prettily arranged bib; skirt finished with broad hem. Price 1/11½
French Coronet Cap, with frills, edged Val. lace. Price 1/0½

No. 43. **White Spotted Muslin Apron**, bib prettily trimmed insertion and embroidery, skirt finished with hem and tucks. Price 3/11½
Pretty Muslin Cap, crown of insertion and tucks, made to draw up; with long ends. Price 2/6

New "Judge" Cravat, *as illustration,* in Pleated Point d'Esprit Net, trimmed square ground lace and insertion; Neckband threaded with Bébé Velvet.
Prices 8/11, 9/11
Also in Silk, in place of Net.
Price 10/9

Dainty Lace Jabot, *as illustration.* Price 3/6
Or in **Real Lace.** Price 13/9
A large variety of other styles, 4/11 to 3 Guineas.

Servants' French Cap. *as illustration,* 7½d. each.
Other prices, 11¼d., 1/*¼, 1/9 and 1/11
For other Servants' Caps and Aprons, see sheet of Illustrations, which can be had post free.

No. 44. **Maids' Lawn Apron**, bib and epaulettes of fine tucks, with insertion and embroidery; tucked hem on skirt. Price 2/11.
Pretty Muslin Cap, trimmed embroidered frills and made to draw up, without ends. Price 1/9

No. 45. **Maids' Hemstitched Lawn Apron**, with frilled bib and deep hem on skirt. Price 2/6
Pretty Coronet Washing Cap, with crown of tucks and insertions, goffered frills and long ends. Price 1/2½

Lawn Puritan Sets of Collar and Cuffs, with rows of hemstitching and 2 tucks, *as illustration,* 3/6 per set. Others at 2/6, 3/9 and 3/11 per set.
Collars separately 1 3½, 1/6½, 1/0, 1/11½ each.

DICKINS & JONES, LTD., REGENT STREET, LONDON.

were called up and women and youths admitted to more responsible positions. Fortunately Dickins & Jones escaped major bomb damage but public air-raid shelters and a canteen were opened in the sub-basement and the third floor was requisitioned by the post office for telecommunication purposes. The postwar years witnessed gradual modernisation of the store which, in the 1930s, had had a rather traditional image which discouraged casual browsing. From 1947 the sales floors were refurbished to suggest intimate and prettily decorated rooms. Heavy wooden fittings were replaced by glass counters, and in 1952, after the introduction of new advertising agents, the 'Lady in the Rose' trade mark was adopted. In 1947 the Lincoln Room was created as an extension to the restaurant, and a 'Younger Londoner' department was opened to attract new customers. Cash registers were later introduced, and in 1955 the first escalators were installed. Major promotions were held for the Festival of Britain in 1951, when late night opening on Thursday was introduced, and for the Coronation in 1953. At that time the store employed around 1,000 staff.

In 1959 Harrods Ltd, the store's owner, was acquired by House of Fraser. Dickins & Jones was, however, little changed and remained predominantly a ladies' fashion store until 1969 when menswear and china and glass departments were opened. In 1968 the restaurant was refurbished and renamed the Rose Restaurant. The following year the first branch store opened in Richmond in purpose-built five-storey premises, one third the size of the Regent Street building. In 1972 the first concession departments were introduced and in 1973 the hairdressing department which, along with the library, had closed after the war, was re-opened. In 1975 the two basements were redeveloped to convert the lower ground area into a sales floor for home requisites. The basement opened in 1976 and, at the same time, the ground floor was completely refurbished. In 1977 a major promotion was launched to mark the Queen's silver jubilee. In September 1981 a second branch store, comprising 70,000 square feet on two floors, opened in a brand-new shopping centre in Milton Keynes. During the early 1980s efforts were made to create a younger image for the Regent Street store, which was totally refurbished, between 1986 and 1988, by leading American designers.

The ladies' lingerie department in 1955.

E. Dingle & Co Ltd, Plymouth

In 1880, a 39-year-old Cornishman, Edward Dingle, became dissatisfied with his position as the manager of Spooner & Co's drapery store in Bedford Street, Plymouth. Prompted by his wife, Annie, Dingle asked his employers to reward his contribution to the success of the business by making him a partner. The Spooner family refused and Dingle subsequently handed in his notice and opened his own drapery shop nearby at 30 Bedford Street, in premises formerly occupied by a clothier, John Adams. Dingle was aware that the class of customer which he wished to attract would frown upon newspaper advertising, but soon hit upon another, highly effective way of drawing the public's attention to his new shop. He had become a well-known figure while working at Spooners, where, dressed in his long black tail-coat, he greeted customers and helped them make their purchases. Similarly attired, he now stood outside his new premises, and those who recognised him and stopped to chat were invited inside to view his range of merchandise.

Within a year of starting out in business, Dingle employed thirteen shop assistants, twelve dressmakers and two boys. He persuaded a young man named Tom Baker to leave Perkins Brothers' hosiery shop to take up the position of floor-walker and, when Baker married his new employer's sister, he was made a partner in E. Dingle & Co. Baker was ambitious and inventive and the partnership flourished. By 1900 Dingles had an uninterrupted frontage from 29 to 31 Bedford

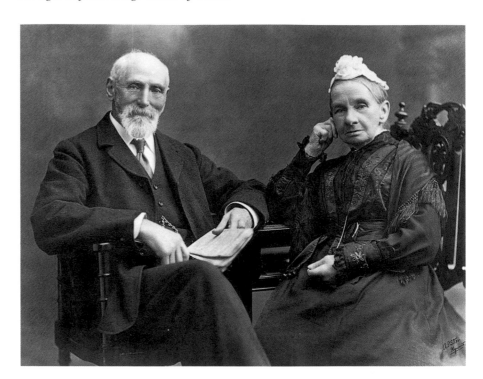

Edward Dingle, the store's founder, and his wife.

BELOW *The store's main entrance before the First World War.*

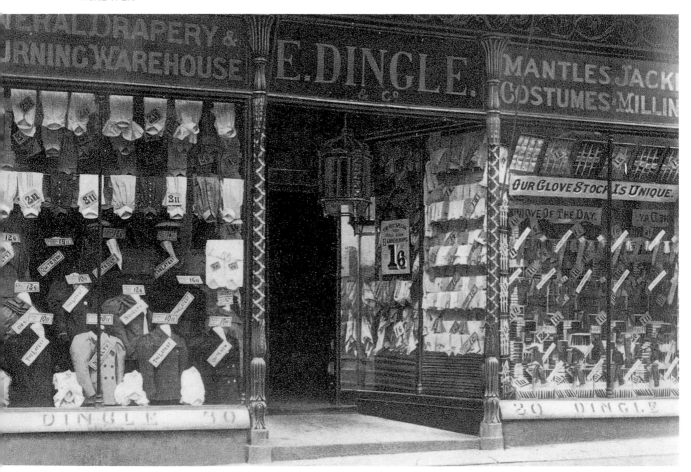

CHARLTON HOUSE

One of the houses used as temporary accommodation during the war.

Street, and a shop behind, at 5 Cornwall Street, had also been connected to the Bedford Street premises.

At the turn of the century, Dingle's second son, Frank, and Baker's sons, John and, until his early death, Harold, began working at the store. Tom Baker became increasingly involved in local politics, as a Justice of the Peace, a Liberal councillor and, from 1913 to 1916, as Mayor of Plymouth. In 1919 he was knighted for his services to the town. As Sir Thomas devoted more of his time to politics and to his civic duties, and as Edward Dingle approached his seventies, Jack Baker and Frank Dingle took greater responsibilities in the running of the business. When Sir Thomas died in 1926, the store occupied 28–31 and 33 Bedford Street and 4–6 Cornwall Street. In 1935, seven years after the founder's death, Dingles was registered as a private limited liability company. The purchase of the freehold corner site and business of W.J. Vickery & Co Ltd, gentlemen's outfitters, at 26 and 27 Bedford Street and 8 Cornwall Street, was negotiated that year, and the brothers Stanley and Ralph Vickery joined Jack Baker and Frank Dingle as directors of E. Dingle & Co Ltd. Three years later, Dingles acquired the lease of 32 Bedford Street and 4 Cornwall Street, the premises which had been occupied by the grocers, Underwood & Co Ltd. By 1939, Dingles also owned a florist's shop at 1 Cornwall Street and a boot shop next door, comprised eighty departments, employed over 500 people and had grandiose plans to rebuild the store along the lines of the Harrods and Selfridges buildings in London. These plans had, however, to be shelved when war broke out later that year.

Plymouth suffered badly during the Second World War, and a total of fifty-nine German air-raids left the city centre in ruins. The most destructive attacks were launched on 20 and 21 March and on five nights at the end of April 1941. Dingles survived the first of these air-raids, which resulted in the destruction of Spooners, but on the night of 21 March, a fire started by incendiaries in Yeos department store across the street, spread to Dingles and burned the premises to the ground. The partners were determined to continue trading, and purchased and leased shops and houses throughout Plymouth and the surrounding area, where most of the departments resumed trading. Fourteen of these forty-eight temporary units were destroyed during air-raids on 21 and 22 April, but Dingles again found premises in which to relocate the affected departments. By the end of the war, 'the store that was bombed but not beaten' employed over 600 people, and had become a symbol of Plymouth's defiant determination to survive.

Under Patrick Abercrombie and J. Paton Watson's famous Plan for Plymouth, the city centre was completely remodelled and rebuilt during the late 1940s and early 1950s. Dingles secured a prime site from the City Council, close to the spot where the old store had stood, and plans were quickly laid for the construction of a modern department store. To assist the executive directors, Jack Dingle and Frank Baker, with the enormous task of financing and organising a major construction project at a time of strict government controls on building, two new directors were appointed in January 1948. Winston Brimacombe, who had begun his career with Harrods and later became assistant general manager at D.H. Evans, was made assistant managing director. Jeffrey Baker, a senior partner in the company's firm of accountants, was also made a director and brought additional financial expertise to the business. In the same month that these appointments were made, the company was reconstructed. Staff members were invited to invest in the company and the share capital was increased from £100,000 to £300,000. The clearing of the site began in the autumn of 1949 and the construction of the steel-framed, Portland stone building commenced in November. In January 1950 a new building was opened in Beaumont Road, Plymouth, by St Teresa's Industries Ltd, a wholly-owned manufacturing subsidiary of Dingles. Bread, confectionery and meat products were made there, for Dingles and other customers, and the building also housed ancilliary service workrooms, including those for soft furnishings and shoe repairs.

Frank Dingle retired as chairman of the company in 1950, and his cousin, Jack Baker, assumed the chairmanship while remaining managing director. Dingle died in May 1951 and did not live to see the completion of the store, which was opened by Baker and Brimacombe on 1 September. The building was completed eight months ahead of schedule, and it was the first new department store to open in Great Britain since 1938. Designed by John Burnet, Tait & Partners, the store was 293 feet long by 127 feet deep, providing 35,000 square feet of sales space on four floors. It had a facade of Portland stone and the interior was designed to maximise opportunities for the display of merchandise. The design had initially included a basement floor, down escalators and air conditioning, but these had to be abandoned in 1950 in the face of rampant inflation. Nonetheless, the building was constructed horizontally so that new floors could be added at a later date. On the opening day nearly 40,000 people visted the store. Nylons, groceries and tinned fruits were in greatest demand as, due to government restrictions, many foodstuffs and luxury goods were still in short supply. Other shoppers were attracted to the building simply to take a ride on the escalators, the first installed in a West Country shop. Profits increased considerably during the following years.

Jeffrey Baker became vice-chairman of Dingles in May 1952, and when Jack Baker died in 1955 he succeeded him as chairman. Winston Brimacombe, who became managing director in October 1954, continued to mastermind trading operations and, convinced that the construction of the Tamar Bridge and a new civic centre in Plymouth would boost trade considerably, he made plans for expansion. Such growth prompted the adoption of public company status in

General view of the store during the 1960s.

1954. Later Dingles acquired Pophams' new store, trading from the premises under the Dingles name for eighteen months until they were leased to help finance the construction of a fifth floor at the Royal Parade building in 1961. It was in that year that the company acquired stores in Falmouth (Cox & Horder) and Newquay (Hawke & Thomas), the first of a group of Dingles stores in Devon and Cornwall, and a central buying office was set up in Plymouth. Meanwhile the ground floor of the parent store was reorganised, improving the food hall and creating extra sales space. Between 1966 and 1969 the group was extended by the acquisition of Criddle & Smith of Truro; John Polglaze of Penzance; B. Thomas of Helston; and Henry Warren & Son and William Badcock & Son of Newton Abbott. Several of these stores were refurbished and extended and, by 1969, when Jeffrey Baker resigned as chairman, the group's pre-tax profits had increased to £386,115, having risen every year, save one, since 1951. In 1970 a further significant step was taken when E. Dingle & Co amalgamated with Jolly & Son, owners of an old-established and prestigious store in Bath.

Winston Brimacombe, who had become chairman on Baker's retirement, was acutely aware of the problems which would face small stores groups such as Dingles once Britain joined the European Economic Community, and so, in 1971, when Sir Hugh Fraser announced his intention to bid for the business, Brimacombe was concerned only to secure the best possible deal for the share-holders and staff. Finally, in July, he recommended acceptance of the latest offer from House of Fraser, having obtained assurances that 'the future of Dingles as a store group with particular regional skills and loyalties will be preserved.' Brimacombe moved on to become non-executive chairman of the Army & Navy Division and his son, Peter, a director of Dingles since 1966, took his place as managing director with Peter Humphries as chairman. Under House of Fraser, the construction of a sixth storey at Dingles, begun before the takeover, was completed in 1975. The Dingles Division, set up that year eventually numbered seventeen stores.

During the following decade the Plymouth store traded strongly until, on the evening of 19 December 1988, a small fire broke out on the fourth floor. It caught hold as furniture, bedding and fittings were set alight and the top three floors of the building were quickly engulfed in flames. Around 120 firemen were called in to tackle the blaze and, although no-one was killed, the upper half of the store was reduced to a charred shell by morning. Responsibility for starting the fire was claimed by a militant animal rights group, but the culprits were never apprehended.

The Dingles fire of 1988 was the largest seen in Plymouth since the Second World War, with damage initially estimated at £13.2 million, but the staff refused to accept defeat despite the temporary closure of the entire building. On 19 January 1989, 5,000 people queued up for the opening of Dingles' fire clearance sale, in temporary premises secured at Estover. The old Habitat premises in Campbell House were purchased as an outlet for furnishings and electrical goods, and the ground and first floors at Royal Parade were finally re-opened, after rigorous structural tests, at the end of March, with customers being permitted on to the second floor in early April. In May, it was announced that a contract worth £12 million had been awarded to rebuild the gutted floors of the store and House of Fraser made it known that it hoped to launch the completed store in September 1990.

The hosiery department in 1970.

D. H. Evans & Co Ltd, Oxford Street, London

Dan Harries Evans was born in south Wales around 1856. He was apprenticed to a draper near Merthyr Tydfil and moved to London in 1878 to start up in business on his own account. For a few months he traded from premises in Westminster Bridge Road but found the location too remote to attract sufficient custom. Consequently, in 1879 Evans rented a small shop at 147 Oxford Street (renumbered as 320 in 1880), for the sale of linen drapery and fancy goods, where he employed two assistants. In 1882 Evans leased 314 and 316 Oxford Street and by 1885 had also acquired 318. The trade grew extraordinarily quickly, imitating the low-price ready-money policies of the West End middle-class co-operatives. Most of the staff lived-in and Evans, a supporter of the early closing movement, proved a paternal employer.

During the latter part of 1892 Evans acquired the leases of shop premises formerly owned by a cabinet maker at 290–294 Oxford Street, on the opposite side of Old Cavendish Street. A refurbishment programme was immediately put in hand and the store was opened to the public in May 1893. The new showrooms, flooded with natural light from well-placed windows, were attractively fitted out in oak and amply equipped with tables and showcases for display. The impression of spaciousness was enhanced by the skilful arrangement of the various shop entrances which allowed a clear view through all the showrooms. The ground floor comprised the silk, costume and mantle departments with the children's clothing, baby linens and ladies' underclothing on the first floor. A large room had also been set aside for later use as a restaurant. From the basement a subway, fitted out as a china and fancy goods department, led to the original shop where the curtain, cretonne and rug departments were installed. The store at that time employed some 400 staff. The new showrooms, known as the west block, were a huge success. Profits for 1894 amounted to £26,623, an increase of some £10,000 over the previous year.

Evans was determined to continue to develop the business by the introduction of new lines, such as groceries, general provisions, ironmongery and glassware. This growth required a considerable capital investment and in April 1894 Evans announced the creation of a limited liability company, D.H. Evans & Co Ltd. The new company had a capital of £202,000 divided into 120,000 £1 ordinary shares, 2,000 £1 founder shares and 80,000 per cent cumulative preference shares. Evans retained a majority holding and the remaining shares, offered to staff and customers, were subscribed several times over. Evans received £160,000 for the premises, plant, machinery and goodwill. Alderman Alfred James Newton, chairman of Harrod's Stores Ltd, was appointed chairman of the new company, assisted by James Bailey, James Boyton and Richard Burbidge, who were later joined by Edgar Cohen and William Mendel as directors. Evans was appointed managing director, at a salary of £750 per annum, and attended board meetings as an observer.

During the following year the directors consolidated and extended control over the store's site by acquiring 296–306 Oxford Street in 1894/95 and number 308 in 1898. Such expansion, coupled with moves to improve the terms of the existing lease, was costly and, despite buoyant trade, the directors were obliged to loan the company sufficient funds for payment of the dividend. The lack of operating capital was remedied in early 1898 by the issue of £100,000 of $4\frac{1}{2}$ per cent first mortgage debenture stock and 80,000 cumulative 6 per cent £1 preference shares. In 1897 Evans resigned as managing director, although remaining on the board, and Richard Burbidge assumed an executive role until a successor could be found. Since Burbidge was managing director of Harrods, it was not surprising that he proposed one of his own managers from Knightsbridge, Ernest Webb, as Evans' replacement. Burbidge was also convinced of the value of advertising and masterminded a major promotional campaign in December 1898. A few months later he retired from the board in order to concentrate on his growing responsibilities at Harrods. Improvement of the premises continued with the refurbishment of the first floor of the east block and the rebuilding of 5–7 Chapel Place in 1900.

In July 1903 the board conceived a plan to sell the shares in D.H. Evans Founders Share Co Ltd, each worth around £100, in order to raise further capital. This was an unusual procedure and the bank expressed its extreme reluctance to assist in the sale. In December 1904 the company acquired the premises and goodwill of James Goodman of 310 Oxford Street. Later, in June 1906, the leasehold property and stock of Arthur Saunders were also purchased and the premises at 3 Chapel Place rebuilt. By mid-1906 plans were in hand for the erection of new buildings to replace the rambling collection of shops on the west side of Old Cavendish Street. By the end of the year John Murray, architect, had produced designs for a five-storey building at 308–320 Oxford Street. In March 1907 the board announced its intention to finance the expansion by the issue of 40,000 £1 ordinary shares at a £2 premium. The list opened in April and was subscribed twice over. Further share issues were made in 1909 and 1910. The first section of the new building was opened in May 1907 and the final construction work was hastened by the opening, in March, of Selfridge's new store at the western end of Oxford Street. The rebuilt D.H. Evans store with its highly decorated facade of Italian marble cost in excess of £131,000. The showrooms extended to the first floor with general drapery on the ground floor and ladies' mantles, jackets, costumes and millinery above. Curtains, rugs, china, glass, novelties and stationery were available in the basement. In 1913 Evans Leases Trust Ltd was created to take advantage of an opportunity to acquire a 999-year lease on the east and west blocks.

In January 1915 D.H. Evans retired from the business. He died penniless in 1928 after a series of ill-advised property deals. He was succeeded by Ernest Webb's son, William Wallace Webb. By this time the founders' shares had become an obstacle to the raising of sufficient capital. Mindful of the need to take advantage of the expected postwar boom, a scheme was devised, in 1918, to convert the founders' shares to ordinary shares by means of a private parliamentary bill. Profits which had been depressed during the war peaked at £169,280 in 1919, a level which was not reached again until 1946. In 1921 Newton, the company's chairman, died and was replaced by Ernest Webb. During 1923 the company acquired the freehold of much of the west block and built showrooms to the rear in Chapel Street. Plans were also laid for the creation of a French company, Établissement D.H. Evans, to operate the existing office in Paris where premises had been acquired as early as 1905. By the late 1920s it had become clear that the company lacked both sufficient capital to fund further expansion and the innovative leadership of its earlier years. Under such circumstances, and, in the light of the long-established personal links between the two firms, when Harrods Ltd proposed merger in mid-1928, its approaches were welcomed. Harrods acquired the entire ordinary share capital, Woodman Burbidge became chairman and Frank Chitham, a Harrods director, also joined the board. William Webb became managing director and C.H. Bromhead, who had joined the company the previous year, became general manager.

Burbidge increased turnover by lowering margins, introducing new systems of control, launching progressive fashion departments and creating more exciting window and departmental displays. Shoppers began to flock to the store. Burbidge was, however, acutely aware of the problems of trading in two buildings and determined to consolidate the business in a new west block. By 1935 a huge island site, bounded by Oxford Street, Old Cavendish Street, Henrietta Street and Chapel Place, had been acquired and demolition of the rear portion had begun. Meanwhile John Spedan Lewis, founder of the John Lewis Partnership, had made an offer of £848,500 for the east block. This was accepted and the building was gradually vacated. During October to December 1934 Louis Blanc, architect, discussed his designs for the new store with the board, who commented on every aspect of the plans from the floor layouts and escalator locations to the facade details. The building was to cost over £600,000 and the entire sum was loaned by Harrods at three per cent interest.

The rear portion of the new building was opened in February 1936 and departments were gradually moved from the front site. Amazingly, trade increased during 1935 and 1936 despite the chaos. Meanwhile Bromhead and some of the more important buyers were sent to America to assimilate ideas for use in the new store. The new building, with a 140-foot frontage on Oxford Street, was

Artist's impression of the escalator hall from a brochure produced for the opening of the new store in 1937.

A battery of ten escalators conveys customers smoothly and quickly up and down to all six floors.

Page 7

triumphantly opened in February 1937. It comprised eight and one-quarter acres of selling space on eight floors, more than twice the accommodation offered by the west and east blocks combined. The exterior was striking and typically 'thirties' incorporating a large amount of glass to maximise the admittance of natural light. A novel feature was the permanent canopy which was installed around the entire building replacing the traditional blinds. Inside it was fitted out with the most modern equipment, including a battery of ten escalators and air conditioning throughout. Each floor was laid out along broad corridors facilitating the circulation of customers and maximising opportunities for display. The entire fifth floor was devoted to a vast restaurant able to seat 800 diners.

In March 1937 the capital of the company was increased to £1,200,000 by the creation of 680,000 ordinary £1 shares. Trade was brisk during 1938 and 1939 but the outbreak of war heralded a period of shortage and control. Turnover in 1941 was the lowest since 1917/18. On 17 September 1940 the former east block, which had been sold to the John Lewis Partnership, was wiped out overnight by a direct bomb hit, but the new D.H. Evans store escaped serious constructional damage. William Webb died in 1944 and Woodman Burbidge in 1945. In June 1945 Sir Richard Burbidge succeeded the latter as director and chairman. Despite the persistence of controls, particularly the restraints on gross profit margins, sales soared after the war with net profits reaching £288,668 in 1948. In December of that year the company acquired the drapery business of J.F. Rockhey Ltd of Torquay and Newton Abbott for a purchase price of £259,556. The stores continued to trade as a separate entity under their own name. During these years D.H. Evans began to cut back its linen department in order to specialise on ladies' and children's clothing and initiated an unusual advertising campaign on the London underground with the slogan 'Fashionwise D.H. Evans'. In 1950 a Jaeger shop was launched within the store, in 1951 a new-open plan hairdressing salon was installed and in 1952 the Bentinck Room was opened as a fashion-show venue. In February 1954 the entire preference share capital of the company was also acquired by Harrods and converted to ordinary shares, and D.H. Evans became a wholly-owned subsidiary. The following year central buying was introduced for the fabric departments of all the Harrods group stores. The store

A 'Fashionwise' advertisement dating from the late 1950s.

319

D. H. Evans' Oxford Street facade decorated for the Christmas season in 1987.

traded successfully during the following decades and in 1979 a new furniture department was created on the fifth floor to augment sales of fashion goods. In February 1980 a branch store was opened in a new shopping centre in Wood Green in north London, comprising 60,000 square feet of sales space on two floors. The following year both the Oxford Street and Wood Green stores were integrated into the Dingles Division. Between 1982 and 1984 the Oxford Street store was extensively refurbished with the opening of a Lifestyle department, redesigning of the ground and lower ground floors, and refitting of the first and second floors. In 1985 the store was again refurbished, with the opening of a major Astral sports department in the basement and an enlarged men's department on the ground floor. In 1987 the store was renamed House of Fraser Oxford Street.

Harrods Ltd, Knightsbridge, London

Charles Henry Harrod was born in Essex in 1800. It is not known precisely when Harrod moved to London, but by 1834 he had begun trading as a wholesale grocer and tea dealer from premises in Cable Street, Stepney, where he married Elizabeth Digby, daughter of a pork butcher. The business grew rapidly and in 1849 Harrod acquired a further warehouse in Eastcheap in the City of London. Four years later, in 1853, he took over the house and grocery shop of Philip Henry Burden in the Brompton Road at 8 Middle Queen's Buildings. Burden is believed to have been one of Harrod's customers who sold up after getting into financial difficulties. Charles Harrod had no great ambitions for the shop and was content to retail on a small scale whilst continuing his wholesale tea business. During the mid-nineteenth century Knightsbridge was an unsalubrious district surrounded by fields, and most of the shops in Middle Queen's Buildings were no more than single-storey additions to the fronts of older houses. The holding of the Great Exhibition in Kensington in 1851 had, however, already brought some improvement. A large number of public buildings had been constructed between Kensington Gardens and Cromwell Road and to the west an enclave of smart middle-class housing was developing, providing an excellent market for shops in Brompton village and Kensington High Street.

In 1861 Harrod retired and his son, Charles Digby Harrod, born in 1841, apprenticed to a City grocer and trained as a commercial clerk, assumed control. Charles was more ambitious than his father and, assisted in the shop by his brother, determined to expand the business. By 1864, when the premises were renumbered as 105 Brompton Road, Harrod had built up a large trade, particularly in tea. His brother later commented that they had developed 'a very nice counter trade which, you know, was when I left it [circa 1866] about 200–250 per week and very profitable.' By the late 1860s more space was sorely needed for the retail departments. Harrod's family (he had married a grocer's daughter in 1864) moved out to Esher, and a new shopfront was erected and departments for the sale of stationery, perfumery and patent medicines installed. Later, in 1873, a two-storey roof-lit extension was built over the garden to the rear where flower, fruit and vegetable departments were opened.

Harrod's success was based upon an insistence on ready money and low prices along the lines of such middle-class co-operatives as the Army & Navy Co-operative Society which had proved so popular in the West End. His shop, however, was even more attractive than the co-operatives as it was open to all, offered free delivery and provided clerks to make out order sheets on customers' behalf. Harrod advertised his 'co-operative prices' widely and deliberately adopted the title of Harrod's Stores because of its co-operative connotations. As the business grew, extra managerial help was required and Harrod was joined by his cousin, William Kibble, formerly of Clapham Stores. In 1879 adjoining shops at 101 and 103 Brompton Road were acquired and rebuilt to accommodate new departments. By 1883 the store had over 150 staff and offered departments for groceries, provisions, confectionery, wines and spirits, brushes and turnery, ironmongery, glass, china, earthenware, stationery, fancy goods, perfumery and drugs.

On 6 December 1883 the entire store was destroyed in a massive fire. Within twenty-four hours temporary offices had been set up with a small stock and three days later Humphreys Hall in Brompton Road, where the departments were to trade for nine months, was hired. The original store was reconstructed on five floors to the designs of Alfred Williams, assistant district surveyor of Kensington,

Charles Henry Harrod (1800–1885), the store's founder.

BELOW *Richard Burbidge (1847–1917), the store's managing director.*

with a handsome facade and interior. It opened in September 1884 to universal acclaim. On the ground floor a central circular counter, where clerks made out orders, was surrounded by well-stocked departments for wines, tea, groceries, fruit and flowers, poultry and game, and cheese. A broad staircase led to the first floor where departments for silver, electric goods, lamps, saddlery and portmanteaus were located. On the second floor, perfumery, patent medicines and toys were available, and on the third, furniture and bedding. The basement

was used entirely for storage. Sales increased rapidly, averaging net profits of
around £16,000 per annum during the late 1880s, when the store was already
issuing comprehensive price lists.

In 1889 Harrod, troubled by ill-health, determined to withdraw from the
business and in November sold the store to a new limited liability company,
Harrod's Stores Ltd, with an authorised capital of £141,400. The board of
the new company comprised Alfred Newton, a well-known City merchant, as
chairman, and four local businessmen. William Smart, previously one of Harrod's
floor managers, became general manager and the store was enlarged by the
acquisition of premises to the rear and the addition of chemistry, hosiery and
boot and shoe departments. In addition, plans were laid for the erection of a
handsome frontage. Smart's appointment was not, however, a success and in
March 1891 he was replaced by Richard Burbidge, a hard-working and ambitious
warehouseman, who had considerable experience in the provision departments
of Army & Navy Co-operative Society, William Whiteley's and West Kensington
Stores. During 1891 new premises were acquired, leases extended, basements
remodelled and five new departments, fish, bakery, cooked meats, refreshments
and oriental, were opened. In April 1892 Harrod's Stores Ltd made an offer for
Bon Marché of Brixton, a south London department store which had been
founded in 1872 but was then in liquidation. The price was, however, too high
and a few months later Harrods, instead, opened a City depot for the sale of
packet tea and other goods.

During 1893 Harrods expanded dramatically with the acquisition of 91–99
Brompton Road between January and April and the purchase of ten acres of land
and an old soap works in Barnes, for use as a depository, in November. The
furnishing and drapery departments were also extended and a new banking
department opened. In March 1894 the store acquired the lease of 87 Brompton
Road, the easterly corner of the block bounded by Brompton Road, New Street
(now Hans Crescent), Queen's Gardens and North Street, and determined to
erect premises 'of very substantial character'. Later the store negotiated the
rebuilding of North Street (now Basil Street) further south, whilst acquiring

The Brompton Road frontage during the 1890s.

BELOW *Construction of the new Brompton Road building underway in around 1901.*

most of the new street's northern frontage and thereby extending the store into Chelsea. It was not until the late 1890s that interest was shown in extending west of Queen's Gardens, a narrow lane which then dissected the modern site. C.W. Stephens was appointed architect, designing a flamboyant facade in Doulton terracotta with five storeys of residential flats above a ground-floor shop. The rebuilding, financed by successive share issues and profit plough-back, proceeded piecemeal between 1894 and 1912 in a general anti-clockwise direction, from Basil Street into New Street and Brompton Road. The first portion completed in the new style was a side entrance at 8–9 New Street. Most of the Basil Street frontage was finished by 1896. Meanwhile, in 1894, small improvements were made to the windows on Brompton Road. In 1894 hairdressing and manicure departments were opened, followed by photographic and estate departments and cycling and dairy departments in 1895 and 1896. Between 1890 and 1896 profits showed a five-fold increase, from £12,479 to £61,959.

In 1897 Harrods secured the leases of 111–115 Brompton Road and a school site to the rear, with entry, from 1902, upon the expiry of existing agreements. With the acquisition of these new properties west of Queen's Gardens, Stephens redesigned a more ornamental Brompton Road frontage featuring a central dome and carved pediment. The trade had grown massively since the original plans were laid and the store was now entirely replanned to accommodate showrooms at both ground- and first-floor levels with exclusive residential flats above. The flats, arranged around light-wells giving access to showroom skylights, had been quickly let on the New Street frontage and the board was confident of a substantial rental income. The Brompton Road facade was built in five sections between 1901 and 1905 and incorporated a delightful Art-Nouveau shop front. Meanwhile between 1902 and 1903 the famous meat hall was built on the site of the former school to the rear of the block. Decorated with Doulton tiles depicting scenes of animal life in Art-Nouveau style, the design of the food hall was the work of W.J. Neatby. Leases on the Hans Road frontage proved more troublesome to acquire, as the property largely comprised new houses, and it was not until 1911 that the penultimate portion of the modern island site was acquired. Inside, the warehouse was laid out as separate shops connected by archways and lavishly fitted out with marble, inlaid woodwork, glass, ornate plasterwork, painted ceilings and thick carpets. The shopfittings, extraordinary in their opulence, were largely the work of Frederick Sage Ltd.

In 1905 a book department was opened and an agency established in modest premises in Paris, France. By this time the range of merchandise was immense. The store was publishing an annual illustrated price list running to more than a thousand pages and had confidently adopted the telegraphic address 'Everything, London' and the trade-mark 'Harrods Serves the World'. By 1908 more sales space was urgently required and plans for many of the flats on the Brompton Road frontage were abandoned. Others were converted during succeeding years, the entire building being turned to commercial use during the late 1920s. Meanwhile profits contracted in 1909 with fierce competition from Gordon Selfridge's brash new store in Oxford Street. However, sales quickly recovered and in 1910 the company purchased 25–35 Hans Road, thereby acquiring much of the fourth side of the block. Rebuilding began immediately. In 1912 a two-acre site near Trevor Square was purchased for the erection of storage and despatch facilities, bakeries and factories. The same year a new subsidiary, Harrods (South America) Ltd, was set up to trade in Buenos Aires. The new company, with a capital of £25,000, was wholly owned by Harrod's Stores Ltd. In July 1914, upon the retirement of the chairman, Harrods also acquired Dickins & Jones Ltd, with its prestigious Regent Street store.

After the outbreak of the First World War, Harrods experienced considerable difficulty in sustaining services and stock at prewar levels. By 1916 3,000 staff had joined up and Harrods was also contributing to the war effort by supplying and equipping hospitals in France. In May 1917 Richard Burbidge, who had been awarded a baronetcy the previous year, died. Burbidge had visited American stores frequently and it was his vision of a massive diversified department store on a huge island site which had been responsible for the growth of the business during the previous quarter of a century. He had introduced aggressive advertising and promotion, a range of new merchandise and services, and a vast improvement in staff conditions whilst also engineering the geographical expansion of the business. Between 1891 and 1913 profits had risen from £16,071 to £309,227. He was succeeded as managing director by his son, Woodman Burbidge, who had joined Harrods in 1893 and acted as general manager since 1901.

With the cessation of hostilities, trade soared and in 1919 Harrods achieved a record sales increase in excess of £1,850,000. That year the company acquired Kendal Milne & Co with its large department store in central Manchester, the first in a network of provincial stores. The company also began to expand its operations abroad. During the war Harrods had carried out large contracts for the Belgian government, erecting hospitals, laundries and aeroplane sheds and supplying provisions. In 1919 Harrods (Continental) Ltd was established with warehouses in Antwerp and Brussels to carry on a wholesale trade in Belgium. The experiment, largely due to adverse exchange conditions, was not a success

OPPOSITE *An attractive carpet department catalogue dating from the 1920s.*

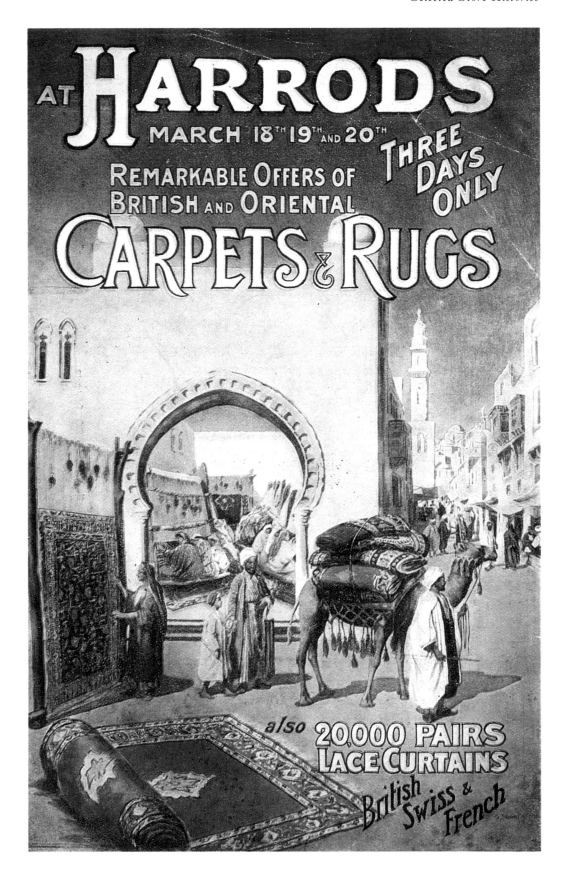

and the company was wound up in 1922. During the same year an office was opened in New York and in 1920 Harrods (North America) Ltd was registered in the United States of America. This project was short lived and the New York business closed in 1922. Also in 1919 the company acquired the freehold of 78–94 Brompton Road opposite the principal block.

In 1920 the company's name was changed to Harrods Ltd. That year centralised purchasing for the entire group was introduced as a means to control costs, and Walter Carter Ltd, a Manchester removal business, was acquired and its business merged with that of the Kendal Milne store. In May 1920 an agreement was signed for the purchase of Swan & Edgar Ltd, which owned a large department store in London's Piccadilly. In addition negotiations were concluded for the purchase of the freehold of the Brompton Road site. The early 1920s were, however, difficult years when the onset of a general trade depression forced Harrods to reduce prices in order to dispose of surplus stocks. During the first half of 1920 the company experienced a trading loss and the store initiated a food campaign reducing prices of groceries and provisions. By this time the main store covered four-and-a-half acres and had twenty acres of floor space. Moreover, the company was not merely a retailer but also operated a large manufacturing business for textiles and tailoring, furniture and upholstery, boots, and silver-plating; bread and confectionery bakeries; a printing works; a model chocolate factory; and box-making workshops. In 1921 the building in Trevor Square, commenced in 1913, was finally completed, thereby freeing sales space in the main store. That year the freehold of the main block was finally acquired. During 1924, in an effort to stimulate sales, the Knightsbridge premises were extended and departments re-arranged in the interest of customers' convenience. The food departments were grouped together, and the furniture and carpet departments were moved into three acres of space on the second floor. In 1925 a new battery of eight lifts serving all floors was installed, and parking space for 100 customer cars was acquired close to Brompton Road.

In February 1927, with the depression still biting hard, Swan & Edgar was sold to Charterhouse Investment Trust Ltd at a profit of £321,320. Meanwhile, at Knightsbridge, trade had begun to recover and the third floor of the Brompton Road frontage, hitherto residential flats, was thrown into commercial use for furnishing galleries, increasing the selling space by two and a half acres. During the summer of 1928 expansion continued with the acquisition of D.H. Evans & Co Ltd of Oxford Street. Harrods had had a long and intimate connection with the firm, Alfred Newton acting as chairman and Richard Burbidge as director from 1894 when the company was formed. As with the other group stores, D.H. Evans retained its own distinctive style whilst benefiting from the economies of group purchasing. Meanwhile alterations to the Knightsbridge premises between 1926 and 1930, particularly the reconstruction of the Basil Street block, increased selling space by three-and-a-half acres, introducing a new men's clothing and outfitting section and a new battery of six lifts.

By 1930 trade was again extremely depressed and the board became concerned that customers were staying away in the mistaken belief that Harrods' prices were too high. Consequently the company announced a scheme to refund the difference in price if the same articles could be bought elsewhere, and at the same time, at a lower price. The high prices were, in fact, a reflection of Harrods' continuing insistence on quality and buying British. By 1931 several large London stores were in financial difficulties and Harrods bought the stock and goodwill of both James Shoolbred & Co Ltd of Tottenham Court Road and of the Civil Service Co-operative Society of Haymarket. Both shops were closed and their merchandise profitably sold off. Despite this success Harrods' profits fell further in 1932 and the store introduced a policy to increase the assortment of inexpensive quality merchandise in each of the 200 departments. Trade did not improve until early 1934 when a project was launched to rebuild the entire central block, thereby doubling the sales space available there. Meanwhile plans were also in hand to rebuild D.H. Evans' Oxford Street store and the Kendal Milne building in Manchester. In 1935 Woodman Burbidge retired as managing director and was replaced by his son, Richard Burbidge, who had held a managerial position in the store for fifteen years. In early 1939 the reconstruction of the Hans Crescent buildings and the installation of a battery of escalators, completed Harrods' major rebuilding programme.

The outbreak of the Second World War was particularly detrimental to Harrods' class of trade. Many of the store's customers left for the country, petrol shortages and restricted railway travel inhibited shopping trips to town, the black-out shortened business hours and wartime restrictions disrupted supplies. In 1946 the company was approached by John Walsh Ltd concerning the purchase of the company's Sheffield store which had been destroyed by bombing during the war. Walshs' entire share capital was quickly acquired, although restrictions delayed rebuilding until 1952. Three years later, in 1949, Harrods acquired William Henderson & Sons Ltd of Liverpool. Thirty years earlier, Harrods had been involved in abortive negotiations for the acquisition of a site in Liverpool,

A home farm display in the food hall in 1936.

The Younger Set gown salon in 1939.

but now the opportunity to purchase a thriving store in the city was welcomed. Plans were quickly laid for the development of the Liverpool store and a new extension was completed in 1954. Meanwhile the building of Walshs of Sheffield was finished in 1953. The expansion of the group was resumed in 1955 with the acquisition of a large block of properties in Birmingham along with Rackhams department store which traded on part of the site. The Rackhams board had already laid plans for the construction of a new store. These were carried through by Harrods, and the rebuilt and enlarged store opened in several stages between 1960 and 1966.

During the late 1950s Harrods was responsible for about half of the group's turnover and in all stores efforts were made to attract new customers, particularly

younger ones, by the sale of budget merchandise. In August 1959, despite competitive offers from Debenhams and United Drapery Stores, the entire Harrods group was acquired by House of Fraser. Richard Burbidge left soon after the takeover and was succeeded as managing director by Alfred Spence. Throughout the 1960s the group's performance was undermined by changes in shopping habits, staff shortages and the poor performance of some of the provincial stores. Efforts were made to control costs and revitalise the Knightsbridge store with the launch of the Way In boutique in 1967. By 1971 Robert Midgley, recently appointed managing director, had determined to improve sales by changing the store's traditional lay-out and systems. The large banking hall on the ground floor was converted into sales space, creating an elegant perfumery department furnished with marble and red velvet. The food halls were refurbished, with an emphasis on self-service; the paperback book and china departments expanded; the fashion floor refitted and the restaurants redesigned. In December 1974, with these improvements underway, a bomb exploded in the garden tools department. Fortunately the package had been spotted and fire doors were able to contain the blast. Normal trading resumed within months. Redevelopment continued with the opening in 1976 of a new sports department, Olympic Way, on the fourth floor (in an area previously occupied by the directors' suite) and an American ice cream parlour on the ground floor.

In 1980 Aleck Craddock was appointed managing director, presiding at the opening in 1981 of Midgley's second bank of escalators at the west end of the store. That year work on 'Harrods' major project' was commenced. The scheme, masterminded by Craddock, involved the creation of 40,000 square feet of new selling space on the fourth floor, establishing a hair, feet and beauty salon on the fifth floor, introducing a Cook's Way department and international crystal room, creating two new food halls and refurbishing the existing bakery, charcuterie and meat hall. In 1981 *Harrod's Magazine*, a glossy colour catalogue, was launched. Between 1982 and 1984 Harrods' shops were opened within the Mitsukoshi department store in Tokyo, in Illums in Copenhagen and on the *QE2* liner. Further efforts were made to encourage international trade with the launch of an experimental United States mail order scheme in 1984. The IRA bomb which severely damaged the eastern end of the building in December 1983, at the height of the Christmas shopping rush, shocked the nation and was a severe setback to the store. However, refurbishment of the Knightsbridge building continued with the completion in 1985/6, of a large battery of high-speed escalators serving all floors.

During mid-1987 Harrods announced plans to spend £200 million, over five years, on recreating the original grandeur of the store and relocating related departments. The budget included a spend of over £15 million on new marble floors and carpets and £56 million on such fittings as counters and showcases, copying the hardwood and bronze Art-Deco finishes of the original furnishings. The first stage, work on the new leather room and men's shop, was completed in July 1988. Alongside the interior renovations the organisation of the business was updated to separate the selling and buying functions, and improve customer service and staff training. In addition, in 1987 work began on the construction of a new computerised distribution centre in Osterley, West London. The depository at Barnes was no longer adequate and the new centre was planned to improve stock control and make more selling space available in Knightsbridge. Thus Harrods, probably the best known shop in the world, continues to trade strongly upon the twin foundations of modern technology and the elegance of the Edwardian department store.

James Howell (1835–1909), the store's founder.

James Howell & Co Ltd, Cardiff

James Howell, son of a farmer, was born near Fishguard, Pembrokeshire, in 1835. Apprenticed to a local draper he proved to be an ambitious and able entrepreneur. From 1858, eager to gain further experience, he worked in similar establishments at Milford Haven and for Ben Evans at London House, Newport, before securing a situation at Shoolbreds of Tottenham Court Road, London. There he became familiar with the running of a major warehouse. After a few years Howell entered into partnership with D. Jenkins and set up a drapery business in Pembroke Dock. The arrangement did not prove to be satisfactory and by the early 1860s Howell had returned to London where he entered into service with William Tarn & Co, drapers of Newington Causeway near Elephant and Castle. Shortly afterwards he married Fanny Logan and opened a linen drapery shop on his own account in Portman Place, off Edgware Road. After the first difficult year trade began to pick up but Howell was already impatient to return to Wales. In 1865 he learned that suitable premises were available in Cardiff.

On 21 October 1865 James Howell opened a new shop for the sale of drapery and fancy goods in a building called Stuart Hall, in the Hayes, and appears to have secured a guarantee for the first twelve months' rent from Ben Evans, his former employer. The venture was an immediate success. Howell's insistence on ready money, at a time when most Cardiff shopkeepers sold on credit terms, allowed him to offer merchandise more cheaply than his competitors. Within months he was confident enough to advertise his business as 'linen drapers to the million by universal appointment.' In August 1867 Howell moved to larger premises at 13 St Mary Street, the site of the present building. In early 1869 new carpet, furnishing, millinery and mourning departments were opened next door at number 12, and in 1870 Howell employed around thirty shopmen. Expansion continued throughout the following decade with the acquisition of a furniture warehouse in Wharton Street and further shops on St Mary Street itself. By 1883 the store occupied 9–14 St Mary Street and had also acquired Biggs Brewery to the rear, which afforded a small frontage on Trinity Street. Further premises abutting Trinity Street were quickly secured to house the growing furniture departments and by 1892 the store, with its striking facade on St Mary Street, comprised almost 36,800 square feet. It was one of the largest retail establishments in Wales and had become popularly known as 'James Howell & Co, the Cardiff drapers'. Cardiff flourished during the latter half of the nineteenth century, not only as a port but also as an important centre for coalmining and iron smelting. By 1891 the city's population was four times as great as it had been forty years earlier and half the inhabitants of Wales were concentrated within twenty-five miles of the city. New shops sprang up to cater for the growing demand for consumer goods. Cardiff's streets were cleansed, paved and lit for the first time and horse-drawn buses began to ply regular routes from the suburbs and railway stations to the emerging shopping centre in St Mary Street.

By the 1890s it was evident to Howell that his plan to occupy the whole block, between St Mary Street and Trinity Street, would be frustrated by tenants who were unwilling to move. He therefore turned his attention to premises on the opposite side of Wharton Street where he erected several warehouses and workshops. Stables and stores were also acquired in Charles Street. By 1905 Howell was also trading in ironmongery and china in Castle Arcade and later opened a hairdressing salon and refreshment rooms in the main building. Trade was brisk, with a busy mail-order business and a staff of over 400, most of whom lived in. James Howell died in May 1909 leaving an estate of nearly £312,000. His success engendered a growing sense of responsibility as he became more actively involved in civic life. Howell, vehemently proud of Cardiff, frequently lent his support to the improvement of the city's amenities. In 1882 he speculated on a land purchase in Crockherbtown to build a magnificent hall for public concerts and lectures with a new hotel, shop and office complex. A separate company was set up to manage the project in which the Howell family retained a controlling interest for many years. In 1892 Howell gave massive financial support to help present Cardiff's case to host the proposed Welsh national museum and library. He was a justice of the peace for the County of Glamorgan and a generous subscriber to local charitable causes, particularly those involving the non-conformist church. A keen farmer and horse breeder he was also responsible for initiating, in 1883, the annual Cardiff and South Wales horse show. Howell had always remained in direct control of every aspect of the store's operation and his death prompted far-reaching reorganisation. The terms of his will required that ownership of the store be divided equally amongst his eleven children. In order to comply with this, in December 1909 the business was turned into a private limited company, James Howell & Co Ltd, with a capital of £185,000. Thomas Francis Howell, a London barrister and Howell's eldest son, became chairman of the new concern and John Hugh Howell, Frederick William Howell and James Howell, already involved in the business, assumed active management in Cardiff. James Howell's executors were paid £26,000 for the goodwill of the business alone.

Trade was buoyant. A new grocery and provisions department in Wharton Street proved popular and was promptly followed in 1913 by the opening of an experimental motor showroom and repair depot in premises on the opposite side of Bakers Row. Frederick Howell, a keen motorist, took charge of the new department. The outbreak of war in 1914 thwarted further developments and plans for a new arcade to link the busy Wharton Street premises with the main store had to be shelved. The war years were not without their problems – huge numbers of staff joined up and the entire delivery fleet was requisitioned by the War Office. Profits, however, increased steadily and turnover more than doubled between 1916 and 1920. In 1919 the issued ordinary capital was increased to £240,000 and in 1920 to £295,000. It was clear that more profound organisational change was required to sustain such phenomenal growth. Between 1911 and 1920 profits had increased from £20,589 to £73,246 and between 1916 and 1920 the turnover had more than doubled, peaking at £913,942 in 1920.

In November 1920 the company went public with a share capital of £500,000 of which £295,000 was issued and fully paid. Thomas Francis Howell remained chairman and John Hugh Howell and William Frederick Howell directors. During the early 1920s a building department was set up to handle building, decorating and plumbing work, and in 1922 a soda fountain was installed on the ground floor. The Wharton Street arcade, planned ten years earlier, was finally opened in 1924, along with a new motor showroom on the corner of Wharton Street and Bakers Row, dealing, from 1930, exclusively in Austin cars. Meanwhile the store's fleet of delivery horses and carts were gradually sold off and replaced with motor vehicles. In 1931 a new four-storey building was opened on the corner of Wharton Street and St Mary Street to house the menswear section. The fine design, by Percy Thomas, won an architectural award. Inside the store remained rather traditional, wooden counters with seats for customers, walls lined with shelves and simple displays of merchandise on open tables.

The staff annual outing by charabanc in 1925.

The glove department during the late 1920s.

The St Mary Street frontage during the 1930s.

The years of depression and war during the 1930s and 1940s were the most difficult the store had ever experienced. In 1932 sales plummeted, but trade had begun to recover by the mid 1930s when the entire store was refurbished. The outbreak of the Second World War was, however, to prove a major setback. Price regulations, rationing and the introduction of utility goods all affected sales detrimentally. The costume workrooms were taken over for the production of uniforms and parachutes and the garage was requisitioned for official repair work. In addition one-quarter of the staff enlisted, forcing management to rely on juvenile and part-time labour to maintain standards of service. New lines in perambulator manufacture and second-hand furniture were developed. Fortunately the building did not suffer major bomb damage and customers continued to be drawn by such events as ARP exhibitions and 'warship weeks'. After the war rationing persisted, trade was slow and several unprofitable departments were wound up. The most successful development was, undoubtedly, the conversion of the wartime parachute factory into a restaurant. The Orchid Room, which seated 300, became a popular meeting place and was later complemented by the Argosy Room, a self-service cafeteria on the ground floor decorated in a nautical vein.

In 1953 a new management team assumed control with Alfred Thorpe as chairman and managing director, assisted by his son, Victor Thorpe. During the mid-1950s the entire store was extensively modernised. Sales floors were opened up to create an impression of spaciousness and to allow customers access to the largest possible selection of goods. A luxury hairdressing salon was opened in 1954. In 1955 a motor division, Howell's Garage and Commercial Vehicles Ltd,

The store entrance in 1984.

commenced business at a new garage in Newport Road. During the late 1950s it acquired several other Austin dealers in the area and was renamed Howell's Garages (Cardiff) Ltd. The retail side of the business also expanded with the acquisition in 1959 of a branch store, Reynolds & Co, of Newport, and the purchase of the remaining corner of the main block was finally realised. Plans were immediately made to incorporate the new premises and to build a two-storey bridge linking them with the buildings on the opposite side of Wharton Street.

In October 1961 J.J. Allen Ltd, a Bournemouth-based store group, acquired a controlling interest in James Howell & Co Ltd, reselling its shareholding at a substantial profit in March 1962 to the Hodge Group, managed by Sir Julian Hodge, a Welsh merchant and banker. Reynolds & Co was disposed of later that year. Meanwhile building work continued, and in 1963 the Bethany Chapel, one of Cardiff's oldest non-conformist churches, which had previously been surrounded by the store, was finally converted into sales space featuring a cobbled courtyard, Wharton Court, in Regency style. The store now boasted around ten acres of floor space, and a new chemist shop and wine shop were also introduced. The modernisation of the store continued with the introduction of credit facilities and the installation of escalators in 1964. In April 1972 the department store operation was separated from the motors division and sold to House of Fraser for almost £5 million.

Trade continued to grow under House of Fraser's control. The store joined the Dingles Division and soon became the premier store in south Wales. In 1977 Mair Barnes was appointed general manager, the first woman to run a British department store. Between 1977 and 1979 a major refurbishment programme was carried out, incorporating the creation of new sales space, installation of modern escalators and a third licensed snack bar. In 1985 the ground floor was reorganised and a major £12 million refurbishment is planned for 1990/1991, which will revitalise the store and provide a glass roof over the former chapel.

Jolly & Son Ltd, Bath

James Jolly was born in the Norfolk village of Brockdish in 1775. His father was a linen draper, and, as the eldest son, James was apprenticed in the same trade. He was an ambitious youth, and by the early 1800s had left the village to set up his own shop in Winchester, Hampshire. After trading there for some years he entered into a partnership as a wholesale woollen merchant in the City of London. During the 1810s James moved to Kent where he opened a linen drapery shop at Deal, trading as Jolly & Co. Ten years later he also established a bazaar in nearby Margate. The idea of multiple branches was relatively new but both towns held promise. Deal had prospered during the French wars as the navy's principal anchorage and embarkation point and Margate was fast becoming a popular seaside resort. The Margate business thrived but James now had help in the shop from his son, Thomas, and was determined to find a suitable place to conduct a higher class of holiday trade. In about 1823 Jolly, therefore, took seasonal premises in Bath for the first time. A few years later father and son leased a permanent shop at 20 Old Bond Street, largely to sell foreign drapery and other fashion novelties to the carriage trade.

Throughout the eighteenth century Bath had remained the most fashionable resort in the country, an alternative capital to London. Shortly before the arrival of Jollys it had, however, begun to be superceded by a number of coastal resorts. Royal dips at Worthing loosed a new passion for sea bathing and towns like Brighton and Margate began to flourish. Bath was, nevertheless, to prove an ideal place for the new shop. It was unique amongst the spas in being an important provincial centre in its own right and many wealthy visitors continued to come for the season. Moreover, shopping in Bath had always held a particular attraction. The fashionable social regime devised for the town by Richard Nash and set out in his 'rules of conduct', specified not only times of day for bathing and taking the waters, but also for such pastimes as driving and shopping. Whilst the streets, paved and sewered long before it was common elsewhere, were very attractive promenades. Jolly & Son's new branch was consequently a great success and from 1830 the Parisian Depot, as it was known, remained open during the entire year rather than for the winter season only. During the same year Jolly's Bazaar at 26 High Street in Margate was refurbished on a lavish scale and considerably extended.

In 1831 Thomas, who had taken effective control in Bath, moved the branch business to larger premises at 12 Milsom Street. Built as fine houses for the wealthy, the street had become one of the most fashionable shopping places in the spa by the 1830s and was lined with the most exclusive costumiers and silk mercers. In November 1831 Thomas placed a large advertisement in all of the four local newspapers, announcing the opening of the new shop. 'Economy, fashion and variety' were to be the watchwords of the establishment which was grandly called the 'Bath Emporium'. The new shop sold not only the foreign fashion novelties in which Jolly had previously specialised, but also regular linen drapery, silk mercery, hosiery and lace. In addition it offered the bazaar stock, china, jewellery, perfumery, stationery, toys and cutlery, which would have been on sale in Jolly's Bazaar in Margate. All goods were to be sold for ready money only.

The new showrooms were an immediate success, and within a few years Thomas had acquired the lease of the shop next door and fine roof-lit showrooms were built in the garden behind. In 1834 an imposing frontage was erected to unite numbers 11 and 12, with large plate-glass windows framed by pilasters and

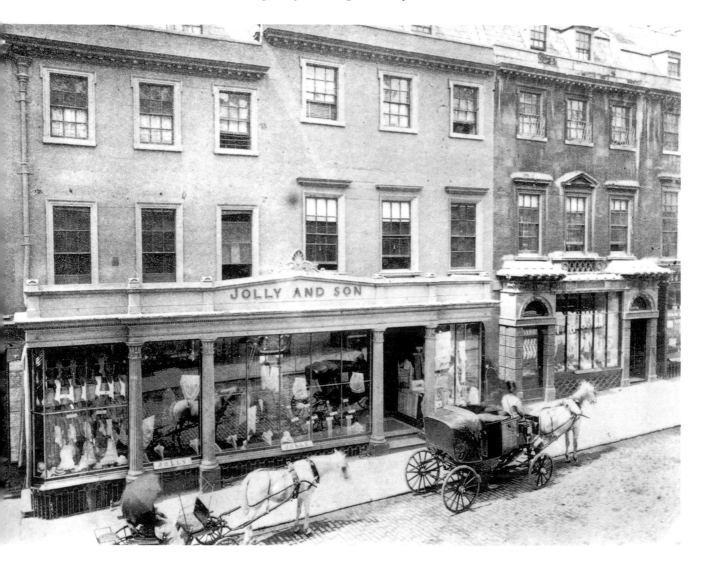

A carriage outside the store in Milsom Street during the 1870s.

a fine fascia board with the words 'Jolly & Son'. In 1836 the shop was sufficiently well established to feature in a series of poetical letters entitled *The Fusseltons in Bath*, which described the shop in some detail: "Twould take more time than I can spare if half these wonders I declare; but if you come to Bath, 'twere folly not to buy all you can of Jolly.' The success of the venture meant that the Bath business had begun to demand Thomas Jolly's entire attention. By 1838 the Deal business was managed by William Hutchinson, the husband of James Jolly's deceased sister, Harriet, and the Bazaar at 26 High Street in Margate was managed by James Jolly himself who had never removed permanently to Bath.

The Bath business continued to grow, adding new lines like furs to the goods sold and providing additional services such as funeral undertaking. Thomas Jolly travelled regularly to Paris to buy silks, shawls and ribbons. By 1851 the shop had a large staff of sixteen male and forty-two female assistants, of which twenty-six lived-in above the showrooms. Around 1852 Jollys opened a branch in College Green, Bristol, under the management of Thomas' second son, Frank. William, the elder son, was already totally preoccupied with the Bath store. In 1858 Thomas Jolly, who had largely retired from active involvement in the firm, acquired the freehold of 11 Milsom Street. By the late 1850s Thomas had had a

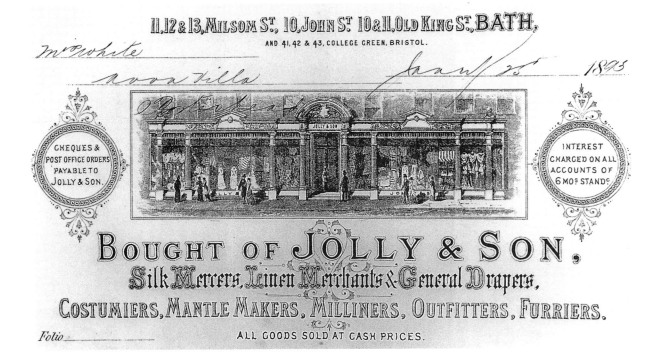

The store's frontage as illustrated on an 1893 billheading.

long and active involvement in Bath civic life, where success in business had brought him social acceptibility. By 1851 he had moved from his small house near Milsom Street to a large villa on the Oldfield Road. As early as the 1830s he had advocated early closing, to allow his shop staff opportunities for recreation and self-improvement, and in 1860 he tried to establish a public library for their use. Yet Thomas was more than a well-meaning philanthropist. As a successful and energetic tradesman he had resuscitated Bath's dwindling commercial community, and as a town councillor he had reformed the borough's police force and land-holding system and saved the neglected baths and pump rooms from decay. In 1860 he became the first tradesman to be elected mayor of Bath, a position to which he was returned in 1868 by popular demand.

During the 1860s Jollys developed a speciality in silks which were ordered from agents in France and Switzerland who dealt directly with the manufacturers.

The peacock trade-mark adopted by the store.

These buyers provided advice on the quality, price and fashionability of cloths and negotiated for discounts and exclusive designs. In 1873 Jollys' silks won a medal at the International Exhibition in London. Other stock was also acquired overseas, including linens from Belgium and Ireland and model millinery from Paris. In 1879, 13 Milsom Street was added to the premises and a fine arched doorway was erected to unite the new shop with the old. By 1880 the store enjoyed a large and aristocratic connection, regularly despatching more than 4,500 copies of the quarterly price list to both regular customers and seasonal visitors. The store's travellers made personal visits to towns like Bournemouth, and in 1881 an agency was opened in Bombay for 'ladies who have commissions from friends in India.' In 1888 the showrooms were extensively altered, with fitting rooms and lavatories added to the costume departments and a separate department for mourning goods created. By this time Jollys had adopted the peacock as a trade emblem in the decoration of the showrooms and the design of the store's stationery and packaging. By the 1890s the mail-order business was extensive. Annual fashion shows were held as far afield as Birmingham and Swansea and more than 14,000 orders were received each year.

In June 1903 Jolly acquired the adjoining premises of Pearson & Son at 14 Milsom Street which was converted into a handsome showroom. The acquisition was celebrated with an exhibition of modern and antique lace. That year the proprietors, Jolly and his son, Paul, sold the firm to a private limited company, Jolly & Son, Bath, Ltd, whilst retaining the majority of the shares. William Jolly had moved to Hampstead in 1899 but remained nominal head of the company until his death in January 1904 whilst executive control was assumed by Paul Jolly.

OPPOSITE ABOVE
The fashion department in around 1932.

OPPOSITE BELOW
Illustrations from the centrefold of a 1920s ladies' costume catalogue.

BELOW *The bridal gown salon during the 1890s.*

Z.4

COSTUME in Angora-finished cloth. In navy, black and lido shades ... **75/-**

Z.1

NEW line edge-to-edge COAT, trimmed motifs and piped with soft patent leather. Belted waist. Navy, black and new brown .. **4½ Gns.**

Z.5

COPPER-COLOURED CARDIGAN SUIT, in novelty cloth, fastened to neck, with wooden buttons dyed to tone ... **4½ Gns.**

Z.2

VERY SMART COAT, in Botany wool and alpaca. Camel colour, suitable for town or country .. **69/6**

Z.6

THE favourite TAILORED COSTUME, link fastening, with double-wrap Skirt. Colours: Copper, blue and grey, and brown mixtures. **79/6**

Z.3

HOMESPUN SWING COAT, in soft shades of brown, blue and green check ... **4 Gns.**

Z.7

FUR COAT, in the new box shape, in Mocca Lapin. S.W. size. **8½ Gns.**

Z.8

SILVER FOX TIE, in nice dark skin, well silvered. **10 Gns.**

Z.9

HIP-LENGTH COAT, in Scotch mole-skin, useful pockets. **9½ Gns.**

By 1905 the showrooms had grown too small for the volume of trade conducted and work began on a major refurbishment designed to increase sales space and improve the costume, millinery and outfitting rooms. Rebuilding work continued throughout 1906 when sales amounted to £83,050. The growth of the store continued unabated and in early 1907 the adjoining premises of Messrs Jackman at 9 Milsom Street were acquired. In 1912 the firm also purchased the business, premises and stock of T. Knight & Son, adding carpet, furniture, auctioneer and estate agency departments. In addition, a circulating library and cold rooms for fur storage were launched. During the First World War acute trading difficulties were experienced and the high-class costume and furnishing departments were particularly badly affected. Attempts were made to boost sales by the organisation of special train excursions and the store's reputation was enhanced by Queen Mary's regular visits whilst at Badminton. Sales increased dramatically in 1919 and by 1920 the company had purchased the entire Milsom Street premises outright.

In January 1922, upon the death of Herbert Jolly, the Bristol store, which had been hived-off for family reasons in 1889, was acquired at a cost of £80,000. The purchase price was paid in two parts, £50,000 cash and £30,000 as a short-term loan. A year later, in February 1923, the company went public, as Jolly & Son Ltd, in order to raise finance for the Bristol purchase. Paul Jolly remained chairman of the new company and the new board comprised Russell Jolly, a Birmingham solicitor, and three former departmental heads, as managing directors. Meanwhile a small furniture shop had been opened in Charles Street, Cardiff. In 1924 sales of the three stores amounted to over £264,000. Trading conditions became difficult during the depressed years of the mid-1920s and early 1930s, although small improvements continued to be made at both Bath and Bristol. In 1928, for example, tea and rest rooms were opened at Bristol and in 1937 structural alterations were made at Bath to allow the regrouping of the drapery sections. Most of the departments at Bath were, however, still located only on the ground floor.

In 1940 the Bristol store was totally destroyed by enemy action and smaller, temporary premises were found in Whiteladies Road where the store was eventually relocated on a permanent basis. Later, in 1961, the Bristol site was greatly enlarged by the acquisition of an adjoining three-storey building. In 1968 Jolly & Son (Holdings) Ltd was formed as a holding company for the group with a capital of £150,000. In 1963 purpose-built auction rooms were opened in New King Street and a local transport company, Bath Parcel Services Ltd, was acquired. In early 1964 the group also purchased The Commercial Garage in order to service the store's growing vehicular fleet. In May 1965 a new restaurant was opened at the Bath store. In 1970 E. Dingle & Co Ltd of Plymouth acquired Jolly & Son (Holdings) Ltd and was itself taken over by House of Fraser in 1971. In 1972 the front portion of the store was redeveloped in a manner which preserved the traditional style of the store whilst also attracting younger customers, expanding, for example, the perfumery and hosiery departments. In 1973 a food hall and coffee bar opened in the basement. In 1975 the Bath premises of Cavendish House of Cheltenham, which were also owned by House of Fraser, were merged with the adjoining Jollys' showrooms. The extra refurbished space allowed the opening of several new departments. Subsequently activities outside the mainstream retail business were disposed of with the sale of the auction rooms in 1976 and of the estate agency in 1980. Jollys was partially refurbished in 1985 and 1987, in a manner which matched modern shop fittings with the store's traditional architecture.

Kendal Milne & Co, Manchester

The store was founded by John Watts, a farmer from Didsbury, near Manchester, who taught his six sons hand weaving and spinning in order to eke out the family income. Woven ginghams and regattas had a ready market during the French wars when home-produced fabrics were in great demand. In 1796 John Watts opened a small drapery shop on the Salford side of Deansgate in Manchester. The business expanded and larger premises were rented on the opposite side of the street at 272 Deansgate, where John Watts traded as a wholesale and retail linen draper, silk mercer, glover and agent for Urling's lace. By 1821 Watt had appointed a buyer in London to procure the most fashionable goods for his Manchester customers.

By the late 1820s Samuel and James, John Watts' youngest sons, had joined the business. The continued growth of the trade prompted the removal of the retail store to 64 Deansgate by 1832 and to a corner site at 99 Deansgate and Police Street by 1834. In 1835 the Watts family determined to withdraw from the retail trade in order to concentrate exclusively on the wholesale side of the business (S. & J. Watts & Co later became one of the largest wholesale businesses in the city). The bazaar was consequently sold to three young men in the Watts' employ – Thomas Kendal, trained as a draper in London, and James Milne and Adam Faulkner, who had both been apprenticed in the textile trade. The transfer of ownership was announced in the local newspapers and the new partners re-opened the bazaar on 2 January 1836, trading as Kendal, Milne & Faulkner.

Trade card dating from around 1850.

*An 1897 billheading
featuring the store's royal
warrant.*

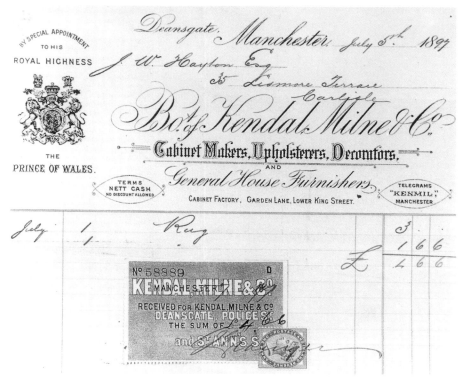

They marketed the bazaar aggressively, advertising in nearby towns like Stockport and Bolton and making a speciality of sales of both regular goods and the discounted stocks of bankrupts. During the 1840s the firm installed the most up-to-date gas lighting, and developed a substantial delivery fleet, stabling more than fifty horses in Wood Street by 1847. The business thrived, trading as Kendal, Milne & Co after Adam Faulkner's death in 1862.

By 1870 the range of goods and services which the firm offered had been greatly increased from drapery to cabinet-making and funeral undertaking and the supply of such consumer goods as sewing machines. The firm had also begun to issue a printed catalogue and to develop a considerable mail-order connection. New cabinet showrooms were taken on the opposite side of Deansgate where the store also owned a cabinet factory in Garden Lane. Later upholstery workrooms were also established in Back Bridge Street. During 1872 and 1873 the old bazaar was extensively rebuilt, as part of the Deansgate improvement scheme, with four floors housing drapery and fashion departments. The new cabinet showrooms were refurbished and, by 1882, a special arrangement had been made with Morris & Co of Oxford Street for the display of their wall coverings and fabrics in a special showroom where interior design advice was also available.

In 1884 Thomas Kendal retired from active involvement in the trade and control passed to John Dewhurst Milne, son of James Milne, working in partnership with James Herbert Milne, his brother, Samuel Kendal and Thomas Herbert Kendal. By 1890 the store employed over 900 staff and was described as 'the largest showrooms out of London.' Tearooms were opened, extravagantly decorated in Moorish style, and the store became one of the most fashionable social venues in the city. In 1893 new departments were created for the sale of ladies' and children's shoes. During the late 1890s the firm acquired a small building facing King Street, which was divided from the main store by Hatter's Alley, and the two were linked by an underground passage and a bridge at first-floor level. By the 1900s the business was advertising widely, as far afield as Southport and Preston, and in 1901 was appointed upholsterers to the royal household. In 1908, after the death of Herbert Kendal and James Herbert Milne, John Dewhurst Milne and Samuel Kendal managed the company as senior partners.

In July 1919 the store was acquired by Harrod's Stores Ltd, which was beginning to develop a network of provincial stores. Extensive refurbishment followed and in 1921 a fifth storey was added to the Police Street building, Hatter's Alley disappeared, the King Street site was joined with the rest of the premises and a subway under Deansgate was completed. In April 1920 Harrods had acquired Walter Carter, a removal firm in Rusholme. Its business was subsequently merged with that of the store and its premises used for the storage of furniture stock. In 1936 a major extension to the Deansgate store, the Centenary Building, was completed. During 1938 work began on the rebuilding of the store on the Salford side of Deansgate, but in February 1939 the remaining buildings were gutted by fire. Work continued and the new store was finally completed in 1940. Although much of the store was requisitioned during the war for use by the Civil Service, drapery and fashion departments were gradually opened on two floors and air-raid shelters created in the basement. The furnishing business was transferred to the former main building on the other side of the street. The new store offered a variety of services, including hairdressing, library, funeral undertaking, travel agency and estate agency departments. In 1959 Harrods Ltd was acquired by House of Fraser, trading as part of Harrods Provincial and subsequently within the Group's Midland Division. In 1981 the household store on the opposite side of Deansgate was disposed of and all the departments consolidated within the main store. Between 1983 and 1984 the store was progressively refurbished, installing a new food hall on the ground floor and redesigning the first and second fashion floors. In addition the striking stone facade was cleaned. Most of the floors were refurbished once again between 1985 and 1988.

McDonalds Ltd, Glasgow

Stewart & McDonald was established in 1826 as a small wholesale drapery warehouse in Glasgow. The firm was founded by Robertson Buchanan Stewart of Rothesay, who had recently quit the army after an injury, and John McDonald, an experienced tailor from the Vale of Leven. The original premises, in a rented tenement on the first floor of 5 Buchanan Street, consisted of a room about thirty-one feet long by fifteen feet wide. By 1847 the partners had also acquired premises at 152 Argyle Street and 4 Mitchell Street. In 1859 the founders' sons, Ninian Bannatyne Stewart and Alexander McDonald, were assumed as partners, and upon John McDonald's death, around 1860, Robertson Stewart's eldest son, Alexander Bannatyne Stewart, abandoned his career in the legal profession to join the firm.

By 1866 the business boasted an immense turnover in excess of £1 million pounds per annum, and a fine retail warehouse was erected north of the original site at 21 Buchanan Street. Designed in Italian style with an eighty-foot frontage on to Buchanan Street the retail showrooms were substantial, comprising, at ground-floor level, an open salon with staircase and central well bordered by marble pillars. From 1860 the wholesale departments were also greatly extended, both in Buchanan Street and Argyle Street and along the east side of Mitchell Street. During the late 1860s the firm acquired a block on the west side of

Mitchell Street where a shirt manufactory was established. Later a packing area was installed in Union Street, connected to the main building by a new subway.

Robertson Stewart died in 1871 and, after Ninian's retirement in 1874, Alexander Stewart became senior partner, at which time he took Archibald Crombie, formerly the cashier, into partnership. Alexander Stewart died in 1880 and was succeeded by the founder's nephew and grandson, John R. Stewart, and later, in 1882, by Robert Keddie, manager of several of the principal departments. During the 1880s it was Keddie who initiated the establishment of supply factories and the improvement of the Buchanan Street frontage. By 1889 Stewart & McDonald was a huge business with thirty-three wholesale drapery departments and a thriving retail business, operating from a six-storey warehouse with massive frontages on Argyle Street and Buchanan Street. Three years later the sales area was greatly extended by the excavation of a lower ground floor. Each department had its own manager and buyer and the company specialised in dress materials, with four departments for English, French, German and Scotch goods, and ready-made clothes. It employed 500 staff in the warehouse and around seventy commercial travellers. The company also owned three factories in Dunlop Street, Glasgow, for ready-made shirts, costumes and mantles (later removed to Rutherglen Road); in Leeds, for ready-made clothing; and in Strabane, Ireland, for shirts, collars and ladies' underclothing. Branch establishments were operated in London, Edinburgh, Liverpool, Rochdale, Birmingham, Belfast, Dublin, Newcastle, Leeds, Preston, Hull, Montreal, Toronto, Melbourne, Sydney, Dunedin and Port Elizabeth. The firm's retail warehouse was extremely popular, and was voted the second most fashionable shop in Glasgow in a London magazine poll in 1896.

In 1900, in order to furnish capital for further expansion, the firm was registered as a limited liability company, Stewart & McDonald Ltd, with a capital of £1 million. During the previous five years the net profit had averaged £64,000. In 1898 plans had been laid for the rebuilding of the southern portion of the warehouse fronting Argyle Street and the corner of Buchanan Street, and compensation of £8,000 was awarded to Stewart & McDonald by the Council for setting back the frontage in line with the rest of Buchanan Street. The new premises, completed in 1903, were designed by the architect Horatio Bromhead

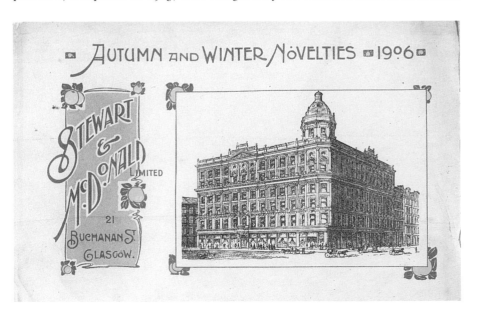

A 1906 trade card illustrating the new building.

Bridal Gown.

Gown of mousseline, veiling
bodice, and apron of real lace,
edged seed pearls ; underskirt
of satin ; train of satin, with
raised embroidery of ribbon
and garlands of roses, touches
of silver thread, train lined
gauged mousseline.

— 1 —

and incorporated a fine domed corner section and a central pediment feature. The warehouse had 235,000 square feet of floor space on six storeys with the ground floor reserved for shop premises.

In 1913 the retail section of Stewart & McDonald Ltd, trading at 21/31 Buchanan Street, was hived off from the larger wholesale business as a separate private limited liability company, McDonalds Ltd. 'It is the express purpose of the new company', announced the independent store's first price list, 'to inaugurate this change of control by a complete clearance of stock at reductions upon a scale which cannot fail to extend their business far beyond its present boundaries.' More than £40,000 worth of merchandise was offered in the sale.

The business was essentially a ladies' fashion store although it also carried household linens and a few lines in menswear. Four years earlier the showrooms had been considerably improved by the installation of fitting and waiting rooms, after the appointment of a new manager from a London store.

The retail branch had always conducted a high class of trade and, despite falling sales during the First World War, the directors adamantly refused to experiment with cheaper lines. Business recovered after the war and in 1921 the store expanded into new premises in Argyle Street, connected to the principal showrooms by a large doorway. Several departments were augmented and a new boot department established. The following year McDonalds opened a branch store upon the acquisition of Edward J. Clarke's family drapery shop in James Street, Harrogate, in Yorkshire. The acquisition was described by the board as 'a high class business of a similar character to our Buchanan Street business.' The new branch, renamed McDonalds, was considerably enlarged but continued to operate as a separate concern advertising as 'the house for courtesy, service and quality and outfitters to gentlewomen of taste.'

Trade was slow during the depressed years of the mid-1920s, but in 1926 McDonalds embarked upon a massive extension of the Glasgow store, adding several new floors and increasing the sales area four-fold. In preparation for this

The spacious ladies' costume department in 1929.

*The arcade entrance in
around 1935.*

expansion the Buchanan Street property had been bought outright in 1925 and
the issued capital increased from £140,000 to £265,000. Despite the economic
recession the share issue was well subscribed. Work on the refurbishment of the
building continued for many months, and in 1927 a restaurant, ladies' hairdressing
salon, new ready-made clothing department and private arcade were opened.
The following year these were joined by a coffee lounge, men's hairdressing
department, new lifts and, in Mitchell Street, carpet and furniture departments.
Bathrooms and dressing rooms were also provided for those who had travelled
from a distance in order to attend weddings and other functions.

By 1930 the alterations were complete but sales had been undermined by the
poor economic outlook. The board determined to lower prices, explaining that
'the quality of the firm's goods will, of course, be maintained as a first principle.
We believe a still larger section of the shopping community would be delighted
to shop at McDonalds, but for the false impression that the prices are beyond
their pockets.' The following year the turnover of the Glasgow store increased,
but that at Harrogate suffered sorely from the lack of visitors and the depressed
state of local agriculture. In 1933 a new arcade and canopy was opened at the

northern end of the Buchanan Street store in order to increase the display area and attract shoppers. By the late 1930s, although the unhelpful high-price image persisted, trade had increased to such an extent that the area of the restaurant had to be extended by converting the board-room into a coffee lounge. In 1937 the ailing Harrogate business was placed under the direct control of the main Glasgow store. Turnover continued to increase during the war, although price controls and rising operating expenses suppressed profit levels.

In April 1951 McDonalds Ltd was acquired by House of Fraser, owners of a similar business on the opposite side of Buchanan Street. The store retained its original character until, in 1966, it was linked with Wylie & Lochhead, a neighbouring furnishing store which had been acquired by House of Fraser in 1957. Together the two stores traded as McDonalds, Wylie & Lochhead. In 1975 this merger was taken a stage further by the amalgamation of Fraser Sons & Co, Wylie & Lochhead and McDonalds as a single department store, Frasers, on the west side of Buchanan Street. The showrooms were totally refurbished at a cost of £2 million, and new departments, such as a food hall and designer rooms, added. By 1981 the store had secured a Barratt national furnishing contract, fitting out over 2,000 studio flats nationwide, and a show flat was opened in the store. The following year a new Lifestyle department was created on the fourth floor, selling a wide range of goods, from fashion to furniture, and aimed at younger customers. In 1983 the second floor was revitalised by the introduction of Innovations, a cookware, china and glass shopping mall, and the following year a huge Astral sports shop was opened on the lower ground floor. The store has major plans for a £6 million facelift, including the restoration of the galleried hall to its former grandeur.

The Buchanan Street frontage during the 1950s.

Robert Maule & Son Ltd, Edinburgh

Robert Maule opened his first retail drapery business at 2 Kirk Street, Kincardine-on-Forth, in 1856, whilst continuing to manufacture woollen shawls and tartans in his own factory. In 1872 he transferred the business to Tolbooth Wynd, Leith, and admitted his son, Robert, into partnership. The shop was a great success. The premises were extended in 1878 and again in 1892. In 1893 the firm bought a large building at 146–148 Princes Street and 1–5 Hope Street, Edinburgh, formerly occupied by the Scottish Liberal Club. It was a fine site at the end of Princes Street opposite the Caledonian Station but the premises required total refurbishment. The new warehouse, described as 'one of the largest and best appointed drapery house, furnishing and fashion emporiums in Scotland,' attracted huge crowds on the opening day in February 1894. The store offered a diverse range of stock, including china, glass, household linens, furnishings, gentlemen's and children's wear, and possessed one of the first tearooms and electric lifts in Edinburgh. During the following years Maule determined to extend the showrooms, acquiring two more shops at 145 and 145A Princes Street and occupying premises, from the first floor upwards, along Hope Street. These extensions, completed by 1898, cost around £25,000. The store became an

important social centre, the restaurant was called The Rendezvous, and adopted the advertising slogan 'Meet me at Maules'.

In 1901 Maule's son became sole partner and continued to conduct the business with imagination and enterprise. The award of a Royal Warrant served to underline the store's excellent reputation. In 1908 the firm made a magnificent display at the Scottish National Exhibition. Maule was well known as a philanthropist, sitting on the boards of many charitable institutions and regularly distributing provisions to the poor. He was also chairman of the Scottish Reform Club and vice-president of the Scottish Liberal Club. For this work and the many other civic and public duties he performed he was awarded a knighthood in 1913.

During the early 1920s a large adjoining block was built in Hope Street, incorporating a new system of window lighting. In June 1929 the business was incorporated as a private limited company, Robert Maule & Son Ltd, with an authorised capital of £60,000. Sir Robert, who was allocated a majority

OPPOSITE ABOVE
*A view of the store today,
still known locally as
'Binns' corner.'*

OPPOSITE BELOW
*A 1930s advertisement for
the tearoom.*

shareholding, died in December 1931. He had no son to succeed him and the business, managed by Robert McPherson since 1929, passed into the hands of trustees. McPherson, a chartered accountant, had previously been managing director of Anderson's Royal Polytechnic in Glasgow and had negotiated the sale of that company to Lewis's Investment Trust. In 1934 he similarly arranged the acquisition of Robert Maule & Son Ltd by H. Binns Son & Co Ltd of Sunderland. Thereafter the store traded as Binns and was rebuilt to create an up-to-date department store with large open showrooms on six floors. The work was carried out in two phases to minimise disruption, and elegant lounges and refreshment rooms were installed on the third floor together with a new furniture department on the fifth floor. In 1953 House of Fraser took over the Binns group and assumed control of the store which then comprised fifty departments on seven floors.

In 1976 the store was renamed Frasers and given a major facelift with the opening of several new departments, including a man's shop, cook shop and Impact boutique. In 1981, following the closure of Arnotts in Edinburgh, the store was extensively reorganised, with the installation during the early 1980s of twelve new escalators and the opening of a new restaurant on the top floor.

Rackhams Ltd, Birmingham

In 1851 William Winter Riddell and Henry Wilkinson opened a retail drapery shop at 78 Bull Street, Birmingham. The business was successful and in 1863 a wholesale branch was also established in Temple Row. John Rackham and William Matthews were apprenticed to Wilkinson & Riddell in 1861 and eight years later both were promoted to positions as floor walkers. By 1878 Rackham had been appointed as dress buyer and Matthews as linen buyer. In 1881 management of the retail business was transferred to Rackham and Matthews and the wholesale trade was hived off as a separate concern. Shortly afterwards Wilkinson withdrew completely, in order to concentrate on the prospering wholesale trade, selling the retail shop to its new managers.

The shop, trading as Rackham & Matthews, flourished as town improvements began to attract a large amount of trade to the area, particularly upon the completion of part of a new thoroughfare, Corporation Street, in 1882. In 1888 William Matthews retired, followed by John Rackham in 1889. In 1890 the business, re-named Rackham & Co, was acquired by Charles Richards, a trader in Snowhill, who managed the store until 1907. The premises were extended in 1898 into the North Western Arcade and two years later a dressmaking business was launched. In 1907 Frank Matthews, William's son, who had worked in the store during the 1890s, married Charles Richards' daughter, Hettie, and was appointed manager. Richards also owned a cut-price clothing warehouse, called the Beehive, in Albert Street.

In 1913 a limited liability company, Charles Richards Ltd, was formed to incorporate both Rackham & Co and the Beehive. Charles Richards became chairman, retaining one-third of the shares and the remainder were distributed equally between his two daughters. Frank Matthews was appointed general manager at a salary linked to the profits. The following year work began on the rebuilding of the Bull Street frontage. The premises then included shops on Temple Row and Bull Street and in the Windsor and North Western Arcades. In 1921 Matthews was succeeded by Charles Phillips, Richards' nephew. In 1926 the property on Temple Row was massively expanded and the store refurbished.

In 1927 Charles Richards died and was replaced by Maurice Clutterbuck. The store was in sore need of further modernisation and the sale of the business was

The store's refitted soft furnishings department today.

contemplated as an alternative to capital investment. In 1928 the board agreed 'that only a fancy price should be accepted' and several offers for purchase were refused through the early 1930s despite the difficult trading conditions. Meanwhile the company was quite unable to carry out the vital refurbishment or to exercise options for the purchase of the Bull Street and Temple Row freeholds. During the Second World War the store suffered a direct hit in 1940 which destroyed one-third of the premises.

After the war some improvements were made and a new model coat salon was opened in 1954. In 1955 Rackhams was acquired by Harrods Ltd which was able to purchase a large island site, and the construction of a new store began in 1957. In 1959 Harrods was itself taken over by House of Fraser. House of Fraser proceeded with the plans for the new store which was opened in several stages between 1960 and 1966. The new enlarged store was extremely successful, becoming one of the most important department stores in the city. It was the first store to be redeveloped during House of Fraser's refurbishment programme in the early 1980s. In 1982 the furniture floor was redesigned and the following year a Lifestyle department was opened on the fifth floor and a restaurant on the top floor. During the following two years a further £6 million was spent on redeveloping the ground floor, enlarging the perfumery department and creating a new food hall, and on installing a china and glass department on the lower ground floor. In 1984 the growing importance of the store was reflected in the launch of a colour magazine advertising the store's departments and services.

The menswear department of the new store in 1961.

Schofield Ltd, Leeds

Snowden Schofield was born in 1870 at Horton in Bradford. After leaving school he went to work in Albert Priestley's drapery store in Manchester Road, and in 1889 he applied successfully for a job with Brown & Muff in Bradford's town centre. Schofield spent less than nine months with Brown & Muff before moving on to work for Affleck & Brown of Manchester. He then spent a short time with Harvey Nichols in London before returning north to take up a position as a lace buyer with Owen Owen of Liverpool. In 1901, with savings of £300 to invest, he decided to exploit his wide experience of the drapery trade by setting up in business on his own account. A former colleague advised him of attractive premises lying vacant at the corner of Upperhead Row and the recently opened Victoria Arcade in central Leeds, and Schofield quickly secured the lease for £50 per annum. He opened his small shop in May 1901, selling laces, frillings, ribbons, neckwear and other fancy goods on the ground floor and millinery upstairs. The store, which was launched with an opening sale, took £112.11s. during the first week.

Schofield was a shrewd buyer, with a talent for creating attractive merchandise displays and an appreciation of the value of newspaper advertising. His business prospered, and by 1910 he had taken the leases of the five shops next to his own, and possessed an unbroken frontage from numbers 1 to 6 Victoria Arcade. In 1911 he doubled the size of the premises by acquiring a seventeenth-century mansion, called the Red Hall, which lay behind his shop on the corner of

A corner of the store in the Victoria Arcade in around 1910.

Victoria Arcade during the late 1940s.

Guildford and King Charles Streets. Gloves, ladies' underwear, hosiery and baby linen departments were opened there, as well as a fashionable café restaurant in the splendidly re-appointed King's Chamber. In 1916, the business was transformed into a private limited company, Schofields (Leeds) Ltd, and six years later, on the twenty-first anniversary of the store's opening, it possessed a sales area of 40,000 square feet and employed 250 people.

During the 1920s, the nineteenth-century mock-Tudor frontage of the Red Hall on Guildford Street and the courtyard which lay behind were acquired and incorporated into the store. More shops were leased in the Victoria Arcade and a large extension was completed next to the Red Hall on King Charles Street. The Corporation's plans to improve the central area of Leeds involved an extensive road-widening programme, and Guildford Street, Upperhead Row and Lowerhead Row were swept away in 1931 to be replaced by a magnificent new thoroughfare, The Headrow. When Lewis's opened a new department store opposite his own in The Headrow the following year, Snowden Schofield was spurred into making further plans for expansion. The Hippodrome in King Charles Croft was leased in 1934 and connected by a tunnel to the main store, and the staff workrooms, cloakrooms, and canteen, as well as the warehouse and despatch office, were transferred to the former theatre. Since 1918 Schofield had made several attempts to acquire the Cock and Bottle Inn, which interrupted The Headrow frontage of the store. In 1938 these premises were finally purchased at a cost of £32,000. Proposals to spend £100,000 on rebuilding the frontage, from the Victoria Arcade up to King Charles Street, were subsequently announced to

357

The Headrow frontage in 1959.

the press. These plans had to be shelved, however, when it became clear that war was imminent.

Schofield was able to resume his plans for expansion in 1946, when he purchased the Victoria Arcade. Two years later the arcade was extended and bridged, but Schofield died in March 1949 and did not live to see the successful completion of the project. Control of the business, which was by then Leed's best-known department store, with 100,000 square feet of floor space and a

workforce of 600, passed to Schofield's sons, Ronald and Peter. Schofield had for many years been content to delegate authority whenever necessary, and Ronald, Peter and their fellow directors, Ernest Woods and Alfred Ambler, were well prepared for the task of guiding Schofields through the difficult, postwar years.

The Schofields board was well aware as early as 1949, of the need for further expansion, but government restrictions on borrowing and materials supply prevented them from embarking upon new building programmes. By 1957, however, with government controls removed, Schofields were finally able to proceed with the enlargement and improvement of the store. The vacant Theatre Royal in Lands Lane was purchased and a new building erected on the site to house the linen, soft furnishing, china, carpet and furniture departments and new hardware and electrical appliances departments as well as the Café Royal self-service restaurant. Schofields' furnishing centre was opened in November 1958. In January 1959 the Victoria Arcade was demolished and the north-eastern portion of the store totally rebuilt. Subsequently the Red Hall area, which housed the main entrance, staircase and lifts, was reconstructed. It was originally intended to build the new store on two storeys, but continuing pressure for space and satisfaction with the economical progress of the work, encouraged the firm to proceed with further floors. The rebuilding was completed in June 1962.

The reconstruction of Schofields was a triumph for the board of directors and in particular for the chairman, Ronald Schofield, who had worked closely with the architects and contractors on the project. Within four years, however, the furnishing centre was already becoming overcrowded, and the furniture warehouse and despatch department at the Hope Warehouse, one and a half miles from the store, was proving unsuitable. In 1965 Schofields acquired the lease of Merton House, situated on Albion and King Charles Streets and stockrooms and food halls were located there. In 1967 it was decided to proceed with the demolition of some buildings on Albion Street, and of the old Hippodrome, and to erect a new extension to the furnishing centre in their place. The extension opened in 1970, by which time King Charles Croft had been bridged to connect the furnishing centre with the main store at first- and second-floor levels. During the early 1970s, a new warehouse was built at Pontefract Lane, with easy access to the local motorway system to facilitate expansion into other towns and cities. In 1974 the company's name was changed to Schofields (Yorkshire) Ltd. Schofields' attempts at expansion beyond Leeds met with mixed success. In November 1972 a store in Angel Street, Sheffield, was acquired from T.B.& W. Cockayne, and in June 1980 Schofields purchased the Ledgard & Wynn furnishing store in Skipton. The Sheffield store closed in 1982 and the Skipton venture followed in 1986. Schofields met with greater success in Harrogate, where the company acquired the Cresta House women's store from Debenhams in 1980. That store continued to trade under the Schofields name until it was sold in 1989.

In 1984 Schofields was acquired by Clayform Properties plc, and the new owners announced ambitious plans to redevelop the store site, creating a new shopping mall. In 1987 Schofields moved to the former Woolworths premises in Briggate to permit Clayform Properties and Tarmac Properties Ltd, through their jointly owned subsidiary, Schofields Centre Ltd, to proceed with the rebuilding work on The Headrow site. In 1988 House of Fraser purchased the business. Schofields will re-open on four floors at the Schofield Centre in 1990 and House of Fraser will continue to use the Briggate premises after the completion of a major refurbishment programme.

John Walsh Ltd, Sheffield

John Walsh, a young Irishman, bought lace, underclothing, ladies' costumes and baby linens for T.B. & W. Cockayne, Sheffield drapers, for nine years before leaving in 1875 to set up on his own account at 39 High Street. His shop, selling ladies' clothing, baby linen, lace, muslin and embroidery, comprised a ground floor and cellar rented for one year only. The staff included Walsh's wife, Harriet, who was to prove an invaluable manager and buyer, and two female assistants. The shop opened on 19 June 1875 and the first year's sales amounted to £5,000, more than four times his invested capital. Walsh, his wife and four children lived over the shop until 1879 when the showroom was extended to the rear and a new millinery department launched. By 1880 lack of room had again become a problem and Walsh rented number 58 on the opposite side of the High Street. The new venture was an immediate success. *The Sheffield Daily Independent* later reported: 'Customers crowded the shop and overflowed into the street, and closing time regularly came with the shop full of purchasers so that an occasional wet day with its dearth of custom was a necessity, as well as a relief, in order to go through the stock.' The business then employed five men and nineteen women and grossed sales of £12,000 a year.

In 1883 Walsh turned his attention to the north side of High Street and secured number 37, next door to his original shop. The extra window space was a great boon and the ladies' outfitting department moved into the new showroom. In 1887 Walsh took over the lease of 45 and 47 High Street, from J.E. Grundy's mourning goods warehouse, and installed the mantle department there. In 1889 he also secured the lease of 41 and 43 High Street which were used initially as a store room. Until 1887 the premises, all held on short-term tenancies, had been little altered and the departments were still divided by the walls of the original shops. During the following year, certain properties on the north side were knocked into a single showroom, and new glass roofs were constructed to illuminate sales areas to the rear, an investment prompted by the negotiation of a fourteen-year lease. Walsh clearly intended to reconstruct all his properties on the north side of High Street. These plans were hastened by the Corporation's proposal to set back Walsh's frontage and thereby demolish an awkward projection into the street known as 'Grundy's Corner'. Walsh was awarded £6,000 toward the cost of rebuilding, but the leaseholder of the upper portion of the premises, The Star Hotel, refused to come to terms and consequently the reconstruction had to take place in two phases. Furniture, ready-to-wear clothing and travel requisite departments were soon opened but the total rebuilding was not completed until 1899. Such a delay must have been an annoyance to Walsh whose vision of a single magnificent warehouse was scarcely nearer its achievement. In 1889 he had found some consolation in setting up a branch establishment in Halifax but the experiment was not a success and the new shop closed four years later. Once again Walsh began to seek property on the south side of High Street, and by 1895 had not only acquired 52 to 66 High Street but had also purchased land in Trippet Lane (for stabling horses and storing furniture) and nineteen rooms in Fargate for assistants for whom there was no accommodation at the shop.

By 1895 the store had thirty-six departments ranging from feathers to furniture. The premises on the south side of High Street were the most important, for the twenty-four departments there took two-thirds of the trade. Consequently the whole undertaking was threatened when, in 1895, Walsh was forced to surrender to the Corporation the leases of all his premises fronting the southern

Walter John Walsh.

side of High Street. The buildings were to be demolished as part of a scheme, first mooted in 1892, to widen the street. Walsh demanded £66,248 in compensation. The arbitration lasted several days and the final award amounted to a mere £28,844. Walsh, unabashed, began negotiations to buy or lease back a large block of his former properties. In 1896 he invited Sheffield architects Messrs Flockton & Gibbs to draw up plans for the new store. The premises, with a frontage of 173 feet along High Street and of 200 feet of covered arcade along Mulberry Street, comprised three-and-a-half acres of floor space. Completed in 1899, the building cost more than £60,000. By this time Walsh was trading in a wide variety of goods – silks, dresses, millinery, ribbons, laces, flowers and feathers, furs and umbrellas, ladies' hosiery and gloves, boots and shoes, trimmings, haberdashery, foreign fancy goods, Berlin wools, household linen, family drapery, flannels, prints, carpets, house furnishings, glass and china, ironmongery, men's and boys' ready-to-wear clothing, travelling requisites, gentlemen's outfitting, mantles, furniture, baby linen and ladies' outfitting. All these departments were moved into the new building where lines like patent medicine, stationery, books, silver, cutlery, oriental goods and toys were launched. The evacuated premises on the north side of High Street were retained by Walsh and let to tenants. In addition to the selling departments there were ladies' cloakrooms and writing rooms and a restaurant where coffee was served throughout the day.

Around 1901 John Walsh retired from active management, and his son, Walter John Walsh, assumed control. Walter had already worked in the store for some time and was, despite his relative youth, described in the local press as 'a thorough businessman, who knows how to treat his workers and how to cater for the requirements of the public.' On 11 July 1902, he converted the firm into a private limited company, John Walsh Ltd, with a nominal capital of £350,000. No shares were offered to the public. The founder divided his shareholding amongst members of the Walsh family and it was from the family that the five directors were also drawn – John Walsh, chairman; Walter John Walsh, managing director; Thomas Walsh (John Walsh's second son); Patrick Benson and J. Barker Norton (his sons-in-law). Despite changes in management the store continued to rely on the same formula of selling reputable goods at reasonable prices. Every day carriages lined the street outside the store and the post-free distribution of catalogues attracted a huge mail-order trade. In 1902 new decorating, sanitary, gas and electrical departments were opened. Food remained the only regular commodity that Walshs did not carry. In December 1902, John Walsh's wife, Harriet, died and the store closed for a day as a sign of respect. Three years later John Walsh also died leaving legacies of between £50 and £200 to seventeen of the store's buyers, porters and packers. The Sheffield papers carried lengthy obituaries praising his remarkable energy and talent.

Walshs, however, continued to grow. In 1906 a new cabinet factory, warehouse and furniture depository was built in Pinfold Street replacing a number of small scattered properties. The first removal had been carried out around 1893 and seventeen shire horses, stabled nearby, were used to pull the carts and vans. Remodelling of the High Street windows began in June 1914 and a new arcade was built to provide a total window frontage of 500 feet, the largest in Sheffield. Work was completed in November 1914, a few months after Britain entered the First World War. Ladies' and gentlemen's hairdressing salons were also opened at this time and a mansion house called The Mount was purchased in Glossop Road. Previously owned by a city magnate the property was furnished by the store as a residence for senior female staff. The war years were not without problems. Nearly 140 staff, around a quarter of the workforce, joined up, and,

One of the
Cabinet Galleries

although many returned after the war, it was a struggle to maintain standards of service. Despite these difficulties sales grew during the latter years of the war. Annual turnover increased from £18,000 in 1914/15 to £37,000 in 1916/17 and £74,000 in 1918/19.

Once again the firm's expansion prompted organisational change. In April 1920 the business was incorporated as a public limited company with an authorised capital of £500,000. Most of the ordinary and preference shares were acquired by Walter Walsh and other members of his family. By this time Walshs was undoubtedly the city's premier shop. The main departments, on the basement, ground and first floors were beautifully appointed – spacious, well lit, amply supplied with chairs for weary customers and lined with polished glass show cases and wooden counters. On the second floor were the restaurant, ladies' cloakroom, hairdressing salons and furniture showrooms and, on the third floor the removal office along with further furniture showrooms. The top two floors were devoted to rest rooms, dining rooms and bedrooms for staff. In 1925 the store celebrated its fiftieth anniversary with an anniversary promotion, extension of the hairdressing salon and restaurant and provision of a sports ground for staff.

The store's fleet of delivery vans in 1925.

In 1928, despite the continuing recession, the entire ground floor was refixtured in anticipation of an improvement in trading conditions.

The years of depression and war during the 1930s and 1940s were the most difficult the store had ever experienced. Sales plummeted in 1931 and the board began to question 'whether we were not catering for too high a class of trade in the present conditions.' A special, fixed-menu luncheon was introduced in the restaurant, the lease of property on the northern side of High Street, due to expire in 1936, was not renewed, the share capital was reduced and reorganised and the staff sports ground was sold to the Corporation. Nonetheless, an offer for the store property from a multiple retailer was declined and an extension programme of refurbishment was embarked upon, filling in the well-hole spaces and altering the basement floors. In 1937 Walter Walsh retired from active management and was succeeded by his brother Thomas with J.D. Fraser Johnson as general manager. Walter Walsh died in July 1938. By the mid-1930s Walshs' trade was recovering. The entire basement and ground floor were refurbished and neon signs were installed outside. In 1935 *The Star* described it as 'one of the most comprehensive stores it is possible to imagine.'

The outbreak of the Second World War was, however, a major setback for it heralded a long period of control and shortage. Again many of the male staff were

called up, and women and youths admitted to more responsible positions. An air-raid shelter was installed on the lower ground floor. Plans were in hand for the extension of the food hall and redecoration of the entire store when, in December 1940, Sheffield suffered one of the heaviest air raids of the Blitz and the entire store was gutted. The cabinet factory was untouched as was the residential property known as The Mount on Glossop Road. The Ministry of Works refused permission to rebuild the premises on High Street but within seven weeks Walshs' wartime store was opened at The Mount by the Lord Mayor. It was a remarkable achievement. At The Mount each department had its own private room. Gowns, underwear, shoes and cosmetics in the old staff bedrooms, gloves and handkerchiefs in the drawing room, and so on. A month later in February 1941 the man's shop opened at 41 to 43 Fargate and the furniture and carpet galleries in the banqueting rooms of Cutlers' Hall. Later that year premises were purchased at 45 Fargate providing more space for the man's shop and for a few ladies' wear departments. By May only one of the fifty-two departments which had existed before the Blitz had not been reinstated. In December 1941, the Cutlers' Hall departments were moved to new premises in Church Street where the sale of household goods was centralised. In 1944 the Pinfold Street factory was, for administrative reasons, made into a separate company, John Walsh Manufacturing Co Ltd. It continued to make furniture until the factory was closed in 1957.

In 1946, mindful of the problems attendant upon the rebuilding of the store, the Walshs' board approached Harrods Ltd of London which made an offer for the company's entire share capital. Sales had increased gradually during the war years but the existing premises were quite inadequate, and The Mount, where most of the departments were concentrated, was inaccessible by public transport. However, with the financial resources of Harrods behind the store, plans could be laid for the future. J.W. Beaumont & Sons, Manchester architects, designed a new building, and in 1950 George Longden & Sons began demolition of the derelict premises in High Street. Work was hampered by shortage of labour and materials but the foundation stone of the new store was laid in September 1952. The frontage of Portland stone had recessed windows to create covered arcades and the vertical lines of the structure served to counterbalance the sloping site. The interior was carefully designed in contemporary style both to please the eye and allow flexibility in the location of departments, and low-level fixtures created an impression of spaciousness and the unusual colour schemes attracted some interest. There were three selling floors (it was intended that two more should be added later) and a balcony which ran the length of the store frontage above ground level. The escalators, air-conditioning and lighting systems were all the most modern installations available. The new store was opened in May 1953 to universal acclaim. During the following three years the wartime premises in Fargate, Glossop Road and elsewhere were sold off.

In 1959 Harrods Ltd was itself taken over and Walshs passed into the control of House of Fraser. Trade was buoyant during the early 1960s, and by 1966 plans were in hand for the alteration of the store to conform to Sheffield's plans for the development of Castle Square as a focal point for the city centre. The altered building, which opened in March 1968, had an extra 25,000 square feet of selling space and a new subway entrance from Castle Square. Walshs continued to trade successfully during the following two decades and was renamed House of Fraser Sheffield in 1987, after a £2 million refurbishment of the entire store was completed during the previous three years.

Wylie & Lochhead Ltd, Glasgow

In 1824 Margaret Downie married Robert Wylie, feather and hair merchant in Saltmarket. The following year her sister, Janet, married William Lochhead, partner in his father's undertaking and cabinet-making business in Saltmarket. Mrs Robert Downie died in 1827, leaving all her property in Saltmarket and Bell Street to her daughters, Margaret and Janet, under the charge of William Lochhead. In 1828 Robert Wylie determined to expand his business and was provided with capital of £150 from the family funds administered by Lochhead. In September 1829 Lochhead himself left his father's firm to join Wylie in partnership, trading as Wylie & Lochhead, feather merchants, in a rented second-floor flat at 164 Trongate. Lochhead immediately set up a complete funeral undertaking service, ranging from the provision of coffin and hearse to mourning stationery and catering. Indeed, Wylie & Lochhead established a fine local reputation during an outbreak of Asiatic cholera in 1832 by continuing to handle corpses which others would not touch.

In 1833 the partners bought the top flat and attic at 164 Trongate, and during 1837 also rented the first-floor flat and a single shop below 160 Trongate. By this time Wylie & Lochhead were operating a suburban omnibus service to Rutherglen and the Townhead railway depot, hiring post horses and selling paperhangings in addition to upholstery and furnishings. In March 1843 Wylie proposed admitting Archibald Hill, his son-in-law, as a partner. Lochhead did not favour the idea and the issue was to cause unpleasantness between the partners for the next fifteen years. During 1844, 160 and 164 Trongate were devastated by fire, giving rise to massive stock losses. The partners were already planning to move

Founding partners Robert Wylie (1798–1866) left, and William Lochhead (1796–1875) right.

west and had acquired a vacant site in Argyle Street. Whilst the new warehouse was built, temporary premises were found for the omnibus and funeral undertaking departments at 171 Argyle Street and for the carpet and upholstering departments at 169 Argyle Street. Other lines continued to be sold at Trongate, where a temporary roof was erected.

In May 1845 a massive clearing sale marked the removal of many of the departments to the new warehouse at 28 Argyle Street, which was the first significant iron-framed warehouse in Glasgow and boasted an immense window covering the entire upper storeys. In February 1846 Wylie & Lochhead also leased the Eagle Hotel and stables in Maxwell Street to house the post-hiring and funeral undertaking businesses, letting out the hotel itself as a separate concern. The omnibus business was temporarily abandoned on account of the escalating price of corn. In May 1846 the remainder of the retail departments were accommodated in Argyle Street which was itself extended in 1848 by the acquisition of the adjoining National Bank property in Virginia Street.

The trade grew steadily, and in December 1853 new premises were acquired in Kent Road, west of Elmbank Crescent, to house the funeral undertaking and carriage-hiring businesses. By 1854 Wylie & Lochhead had determined to move the retail business further west to Buchanan Street, which was quickly becoming the most fashionable shopping promenade in the city. The new building, designed by William Lochhead himself, was described in the contemporary press as 'without doubt the most handsome erection for business purposes in Glasgow.' The warehouse, which was iron-framed, had a facade of Corinthian pillars and plate glass and an arched glass roof. Inside, the departments were deployed on three handsome galleries ranged around a central well, with furnishing fabrics on the ground floor and carpets, paperhangings and cabinets on successive galleries above. Around 500 shopmen were employed in the store which also featured a steam-powered lift.

During the following year the firm erected a large building in Union Street to house the funeral undertaking department. However, despite the huge success of the business the relationship between the partners remained uneasy. Wylie was still keen to recruit Archibald Hill and there were also squabbles over how the partners' respective shares in the business might be equitably passed on to their sons, William Lochhead, Robert Downie Wylie and John Wylie. By 1862 the firm was extensive, offering a wide range of departments and services – upholstering, bed and table linen, feathers, carpets and floor cloths and paperhangings at 43–47 Buchanan Street; funeral and undertaking and post-horse hiring at Kent Road and Whiteinch stables; cabinetmaking and paper staining also at Kent Road; and upholstering, carving and gilding at Mitchell Street. During the 1860s Wylie & Lochhead gave up the omnibus service because keen rivalry with other businesses had begun to damage the firm's goodwill. Meanwhile the partners had started paper staining at Kent Road in 1854, acquiring a special factory in Whiteinch around 1862 where the firm began block-printing, and later machine-staining, paperhangings on a massive scale. Wylie & Lochhead papers were well known all over Britain and the firm were exclusive manufacturers of the popular 'stamped gilds'.

Robert Wylie had long suffered from poor health when, in December 1863, Lochhead's only son, William, died. Within months Robert Wylie and William Lochhead had agreed terms for the dissolution of the partnership. Robert Downie Wylie and John Wylie, who were effectively already managing the business, were to take over the firm, continuing to trade as Wylie & Lochhead. The proceeds of the sale were to be divided between Robert Wylie and William Lochhead in

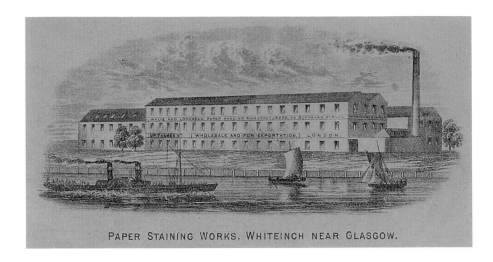

PAPER STAINING WORKS, WHITEINCH NEAR GLASGOW.

a proportion of three to two. The new partners were unable to purchase the business outright but agreed to pay off the debt in instalments and were given a nine-year purchase option on the Buchanan Street premises. Wylie retired entirely from the concern but Lochhead continued to retain an interest and the managing partners were obliged to seek his sanction in such matters as alterations to the building. Robert Downie Wylie died in June 1866, leaving John Wylie in sole charge of the concern. Robert Wylie, the founder, also died a few months later and at his death still retained an interest of over £58,290 in the business. The trust set up by his will provided for funds to be made available to John Wylie for the purchase of the Buchanan Street premises or for the annual monthly instalments to Lochhead, if such borrowing became necessary.

In August 1867 Wylie & Lochhead suffered a considerable setback when a major fire broke out in Buchanan Street, completely destroying the Mitchell Street wing of the warehouse and causing the glass roof of the principal showroom to collapse on to the galleries below. Fortunately the business was able to carry the loss despite the reluctance of the insurance companies to furnish full compensation. Turnover continued to grow and a London office was opened in Cannon Street during the late 1860s. In 1874 the Buchanan Street premises were altered, extending the floor space by the addition of flats for the display of furniture. During mid-1882 an intermediate gallery was also created to provide more accommodation for the bedroom furniture department.

John Wylie, like his father, was a shrewd and inventive entrepreneur quick to identify potential new markets. He was a keen sailor and from the 1870s Wylie & Lochhead were amongst the first of the Glasgow furnishers to specialise in ship and yacht interiors, catering for the busy shipyards developing along the Clyde. John Wylie, having no sons, wanted to safeguard the interests of his daughters and to ensure that the control of the business passed to Robert Downie Wylie's four sons, John, William Adam, Robert and Samuel. He was also acutely aware of the need for both more capital to fund expansion and for some spreading of the financial risk. Consequently, in August 1883 he floated the business as a private limited company with a capital of £200,000 divided into 2,000 £1 shares of which 500 were cumulative preference shares. Wylie retained the entire preference stock and 500 of the ordinary shares, the remainder being allocated to members of the Wylie family. John Wylie became chairman of the new company, with John Steel Wylie as managing director and William Adam Wylie and John Wylie as directors.

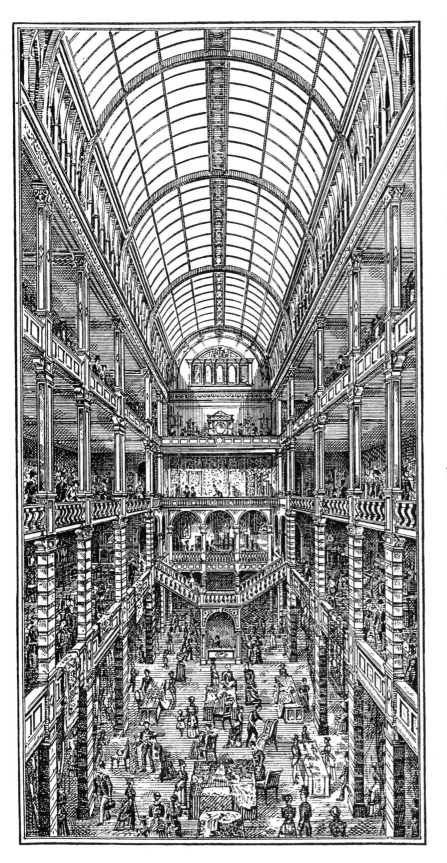

The Buchanan Street
frontage and galleried
interior in 1885.

*Illustrations from the store's
furnishing catalogue for
1900.*

A 1901 customer's bill.

Within months of the creation of the new company the entire Buchanan Street warehouse was totally destroyed in an immense fire which broke out in the linoleum department on the evening of Saturday 3 November 1883. The fire burned for hours and the spectacle attracted huge crowds from all over the city. The damage was estimated at around £150,000. Within weeks Wylie & Lochhead had found temporary premises at 111 Union Street, and Glasgow architect James Sellars was commissioned to design a new building for the same site. Douglas & Sellars had earlier been responsible for the design of the new Kent Road cabinet-making factory in 1872. The new warehouse, completed during early 1885, its iron frame sunk in hard burned brick and fireclay, was constructed of fireproof materials within an ornamental terracotta facade. Inside were four galleried storeys lit by a fine arched glass roof, reminiscent of the earlier design.

John Wylie died in August 1888, his entire estate passing to his wife, Minnie. Thereafter John S Wylie became chairman of the company and was succeeded, upon his death in September 1895, by Robert Wylie. In 1889 a branch business had been established in Manchester. By the 1890s the cabinet-making business was not only the largest in Scotland but was also pioneering Scottish *avant garde* design alongside more traditional furniture styles. Many remarkable designers worked for Wylie & Lochhead, including Ernest Archibald Taylor and George Logan, and the firm's Art-Nouveau pavilion designed for the 1901 Glasgow International Exhibition excited considerable interest. During that year Wylie & Lochhead was awarded a Royal Warrant as cabinetmakers and upholsterers to Edward VII.

The years before the First World War were difficult. The retail trade was severely depressed, particularly at the important luxury end of the market; the lower death rate had diminished the funeral business; there was severe competition from price-cutting wallpaper manufacturers; and the London branch was performing badly. The board determined upon retrenchment, instituting economy measures to reduce overheads and sustain profits. In 1904 the paper-staining business was transferred in its entirety to Wallpaper Manufacturers Ltd and removed to Lancashire. Many new ideas were adopted including the introduction of ticketed goods and sales visits to shipyards and naval architects in 1913; the adaptation of the basement for bargain merchandise in 1914; the provision of a ladies' washroom in 1915; and the establishment of surburban funeral parlours offering plainer funerals and institution of a wholesale mail-order business in 1916. The stringencies of the First World War brought a new set of problems. The younger directors, including Frank and John Wylie, and many of the staff enlisted; the carting and cab branch suffered from a shortage of drivers and rising costs of petrol and horse-feed; and the manufacturing

OPPOSITE *Frasers' famous galleried hall stunningly decorated for Christmas 1984.*

departments were acutely affected by severe supply problems. However, the war also created new opportunities and the Kent Road factory, registered as a controlled establishment, was quickly and profitably engaged upon the manufacture of aeroplanes.

Despite the postwar problems of converting from munitions work to the regular cabinet trade, the board began 1919 in confident mood, opening a new estate agency and extending the retail showrooms by the acquisition of Kemps warehouse at 37 Buchanan Street. In early 1920 the company also purchased 49/53 Buchanan Street and 46/48 Mitchell Street in order to safeguard the workshops and carpet salon located there. However, within a few months the postwar depression had made itself felt. In early 1921 prices were reduced throughout the warehouse by a general ten per cent. Stock levels were reduced to a minimum and, with buyers instructed to purchase only against firm orders, long credit was severely restricted. The possibility of holding general sales was even considered. In February 1921 Robert Wylie died and John Hunter, of William Arrol & Co, was appointed chairman and director.

The outlook remained gloomy throughout the 1920s and early 1930s with prices falling, diminished spending power, limited new house building and virtually no shipwork. Popular tastes in furnishings were also changing, forcing the store to alter its approach. Cheaper, man-made furniture was brought in, hire purchase introduced, a tearoom opened, surplus property disposed of and the management structure reorganised. By 1936 sales had begun to recover and an arcade and bronze canopy were built in Buchanan Street. During the Second World War an air-raid shelter was installed in the store's basement and the cabinet factory embarked upon the production of utility furniture. After the war, the store was refurbished with the introduction of a new smoking room and lift. By 1953 the board was considering the flotation of the firm as a public company in order to raise funds, and received takeover offers from Waring & Gillow, Great Universal Stores Ltd and House of Fraser. In September 1957 the House of Fraser offer was accepted. Meanwhile, branch businesses were opened in Aberdeen and Edinburgh.

The Glasgow store retained its original character until, in 1966, it was linked with McDonalds, a neighbouring fashion store which had been acquired by House of Fraser in 1951. Together the two stores traded as McDonalds, Wylie & Lochhead. [See McDonalds Ltd for post-1966 history]

Sources

ARCHIVES

The records of House of Fraser plc and the various companies which it acquired, including minute books, directors' and members'; prospectuses; directors' reports and accounts; ledgers, journals and other books of account; catalogues; press cuttings and photographs. Enquiries concerning the collection should be addressed to the Archivist, The Archives, The University, Glasgow G12 8QQ.

The records of Harrods Ltd, including catalogues and photographs. Enquiries concerning the collection should be addressed to the Archivist, Harrods, Knightsbridge, London SW1X 7XL.

The records of the Scottish Retail Drapery Association, Glasgow.
The records of the Bank of Scotland, Glasgow.
Wills and administrations.
Registers of sasines.
Birth, marriage and death certificates.
Trade directories.
National census enumerator books.
Rate books.
Parish registers.

PRINTED BOOKS

Alison Adburgham, *Liberty's: A Biography of a Shop*
   (George Allen & Unwin, 1975)
Alison Adburgham, *Shopping in Style* (Thames and Hudson, 1979)
Alison Adburgham, *Shops and Shopping*, second edition
   (George Allen & Unwin, 1981)
David Alexander, *Retail Trading in England During the Industrial Revolution*
   (Athlone Press, 1970)
John S. Barclay, *The Story of Arthur and Company Limited, Glasgow*
   (priv.pub., 1953)
David Bond, *Guinness Guide to Twentieth Century Fashion*
   (Guinness Publishing, 1988)
Asa Briggs, *Victorian Things* (Batsford, 1988)
J. D. Burn, *Commercial Enterprise and Social Progress* (1888)
Maurice Corina, *Fine Silks and Oak Counters: Debenhams Ltd 1778–1978*
   (Hutchinson, 1978)
David Daiches, *Glasgow* (Andrew Deutsch, 1977)
Dorothy Davis, *History of Shopping* (Routledge & Kegan Paul, 1966)
J. W. Ferry, *A History of the Department Store* (MacMillan, 1960)
Alan Flanders, Ruth Pomeranz and Joan Woodward, *Experiment in Industrial Democracy. A Study of the John Lewis Partnership* (Faber & Faber, 1968)
W. Hamish Fraser, *The Coming of the Mass Market 1850–1914*
   (MacMillan, 1981)

Philippe Garner (Ed.), *Phaidon Encyclopedia of Decorative Art 1890–1940*
(Phaidon Press, 1988)

Hermione Hobhouse (Ed.), Survey of London, *Southern Kensington: Kensington Square to Earl's Court*, Vol. 42 (The Athlone Press, 1986)

Gordon Honeycombe, *Selfridges: The Story of the Store 1909–1984*
(Park Lane Press, 1984)

James B. Jefferys, *Retail Trading in Great Britain 1850–1950*
(Cambridge University Press, 1954)

William King, *Battle for the High Street* (Corgi, 1989)

F. MacCarthy, *British Design Since 1880* (Lund Humphries, 1982)

Neil McKendrick, John Brewer and J. H. Plumb, *The Birth of a Consumer Society* (Hutchinson, 1982)

A. H. Millar, *Glasgow Sketches* (1889)

Michael B. Miller, *The Bon Marché. Bourgeois Culture and the Department Store 1869–1920* (George Allen & Unwin, 1981)

Jane Mulvagh, *Vogue History of Twentieth Century Fashion* (Vogue, 1988)

H. Pasdermadjian, *The Department Store. Its Origins, Evolution and Economics* (Newman, 1954)

Peter Pagnamenta and Richard Overy, *All Our Working Lives* (BBC, 1989)

Reginald Pound, *Selfridge* (Heinemann, 1960)

O. E. Schoeffler and William Gale, *Esquires Encyclopedia of Twentieth Century Men's Fashions* (McGraw-Hill, 1973)

F. H. W. Sheppard (Ed.), Surveys of London, *Southern Kensington: Brompton*, Vol. 41 (The Athlone Press, 1983)

Wilfred B. Whitaker, *Victorian and Edwardian Shop Workers* (David & Charles, 1973)

Arthur Wilson, *Walter Wilson, Merchant, 1849–1917* (1920)

Michael J. Winstanley, *The Shopkeeper's World*
(Manchester University Press, 1983)

JOURNALS

The Drapers' Record (London). First published in 1887, to furnish provincial drapers with general trade news, descriptions of novelties and information on registered patents and trademarks, this journal quickly achieved a large circulation. One of the most widely read trade periodicals, it contains a wealth of information about the drapery trade as a whole as well as about individual shops.

Scottish Retail Drapery Journal (Glasgow).

Local newspapers, particularly the *Glasgow Herald* (Glasgow).

The Bailie (Glasgow).

Punch (London).

Index

Aberdeen, 143, 203, 214, 236, 242, 273; Isaac Benzie of, 183, 217; Falconers of, 86, 139, 181, 217; Frasers of, 258; Reid & Pearsons of, 177, Watt & Grant of, 130, 177, 200; Watt & Milne of, 183, 209

advertising, 16, 21, 23, 31, 35, 72–6, 78, 95, 141, 216; Army and Navy, 275; Arnotts, 278; Barkers, 285; Binns, 291, 292; Brown Muff, 295; Chiesmans, 303; Dingles, 309; D.H. Evans, 319; Fraser Sons, 47, 49, 146; Harrods, 326; Schofields, 356

Air Raid Precautions (ARP), 157, 160

Airdrie, 212

Aiton, John, 217, 233

Al Fayed, Mohamed, 254, 255, 257–8, 261–2, 265, 266, 268

Aldershot, 219, 277

Alexander shops, 195

Alfayed Investment and Trust (U.K.) Ltd (AIT), 254–5, 266

Allan, Elizabeth, 181

Allan, J. & R., 117, 135, 177, 217

Allan, Peter, 162

Allander brand, 218, 228, 232

Allander, river, 204, 203

Allders, 248

Allen, J.J., 82, 210, 212, 214, 216, 301, 336

Allied International Designers (AID), 252, 258

Altrincham, 230, 297, 330

Allied Trades Association of Edinburgh, 166

Amalgamated Caledonian Assets, 226

Amalgamated Investment and Property Ltd (AIP), 216, 219

America, Bank of, 246

American stores, 54, 75, 190, 208, 285, 290, 303

Anderson, John, 30, 31, 34–5, 36, 39, 40

Anderson's Arcade, Edinburgh, 166

Anderson's Royal Polytechnic, 93, 101, 117, 135, 139, 141, 153, 353

Anglo Continental Investment and Finance Co, 217

Anthony, Gordon, 207, 210

Argyle Securities Ltd, 225

Argyle Street, Glasgow, 15, 24, 32, 35, 117; Arnotts of, 153, 155; Arthur & Fraser of, 35, 39, 41; Fraser & McLaren of, 42, 44–5, 47, 49, 50, 91; Fraser Sons of, 123, 137, 143; Stewart & McDonald of, 26, 345, 346; Wylie & Lochhead of, 36, 54, 367

Argyll Arcade, Glasgow, 24, 32, 49

Army & Navy Auxiliary Society Ltd, 373

Army & Navy, 97, 99, 107, 136, 150, 157, 192, 236, 242, 272–6, 321, 323; history of, 272–7; House of Fraser takeover of, 216, 219–20, 277; manufacturing activity, 65, 66–7, 273; merger with Barkers, 224, 277, 287; merger with Chiesmans, 243, 304; price lists, 66, 76, 78, 96, 108, 109–11, 113, 272, 275; prices, 79, 273; site redevelopment, 226, 277; store refurbishment, 101, 261; survey of operations, 242; tearoom, 60; wages dispute, 117, 277

Arnott & Co, 35, 44, 58, 80, 93, 153, 155–6, 173, 174, 279–80; displays, 69, 71, 72; history of, 278–80; store refurbishment, 91, 99, 261, 278; see also Arnott Simpsons

Arnott Simpsons, 152, 155–6, 173–4, 181, 183, 193, 197, 198, 217, 280, 280

Art Nouveau, 87, 89, 141, 371

Arthur & Co, 39–42, 190, 192, 206–7

Arthur & Fraser, 4, 33, 35, 39–42, 40, 41, 190

Arthur, Evelyn (Col.), 190, 192

Arthur, James, 26, 32–3, 35, 38, 39, 190

Arthur, William, 41

ASDA, 216, 233

Ashley, Laura, 210, 216, 244

Associated Fisheries Ltd, 200

Astral Sports & Leisure Ltd, 230, 263

Atlee, Clement, 172

Austin Reed, 216

Australia, 258, 261, 262, 265

Austin Friars Investment Trust, 130

Automobile Association, 195

Aviemore, 230

Ayr, 174, 183, 200

Badcock, William & Son, 313

Bainbridges, 198, 224

Baird, T. & Son Ltd, 211–2

Ballantyne, D. Brothers, 199

Banff, 192

Barbados, 220

Barker, John (Sir), 59, 281–3, 282

Barker, John (Construction & Development) Ltd, 287

Barkers, 59, 65, 101, 112, 165, 185, 191, 195, 196, 199, 207, 208, 283–5; acquisition of Derry & Toms, 117, 212, 284; acquisition of Pontings, 209, 283; adoption of limited liability, 82, 282; fire, 106, 106, 283; history of, 281–7; House of Fraser takeover of, 184–5, 192, 286–7; merger with Army & Navy, 224, 277, 287; store reconstruction, 91, 123, 190, 229, 236, 243, 245, 258, 283, 284, 286, 287; young fashions at, 205, 208

Barkers Centre, 258, 260, 287

Barnes, 323, 331

Barnett-Hutton, 177

Basildon, 233, 261

Bassingshaw, 248

Bath, 19, 20, 24, 44, 212, 261, 298, 313, 337–42

Bath Parcel Service Ltd, 342

Bayswater, London, 59, 97, 134

Bedford, John, 195

Belfast, 93, 210, 231, 278

Bennetton, 244, 250

Bentalls, 254

Benzie, Isaac Ltd, 183, 217

Benzie & Miller, 192, 200, 217

Berkertex, 164, 181

Biba, 225

Bingley, 297

Binns, 82, 119, 128–9, 160, 198, 199, 209, 214, 230, 288–91; acquisitions of,

Binns—*cont.*
126, 130, 139, 147, *178*;
directors of, 184, 210, 233;
Edinburgh, 156; history of,
287–93; House of Fraser
takeover of, 178–9, 183,
292, 353; Hull, 261, 262,
262; Middlesbrough, 187–
9, 190, 196, 291, 292;
shares, 83, 208; store
redevelopment, 123, 130,
141, 193, 258, 261
Birkenhead, 197
Birmingham, 11, 195, 196,
236, 242, 250, 258, 330,
353–5
Birtchnell, Richard, 245
Blackpool, 224
Blair, J.D. & Sons, 177
Blanc, Louis, 317
Body Shop, 269
Boer War, 84, 87, 275
Bolton, Ian (Sir), 168
Bombay, 273, *274*, 277, 340
Bon Marché; Brixton, 303,
323; Gravesend, 304
Bonwit Teller, 200
Booker Brothers McConnell
& Co, 187
Boots Ltd, 87, 210, 220–2,
225, 241
Bournes, 233
Bournemouth, 76, 82, 210,
242, 301
Bowen, Trevor, 185, 190, 285,
286, 287
Bowes-Lyon, Elizabeth, *see*
Elizabeth, Queen Mother
Bowie, J.A., 152
Bowie, Patricia, 200, *203*
Bradford, 100, 101; Brown
Muff of, 20, 44, 149, 222,
229, 293–7, 356
Braemar Knitwear, 199
branded goods, 79, 181–2,
192, 199, 202, 217, 232, 285
Bridlington, 216
Brights, *180*, 210
Brimacombe, Peter, 243, 244,
313
Brimacombe, Winston, 216,
312, 313
Bristol, 22, 210, 231, 242, 338,
342
Britchnell, Richard, 245
British American Tobacco
(BAT), 218
British Broadcasting
Corporation, 125
British Empire Exhibition
(1924), 125–6
British Expeditionary Force,
107
British Home Stores (BHS),
197, 257, 266
British Shopping Weeks, 100–
1, 126
British Standards Institute
(B.S.I.), 182
Broadway Hale Inc, *see* Carter
Hawley Hale Inc
Bromley, 219, 236, 250, 261,
277

Brown, D.M. Ltd, 130, 177,
181, 217
Brown, John & Co, 146
Brown Muff, 20, 44, *44*, *65*,
149, *163*, *170*, 222, *223*,
228, 229, 230, 293–7, *293*,
295–7, 356
Brown Smith & Co, 91, 174
Browns of Chester, 224
Bruno Magli, 258
Buccleuch, Duchess of, 173
Buchanan Street, Glasgow,
25, 39, *40*, 44, *46*, 48, *154*,
203; Arthur & Fraser of,
32–3, 35, 39, 41; declining
fashionability of, 83, 91;
development of, 15, 24, 32;
Fraser & McLaren of, 42,
44–5, 47, 49, 50, 91; Fraser
Sons of, 113, 123, 135, 137,
143, 153, 170, 173, 181, 205,
225; Frasers of, 243, 250;
Stewart & McDonald of,
24, 26, 84, 345, 346, 349,
350; Wylie & Lochhead of,
36, 54, 117, 187, 367, 368,
371, 373
Bunting, Jane, 33, 45
Burbidge, Richard (Sir) I, 58,
75, 306, 315, 316, *322*, 323,
326, 328
Burbidge, Richard (Sir) II,
173, 194, 195, 196, 197,
313, 319, 329
Burbidge, Woodman (Sir), 95,
123, 141, 316–7, 319, 326,
329
Burgis & Colbourne Ltd, 277
Burke, George, 217, 218, 221
Burlington Arcade, London,
21, *21*, 258
Burton Group, 243, 245, 248,
250, 252, 257, 258
Burton, Montague, 143
Butler, R.A.B., 175
Buy British campaigns, 100–
1, 227, 232–3

Callaghan, James, 227
Camberley, 219, 250, 277
Cambridge, 76
Cameron, A.I., 178–9
Cameron, Neil, 179
Campbell, John, 130, 139
Campbell, J. & W., 35, 120
Canterbury, 303
Capell Cure Myers, 255
Cardiff, 76, 192, 342; Howells
of, 91, 123–4, 216, 217, 261,
332–6; Seccombes of, 224,
230
Cardross, Dunbartonshire, 26
Carlisle, 177, 236, 292
Carrefour, 216
Carswell (The Modern Man's
Shop) Ltd, 184
Carter, Edward, 225, 229
Carter, William Ltd, 328, 345
Carter Hawley Hale Inc, 222,
225, 229, 233
Carvela, 258
cash carrying system, 58, 84,
278

Cassidy, Dennis, 257
catalogues, *see* price lists
Cattanach, John, 32
Cavendish House, *23*, 80, *81*,
99, 210, *211*, 258, *298–301*,
298–301, 342
Cazenoves, 233
central buying, 130, 167, 170,
200, 202, 209, 212, 214,
218, 234
chain stores, *see* multiples
Chanelle fashion shops, 210
Channon, Paul, 266
Charles, Price, 240
Charterhouse Investment
Trust, 135
Chichester, 219, 236
Cheltenham, 24, 80, 99, 210,
258, *298–301*
Chester, 224
Chicago, 95
Chichester, 236, 277
Chiesmans, 141, 224, 225,
236, 243, *302–4*, *302–2*
Chitham, Frank, 156, 316
Christmas bazaars, 72, *72*
Churchill, Winston (Sir), 161
City of Glasgow Bank, 47–8,
278
Civil Service Co-operative
Society, 272, 328–9
Civil Service Supply
Association, 272
Clarke, Edward J., 175, 348
Clarkson, Thomas Ltd, 277
Clayform Properties plc, 359
Clore, Charles (Sir), 179, 184
Coatbridge, 212
Coats, J. & P., 102
Cochran, Robert & Son Ltd,
200
Cochrane, James D., 172
Cockayne, T.B. & W., 359,
360
Collier, John shops, 195, 248
Comet, 233
Commercial Corporation of
London, 130
Commercial Garage, The, 342
Conran, Terence (Sir), 216,
244, 250, 252, 257, 266
Conran Associates, 228, 245
Consumers' Councils, 139, 141
co-operative societies, *see* co-
operative stores
co-operative stores, 87, 95,
139, 149, 182, 272, 273,
315, 321
Co-operative Insurance
Society Ltd, 179
Copenhagen, 217, 222, 231,
331
Copland & Lye, 72, 83, 93, 99,
101, 116, 118, 123, 156,
212, 217, 230
Corbett, Cameron, 99
Cork, 210, 231, 258, 278
coronation; 1911, 101, 126,
227; 1953, 179, 181, 307
Cottage Homes, *see* Linen and
Woollen Drapers'
Institution and Cottage
Homes

Cotterill, Seton, 173
Courrèges, André, 208
Cox & Horder, 313
Coxon, James & Co, 139, 292
Craddock, Aleck, 236, 240, 248, 261, 331
Crawford, D.S. Ltd, 208
Criddle & Smith, 313
crinoline, 42, 43
Cripps, Stafford (Sir), 172
Crossan, Bill, 218, 220, 229, 234, 240, 243, 254, 255; management committee, chairmanship of, 222, 225, 226, 231; promotions, 212, 214, 216, 217, 218; retires, 258
Croydon, 197
Crystal Palace, *33*, 33–4, 38

Daily Mail, 72
Daily Telegraph, 72, 75
Dallas's, *77*, 95, 97, 105, *105*, *107*, *108*, 123, *127*, 164, 165, 211
Dalmore Whyte & MacKay, 206
Dalton, Hugh, 166
Dalys, 35, *36*, 83, 116, 147, 177, 230
Darling & Co, 200
Darlington, 123, 291, 293
Dash, 250
Davies, George, 244, 257
Debenhams, 202, 225, 254, 266, 359; bids for Harrods, 331; central buying, 200, 209; Debenham & Freebody, 117; Debenham & Hewitt, 299; Debenham, Pooley & Smith, *23*, 298; Drapery Trust and, 135, 139; House of Fraser possible takeover of, 183, 199, 230, 257–8
Defoe, Daniel, 11, 15
delivery, 64, *64–5*, 112, *112*, *191*, 216, 272, 275, 282, *289.297*, 306, 321, 344, *364*
Denmark, 217
depository, 282, 299, 303, 323, 331
Derry & Toms, 184, 190, *193*, 225, 284–7, 303; Barkers takeover of, 117, 284; closure, 212, 214, 287; store reconstruction, 123, 141, 286
Dickens, Charles, 23
Dickins & Jones, *73*, 82, 84, *85*, *88–9*, *92*, 94, 95, 97, 102, 102–3, *173*, 194, 208, 250, 265, *304*, 307–9; acquisitions, 83, 306; branches, 207, 208, 212, 216, 233, 308; Harrods and, 105, 195, 248, 306, 308, 326; history of, 305–8
Dingles, 171, 212, 213, 214, 216, 236, *243*, 258, 309–14, *310–1*, *313–4*, 342
Dior, Christian, 168
discount associations, 139

discount houses, 199
display, 22, 33, 68–71, 69, 78, 106, *151*; window, 15, 21–3, 33, 51, 70, 71–2, *125*, *182*, *183*, *185*, *193*, 196, *201*, *227*, *283*, *303*
Dixons, 225
Dobson, Richard, 218
Dollar Export Council, 182
Doncaster, 230, 297
Dorchester, 219, 277
Drapers' Record, 60, 71, 76, 83, 84, 95, 113, 139, 199, 207; on demand, 91, 111–2, 117, 161; on fashion, 120, 132; on Fraser Sons, 49, 50, 91; on Glasgow shops, 50, 73, 84
Drapery and General Investment Trust, 130, 134–5, 139
Drew, James, 258
Drew, Richard, 218
Drumchapel, 212
Dublin, 130, 212, 258, 278
Dumfries, 177, 292
Dunbartonshire, 26
Duncan-Sandys, Edwin, 229, 233, 252, 254
Duncans, 175
Dundee, 130, 152, 162, 170, 177, 181, 217, 243
Dunnings, 224

Early Closing Association, 99–100
East Kilbride, 212
Eastbourne, 184, 277, 286
Edinburgh, 31, 123, 166, 167, 192, 280, 373; J. & R. Allan of, 117, 135, 177, 217; Peter Allan of, 162; Binns of, 214, 353; Blairs of, 177; Darlings of, 200; Mackie & Sons of, 199; McLarens of, 174; Frasers of, 243; Maules of, 60, 147, 292, 351–3; Smalls of, 183, 230; Patrick Thomsons of, 130, 177 *see also* Princes Street
Edward VII, King, 87, 89, 99
Elgin, 200
Elizabeth, Queen, 156, 177, 179, 181; coronation of, 179, *180–1*, 181, 307; silver jubilee, 227, *227*, 308
Elizabeth, Queen Mother, 120, 151, 156
Empire Exhibition, Glasgow (1938), 155
escalators, *57*, 58, 141, 280, 301, 307, 312, 318, 329, 331, 336, 353, 365
Escourt, Iris, *see* Picken
European Economic Community (EEC), 211, 217, 313
Evans, D.H., 72, 79, *134*, *158*, *176*, *208*, 212, *238*, 243, 250, 312, *318–20*; adoption of limited liability, 80, 82–3, 315; Harrods and, 135, 195, 328; history of, 315–

20; new building, 91, *148–9*, 149, *155*, *317*; possible sale of, 236; store refurbishment, 261, 329
Evans, D.H. Founders Share Co Ltd, 316
Evans, David & Co, 231
Evans Leases Trust Ltd, 316
Ewing, Alexander & Co, 162
excess profits tax, 115, 117

Fagan, B. P., 216
Falconer, John & Co, *86*, 139, *144–5*, 181, 217
Falmouth, 212, 313
fashion, *17*, 27, 50; changes in, 207, (18th century) 16, (1890s)90, (1900s) 93, (1910s) 103, 105, 111, 113, 116–7, 118–9, (1920s) 120, 121, 131–2, (1940s) 157, 160, (1950s) 177, 193, (1970s) 228; in departments stores, 151, 181, 207, 210–1, 230, 306; royal family and, 151, 156, 179, 240; shows, *203*, *205*, 340; *see also* crinoline
Fayed, Ali, 255, 257–8, 261, 265, 266, 268
Federated Department Stores Inc, 207
Festival of Britain, *176*, 307
Fine Art Institute, Glasgow, 101
Fine Fare, 216
fires, 54; Barkers, 106, *106*, 283, 285; Binns, 291, *291*, 292; Brown Muff, 294; Dingles, 314; Frasers, 44, 49; Harrods, 321; Hendersons, 197; Kendal Milne, 345; Pettigrew & Stephens, 200; Wylie & Lochhead, 366, 368, 371
First World War, 106–17, 275, 284, 294, 301, 303, 326, 333, 342, 348, 361, 371
Fleming Reid, 87
Flint & Palmer, 20
Forresters (Outfitters) Ltd, 183, 192
Forum des Halles, 244–5, *245*
Fowler & Brock, 130, 292
France, 35
Fraser, David, 45, 48, 83
Fraser, Emily Florence (McGowan), 135, 199
Fraser Estates Ltd, 153
Fraser Foundation, 199
Fraser, Hugh (1815–73), 26, *27*, 32–3, 35, 39, 41–2, 45, 47
Fraser, Hugh (1860–1927), 45, 47, 48, *48*, 83, 91, 93, 113, 117, 121, 123, 135
Fraser, Hugh (Sir), Lord Fraser of Allander (1903–66), *9*, *137*, 161, 167, *168*, 170, 172, 175, 181, *197*, 200, 210, 226; acquisitions, 153, 161, 162, 164, 166, 174, 175, 177, 178–9, 183–

Fraser, Hugh (Sir)—*cont.*
5, 187, 190, 192, 194–6,
199, 280; at annual
meetings, 153, 168, 206;
assumes control of
company, 135; attacks
government, 166, 172;
baronetcy, 199; creates
House of Fraser, 168; dies,
205, 206, 218; education,
121; illness, 165, 184, 203;
improves stores, 123, 135,
137, 143, 146, 147, 153,
155–6, 165, 177, 181, 193;
marries, 143; peerage, 203;
promotions, 121; and
Scottish tourism, 195, 200,
230; and SUITS, 170, 199;
supports war work, 157;
trade bodies, presidency of,
162, 164, 166, 172, 175, 177,
193, 200; trading policy,
182–3, 190, 199, 202
Fraser, Hugh (Sir) (1936–88),
9, 197, *197, 203*, 208, 209,
217, 222, *228*, 240, 241–2;
acquisitions, 210, 212, 216,
217, 222, 287, 313;
appoints directors, 206,
210, 214; and Boots
merger, 210, 220, 221, 222;
buys shares, 225;
confirmed as father's
successor, 205; contravenes
Companies Act, 226, 229;
develops young fashion
shops, 200, 203, 205, *206*,
207–8; elected chairman,
206; desires reduced
commitments, 218, 219,
220, 222; disposals, 206–7;
forecasts retail
developments, 210, 212,
214; and Lonrho, 229, 233,
234, 236, 238, 239; marries,
200, 220; opens McLarens,
174; promotions, 184, 199,
206; resigns from board,
241; retires from
chairmanship, 239, 240
Fraser, James Arthur, 45, 47,
48, 83, 91, 93, 101
Fraser, John, 45, 47, 48, 83,
91, 93, 113, 121, 123, 135,
137
Fraser, Katie (Lewis) (Lady),
143, *204*
Fraser & Love, 200
Fraser & McLaren, 42, 44–5,
47
Fraser, Matthew Pettigrew,
45, 48, 83, 135
Fraser Sons & Co, 47–50, *50*,
58, 65, 71, 76, 83–4, 91, 93,
113, 116, 135, 137, *143*, 153;
acquisitions, 153, 278;
advertising, 101;
anniversaries, 161, 173;
extensions, 91, 153; House
of Fraser and, 153, 168;
profits, 112, 117, 118, 121,
147; store refurbishment,
123, 143, 146–7, 205

Fraser (Stores) Ltd, 234,
258
Fraserburgh, 192
Frasercard, 243, 258
Frasers (Glasgow) Bank Ltd,
153
Freeman Hardy & Willis, 87
furnishings, home, 27, 42,
132, 132, 134, *370*

Galway, 258
Gamages, 258
Gamble, Elson, 153, 156, 165,
167, 168, 170, 172, 179,
184, 205, 206, 210, 214
Gardiner, A. H., 179, 184
Gateshead, 261
General Strike, 130
Genge & Co Ltd, 277
George V, King, 99, 101, 115;
coronation of, 101, 126, 227
George VI, King, 120, 156,
177
George, Bernard, 141, 286
Germany, 35, 107, 116, 118,
120–1, 156–7
Gieves & Hawkes, 216
Glasgow, 16, *28–9*, 39, 58, 80,
100, 113, 116, 117, 139,
146, 147, 153, 165, 192, 200;
advertising in, 73; Arnotts
of, 58, 69, 71, 183, 217, 261,
278–80; Dalys of, 147, 177;
during the eighteenth
century, 11, 15; Forresters
of, 183; Fraser Sons of, 71,
93; International
Exhibition, 49, 72, 84;
McDonalds of, 209;
Muirheads of, 217;
Pettigrew & Stephens of,
177; shops in, 15, 18, *19*,
35, 23–31, 58, 59, 91, 93,
101, 105, 120, 123, 214;
Stewart & McDonald of,
71, 345–50; Walter Wilson
of, 58, 60; Wylie &
Lochhead of, 65, 366–73;
see also Argyle Street;
Buchanan Street;
Sauchiehall Street;
Trongate
Glasgow Academy, 121
Glasgow Herald, 33, 37, 39, 44,
47, 57, 93, 203
Glasgow Industrial Finance
Ltd, 168, 172
Glasgow International
Exhibition, 1888, 49, 72;
1901, 84, 87
Glasgow Royal Polytechnic,
see Anderson's Royal
Polytechnic
Glasgow & West of Scotland
Drapers, Outfitters etc.
Association, 120
Glasgow & West of Scotland
Retail Garment Makers'
Association, 120
Glasgow & West of Scotland
Retail Drapers' Association,
120
Glaxo, 220

Gloucester, Duchess of, 151
Goorwitch, 160
Gordon & Stanfield, 162
Gorringes, 302
Gosling & Sons Ltd, 184, 207,
286, 287
Grand Metropolitan, 234
Gravesend, 304
Gray Peverill & Co Ltd, 130,
292
Great Exhibition (1851), 33–
4, *34*, 49, 126, 321
Great Universal Stores, 187,
195, 245, 373
Greenock, 30, 165, 170, 177
Griffiths, John, 254
Grimsby, 103, 209, 258, 293
Guildford, 219, 261, 277
Guy & Smith, 103, 209

Habitat, 216, 225, 228, 243,
244, 257, 266
Haldane, Richard (Sir), 95
Hale, Prentice C., 225, 229
Hall, John (Sir), 261
Halpern, Ralph (Sir), 248,
257, 258
Hamilton, 212
Hamleys, 257
Hammonds Ltd, *118*, 216
Hampson, Robb, 265, 266,
268
Hanson Trust, 248–9, 250
Harding, Howell & Co, *22*
Harker, Cecil C.S., 165, 167
Harrison Gibson Ltd, 277
Harrod, Charles Henry, 36,
321, *322*
Harrodian Gazette, 194
Harrods, 100, 101, *118*, 130,
141, 165, 197, 199, 206,
208, 210, 211, 216, 233, 234,
239, 240, 262, 265, 266 311,
315, 317; acquisitions, 117,
134, 135, 139, 306, 316,
319, 345, 355, 365;
adoption of limited liability,
80; advertising, 75, 97;
anniversaries: 60th, 95, *97*;
75th, *124*; 100th, 173;
bomb, 252, 253, 331;
branded goods, 78, 79, 182;
concession shops, 151, 258;
demerger issue, 246–50,
252; delivery vans, *64, 112*;
departments, 60, *61–3*, 62,
*140, 142, 163, 237, 267,
323, 329, 330*; escalator, *57*,
58; food halls, *62–3, 234–
5, 237, 329*; frontage,
Brompton Road, *165, 247,
268, 270, 324–5*; history
of, 321–31; House of
Fraser takeover of, 190,
194–6, *197*, 200, 308;
manufacturing activity, 65;
price lists and catalogues,
78, 245, *246, 327*; 79, 99,
273, 275; rebuilding, 54,
91, 105, 149, 282;
refurbishment, 243, 261–2;
telephone ordering, 76, *77*,
95; trademark, *79*; Way

In, *206*, 207, 216; white
sale, 123, *125*
Harrods (Continental) Ltd,
326
Harrods (London) Ltd, 214
Harrods Major Project (1981–
4), 236, 240, 261
Harrods (North America)
Ltd, 328
Harrods (Provincial) Ltd,
214, *215*, 225
Harrods (South America)
Ltd, 326
Harrogate, 175, 177, 298, 299,
348, 349, 359
Hartnell, Norman (Sir), 164,
181, 183, 200
Harvey Nichols, 100, 117,
135, 225, 230, 257, 356
Harvey, William of Guildford
Ltd, 277
Hatry, Clarence, 130, 135, 139
Hawes & Curtis, 258
Hawke & Thomas, 313
Hawley, Philip M., 229
Head, Ron, 233
Healey & Baker, 175, 177
Heath, Edward, 220, 221
Helston, 212, 313
Henderson, Alexander Ltd,
211–2
Henderson, James Arthur
Fraser (Capt.), 135
Henderson, William & Sons
Ltd, 103, *104*, 195, 197,
200, *201*, 329
Henderson, W. Craik, 162
Hepworths, 87, 244
Heron International, 248
Hi Street West Eight
boutique, 208
Hide & Co, 177, 224, 225
Highland Tourist (Cairngorm
Development) Ltd, 230
Hills, R.H.O., *223*, 224
hire purchase, 126, 139, 221
Hitchcock, George, 83, 306
Hobart, Robert (Sir), 186,
187, 196
Hobday, Gordon (Dr), 220,
221
Hodge Group, 336
Hollom, Jasper (Sir), 255
Home and Colonial Stores, 87
Home Office, 107
Hourston, D. & Sons, 174,
183, 200
House of Fraser Ltd, 197, 198,
199, 200, 203, 205, 225,
226, 228, 232, 261;
acquisitions, 166, 199–200,
210, 230, 248–9, 258, J.J.
Allen, 210, 301, Army &
Navy, 219, 277, Bairds,
212, Barkers, 185, 286–7,
Binns, 179, 292, 353,
Brown Muff, 297,
Chiesmans, 225, 304,
Dingles, 212, 313–4, 342,
Harrods, 195–6, 331, 345,
355, 365, Hides, 225,
Howells, 216, 217, 336,
McDonalds, 350,

Schofields, 265, 359,
Scottish Drapery
Corporation, 177, Switzers,
212, 258, Wylie &
Lochhead, 373; central
buying, 202, 209, 211, 214;
Debenhams and, 257–8;
directors of, 210, 216, 218,
225, 229–30, 265;
disposals, 231; financial
services, 258; formation of,
153, 156, 162; goes public,
168; Lonrho and, 229, 231,
233, 236, 238, 239–41, 246–
9, 250, 252, 254–5, 266,
268; property values, 217,
239; rationalisation of, 211,
217; shares, 199, 208, 218–
9, 220, 221, 222, 225, 229,
231; store redevelopment,
243, 245, 257, 261, 355;
supports Buy British, 227;
takeover bids for, 218, 219,
220, 221, 222, 255–6;
trading policy, 218–9, 222,
229, 230, 236, 243, 250,
257, 261, 266
House of Fraser (Northern)
Ltd, 234
House of Fraser Northern
Management, 214
House of Fraser Stores Ltd,
234
House of Fraser (Stores) Ltd,
234, 258, 265
house ownership, 126, 132
Howell, James & Co, 91, 123,
125, 216, 217, *251*, 261,
332–6, *332*, *334–6*
Howells Garage and
Commercial Vehicles Ltd,
335–6
Hull, 216, 261, 293
Humphries, Peter, 230
Hunt, Leigh, 34
Hunter, T.C., 179, 184
Hutcheson, Grace, 93

Ilford, 204
Illum, A.C. 217, 222, 231, *232*,
331
Impact boutique, 209, 243
Imperial Tobacco, 219
In Company, 194, 196
India, 273, 274, 277, 340
Industrial and Commercial
Finance Corporation, 206
International Caledonian
Assets, 219
Inverness, 192, 243
Iona, 241, *241*
Ireland, 35
iron-framed construction, 54
Italy, 108, 250

Jaeger & Co, 153
Japan, 108, 257–8
Jeune, Lady, 51, 59
Jollys, *19*, 20–1, *22*, *33*, 44,
52–3, *74–5*, 76, 80, 91, 261,
313, 337–42, *338–41*
Jones, David stores, 261
Jones, Michael Ellis, 265

Jones, John Prichard (Sir),
102, 305, 306
Jones, Thomas & Co, 123, 291

Keenan, Robert, 167, 168,
178, 179, 184, 199
Kelly, Thomas (Sir), 146
Kelvin Hall, Glasgow, 181
Kemp, David & Sons, 117,
373
Kenbar goods, 285
Kendals, 244
Kendal Milne, 20, 60, 65, *98*,
118, 195, 242, 328, *343–4*;
Harrods takeover of, 117,
326; history of, 343–5; new
building, 139, 141, 149;
refurbishment, 230, 258;
Way In, 208, 209
Kennards, 197
Kensington, London, 141,
250; Barkers of, 59, 65, 91,
106, 112, 116, 117, 184, 190,
208, 236, 277, 281–7;
Laura Ashley of, 10
Keymer, Walter, 199, 209,
214, 217, 218, 221
Kings Ltd, 161
Kingston-on-Thames, 177,
224
Kinross, John B., 206, 214
Kirkcaldy, 236
Kirkpatrick, Thomas, 39, 40
Kirksop, John & Son Ltd, 184
Kleinwort Grievson, 255
kleptomania, *see* shoplifting
Knight, T. & Son, 342
Knightsbridge, London, 36,
225, 230, 248, 257, 282,
321–31
Kurt Geiger Holdings Ltd,
258

Landport Drapery Bazaar,
182
Leamington Spa, 219, 277
Ledgard & Wynn, 359
Leeds, 356–9
Legal and General Assurance
Society Ltd, 175, 177, 183,
236
Leicester, 100, 210, 301
Leeds, 111, 192, 265
Lennox, Elizabeth, 26
Leonards, 304
Lever Brothers, 181
Lewis & Allenby, 83, 306
Lewis, Andrew (Sir), 143
Lewis, Capt., 99
Lewis, Katie (Lady), *see*
Fraser, Katie (Lewis)
(Lady)
Lewis, John Partnership, 141,
161, 224, 254, 304, 317, 319
Lewisham, 141, 224, 231, 236,
302, 304
Lewis's Investment Trust, 79,
139, 141, 153, 165, 182,
198, 200, 286, 353, 357
Lifestyle, 243, 250, *251*, 252,
255, 320, 350
lifts, 54, 57, 84, 190, 282, 287,
328, 349, 367

lighting, 58, 108, 177, 181, 286, 292, 365; electric, 50, 58, 71, 135, 300; gas, 23, 38, *58*, 298, 344; window, 352

Lilley, Thomas, 87

Limerick, 258

Limitation of Supplies Order (LIMISO), 161–2

limited liability, 80–3, 93

Lincoln, 99, 101, 108, 123, 233

Linen and Woollen Drapers'Institution and Cottage Homes, 164, 166, 205, 206

Liptons, *86*, 87

Livesy, Paul, 262

Littlewoods, 181, 245

Liverpool, 58, 103, 130, 182, 195, 197, 200, 320, 329–30, 356

Lochhead, William, 36, 38, *366*, 366, 367, 368

Logie & Co, 166

London, 11, 15, 20, 24, 41, 141, 161, 210, 298, 299, 301; building regulations, 54; shops in, 15, 18, 59, 75, 76, 123, 126, *see also* Kensington; Knightsbridge; Lewisham, Oxford Street; Regent Street; Victoria

Londonderry, 42

Lonrho plc, 229, 230, 233, 236, 238–41, 245–50, 252, 254, 266, 268

loss leaders, 80

Lyle & Scott, 184

Lyons, J. Ltd, 185

McDonald, John, 24

McDonalds Ltd, *114–5, 138*, 175, 177, 184, *209*, 209, 225, 345–50, *348–50, see also* Stewart & McDonald

McDonalds, Wylie & Lochhead, *224*, 225, 350, 373

McGowan, Emily Florence, *see* Fraser, Emily Florence (McGowan)

MacGregor, Miss Irene, 170

Mackie, J.W. & Sons Ltd, 199, 208

Mackintosh, Charles Rennie, 84, 87

McLachlan & Brown, 166

McLaren, Alexander, 41, 42 45, 47

McLaren & Son, 174, *174*

MacLaurin, Ian, 234

McLellan, William, 183, 209

McMaster, Murdoch, 233, 252, 257, 258, 261, 265

mail order, 76, 78, 95, 112, 120, 245, 273, 275, 299, 306, 333, 340, 344, 371

Maidstone, 224, 236, 303

Management Horizons, 242–3, 250, 252, 257, 261

Management Research Group of Department Stores, 141

Manchester, 11, 16; Kendal Milne of, 20, 60, 65, 117, 118, 139, 141, 149, 195, 208, 230, 242, 258, 326, 343–5; Lewis & Co of, 79; Walter Carter of, 328

Mann Byar & Co, 91

Manson, Alexander Ltd, 199

Margaret, Princess, 156

Margate, 337, 338

Marks & Spencer, 153, 181, 182, 202, 231, 232, 234, 244, 250, 252, 254, 261, 269

Marley, Kenneth T., 179, 184, 210, 233

Marshall Fields, 95

Marshall & Snelgrove, 76, 82, 117, 135

Mary, Queen, 100, 125

Maryon fashion shops, 210

Maule, Robert & Sons, *61*, 62, *80*, 147, 292–3, 351–3, *351–2*

Mawer & Collingham, *70*, *98*, 99, *100*, 101, 108, 123, *151*, 233

Meadowhall, 265

Menzies, Andrew, 30

Merchandise Marks Act, 79

Metro Centre, *260*, 261, 265, 269

M.F.I., 233

Michaels, Louis, 210

middle classes, 16, 26–7, 42, 89, 146, 273, 305

Middlesbrough, 123, 183, 190, 196, 291, 292

Midgley, Robert, 206, 210, 217, 229, 236, 240, 331

Milligan, David K., 233, 240, 242

Milton Keynes, 233, 308

Mitchell, Miller & Ogilvie, 41

Mitsukoshi, 245–6

Moffat, 121

Moffat, A.I., 199

Monopolies and Mergers Commission, 220, 222, 230–1, 239, 240, 242, 254, 255, 266, 268

Monte Carlo, 143, 185, 187, 196

Morant, J.D. Ltd, 277

Morgan Squire, 210, 301

Morgan, Tommy, 181

Morris & Co, 344

mortgages, 126, 130

Moss Bros., 216

Mothercare, 216, 225, 244, 252, 257

Motherwell, 212

Muir Simpson Ltd, 162, 170

Muirhead, Thomas & Co, 35, 99, 153, 155, 165, 183, 217

Mugdock Country Park, 241–2

multiple stores, 139, 152, 153, 161, 166, 167, 175, 181, 182, 212, 243, 244; competition with departments stores, 87, 95, 139, 149, 156, 168, 183, 190, 202, 217, 261

Munitions, Ministry of, 113

National Bank of Scotland, 161, 162

National Car Parks Ltd, 229

National Chamber of Trade, 172

National Federation of Credit Traders, 139

National Retail Dry Goods Association of America, 182

National Trust for Scotland, 241

Neatby, W.J., 326

New Lanark, 20

New Look, 168, 193,

New York, 58, 182, 200, 261, 273

Newcastle-upon-Tyne, 139, 141, 192, 198, 224, 230, 261, 269, 292

Newport, Isle of Wight, 304

Newquay, 212, 313

Newton, Alfred, 315, 323, 328

Newton Abbott, 195, 212, 313, 319

Next, 244, *244*, 257, 269

Non-Utility goods, 166, 167, 172

Northern Ireland, 231

Norwich, 35

Now, 252

Nuremberg, 107

Observer, 268

Office of Fair Trading, 241

Ogilvie, William, 41

Osterley warehouse, 262, 331

Otis, Eliza, 57

Owen Owen, 58, 197, 356

Owen, Robert, 20

Oxford Street, London, 76, 160, 161, 301, 305; D.H. Evans of, 79, 91, 135, 149, 195, 236, 243, 261, 315, 316, 317, 320, 328; Selfridges of, 95, 121, 141, 286, 326; shops in, *14*, 15, 22

Paisley, 26, 32, 33, 200, 236

Paisleys Ltd, 139, 241

paperhangings, 27, 366, 367, 371

Paris, 16, 31, 54, 71–2, 93, 244, 273, 302, 326

Paterson & Smith, 117

Patron, F.E., 170

Patterson, T.R., 183, 192

Pearson & Son, 340

Peebles, 199

Penzance, 212, 313

Perkins, Dorothy Ltd, 216, 242

Perth, 162, 166, 230, 236, 240

Peterhead, 192, 217

Pettigrew, Andrew (Sir), 101, 116, 130

Pettigrew & Stephens, 60, 72, 83, 91, 93, 101, 116, 181, 200; closure of, 211; new building, 84, 86–7;

Scottish Drapery
Corporation and, 130, 177;
site redevelopment, 212,
217, 230; store extension,
113, 120
Piat et ses Fils, 58
Picken, Iris, 153, 162, 168
plate glass, 20, 22, 23, 54, 278
300
Plymouth, 212, 258, 273, 277,
309–14
point-of-sale equipment, 232,
236, 262
Polglaze, John, 313
Pollok, Matthew, 91
Pontings, 112, 117, 123, 184,
190, 209, 212, 283, 284,
285, 286, 287
Poole, 250
Pophams, 312
Portsmouth, 100, 182, 277
post office, 76, 120, 307
Powell, Norman H., 217, 222
Prentice, D.& A., 165, 170
Price Commission, 228, 230,
231
prices, 11, 182, 221, 243;
control of, 116, 161, 166;
cutting, 102, 113, 119, 221,
273, 349, 371; fixed 20, 35,
51, 102, 305; high, 18, 24,
116, 134, 141, 328, 350;
low, 18, 26, 31, 35, 36, 78–
9, 95, 274, 281, 315, 321;
rising, 95, 99, 116, 117, 141,
158, 175; ticketed, 20, 35,
51, *see also* resale price
maintenance
Prices and Consumer
Protection, Department of,
225
prices and incomes policy,
222, 231
price lists, 78, 272, 275, 277,
299, 326, 340, 344, 373
Princes Street, Edinburgh,
62, 147, 166, 199, 208, 209,
230, 351
Private Eye, 240
profit sharing, 84
profiteering committee, 118
Prudential Assurance Co, 175,
179
Pudaloff, Miss, 167
Punch, 51, 76–7

Queen, Mary, 146, *146–7*

Rackhams, Altrincham, 230,
297; Birmingham, 195, 196,
236, 242, 258, 264, 353–5,
354–5; Bradford, 223, 297;
Leeds, 266
Railway Clearing House, 76
Rank Organisation, 219
rationing, clothes, 162, 172
ready-made clothing, 44, 78,
103, 121, 125, *131*, 131–2,
278, 285, 293, 346, 349, 361
ready-money, 20, 30, 33, 35,
36, 39, 273, 298, 315, 321,
332, 337

ready-to-wear clothing, *see*
ready-made clothing
Regent Street, London, 83,
105, 195, 257, 305, 306, 308
Reid & Pearsons, 177
Redmayne, Martin (Lord),
210, 214, 218, 220, 222, *228*,
230
Reno Inclined Escalator Co,
58
resale price maintenance, 102,
121, 141, 198, 200
Retail Advisory Committee,
162, 164
Retail Consortium, 218, 221
Retail and General
Discounting Ltd, 172
Retail Trades Education
Council, 205
Reynolds & Co, 336
Richard, Charles Ltd, 353
Richard Shops, 248, 250, 252
Richmond, 184, 207, 208, 216,
286, 308
Richmond, Frederick (Sir),
139
Robertson, James, 156, 167
Robertson, Ledlie, Ferguson
& Co Ltd, 210, 231
Robinson, Peter, 242
Robinson, Terry, 233, 240,
246, 250, 254, 255
Robinson Brothers Ltd, 292
Rochester, 304
Rockhey, J.F. Ltd, 195, 319
Ross, Aileen, 218, 220
Rowland, R.W. (Tiny), 229,
231, 233, 234, 236, 238–41,
246, 249, 252, 254, 266, 268
royal warrant, 306, 345, 352,
371
Ruellen, Andre, 261

Sage, Frederick Ltd, 326
Sainsburys, 216
St Michael, 182
St Theresa's Industries Ltd,
312
Sanders, Arthur Ltd, 123, 291
Sandys, Edwin Duncan, *see*
Duncan-Sandys, Edwin
(Lord)
Sauchiehall Street, Glasgow,
82, 83, 91, 117, 161, 162,
212, 217; Copland & Lye
of, 83, 123, 217; Dalys of,
83, 147, 230; development
of, 26, 83; Muirheads of,
153, 165, 183; Pettigrew &
Stephens of, 60, 83, 211,
212, 217
Savoy Hotel, 195, 203
Scandanavia, 217
Schenley Industries Inc, 183–
4
Schofields Centre, 265, 359
Schofields, *181*, 265–6, 356–9,
356–8
Scotcade, 240
Scotch drapers, 11
Scottish Amicable Assurance,
217
Scottish Appeal for

Warehousemen Clerks and
Drapers' Schools, 162
Scottish Drapery
Corporation, 130, 135, 139,
147, 172, 177, 183
Scottish Motor Traction Co,
184
Scottish National Party, 222
Scottish National Exhibition
(1911), 101
Scottish Retail Drapers'
Association, 117, 120, 164,
166, 172, 175, 177, 183, 184,
193, 200, 202, 205
Scottish Retail Drapers,
Outfitters, Garmentmakers
& Millinery Federation,
120
*Scottish Retail Drapery
Journal*, 120
Scottish Retail Garment
Makers & Millinery Trades
Federation, 120
Scottish & Universal
Investments Ltd (SUITS),
170, 199, 203, 206, 218, 220,
222, 225–6, 229, 230–1, 232
Seager Evans, 183
Seaman & Little, 282
Sears Holdings, 184, 248
Seccombes, 224, 230
Second World War, 158–67,
277, 295, 306, 311, 329,
335, 354, 364, 373
selective employment tax,
206, 210, 211
self sevice, 139, 182, 197, 212
Selfridge, Gordon, 95, 97,
121, 126, 130, 134, 141
Selfridges, 95, 100, 165, 200,
286, 311, 316, 326
Selfridge, Miss, 200, 216, 228
Selincourt & Sons Ltd, 211
Serious Fraud Office, 266
sewing machine, 44
Shannon, J.S. Ltd, 177
Sharp, Ernest, 234, 236, 248,
250, 254, 257
Shawcross, Hartley (Sir), 175
Sheffield, 65, 68, 105, 195,
208, 261, 265, 329, 330,
359, 360–5
Shoolbred, James & Co Ltd,
328, 332
shop fronts, 15, 21, 21–2, *22*,
105, 137, 153, 277, 278, 300
shoplifting, 71, 106
Shops Act, 99–100, 198
Shotts, 212
silks, 35, 131, 158, 161, 281,
305, 306, 339–40
Simpson Hunter & Young,
116, 200, 203
Simon, John (Sir), 161
Simpson, John, 123, 126, 130,
178, 289, 290, 291, 292
Simpson, Robert & Sons, 35,
153, 155, 280
Singer & Co, 44
Sir Hugh shops, 241
Skinner, Sydney (Sir), 185,
283, 285, 286
Skipton, 297, 359